The Problem of Emancipation

ANTISLAVERY, ABOLITION, AND THE ATLANTIC WORLD

R. J. M. Blackett and James Brewer Stewart, Series Editors

THE PROBLEM OF EMANCIPATION

*The Caribbean Roots of the
American Civil War*

EDWARD BARTLETT RUGEMER

LOUISIANA STATE UNIVERSITY PRESS

BATON ROUGE

PUBLISHED BY LOUISIANA STATE UNIVERSITY PRESS
Copyright © 2008 by Louisiana State University Press
All rights reserved
Manufactured in the United States of America
First printing

DESIGNER: Michelle A. Neustrom
TYPEFACE: Adobe Caslon Pro, Giza
TYPESETTER: J. Jarrett Engineering, Inc.
PRINTER AND BINDER: Thomson-Shore, Inc.

LIBRARY OF CONGRESS CATALOGING-IN-PUBLICATION DATA

Rugemer, Edward Bartlett, 1971-
    The problem of emancipation : the Caribbean roots of the American Civil War / Edward
Bartlett Rugemer.
        p. cm. — (Antislavery, abolition, and the Atlantic world)
    Includes bibliographical references and index.
    ISBN 978-0-8071-3338-5 (cloth : alk. paper) 1. Slaves—Emancipation—United States.
2. Slaves—Emancipation—West Indies. 3. Antislavery movements—United States—History—
19th century. 4. Antislavery movements—West Indies—History—19th century. 5. Slavery—
Political aspects—United States—History—19th century. 6. Slavery—Political aspects—West
Indies—History—19th century. 7. United States—History—Civil War, 1861-1865—Causes.
8. United States—Relations—West Indies. 9. West Indies—Relations—United States. I. Title.
    E453.R84 2009
    973.7′114—dc22

                                                                        2008014733

for Kate

... the voice of this nation is loud and incessant against the system of slavery. Its death warrant is sealed, so far as it relates to the British West Indies. The advocates of slavery are trembling, for the signs of the times proclaim that the end of their oppression draweth near.

—NATHANIEL PAUL TO WILLIAM LLOYD GARRISON,
APRIL 10, 1833

The great Slave question has started in England, if realized [it] will transfer a great bearing on the United States: of course, the whole evil will fall on the Southern section. Already does great—though secret—anxiety cloud our atmosphere? Therefore Planters must entertain views of the future different from those of existing times, that they may be prepared to bear the [brunt] of baneful change in the coming state of affairs.

—CHARLES DRAYTON II TO HIS SON,
AUGUST 13, 1833

Contents

Maps

Acknowledgments

I have looked forward to this moment when I could thank all those who helped along the way. The endeavor of historical research and writing has more than its share of solitary moments, but no one could do it without the support of family, friends, and colleagues.

Though I didn't know it at the time, this book has its origins in the late 1990s when I taught at St. George's College in Kingston, Jamaica as a Jesuit volunteer. I became thoroughly captivated with Jamaican culture and society, its vivacity and creativity. Where did all of this come from? Jamaican students, friends, and fellow teachers offered hints, but still, I wondered. As I began graduate school wiser heads told me gently that I might benefit from broadening my interests beyond one island. I branched out into the history of the United States and here we are with this book.

The book began as a dissertation at Boston College. Lynn Lyerly was the ideal adviser. Our discussions of the history of slavery were formative to my thinking, and her sharp insights and careful readings of everything I wrote were invaluable. Few people are as passionate about History as David Quigley. I have benefited enormously from our many conversations, his three-part questions, and his careful readings of my chapters. David Northrup was the first to suggest that I think Atlantically, to dissolve some of the artificial geographies in which we are taught to think. Frank Taylor taught me about Caribbean history and the art of telling a good story. Long conversations with Karen Spalding and Ginny Reinburg shaped my historical consciousness, I will always treasure my time with them. Crystal Feimster, Robin Fleming, Lynn Johnson, Alan Rogers, and Sergio Serulnikov, though not directly involved with this project, all contributed to my training as an historian in important ways. In the early stages of research I met Joan Cashin at the Huntington Library in San Marino, California, where we shared a wonderful month of research and conversation. She read drafts of each dissertation chapter and helped me appreciate prose. Graduate student colleagues have been equally important. Todd Romero has been a steady friend, a gracious groomsman, and a model scholar. Stephanie Kermes, Libby MacDonald-Bischof, Ken Shelton, Dolly Smith-Wilson, and participants in the Americanist writing group at Boston College read chapter drafts, listened, and shared ideas that have made this project better and the study of history fun.

The transition from dissertation to book has benefited from the help of scholars and friends. Jim Stewart agreed to serve on the dissertation committee knowing little about me beyond the title of a conference paper for SHEAR in 2002. Jim read the manuscript several times and his incisive critiques have improved the book immeasurably. Perhaps more important, he provided the wisdom of a senior scholar to a young historian who was a little concerned that he had bitten off more than he could chew. Seymour Drescher read the completed dissertation and his extensive readers report was my guiding light for the first revision. Richard Blackett read the revised version and made a fundamental intervention that made this a far better book. David Brion Davis read the dissertation and the twice-revised manuscript. His scholarship was seminal, of course, in the conceptualization of this study, his readers report proved an invaluable guide for the final revision, and it is hard to convey how important his enthusiasm for this project has been to me.

I have also learned from the scholars and librarians I've met as I researched in archives and shared my ideas. Over the past several years I have been fortunate to meet Denver Brunsman, Caleb McDaniel, and Dave Gellman. All have been working on their own book projects and I have learned much in conversation with each of them. At conference presentations and other forums I have benefited from the commentary of Jamie Bronstein, Stanley Engerman, Julie Roy Jeffrey, James Miller, Jim Walvin, and especially Mark Summers and Ron Formisano of the University of Kentucky. Librarians are perhaps the greatest collaborators in historical research and early in graduate school I had the opportunity to learn from John Attebury of the John J. Burns Library at Boston College. John's enthusiasm for answering research questions is infectious and I learned a great deal as his assistant. The title of this book emerged from a delightful conversation with Caroline Sloat of the American Antiquarian Society.

The librarians and staffs at the following libraries were all extremely help-ful: Thomas P. O'Neill Library at Boston College, Mugar Library of Boston University, John Hay Library of Brown University, Rhode Island Historical Society in Providence, Massachusetts Historical Society in Boston, Boston Public Library, American Antiquarian Society in Worcester, Massachusetts, Huntington Library, San Marino, California, Maryland Historical Society, Baltimore, Maryland, National Archives of College Park, Maryland, Manuscripts Division of the Library of Congress, Washington, D.C., Virginia Historical Society, Richmond, Virginia, South Caroliniana Library at the University of South Carolina, Columbia, South Carolina, Rare Book, Manuscripts, and Special Collections Library at Duke University, Durham, North Carolina, Manuscripts Department and the Rare Books Collection at the University of North Carolina at Chapel Hill, Charles E. Young Research Library at U.C.L.A., and the Sterling Memorial Library and the Beinecke Library of Yale University.

Rand Dotson and Lee Sioles of Louisiana State University Press have guided the manuscript through the publication process, and copyeditor Julia Ridley Smith smoothed out many imperfections in my prose. Stacey Maples of the Map Collection at Sterling Memorial Library at Yale University spent hours finding all those little towns that celebrated the First of August. Institutional support for this study has been provided by short-term fellowships from the John Nicholas Brown Center for the Study of American Civilization at Brown University, Providence, Rhode Island, Huntington Library, San Marino, California, Virginia Historical Society, Richmond, Virginia, the American Antiquarian Society, Worcester, Massachusetts, and the Gilder Lehrman Center for the Study of Slavery, Resistance, and Abolition at Yale University, where the staff is particularly fun. Dissertation and teaching fellowships were provided by the History Department of Boston College, and publication support was provided by the Frederick W. Hilles Publication Fund of Yale University, New Haven, Connecticut. Portions of this book have previously appeared as "The Harrisons Go to Jamaica: Race and Sexual Violence in the Age of Abolition," *Journal of Family History* (forthcoming, 2007); "British Abolition, Southern Anglophobia, Robert Monroe Harrison and the Annexation of Texas," *Slavery and Abolition* 28 (August 2007): 169-191; and "The Southern Response to British Abolition: The Maturation of Proslavery Apologetics," *Journal of Southern History* 70 (May 2004): 221-248. I thank the publishers of the *Journal of Family History* (SAGE Publications), of *Slavery and Ab-*

olition (*www.tandf.co.uk*), and of the Southern Historical Association for graciously permitting me to reprint this material.

I am only beginning a new chapter of my career in the departments of History and African American Studies at Yale University. This project was largely completed before I arrived, but I would like to acknowledge the gracious welcome I have received from new colleagues, in particular, David Blight, Joanne Freeman, Glenda Gilmore, Lillian Guerra, Bob Harms, Jonathan Hollaway, Gerald Jaynes, Alondra Nelson, and Steven Pincus. I would also like to thank my students, in Jamaica, Boston, and now in New Haven, for the inspiration to dig deeper into the past, and to explain it as clearly as I am able.

My parents, Ted and Virginia Rugemer, have provided their unconditional love and support from well before my interest in history began. They were my first teachers and I continue to learn from them. My brother John has been the source of much needed levity at critical moments throughout my life. For six years now this book has been shaped by my wife, Kate Cooney, to whom this book is dedicated. How lucky I have been to find a lover of the mind to be my partner in love and in life. She has taught me more than anyone. And Henry came along just in time for the final revisions. He has helped in his own way, by reminding me insistently to remember what is most important.

The Problem of Emancipation

Introduction

The summer of 1833 was a critical moment in the history of the United States. The British Parliament debated a bill that would abolish slavery in the West Indian colonies, ending Britain's great struggle over slavery. A similar contest had only recently begun in the United States, and many Americans waited anxiously for the newspapers, eager to learn the outcome. The black abolitionist Nathaniel Paul and the South Carolina planter Charles Drayton were both in Britain at the time, and their letters home offer a glimpse into the history that would unfold. Both men recognized the significance of British abolition, and their starkly opposed premonitions of its broader impact foreshadowed the growing sectional divide that would end in civil war.[1]

The persistence of slavery in the South was the greatest moral and political issue in the antebellum United States. For some, chattel slavery clearly violated the founding precepts of the Revolution, articulated most clearly in the Declaration's promise "that all men are created equal ... endowed by their creator with certain unalienable rights." But at each decisive moment in the creation of the American republic, critics of slavery were rebuffed. Revolutionary elites saw the possession of property as the foundation of personal independence, virtue, and the success of the republican experiment. Likewise, property in human beings had been legitimate

---

1. Nathaniel Paul to William L. Garrison, April 10, 1833, in C. Peter Ripley, ed., *The Black Abolitionist Papers,* 5 vols. (Chapel Hill: University of North Carolina Press, 1985–1992), 1:37. Charles Drayton II to his son, August 13, 1833, in Drayton Letterbook, Drayton Hall, Charleston, South Carolina, quoted in Joe Bassette Wilkins Jr., "Window on Freedom: The South's Response to the Emancipation of the Slaves in the British West Indies, 1833–1861" (Ph.D. diss., University of South Carolina, 1977), 60.

since the beginnings of Western civilization, and in 1776 the right of slave-holding was protected throughout the globe.[2]

The U.S. Constitution of 1787 was the first compromise in the Anglo-Atlantic world between the liberating tendencies of the Age of Revolution and republican tenets of property rights. The British Parliament's Act of Abolition in 1833 was the second. From the founding until the eve of the Civil War, many Americans believed that—in the words of Abraham Lincoln—"slavery would be extinguished in God's own time." America's founding elites had kept the Constitution free of the word *slavery*, but they had recognized the specific rights of slaveholders in manifold ways.[3] As the years passed the basic obstacles to the opponents of slavery were racism and greed, which denied the full humanity of Africa's descendants and secured private property against the claims of a higher law. Property in slaves represented enormous wealth for powerful southern elites, and slave-grown products were the foundation of American commerce, North and South. After the invention of the cotton gin in the 1790s, and as the land available for southern expansion grew with the Louisiana purchase in 1803, the acquisition of Florida in 1818, the forced removal of the southern tribes in the 1830s, and the annexation of Texas in 1845, the economic potential for the use of slaves seemed boundless.[4]

In contrast, West Indian planters had very little power in the British Parliament by 1833, and in the face of a massive popular movement to cleanse the British Empire of the moral stain of slavery, Parliament abolished the right to own human beings. It was the first time in world history that slavery had been eliminated by governmental fiat in a region with a predominantly slave population whose labor was critical to the economy. But the legislation was still a compromise. Black West Indians would no

2. David Brion Davis, *The Problem of Slavery in Western Culture* (New York: Oxford University Press, 1965), and *The Problem of Slavery in the Age of Revolution, 1770–1823* (1975; New York: Oxford University Press, 1999), 259.

3. Harold Holzer, ed., *The Lincoln-Douglas Debates* (New York: Harper Collins, 1993), 157; Paul Finkleman, *Slavery and the Founders: Race and Liberty in the Age of Jefferson* (Armonk, NY: M. E. Sharpe, 1996).

4. Leonard L. Richards, *The Slave Power: The Free North and Southern Domination, 1780–1860* (Baton Rouge: Louisiana State University Press, 2000); William Freehling, "The Founding Fathers, Conditional Antislavery, and the Nonradicalism of the American Revolution," in *The Reintegration of American History: Slavery and the Civil War* (New York: Oxford University Press, 1994): 12–33.

longer be slaves, but West Indian slaveholders were compensated with money and a significant allowance of nearly free labor from those who had once been enslaved. The planters received financial compensation of about £20 million, and the slaves became bound apprentices required to serve their masters for four to six more years. Perhaps even more important was the recognition of the planters' rights to their property in land. As a Confederate general would put it thirty years later, the former slaves received "nothing but freedom," and the eight generations of black labor that had cleared and improved those lands went completely unrecognized.[5]

As the process of emancipation began to unfold in the West Indies, abolitionists and southern spokesmen articulated contradictory portrayals of emancipation that became key elements of the arguments for and against American slavery. The authors of British abolition had styled it the "Mighty Experiment," and the results of abolition were subjected to a variety of measures. The first test involved the first days of freedom. Would there be rebellions of vengeance? West Indian slaveholders and their American sympathizers believed there would be, and abolitionists were quietly concerned. The second test took place on the sugar plantations. Would free black laborers work? Would sugar be as profitable with free laborers as it had been with slaves? Was the abolition of slavery a viable policy or the soft-minded agenda of humanitarian idealists?

While there were no rebellions, as the years passed there was little question that the West Indian sugar industry had declined. In the large colonies such as Jamaica, Trinidad, and Demerara where the sugar plantations had never monopolized all the arable lands, black peasantries emerged that were largely independent of the sugar industry. Freed people made it clear that they preferred to avoid plantation work, and the number of freehold properties increased consistently throughout America's antebellum decades. In the smaller islands such as Barbados, Antigua, and St. Kitts, where lands were not available and the former slaves came to depend upon wages from the plantations, the sugar industry survived. But on the whole, the West Indian economies suffered. By the end of the apprenticeship period in 1838, sugar production in the West Indies had declined by 9 percent. By 1846 the decline was 35 percent, and on the eve of the American

5. Seymour Drescher, *The Mighty Experiment: Free Labor Versus Slavery in British Emancipation* (Oxford: Oxford University Press, 2002), chap. 8; Eric Foner, *Nothing But Freedom* (Baton Rouge: Louisiana State University Press, 1983), 6.

Civil War in 1860 sugar production in the British West Indies remained 11 percent below the production levels of the last decade of slavery. For American slaveholders, abolition in the West Indies did little to challenge southern wisdom on the superiority of the slave system. Indeed, the clear economic failure of emancipation in the West Indies made the abolitionists even more suspect.[6]

The contrast between the free labor experiments in the West Indies with the economic prowess of American slavery was remarkable. When the British Parliament abolished West Indian slavery in 1833, the Cotton South was on the cusp of an economic boom. The price of cotton jumped four cents by the pound between 1833 and 1834, and investors speculated in the frontier lands of the Southwest as well as the slaves to work them. Individual capitalists as well as the state banks offered lines of credit to planters which fueled western expansion, and a vast portion of the old Indian lands were brought into the production of cotton. These fresh soils promised abundant crops, and they attracted the migration of planters from the older, eastern states, as well as the forced migration of slaves through the expanding domestic slave trade. Populations soared in the new cotton regions, and by 1837 cotton production had doubled from the level of 1826. While this huge expansion lowered prices, the steady increase in production over the next decade showed a firm belief in cotton's future which made slavery's role in the southern economy ever more secure.[7]

Ironically, the British people who felt so strongly about the abolition of West Indian slavery were many of the same folks who fueled (albeit unwittingly) the expansion of American slavery. Cotton cloth had been introduced into British society from India in the mid-seventeenth century, and Indian calicoes became quite fashionable, a popular replacement for the scratchy woolens that had previously characterized British wardrobes. Domestic manufacturers' efforts to meet the rising demand by competing with imported Indian cottons were perhaps the most powerful impetus behind Britain's industrial revolution. And as Britain's textile industry grew, imports of American cotton continued to increase. In 1803 American cot-

6. Stanley L. Engerman, "Economic Adjustments to Emancipation in the United States and British West Indies," *Journal of Interdisciplinary History* 13 (Autumn 1982), 195–200.

7. Lewis C. Gray, *History of Agriculture in the Southern United States to 1860*, 2 vols. (1932; Gloucester, MA: Peter Smith, 1958), 898–900, 1026–27; Robert Fogel, *Without Consent or Contract: The Rise and Fall of American Slavery* (New York: W. W. Norton, 1989), 30.

ton held 45 percent of the British market; by 1860 that figure stood at 75 percent.[8]

The power behind American slavery was formidable, but the United States was never a self-contained entity moved solely by the internal dynamic of American society. As the cotton trade shows, the United States was firmly embedded in an Anglo-Atlantic world that transcended the political boundaries of nation-states. The economic, cultural, and historical connections between the regions of Britain's old Atlantic empire were too firmly established to be broken by the political independence of the United States. Slavery was at the core of the Atlantic economy that allowed Britain's American colonies to thrive, and the movement to abolish slavery developed on the same transatlantic stage. Abolition's first proponents were the Africans who rebelled against their masters, whether on the coast of Africa, on slave ships, or on the plantations of the Americas. They were followed in the eighteenth century by the far-flung Quakers, who had long-standing ties to slavery and the slave trade in Britain, the West Indies, and the North American colonies. As the strength of antislavery grew in Britain, news and events from Britain and the West Indies had a tangible impact upon Americans.

Charles Drayton and particularly Nathaniel Paul—present in Great Britain at the very moment of abolition—were living examples of the international dimensions of this history. Drayton was on vacation, revealing the cultural ties between Great Britain and southern slaveholders. Nathaniel Paul was on an abolitionist mission. He had been appointed to raise funds in Britain for the Wilberforce community of African American refugees, who had settled in British Canada after escaping the brutal racism of their white neighbors in Cincinnati, Ohio. The transnational orientation was intrinsic to black abolitionists, and ever since the Revolution African Americans had taken advantage of the possibilities of British liberty. Each man embodied a transatlantic community—slaveholding and abolitionism, respectively—that had been at war with each other ever since they formed. The American Civil War was rooted in this broader struggle.

While most historians of the Civil War's origins have looked within

---

8. Beverly Lemire, *Fashion's Favorite: The Cotton Trade and the Consumer in Britain, 1660–1800* (Oxford: Oxford University Press, 1991), 12–17; David Eltis, *Economic Growth and the Ending of the Transatlantic Slave Trade* (New York: Oxford University Press, 1987), 39; Fogel, *Without Consent*, 67, 70.

American society, the "road to disunion" cannot be fully mapped within the confines of national history.[9] Britain's abolition of slavery should be understood as a seminal event in the history of the United States, a critical moment in the drift toward the Civil War thirty years later. This understanding requires an Atlantic approach to the antebellum United States. Over the past twenty years or so, many historians have been developing what has come to be known as Atlantic history. Motivated, perhaps, by the increasingly globalized world in which we live, scholars have ventured beyond the political boundaries of nation-states toward histories that emphasize the transnational connections and influences that shape our world today and have done so in the past. The sheer number of articles and book titles featuring the word *Atlantic* led the historian David Armitage in 2002 to boldly proclaim—"We are all Atlanticists now," and in the past five years there have been many more such titles. But as Armitage notes, most practitioners of the Atlantic approach limit their focus to the seventeenth and eighteenth centuries, when the political connections of the European empires remained intact.[10] But Atlantic history has expanded beyond the eighteenth century. The works of David Brion Davis, Richard Blackett, Seymour Drescher, and David Eltis on slavery and its abolition, and Daniel T. Rodgers's study of "social politics" during the Progressive era, have all been set on a transatlantic stage and skillfully treat the nineteenth century and beyond.[11]

An Atlantic approach to the antebellum United States demands the

9. William Freehling, *The Road to Disunion*, 2 vols. (New York: Oxford University Press, 1990–2007). Freehling has acknowledged some of the international dimensions of this history; see, esp., *Vol. 1: Secessionists at Bay*, part 6.

10. David Armitage, "Three Concepts of Atlantic History," in David Armitage and Michael J. Braddick, eds., *The British Atlantic World, 1500–1800* (Hampshire, UK: Palgrave MacMillan, 2002), 11.

11. David Brion Davis, *Western Culture, Age of Revolution*, and *Slavery and Human Progress* (New York: Oxford University Press, 1984); Drescher, *The Mighty Experiment*; Eltis, *Economic Growth and the Ending*; R. J. M. Blackett, *Building an Antislavery Wall: Black Americans in the Atlantic Abolitionist Movement, 1830–1860* (Baton Rouge: Louisiana State University Press, 1983), and *Divided Hearts: Britain and the American Civil War* (Baton Rouge: Louisiana State University Press, 2001); Daniel T. Rodgers, *Atlantic Crossings: Social Politics in a Progressive Age* (Cambridge: Harvard University Press, 1998). It should also be said that Atlantic history is not new. The seminal modern studies of Caribbean slavery and its abolition by C. L. R. James and Eric Williams both employed an Atlantic framework, and R. R. Palmer's *Age of Democratic Revolutions* embraced Europe and North America (while barely touching the Caribbean and Latin America). See C. L. R. James, *The Black Jacobins: Touis-*

recognition of two contemporary realities. First, the boundaries of the United States were permeable. News, goods, money, people, and ideas of transatlantic origin entered the United States through various channels on a regular basis. Furthermore, many Americans lived Atlantic lives that took them beyond the United States. They traveled to Europe and the West Indies where they learned about the wider world and gained a new perspective on their own lives. Second, American society had much in common with the societies of the Atlantic world, especially their divisive struggles over slavery and its abolition. British abolitionists began to agitate for the abolition of the transatlantic slave trade immediately after the American Revolution, and Caribbean slaveholders fought them from the beginning. A similar struggle developed in the United States early in its history, as was evident at the Constitutional convention, but the issue was not fiercely divisive until the mid-1830s. By then, of course, Americans had witnessed the Haitian Revolution, the rise of a popular abolitionist movement in Britain, the abolition of West Indian slavery, and the transformation of Great Britain into an abolitionist empire that attempted to suppress the transatlantic slave trade through military and diplomatic efforts. These were critical lessons for three generations of Americans, useable history for an increasingly divided nation.

This study is divided into two parts. Part One, *The Lessons of Abolitionism*, examines the impact of British abolitionism on the West Indies and the United States from 1804 until 1834. Part Two, *The Lessons of Abolition*, looks at the impact of West Indian emancipation upon the United States. Because of the shared history of these societies, the Caribbean struggle over slavery shaped the coming of the American Civil War. White America's problem with black emancipation had Caribbean roots.

The causes of the American Civil War have been the subject of a vast and contested historiography that began before the war was even over. The principal division within this literature today lies between the "fundamentalists," who emphasize the centrality of slavery in creating two fundamentally different societies—North and South—with opposing interests that made the sectionalization of politics, and thus civil war, almost inevi-

---

saint L'Ouverture and the San Domingo Revolution (1938; New York: Vintage, 1989); Eric Williams, *Capitalism and Slavery* (1944; Chapel Hill: University of North Carolina Press, 1994); R. R. Palmer, *The Age of Democratic Revolution*, 2 vols. (Princeton: Princeton University Press, 1959–64).

table. The "revisionists" counter with detailed analysis of the antebellum political system that uncovers a multitude of factors, not just slavery, which pushed the United States toward political collapse and civil war. Historian Edward Ayers has advanced the concept of "deep contingency" as a means of reconciling this historiographical divide. An emphasis on deep contingency in the antebellum United States focuses upon the "connection between structure and event, on the relationships between the long-existing problem of slavery and the immediate world of politics." One of the central structures in democratic societies is public opinion, particularly as it influences political life, and for the antebellum United States, public opinions about black emancipation were important. This book explores this notion of "deep contingency" by focusing not only on the long-term development of American ideas about emancipation in the Caribbean but also on how those ideas intersected with some of the key events in the coming of the Civil War.[12]

Transatlantic influence upon the American struggle over slavery began well before Parliament passed the Act of Abolition in 1833. Chapter 1 presents the historical connections between the United States and the British West Indies which wove the fabric of the nineteenth-century Anglo-Atlantic. British abolitionism had its first impact upon the United States following the Haitian Revolution, when in 1797, the prominent Jamaican planter-historian Bryan Edwards published his influential account. Edwards argued that the *Amis des Noir*, the French abolitionist society, had acted as the catalyst for the rebellion in Saint-Domingue.[13] A respected scholar and parliamentarian, Edwards's work went through several British and four American editions, and his thesis on the origin of slave rebellions would later seem prescient.

Chapters 2, 3, and 4 analyze three slave rebellions that preceded British abolition in 1834, as well as the American responses to those rebellions.

12. Edward L. Ayers, *What Caused the Civil War? Reflections on the South and Southern History* (New York: W. W. Norton, 2005), 138. A useful exploration of the historiography on Civil War causation can be found in Gary Kornblith, "Rethinking the Coming of the Civil War: A Counterfactual Exercise," *Journal of American History* 90 (June 2003): 76–105.

13. Bryan Edwards, *An Historical Survey of the French Colony in the Island of St. Domingo: Comprehending an Account of the Revolt of the Negroes in the Year 1791, and a Detail of the Military Transactions of the British Army in the Years 1793 & 1794* (London: John Stockdale, 1797).

British abolitionism experienced resurgence in the wake of Napoleon's defeat in 1815, and over the next fifteen years abolitionists in Parliament enacted a series of important reforms to the colonial slave codes. West Indian slaveholders condemned parliamentary intrusions in colonial government. They held public meetings, wrote angry editorials, and talked openly among themselves about "fanatical" abolitionists who sought the emancipation of the slaves. Slaves listened. The planters' reactions told West Indian slaves that they had allies in Britain, and with this opening in the firmament they felt empowered to rebel. Insurrection struck Britain's Caribbean colonies of Barbados in 1816, Demerara (now Guyana) in 1823, and Jamaica in 1831. The latter two rebellions took place within months of the slave conspiracy led by Denmark Vesey in Charleston in 1822, and the rebellion led by Nat Turner in Southampton, Virginia in 1831. The rebellions of 1831 were particularly important, as they dramatically unveiled a black radicalism that had transatlantic dimensions and had been developing throughout the 1820s. From the perspective of American slaveholders, the rebellions in the South followed a blueprint that was chillingly close to the West Indian pattern that Bryan Edwards had first noticed. The conspiracy in Charleston followed close upon the Missouri debates, when the future of American slavery was passionately argued in Congress. And the rebellion in Virginia came a mere eight months after the first publication of William Lloyd Garrison's *Liberator.*

American newspapers reported all of these events in great detail. Most accounts of the rebellions echoed the Edwards thesis—that abolitionist agitation had caused the rebellions. West Indian planters blamed the "fanatics" in Britain. They demanded the abolition of abolitionism, not slavery, and most white Americans agreed. But the slaveholders of the Caribbean lost, for British abolition came a mere two years after the rebellion in Jamaica. The demise of West Indian slavery portended a sequence of events that American slaveholders were determined to prevent, and as rich white men who possessed significant political power, they were more than able to do this. Part One argues that these rebellions in the West Indies, coupled with their treatment in American newspapers, were critical events that widened the American rift over slavery. American slaveholders learned from West Indian history that abolitionist agitation led directly to slave rebellions. American abolitionists learned that agitation led to abolition. Both sides acted on these lessons, and the great clashes of the 1830s were the result. The abolitionist mail campaign, the white mobs who seized and burned the mail, the race riots, the "gag rule," and the inexorable growth of abolitionist organization were all rooted in the broader transatlantic struggle.

Part Two explores the impact of British abolition upon some of the major actors in the U.S. struggle over slavery. Chapter 5 investigates the antislavery portrayal of the postemancipation West Indies. Prominent abolitionists such as William Lloyd Garrison, William Jay, and Lydia Maria Child lauded the safety of abolition, demonstrated by the lack of rebellions in the West Indies. And instead of judging emancipation solely by the performance of the sugar plantations, the abolitionists argued that other factors were more important. Through a series of studies, abolitionist writers demonstrated that by their standards, abolition had been a resounding success. Christianity had spread beyond the missions, and the number of baptisms and Christian marriages was on the rise. Literacy, too, had spread and West Indian children now went to school instead of to the fields. Most importantly, abolitionists explained, unlike the citizens of the United States, the British people were no longer burdened by the sin of slavery.

These arguments had considerable impact upon William Ellery Channing, one of the most influential ministers in the early republic and a representative of moderate antislavery opinion in the North. Abandoning an 1835 stance that conciliated the South and condemned the Garrisonians as irresponsible radicals, in the last years of his life Channing called upon the North to recognize its "duty" to demand the end of American slavery. Channing's reflections on the West Indies were the pivot of this change, and he communicated this transformation through the last seven pamphlets of his distinguished career to a national audience that he had cultivated for more than twenty years. By the time of Channing's death in 1842, the antislavery constituency in the North had grown considerably, changing the face of northern politics and deepening the national rift over slavery.

Chapter 6 views the postemancipation West Indies through the eyes of American slaveholders. British abolition made the American South the last slaveholding region in the Anglo-Atlantic world, a cause for great concern among slaveholders. While southern intellectuals developed the most sophisticated proslavery argument every articulated, a conspiratorial interpretation of British abolition pervaded southern society. Prominent southern politicians such as James Henry Hammond, Abel Upshur, and John Calhoun argued that abolitionism stemmed from a British plot to undermine the United States by dividing the country on the issue of slavery. This was particularly apparent to Robert Monroe Harrison, a Virginian who began his diplomatic career in the Monroe administration, and served in the American consulate in Kingston, Jamaica, from 1831 until his death in 1858. Harrison was appalled by the transition from slavery to freedom and informed his superiors of the dangers of British abolitionism with alarmist consistency.

Harrison became convinced that British abolitionists intended to revolutionize the American South from bases in Jamaica, a plausible theory considering the transnational radicalization of black abolitionists and the growing ties between black communities in Jamaica and the United States. Harrison shared his theories with a series of Secretaries of State, and when the well-known proslavery theorists Abel Upshur and then John Calhoun came into that office under John Tyler, Harrison's views became important. Upshur and Calhoun wanted Texas annexed to the United States, and they shared Harrison's distrust of Britain. Britain, they believed, would support an independent Texas if Texas abolished slavery. The South would be surrounded by abolitionists, and insurrections were sure to follow. The annexation of Texas was the most divisive issue of the mid-1840s. Abolitionists condemned the expansion of slavery that would follow annexation. Northern politicians were concerned with what was coming to be known as the "slave power," as Texas would add to southern representation in both houses of Congress. Annexationists talked patriotically of national greatness and the expansion of "American freedom." And southerners like Upshur and Calhoun pointed to the meddling, abolitionist British as a threat to American (they meant southern) security that necessitated bringing Texas into the American fold. Texas was annexed in 1845. Upshur and Calhoun had achieved their goal, but war with Mexico would follow. Influential historians such as David Potter and James McPherson start here with their accounts of the coming of the Civil War, but clearly, British abolition had been the critical precedent for these developments.[14]

Chapter 7 returns to the influence of British abolition on American

14. David Potter, *The Impending Crisis, 1848–1861* (New York: Harper and Row, 1976); James McPherson, *Battle Cry of Freedom: The Civil War Era* (New York: Oxford University Press, 1988).

abolitionists. Beginning in 1834, African Americans and white abolitionists in the North celebrated August 1, the day Parliament's Act of Abolition took effect in the Caribbean. By the 1840s, First of August celebrations took place in a growing number of communities throughout the northern and western United States, as well as in Canada. The celebrations cultivated the "imagined community" of transnational abolitionism, and in the context of American politics, they were the central popular event for the spread of political antislavery. Historians of antebellum America have described popular celebrations, especially the Fourth of July, as essential components of American political culture. They were the rites of partisanship and nationalism, and all political actors employed them to build support. Coming less than a month later, First of August celebrations responded in kind to the Fourth of July. African Americans and their white allies staged public processions with banners and bands, picnics, orators, and evening toasts that began with "the day we celebrate," the same toast made every Fourth of July. But instead of glorifying Revolution-era triumphs over Britain, abolitionist orators honored British abolition and excoriated American slavery; instead of toasting Washington and Jefferson, these activists raised their glasses to William Wilberforce and Nathaniel Turner. Wherever the First of August was celebrated, abolitionists challenged the complacency of the proslavery status quo. First of August celebrations grew in size and geographic breadth throughout the antebellum decades. They boldly pushed abolitionism into the public square and reminded mainstream America of the egregious hypocrisy of a thriving slavery in a nation that claimed freedom as its sustenance. On the eve of war a critical mass of the northern constituency was antislavery, if not abolitionist. The First of August played an important role in this transformation.

The eighth and final chapter explores how the long-term effects of British abolition continued to shape the American struggle over slavery, and ultimately, the coming of civil war. As slavery came to dominate American politics in the 1850s, arguments about West Indian emancipation played critical roles on either side of the debate. Proslavery spokesmen elaborated an interpretation of West Indian emancipation that seemed to demonstrate the impossibility of a like emancipation in the American South. And for the secessionist David Christy, whose election year reprinting of *Cotton is King* encapsulated thirty years of proslavery thought, the "conclusive arguments" defending southern slavery were grounded in Caribbean experi ence.[15] At the same time, the antislavery spectrum in the North broadened, as new voices representing the emergent Republican Party emphasized the benefits of free labor they saw in the postemancipation West Indies. By 1860, to see the benefits of emancipation in the British West Indies was no longer the preserve of radical abolitionists. Moreover, the decades-long struggle against slavery and racism further radicalized black abolitionists, some of whom moved from agitation to action. British abolition had created a geography of freedom in Canada, the West Indies, and the British islands which appealed to black Americans who were fed up with white American intransigence and who decided to emigrate. The black communities that formed in this era of British abolition created a radicalized "Antislavery International" that acted against American slavery. They agitated, raised funds, and facilitated the rescues of fugitive slaves by radicals willing to bear arms against slave catchers, and some of them joined John Brown's band. At each contingent moment in the coming of the Civil War, the beliefs of the principal actors had been shaped by deep reflection on Caribbean emancipations.

Including British abolition in the history of the antebellum United States recommends several reappraisals of the American struggle over slavery, beginning in the pivotal decade of the 1830s. Based on the British experience, abolitionists and proslavery spokesmen had preconceived ideas of the impact of radical abolitionism. The abolitionists had carefully observed their British counterparts, who had preceded them in the same moral cause and had succeeded. They had accomplished abolition (or so abolitionists believed) through the mobilization of the British people, who had become convinced of the terrible sins of slavery through a public relations campaign based upon antislavery publications, public lectures, and petitions to Parliament. Slaveholders and their political allies learned a very different lesson. They saw the insurrections in the West Indies and believed the allegations of West Indian planters that the abolitionists were to blame. So when American abolitionists began to disseminate their own propaganda and northern congressmen sought to read antislavery petitions from their constituents, slavery's partisans responded forcefully. In the South they burned abolitionist publications, in the North they mobbed abolitionist meetings, and in Congress they quashed any discussion of slavery. Aboli-

15. David Christy, *Cotton is King,* in E. N. Elliot, ed., *Cotton is King, and Pro-Slavery Arguments* (1860; New York: Negro Universities Press, 1969), 139.

tionists sought to recreate British success, but slaveholders knew what they were up to, so they acted and they stopped them.

Although the clashes of the 1830s established the lines of struggle, the British example remained potent. Abolitionists continued to agitate through pamphlets, newspapers, public lectures, and petitions to Congress, which the majority of members tried to ignore. The West Indies themselves became an important subject within the discourse on slavery, as abolitionists and proslavery theorists debated the "experiment" with black emancipation that was taking place not far from American shores. Moreover, the southern fear of insurrection grew. The threat of abolitionist agitation was now backed by Britain itself. The most powerful state in the Atlantic world was now an abolitionist state, with colonies too close for the comfort of the white South. British abolition, then, played a critical role in the campaign to annex Texas, a key moment in the struggle over slavery that foreshadowed the violence to come. And up to the very eve of the Emancipation Proclamation, First of August celebrations reminded communities throughout the North that to Britain's moral credit, slavery had been abolished, and a growing minority in the United States refused to let the matter rest. When the Civil War began in 1861, Americans had been divided over the lessons of British abolition for twenty-seven years. It was a dispute they never resolved.

PART I

The Lessons of Abolitionism

1

The Nineteenth-Century
Anglo-Atlantic World

hree lasting connections between the United States and the British Caribbean—language, religion, and trade—transcended the political division created by the independence of the thirteen mainland colonies in 1783. The people of the United States and the British West Indian colonies shared a culture, a history, and a religious heritage that flowed from their shared experience in the British Empire. The mercantilist system of the eighteenth century made the economy of the Anglo-Atlantic into one organic whole. Trade routes crisscrossed the Atlantic, circulating the goods, people, news, and ideas that formed the English-speaking world. British manufactures went to Bridgetown, Barbados, and Kingston, Jamaica, as well as to New York and Charleston; West Indian sugar sweetened tea from Boston to Bristol; North American fish, wheat, and corn fed West Indian slaves and the city-dwellers of Europe.[1] The literate read the same books and periodicals, and many of the same newspapers. Missionaries evangelized all who would listen, and various forms of Protestant Christianity brought these societies together. The churches spread with the empire, and politics could not divide what God had joined. Methodists and Baptists in the United States, the West Indies, and in Britain all shared a faith and worldview that was at least as important as national identity. The progress of God's work knew no national boundaries, and denominational newspapers and periodicals communicated news of the great work to believers throughout the Anglo-Atlantic. The slavery debate that ultimately

1. Walter Johnson has suggested that it makes "more sense to think about the political economy of the eighteenth- and nineteenth-century Atlantic as one single space." See his "The Pedestal and the Veil: Rethinking the Capitalism/Slavery Question," *Journal of the Early Republic* 24 (Summer 2004): 304.

divided the United States grew within this broader world. Slaves and slave-holders, preachers and merchants, politicians and abolitionists in the British West Indies and in the United States were all participants in this vast debate through their words and actions. If we are to fully understand the politics of slavery in the antebellum United States, we must begin with an understanding of the Anglo-Atlantic world. This chapter explores the origins and contours of the nineteenth century Anglo-Atlantic, the geography for the coming of the American Civil War.

ECONOMIC FOUNDATION

An Anglo-Atlantic world began to emerge in the seventeenth and eighteenth centuries from the economic interdependence that developed among England's American colonies on the mainland and in the Caribbean. The earliest English contacts with North America came through the fisheries off the Great Banks of Newfoundland, which attracted entrepreneurs from all over Europe in the early sixteenth century. Beginning as temporary camps for the catching and salting of cod for Mediterranean markets, the Newfoundland fisheries expanded into what is now southern Maine by 1610 to form some of the first permanent English settlements in North America. The fisheries extended Europe's developing system of merchant capitalism across the Atlantic from its roots in the Mediterranean. Merchants and fishermen built a transatlantic economy and began to lay the foundation for an Anglo-Atlantic world. The settlements depended on a staple—cod—and established the pattern for further English settlement.[2]

The gentlemen soldiers of the Virginia Company trailed the fishermen of the North, but they shunned labor and hoped to repeat the legendary conquests of Cortes and Pizarro. Death and failure lurked until they discovered tobacco, another staple with a growing European market. The Spanish had introduced bourgeois Europeans to tobacco, and the American weed was fashionable and scarce, bringing high prices to early Virginian planters. European demand prompted the first North American plantation revolution, and by 1630 tobacco had transformed Virginia

2. Stephen J. Hornsby, *British Atlantic, American Frontier: Spaces of Power in Early Modern British America* (Hanover, NH: University Press of New England, 2005), 8–16, 28–33; D. W. Meing, *The Shaping of America: A Geographical Perspective on 500 Years of History*, 3 vols., *Atlantic America, 1492–1800* (New Haven: Yale University Press, 1986), 1:29, 58–59.

into a nascent plantation society with a dominant class of tobacco planters whose operations depended upon indentured laborers from Europe and, eventually, African slaves.[3]

England's first Caribbean colonies—Barbados, St. Christopher (St. Kitts), Nevis, and Antigua—were settled in the 1620s in the wake of Virginia's successful experimentation with tobacco. In 1655, English adventurers sent by Oliver Cromwell seized Jamaica from the Spanish as a part of the Lord Protector's "Western Design." The largest island colony by far, Jamaica would become Britain's most valuable American possession by the mid-eighteenth century. Like Virginia, the island economies were at first based upon the labor of indentured Europeans in mixed agriculture and tobacco production. But the tobacco from England's Caribbean tasted awful, and brought a poor return in comparison to the Virginian product. The West Indians diversified into indigo and cotton, but in the late 1630s planters in Barbados, with the help of Dutch and English merchant capitalists, began devoting more of their lands to sugar production, which had proven quite profitable for Dutch and Portuguese planters in Brazil. By the early eighteenth century the intensive production of sugar had wholly transformed the society of each island.[4]

Sugar was far more profitable than tobacco, enabling West Indian planters to purchase increasing numbers of Africans from transatlantic slavers, and the African populations in the West Indies quickly outnumbered their counterparts on the mainland. Sugar's profitability also shaped a distinctive style of management for West Indian estates. While Virginia's planters devoted considerable lands to the production of corn, the managers of West Indian estates focused their resources almost entirely on sugar production. The most fertile lands were dedicated to sugar, leaving only the

3. Jack Greene, *Pursuits of Happiness : The Social Development of Early Modern British Colonies and the Formation of American Culture* (Chapel Hill: University of North Carolina Press, 1989), 8–9; Edmund Morgan, *American Slavery American Freedom: The Ordeal of Colonial Virginia* (New York: W. W. Norton, 1975), 108–30; Ira Berlin, *Many Thousands Gone: The First Two Centuries of Slavery in North America* (Cambridge: Harvard University Press, 1998), 95–111.

4. John J. McCusker and Russel R. Menard, "The Sugar Industry in the Seventeenth Century: A New Perspective on the Barbadian 'Sugar Revolution,'" in Stuart B. Schwartz, ed., *Tropical Babylons: Sugar and the Making of the Atlantic World, 1450–1680* (Chapel Hill: University of North Carolina Press, 2004): 289–330; Richard S. Dunn, *Sugar and Slaves: The Rise of the Planter Class in the English West Indies, 1624–1713* (Chapel Hill: University of North Carolina Press, 1972), 46–49, 59–61, 117.

lesser quality regions to food production. This left the West Indian colonies largely dependent on imported food, an economic reality of vast importance to the future integration of the Anglo-Atlantic world.[5]

The sugar revolution created a wealthy planter class that quickly dominated the islands, owning most of the slaves and much of the land. Opportunity became limited for a significant number of middling whites, prompting a migration from the smaller islands of the Eastern Caribbean (Barbados, St. Kitts, Nevis, and Antigua) westward to Jamaica and onward to the mainland. In 1670, the founders of South Carolina—black and white, slave and free—left Barbados for the southern mainland several hundred miles south of Virginia.[6] These migrants carried with them the experience of forming a lucrative slave society; they understood the new system. The earliest Carolinians experimented with sugar, tobacco, indigo, and cotton, but only the latter two became significant, and these were not enough to create the desired fortunes. With the vital contribution of African knowledge, Carolina's exportable staple became rice.[7] As with Canadian fish, West Indian sugar, and Virginia tobacco, Carolina's primary market was in Europe, where rice was used in an increasing number of industries (starch and paper making, and brewing, for example), and as a dietary staple for the poorer members of European society.[8]

The earliest settlements had established a pattern—English colonies depended upon producing a staple with a reliable European market. To be sure, there were significant differences among the societies that developed in the disparate regions of British America, but economically, politically, and culturally they were all a part of the English-speaking Atlantic world—they were elements of an organic whole.

The West Indian colonies were the most specialized economies in the entire Atlantic world. The extreme devotion to sugar production rendered

5. David Eltis, *The Rise of African Slavery in the Americas* (Cambridge: Cambridge University Press, 2000), 195–200; Lowell B. Ragatz, *The Fall of the Planter Class in the British Caribbean, 1763–1833: A Study in Social and Economic History* (1928; New York: Octagon, 1971), 88–92; Dunn, *Sugar and Slaves,* 188–203; J. R. Ward, *British West Indian Slavery: The Process of Amelioration, 1750–1834* (Oxford: Clarendon, 1988), 19, 39–60.

6. Peter Wood, *Black Majority: Negroes in Colonial South Carolina from 1670 through the Stono Rebellion* (New York: Knopf, 1974), 13–34; Jack P. Greene, "Colonial South Carolina and the Caribbean Connection," *South Carolina Historical Magazine* 88 (1987): 192–99.

7. Daniel C. Littlefield, *Rice and Slaves: Ethnicity and the Slave Trade in Colonial South Carolina* (Baton Rouge: Louisiana State University Press, 1981), 74–114; Wood, *Black Majority,* 35–62.

8. Peter A. Coclanis, "Distant Thunder: The Creation of a World Market in Rice and the Transformations It Wrought," *American Historical Review* 98 (October 1993): 1051–52.

the West Indies dependent upon the importation of food, creating a lucrative and easily accessible market for North American farmers. The expansion of sugar fields deforested extensive regions throughout the islands, creating an elastic demand for North American timber products.[9] Americans' seemingly endless thirst for West Indian rum and the various uses they found for molasses made the trading relationship compatible, creating a commercial web that tied the West Indian colonies to the port cities of the mainland. This trade involved the southern colonies as well. Slave traders from Africa would pass through the West Indies first before heading to the mainland colonies. And the staple crop reliance in the South was never as complete as in the West Indies. A middling class of whites developed—some of them slaveholders—who produced corn, wheat, and timber products for West Indian markets.

The West Indian trade formed an essential part of the economy in every mainland colony. Indeed, Bernard Bailyn has argued that the "real birth" of New England's independent commerce had its origins in the West Indian trade in the early 1640s, precisely when the sugar revolutions transformed the West Indies into import-dependent sugar producers.[10] In 1647, Governor John Winthrop of Massachusetts remarked that it "pleased the Lord to open us a trade with Barbados and the other Islands in the West Indies," as New England merchants found godly profits in supplying the sugar islands with dried fish, lumber products, foodstuffs, livestock, and sometimes African slaves.[11] New York was engaged with the West Indies from its beginnings in the Dutch empire. South Carolina in its earliest years depended almost entirely on the West Indian trade. By 1740, Philadelphia and Newport had regular connections with the West Indies, and by the 1770s, Wilmington, Baltimore, Richmond, and Savannah were also linked to West Indian markets.[12] The accompanying chart represents the

9. David Watts, *The West Indies: Patterns of Development, Culture and Environmental Change since 1492* (Cambridge: Cambridge University Press, 1987), 219–23, 393–95.

10. Bernard Bailyn, *The New England Merchants in the Seventeenth Century* (Cambridge: Harvard University Press, 1955), 83.

11. Quoted in Andrew Jackson O'Shaughnessy, *An Empire Divided: The American Revolution and the British Caribbean* (Philadelphia: University of Pennsylvania Press, 2000), 71.

12. Greene, "Colonial South Carolina and the Caribbean Connection," 198–99; Edwin G. Burrows and Mike Wallace, *Gotham: A History of New York City to 1898* (New York: Oxford University Press), 118–37; Richard Pares, *Yankees and Creoles: The Trade Between North America and the West Indies before the American Revolution* (Cambridge: Harvard University Press, 1956), 24; G. Terry Sharrer, "Flour Milling in Baltimore: 1750–1830," *Maryland Historical Magazine* 71 (Fall 1976): 323–24, 331; Sara Guertler Farris, "Wilmington's Maritime Commerce: 1775–1807," *Delaware History* 14 (1970): 22–51.

Table 1. Mainland Ports and the West Indian Trade, 1771

PORT	PRINCIPAL EXPORTS TO THE WEST INDIES
Salem and Marblehead	Empty hogsheads, dried fish
Boston	Spermaceti candles, bricks, empty hogsheads, hoops, dried fish, pickled fish
Falmouth	Pine boards
Rhode Island	Spermaceti candles, lard, onions, hoops, hogs, sheep, poultry, cheese, pickled fish
New Haven	Cattle, horses
New London	Onions, oak boards, cattle, horses, hogs, sheep, cheese, poultry
Piscataway	Bricks, pine boards, shingles
New York	Tallow candles, corn, lard, loaf sugar, poultry, bread and flour, butter
Philadelphia	Tallow candles, leather, oak boards, staves, loaf sugar, bread and flour, barreled pork and beef
James River	Corn, shingles, staves, barreled pork and beef, beans
Savannah	Rice
Charleston	Rice, leather, butter, beans

Source: This table is an adaptation of the list of figures complied by Richard Pares. See Pares, *Yankees and Creoles: The Trade Between North America and the West Indies before the American Revolution* (Cambridge: Harvard University Press, 1956), 25–26.

Note: The ports listed in column one were either the principal or secondary exporter of the items listed in column two.

principal exports to the West Indies from the North American ports most connected to the West Indies.

Each of these Atlantic ports served an agricultural hinterland that was linked to the Atlantic market by rafts or barges floating along the rivers, or by wagons traveling along the growing road systems.[13] As the diversity of goods indicates, the West Indian trade served as a profitable outlet for

13. John Thornton has noted that in Africa, navigable rivers that emptied into the Atlantic had the effect of expanding the bounds of the Atlantic world. The same was true of colonial North America. See John Thornton, *Africa and Africans in the Making of the Atlantic World,* 2d ed. (Cambridge: Cambridge University Press, 1998), 17–21.

the small surpluses of farmers and artisans throughout the country.[14] The chart should not be read to indicate economic specialization. Most voyages to the West Indies involved a great diversity of goods drawn from many different individuals. Merchants took several months to fill a vessel for the West Indian trade, a process that could involve several hundred exchanges of goods and services. The sloop *Mary Ann*, for example, owned by the Browns of Providence, Rhode Island, sailed to Surinam in 1766 with a cargo that included tobacco, candles, staves, hoops, bricks, horses, pigs, onions, axes, empty hogsheads, barrels of pork and beef, ship bread, flour, butter, oars, tar, and oysters.[15] Such a cargo would have taken months to assemble and would have come from small producers in Providence as well as farmers in the countryside. So while the Browns were the most directly engaged in the West Indian trade, the whole community was to a certain extent involved.

Vessels returned from the West Indies with the products of the sugar plantation—sugars of various qualities, rum, and molasses, as well as secondary products like pimiento.[16] These goods often served as currency in the early American economy, which was often short of specie. In 1764, for example, the Browns paid for the construction of a sloop entirely in molasses—300 gallons as a down payment, 900 more upon completing the deck, and the rest when the vessel was ready for sea.[17] The West Indian trade greased the wheels of everyday local commerce. Most merchants involved with the West Indian trade were also retailers or wholesalers. A New England farmer who sold his surplus wheat to a merchant collecting a cargo for the West Indies would more likely receive a debit with that merchant rather than being paid in cash. Actual payment would come through a series of retail purchases of West Indian goods and European imports. The same would be true of coopers in Salem or Providence, who made hoops and empty hogsheads for West India merchants and took their pay in rum.[18] When the loyalist merchant William Moss of Savannah fled the

14. John J. McCusker and Russell R. Menard, *The Economy of British America, 1607–1789* (Chapel Hill: University of North Carolina Press, 1985), 10–11, 92, 171–73, 193, 371.

15. Pares, *Yankees and Creoles*, 37.

16. North Americans know West Indian pimiento as "allspice," essential for pumpkin pie and gingerbread.

17. Pares, *Yankees and Creoles*, 121–22.

18. For examples of these commercial exchanges, see Pares, *Yankees and Creoles*, 123–25; Janet Siskind, *Rum and Axes: The Rise of a Connecticut Merchant Family, 1795–1850* (Ithaca: Cornell University Press, 2002), 52–55. The most thorough explication of the importance of the transatlantic economy to the American colonists is in T. H. Breen, *The Marketplace of*

country in the heat of the Revolutionary War, he left behind 280 small debts, many of them connected to his dealings in the West Indian trade.[19]

The American Revolution seriously disrupted West Indian trade networks, but once peace was reestablished, American merchants and West Indian planters hoped the trade between the sugar islands and the mainland could be resumed. In April 1783, a committee of the Society of West India Planters and Merchants of London felt certain that the United States–West Indian trade would be preserved, as it was clearly essential to the islands' support. Two months later Vice President John Adams wrote the first secretary of state, Robert R. Livingston, that "the commerce of the West India Islands is a part of the American system of commerce. They can neither do without us, nor we without them."[20] But powerful interests like the British shipping industry combined with the lingering animus against the now independent United States to defeat an attempt in Parliament (led by William Pitt) to liberalize the trade. An order-in-council issued in July 1783 maintained the mercantilist system and banned all American ships from British West Indian ports. Furthermore, salted beef, pork, butter, cheese, and fish from the United States were all banned from West Indian ports. While timber products, livestock, and flour and bread were still allowed, they had to be carried to the West Indies in British ships. Intended to be a boon to British shippers and merchants in Canada, Britain's policies simply redirected the trade in American goods through alternative ports in Canada and the Dutch islands. They also increased smuggling and inspired outrage.[21]

West Indian planters protested the new order almost immediately. Bryan Edwards—the esteemed planter from Jamaica, Member of Parliament, and author of a widely read history of the West Indies—warned in a pamphlet printed in both London and Boston that British policy was "fraught with the most serious consequences." Edwards argued that trade

Revolution: How Consumer Politics Shaped American Independence (New York: Oxford University Press, 2004), 33–192.

19. William Roberts, "The Losses of a Loyalist Merchant During the Revolution," *Georgia Historical Quarterly* 52 (1968): 273.

20. Minutes of the Society of West India Planters and Merchants, April 29, 1783; Charles F. Adams, ed., *The Works of John Adams* (Boston, 1853–56), 8:74–75, both quoted in Ragatz, *Fall of the Planter Class*, 173–74.

21. Sheridan, "Crisis of Slave Subsistence," 628–30; Selwyn Carrington, "The American Revolution and the British West Indies Economy," *Journal of Interdisciplinary History* 17 (Spring 1987): 841.

between the West Indies and the United States was essential to the prosperity of the West Indian colonies and claimed that "every addition to the prosperity of our sugar islands is absolutely and entirely an augmentation of the national wealth."[22] Edwards's pamphlet was followed by pleas from the West Indies for resumption of the trade. Governor Thomas Shirley of the Leeward Islands suggested that the trade be allowed to resume, if only in small vessels. Governor David Parry of Barbados recommended free trade with the United States until the Canadians were capable of supplying the islands. These complaints were for nought. Policy makers in Britain did not heed West Indian cries, and mercantilism reigned.[23]

Ironically, Britain's 1783 ban on American shipping to the West Indies preceded by only a few years the most prosperous period for American merchants engaged in the West Indian trade. The French Revolution and the subsequent wars with Napoleon extended their chaos across the Atlantic, disrupted British shipping, and prompted the West Indian governors to liberalize the trade with the Americans through a series of emergency decrees. The old trade routes were quickly reestablished, and from 1791 until the outbreak of war with Britain in 1812 the patterns of life from the colonial period quickly returned with trade resuming its prewar level. In the *Middlesex Gazette* of Middletown—a mercantile community on the Connecticut river—news from the West Indies went under the heading of "Domestic Politics," while news from Europe was considered "Foreign Politics."[24]

After the war of 1812, however, Britain resumed its policy of banning U.S. vessels from its Caribbean ports. Americans were outraged and more assertive now in the enthusiastic nationalism that accompanied their victory in New Orleans. President James Madison raised the issue in his State of the Union address in 1816, and public meetings in New York, Hartford, Newport, and Portsmouth early in the next year demanded action on the part of the federal government to gain access for American merchants to

22. Bryan Edwards, *Thoughts on the Late Proceedings of the Government respecting the Trade of the West India Islands and the United States of North America* (London, 1784), 6, 26; Sheridan, "Crisis of Slave Subsistence," 629.

23. Carrington, "The American Revolution," 842. See also F. Lee Benns, *The American Struggle for the British West India Carrying Trade, 1815–1830* (1923; Clifton, NJ: Augustus M. Kelley, 1972), 10.

24. Suskind, *Rum and Axes*, 48–49. For numbers on the extent of the trade, see John H. Coatsworth, "American Trade with European Colonies in the Caribbean and South America, 1790–1812," *William and Mary Quarterly*, 3d ser., 24 (April 1967): 263.

these lucrative markets.[25] So in March 1817, Congress passed a Navigation Act that prohibited the entry into U.S. ports of foreign vessels whose countries did not allow the free entry of American vessels. The act was clearly directed at the British and the West Indian trade, but it was unsuccessful. For the next thirteen years the trade ebbed and flowed with the protectionist impulses of Parliament and Congress, and American products generally reached the West Indies only through alternative ports.

In the early 1820s it seemed possible that the trade could be fully renewed. Pressure from West Indian colonists had led Parliament to offer to lower the duties on American goods, but only if the United States reciprocated. The administration of John Quincy Adams refused, and in 1825 Britain interdicted all American trade with the West Indies. The economic interests of Americans linked to the trade were badly damaged, and the issue became an albatross for Adams in his next election battle with Andrew Jackson. Jackson made an election year pledge to revive the West Indian trade, and he made good on his promise with the reciprocity treaty of 1830.[26] In 1833 an English captain on a visit to Kingston, Jamaica, expressed his "painful sense of humiliation" at witnessing the great preponderance of American vessels in this bustling port in the heart of Britain's own empire.[27] The economic interdependence rooted in colonial development was not easily disrupted, and as Britain's Parliament moved closer to the abolition of slavery in 1833, the economic interests of Americans and West Indians were as intertwined as they had ever been.

PROTESTANT BONDS

Protestant Christianity spread along the trade routes of empire as soon as settlement began, and the movement to abolish slavery first took root in the churches of the Anglo-Atlantic. By the time Britain abolished slavery in 1833, communities of faith there, in the West Indian colonies, and in the United States were bound together by common spiritual goals, deepen-

25. Benns, *The American Struggle*, 42–44; Timothy Pitkin, *A Statistical View of the Commerce of the United States of America* (New Haven: Durrie and Peck, 1835), 194.

26. *Baltimore Freeman's Banner*, April 14, 1832; Benns, *The American Struggle*, 46–188; Pitkin, *A Statistical View*, 196–213.

27. J. E. Alexander, *Transatlantic Sketches, Comprising Visits to the Most Interesting Scenes in North and South America, and the West Indies. With Notes on Negro Slavery and Canadian Emigration* (London, 1833), 289.

ing the links that economic development wrought in the English-speaking Atlantic.

One of the most potent connections among communities of faith and Anglo-Atlantic slave societies was the mission to African slaves—an endeavor that began early in the eighteenth century, reached out to the West Indies and the South, and lasted well beyond the American Revolution. Evangelical Christians were the most prominent group engaged in this effort. They embraced a democratic theology and cultivated a pastoral style that made Christianity an attractive solace within the world of slavery. In the nineteenth century, Evangelical Christians formed the backbone of transatlantic abolitionism.

Africans were quintessentially "heathen" to British Christians of the eighteenth century, and in 1701 a group of outward-looking Anglicans who sought to save African souls created the Society for the Propagation of the Gospel in Foreign Parts (SPG), with its mission of spreading the gospel among the slave populations of the Atlantic world. While SPG missionaries were dedicated, they ran into resistance from slaveholding colonists almost immediately. Planters looked unfavorably on their slaves spending time with the missionaries instead of in the fields, and many feared that religious ideas could lead slaves to assert their independence, even to rebel. Rumors of rebellion in Virginia in 1731, and actual rebellions in Stono, South Carolina, in 1739 and in Antigua in 1743 were all associated in some way with Christian slaves. Planters' suspicions of religious instruction were confirmed.[28]

Slaveholders' distrust of evangelization revealed an understanding that slaves might appropriate Christian ideas for their own purposes, a lasting pattern to which we shall return. But the Evangelical project had wide support and energetic workers who firmly believed in their mission to spread the gospel. The first Evangelicals to work in Atlantic world slave societies were the German-speaking Moravians, who started missions in the Danish West Indian island of St. Thomas in 1732, expanded into North Carolina in 1753, and spread to Britain's island colonies of Jamaica in 1754, An-

28. David Brion Davis, *The Problem of Slavery in Western Culture* (1966; reprint, New York: Oxford University Press, 1988), 212–15; Sylvia R. Frey and Betty Wood, *Come Shouting to Zion: African American Protestantism in the American South and the British Caribbean to 1830* (Chapel Hill: University of North Carolina Press, 1998), 70–71; John Thornton, "African Dimensions of the Stono Rebellion," *American Historical Review* 96 (October 1991): 1101–13.

tigua in 1756, and Barbados in 1765.[29] The Moravians believed in universal fellowship and actually lived among the slaves. But language was a barrier, as the enslaved of the mid-eighteenth century were either Africans who spoke a variety of languages or American-born creoles who spoke a patois that was equally difficult for European missionaries to comprehend. Thus the Moravians' most important contribution to the Evangelical mission was their use of "native helpers," converted slaves who helped the Moravians spread belief. They would be indoctrinated with the lessons of the faith and then paired with classes of four or five. Classes were organized by gender and the slaves spread the faith among themselves.[30]

The Moravian approach to slave evangelism had lasting implications, as their methods were adopted by the Methodists, who led the first major expansion of Evangelical Christianity in British America. John Wesley himself inaugurated the Methodist mission to the slaves during his first tour of the southern mainland in the 1730s. Wesley was shocked by the absence of Christian knowledge among the Africans he met in South Carolina. In contrast to most of his white contemporaries, Wesley believed that Africans were capable of receiving the faith, and he resolved to support their evangelization. The work was continued by George Whitefield. While Whitefield never left the Church of England, he shared Wesley's belief in the spiritual capabilities of Africans and perfected the oratorical style of Methodist exhorters which would epitomize the Great Awakening. In the 1740s and 1750s, Whitefield traveled throughout Britain's American colonies. He converted thousands—black and white—and criticized slaveholders who denied their slaves the opportunity of conversion. Prominent planters such as Hugh and Jonathan Bryan were moved to provide their slaves with religious instruction, thus broadening the interracial Christian community. While Whitefield vastly expanded the Evangelical mission to the slaves, he never condemned slavery outright, as John Wesley did in his *Thoughts on Slavery* (1774).[31]

29. Frey and Wood, *Come Shouting to Zion*, 86; Jon J. Sensbach, *A Separate Canaan: The Making of an Afro-Moravian World in North Carolina, 1763–1840* (Chapel Hill: University of North Carolina Press, 1998), 44–47.

30. Frey and Wood, *Come Shouting to Zion*, 83–85; Sensbach, *A Separate Canaan*, 37–39.

31. Frey and Wood, *Come Shouting to Zion*, 90–93; Harry S. Stout, *The Divine Dramatist: George Whitefield and the Rise of Modern Evangelicalism* (Grand Rapids, MI: William B. Eerdmans, 1991), 100–101; Harvey H. Jackson, "Hugh Bryan and the Evangelical Movement in Colonial South Carolina," *William and Mary Quarterly* 43 (October 1986):594–614.

Methodism quickly spread to the British West Indies as well. Nathaniel Gilbert, a planter from Antigua, was introduced to Wesley's writings by his brother in 1758. On a trip to England, Gilbert and three slaves who accompanied him (at least two of them women) heard Wesley preach. All were deeply affected, and when they returned to Antigua, Gilbert established a Methodist mission on his plantation.[32] According to Sylvia Frey and Betty Wood, Methodism probably spread through the work of the women who had traveled with Gilbert to England. Antigua's slave population was still predominantly African born, and just as the Moravians had employed "native helpers" to extend conversion beyond the boundaries of language, so too did the Methodist slave women do the work of conversion in Antigua. In the 1760s and 1770s Methodism spread further into the southern mainland colonies through the evangelizing of more missionaries—black and white—who built upon the earlier work of Whitefield.[33] And in the 1780s, Thomas Coke, a close associate of Wesley's, spread Methodist missions from their base in Antigua to St. Vincent, St. Kitts, Dominica, and Jamaica. Coke also secured the missions from planter antagonism by clarifying the missionary agenda—they would save African souls from Satan, but slaves' bodies belonged to the planters. As the esteemed West Indian historian Elsa Goveia has argued, the Evangelical missions to the slaves provided valuable support to the West Indian planters, for as their coreligionists in Britain began to challenge slavery, and as the French and Haitian Revolutions abolished slavery, the Evangelical missionaries demonstrated that slavery was compatible with the Christian way.[34]

Baptists ploughed the same fields as the Methodists during these years. The first Baptist revivals took place in Virginia and were led by Separate Baptists who had migrated from New England. The Baptists were inspired preachers who encouraged remarkably expressive conversions in which believers would speak in tongues, fall to the ground, and writhe in spiritual ecstasy—much to the chagrin of unconvinced onlookers. The Baptists' emphasis on the physical manifestations of spiritual conversion appealed to white and black communities in the South, and the Bap-

32. Elsa Goveia, *Slave Society in the British Leeward Islands at the End of the Eighteenth Century* (New Haven: Yale University Press, 1965), 289–90.

33. Frey and Wood, *Come Shouting to Zion,* 104–6.

34. Goveia, *Slave Society in the British Leeward Islands,* 292, 300–310; Mary Turner, *Slaves and Missionaries: The Disintegration of Jamaican Slave Society, 1787–1834* (Urbana: University of Illinois Press, 1982), 7.

tist revivals spread rapidly through Virginia, North Carolina, and into Georgia.[35]

One of the most influential slaves to be converted in the Baptist revivals was George Liele. Born in Virginia to parents who were probably American born and Christian, Liele recalled a "natural fear of God from my youth." His master, Henry Sharp, was a devout Baptist who brought Liele with him to Georgia. At some point in 1773 Liele heard a sermon by the Baptist preacher Matthew Moore which inspired his conversion. Liele felt compelled to evangelize "the people of my own color," and his success was noticed by the "white brethren," who called upon him to preach to the whole community. Liele preached for three years on several plantations around Savannah, and his efforts led Sharp to free him. Liele remained with Sharp's family, however, and when the war with Britain began Sharp served in the British army and was killed. When the British evacuated Savannah in 1782 (possibly in the same evacuation that rescued the merchant William Moss), Liele and others from his church went along and ended up in Kingston, Jamaica.[36]

Liele's experience was similar to those of the white missionaries who traveled within British America, the only exception being his forced migration. Although separated from his religious community, Liele found himself in a familiar world and began to evangelize in Kingston's black community. By the time Liele recorded his experience in 1790, he and his American brethren had cultivated a church in Kingston of about 450 members, including a few whites. He had also appointed a deacon, bought land, and begun to build a meeting house.[37] Liele continued to correspond with several black ministers in the United States, and sometime in the 1790s he was joined by at least three—Moses Baker, and two men named Gibbs and Robinson. These men took on the work of spreading the Baptist faith through the island, and in 1802 the free black missionary Thomas

35. Rhys Isaac, *The Transformation of Virginia, 1740–1790* (Chapel Hill: University of North Carolina Press, 1982), 161–77; Frey and Wood, *Come Shouting to Zion,* 99–100; Sobel, *Trabelin' On,* 79–98.

36. George Liele et al., "Letters Showing the Rise and Progress of the Early Negro Churches of Georgia and the West Indies," *Journal of Negro History* 1 (January 1916): 69–71; Frey and Wood, *Come Shouting to Zion,* 115–16; Thomas J. Little, "George Liele and the Rise of Independent Black Baptist Churches in the Lower South and Jamaica," *Slavery and Abolition* 16 (August 1995): 188–204.

37. Liele et al., "Letters Showing the Rise and Progress," 73–74.

Swigle reported that in Western Jamaica the "spread of the gospel" continued at an inspiring pace.[38]

In 1814 Liele's efforts were joined by those of the London Baptist Missionary Society, which had been formed in London in 1792 by William Carey. The society sent missionaries from Britain and also provided financial support, but like the Methodist missions established by Coke, Baptist missionaries were instructed to steer clear of the political questions of slavery and abolition.[39] Other denominations had missionary societies as well, and the 1795 formation of the nondenominational London Missionary Society represented an ecumenical effort to save souls throughout the British Empire. Missionary societies in Britain emerged from an Evangelical revival among dissenters that paralleled the Second Great Awakening in the United States. Historians of Britain have linked the Evangelical revival to the social tensions that sprung from the French Revolution and the early phases of the Industrial Revolution. Likewise, historians of the United States have argued that the Second Great Awakening stemmed in part from the social upheaval associated with the market revolution. In both countries, the awakening of religious enthusiasm spawned a variety of reform societies, many of which had their counterparts on either side of the Atlantic. Missionary societies were a part of this effort, and it was through them that the transatlantic communities of faith became most intertwined with the world of planters and slaves.[40]

While the Second Great Awakening and the formation of missionary societies was clearly a transatlantic development, there was a sectional pattern within the United States that revealed the clear division formed by slavery. At first, the formation of American missionary societies was primarily a northern development, which Donald Mathews has traced to a series of revivals in 1812.[41] In the South, however, the old fears that reli-

38. Ibid., 73, 91; James M. Phillippo, *Jamaica: Its Past and Present State* (London: John Snow, 1843), 280.

39. Turner, *Slaves and Missionaries*, 7–8, 17.

40. Emilia Viotti da Costa, *Crowns of Glory, Tears of Blood: The Demerara Slave Rebellion of 1823* (New York: Oxford University Press, 1994), 3–19; Charles Sellers, *The Market Revolution: Jacksonian America, 1815–1846* (New York: Oxford University Press, 1991), 202–36; Frank Thistlethwaite, *The Anglo-American Connection in the Early Nineteenth Century* (Philadelphia: University of Pennsylvania Press, 1959), 76–102.

41. Donald G. Mathews, "The Methodist Mission to the Slaves, 1829–1844," *Journal of American History* 51 (March 1965): 617.

gious instruction inspired slave revolt found evidence in Gabriel's rebellion in Virginia in 1802 and in Denmark Vesey's conspiracy in 1822. Christian slaves were accused of involvement in both threats to the southern status quo, and many planters—even pious ones—blanched at the project of evangelizing their slaves.[42] Despite these fears, African American Christians were already a prominent feature of the southern landscape, for the Evangelical churches—and the number of black Christians—had been growing since the eighteenth-century Awakening.[43] Conversions among southern planters made them far more amenable than their West Indian counterparts to the Christianization of slaves, and they had allowed independent black churches to develop and grow. Moreover, to suppress the spread of Christianity would have clashed with the "aggressive evangelism" that characterized the southern Evangelical mind.[44] So in 1825 a group of ministers in South Carolina began to advocate the mission to the slaves, and in 1829 they were joined by the prominent planter and Methodist C.C. Pinckney, who announced his desire for Methodist missionaries to work on his plantations. For Pinckney, the purpose of the mission was to cultivate "better" slaves who as Christians would be more obedient and hard working. Pinckney's call was answered by southern Evangelicals such as William Capers and Charles Colcock Jones, who made the mission to the slaves their life-long work. As in the West Indies, the Evangelicals were concerned only with saving slaves' souls, and missionaries provided spiritual support to the secular institution of slavery.[45]

On the eve of British abolition, then, the Evangelical mission to the slaves was a major project throughout the Anglo-Atlantic world. American religious periodicals captured the attention of readers throughout the

42. James Sidbury, *Ploughshares into Swords: Race, Rebellion, and Identity in Gabriel's Virginia* (Cambridge: Cambridge University Press, 1997), 73–79; William W. Freehling, *Prelude to Civil War: The Nullification Controversy in South Carolina, 1816–1836* (New York: Harper and Row, 1965), 72–73.

43. Frey and Wood, *Come Shouting to Zion,* 149.

44. Cynthia Lynn Lyerly, *Methodism and the Southern Mind, 1770–1810* (Oxford: Oxford University Press, 1998), 44.

45. Mathews, "The Methodist Mission," 618–30. I should note, however, that C. C. Jones initially approached his mission to the slaves as an antislavery project, to Christianize the slaves in order to make them ready for freedom. Only later in his career did he abandon antislavery ideas and promote the mission as beneficial to slavery. See Erskine Clarke, *Dwelling Place: A Plantation Epic* (New Haven: Yale University Press, 2005), 90, 355–56.

country with laudatory articles about the Christian work underway in both regions. In a review of Pinckney's *Address*, for example, the *New York Christian Advocate and Journal and Zion's Herald* celebrated the mission work already underway, noting "70,000 [slaves] among the members of the Methodist Episcopal Church, and nearly half that number belonging to the Wesleyan Methodists in the West Indies."[46] The mission to the slaves affirms Donald Mathews's suggestion that the Second Great Awakening be seen as an "organizing process" that created something entirely new—national communities of believers who sought to transform their own lives and the lives of others.[47] For American Evangelicals the community of believers was determined by God—not region or section—a geography revealed in the breadth of humanity discussed in their newspapers. The inclusion of the West Indies in the same reports is telling. The political boundary between the United States and Britain's West Indian colonies was of secondary importance in the Evangelical mind—God's mission was the same in both regions. This unity would be severely challenged in the early 1830s, when many Evangelicals in the northern United States and Great Britain began to see slavery as incompatible with their faith. And in 1833 when British Evangelicals celebrated the abolition of slavery—the cleansing of their national sin—Christians in the North were challenged by the example, while Christians in the South were thrown on the defensive.

PRINT AND PUBLIC OPINION

Evangelicals were not the only American readers whose papers kept them in touch with the British West Indies. News in the Anglo-Atlantic traveled

46. *New York Christian Advocate and Journal and Zion's Herald*, August 19, 1831. More accounts of the mission to the slaves in the West Indies and the South include *New York Christian Advocate and Journal and Zion's Herald*, February 18, 1831, March 4, 1831; *Hartford Christian Secretary*, September 13, 1823; *Boston Recorder*, August 29, 1829; *Boston Christian Watchman*, April 8, 1831, September 30, 1831, February 17, 1832; *New York Christian Index*, November 20, 1830, May 21, 1831, December 24, 1831; "Religious Instruction of Slaves in Jamaica," *Gospel Messenger and Southern Episcopal Register* 10 (June 1833): 188; "The Episcopal Plan of Christian Instruction for the Slaves in the West Indies," *Gospel Messenger and Southern Episcopal Register* 11 (June 1834): 175–81. See also Jeffrey Robert Young, *Domesticating Slavery: The Master Class in Georgia and South Carolina, 1670–1837* (Chapel Hill: University of North Carolina Press, 1999), 175–77.

47. Donald Mathews, "The Second Great Awakening as an Organizing Process, 1780–1830," *American Quarterly* 21 (Spring 1969): 34.

along the same channels that facilitated economic integration, and "intelligence" from the West Indies was a regular feature of American newspapers. The first permanent foreign correspondent for an American paper, hired by James Gordon Bennett's *New York Herald* in 1837, was based in Jamaica, and the *Boston Daily Advertiser* noted in 1841 that the fleet of West India Mail Steamers had recently been expanded to five.[48]

The first English newspapers were official organs of the Crown in the late seventeenth century, and during the first two decades of the eighteenth century newspapers proliferated in provincial Britain and the American colonies. The first newspaper published in the Americas was the *Boston News-Letter*, printed by John Campbell in 1704; the second was the *Weekly Jamaica Courant* of Kingston, begun in 1718. Over the next thirty-five years, ten more newspapers appeared in British America, two of them in the West Indies, and a few of the same printers were involved with the expansion in both regions. The *Barbados Gazette*, for example, was started in 1731 by Samuel Keimer, who had first worked as a printer in Philadelphia. One of Keimer's journeymen in Philadelphia was Benjamin Franklin, who famously learned his trade in London. Early American newspapers were usually based in the ports; they were filled with advertisements, mercantile information, and announcements of ships' arrivals and departures. Their news reports reflected the geography of the British Empire, and most were reprinted whole cloth from London papers.[49]

The newspaper's origin in the royal court reflects its political function, and American newspapers cut their teeth on colonial politics. Indeed, many have argued that the politicization of the newspaper press was a critical factor in the movement for independence in the mainland colonies.[50] Most

48. Michael Schudson, *Discovering the News: A Social History of American Newspapers* (New York: Basic Books, 1978), 23; *Boston Daily Advertiser*, August 3, 1841.

49. Charles E. Clark, "Early American Journalism: News and Opinion in the Popular Press," in *The Colonial Book in the Atlantic World*, ed. Hugh Amory and David D. Hall (Cambridge: Cambridge University Press, 2000), 354–55; Isaiah Thomas, *The History of Printing in America, with a Biography of Printers, and an Account of Newspapers*, 2 vols. (1810; reprint, Albany: Joel Mansell, 1874), 2:188, 192; Benjamin Franklin, *The Autobiography of Benjamin Franklin* (1868; reprint, Mineola, New York: Dover, 1996), 31–38. For more on the West Indian press, see Edward K. Brathwaite, *The Development of Creole Society in Jamaica, 1770–1820* (Oxford: Clarendon, 1971), 31–34; O'Shaughnessy, *An Empire Divided*, 280, n. 59.

50. Arthur M. Schlesinger, *Prelude to Independence: The Newspaper War on Britain, 1764–1776* (New York: Alfred A. Knopf, 1958), 3–303; Stephen Botein, "Printers and the American Revolution," in *The Press and the American Revolution*, ed. Bernard Bailyn and John B. Hench, 11–57 (Worcester: American Antiquarian Society, 1980); Clark, "Early American Journalism," 361–62.

West Indians did not seek independence, but their newspapers were political voices during the tumultuous decade before the Revolution. Some island whites—particularly in St. Kitts and Nevis—were as outraged by Parliament as their mainland cousins, especially after the Stamp Act. But the extreme demographic and political imbalances within the slave societies of the British West Indies left the island colonies prone to slave revolts and therefore dependent on British troops for their own security. These fears became manifest in Jamaica in 1776, when a slave revolt broke out which was clearly timed to coincide with the departure of British regiments for the mainland. During the Revolution, West Indian newspapers proclaimed the loyalty of the island colonies, and worked to secure their place within the British Empire. And when Britain closed the trade between the United States and the island colonies, West Indian newspapers agitated for the renewal of this all-important commerce. In the British West Indies and the early Republican United States, newspapers were political voices.[51]

After independence was achieved in 1783, the newspaper press was fundamental to the political development of the early American republic. The Post Office Act of 1792 allowed newspapers to be shipped to subscribers through the mail system at extremely low rates, which Richard John has likened to a subsidy for editors. The act also mandated the delivery of "exchange papers," whereby printers received at very low cost the newspapers of other regions. John argues that such policies began to unify the United States along a nationwide network of information, where, in Toqueville's famous rendering, the newspaper could put "the same thought at the same time before a thousand readers."[52] Historians Richard D. Brown and Jeffrey Pasley have shown how widespread republican values and the emergence of political parties made the newspaper one of the most important institutions in communities throughout the United States.[53]

The nexus between the U.S. newspaper system and the broader Atlantic

51. O'Shaughnessy, *An Empire Divided,* 89–92, 102–3, 200–202, 240–41.

52. Richard John, *Spreading the News: The American Postal System from Franklin to Morse* (Cambridge: Harvard University Press, 1995), 36–37; Alexander de Toqueville, *Democracy in America,* 2 vols. (1840; reprint, New York: Vintage, 1990), 2:111. See also Donald Scott, "Print and the Public Lecture System, 1840–1860," in *Printing and Society in Early America,* ed. William L. Joyce et al. (Worcester: American Antiquarian Society, 1983), 290.

53. Richard D. Brown, *Knowledge is Power: The Diffusion of Information in Early America, 1700–1865* (New York: Oxford University Press, 1989); Jeffrey L. Pasley, *"The Tyranny of Printers": Newspaper Politics in the Early Republic* (Charlottesville: University Press of Virginia, 2001).

was described by Achille Murat, the Sicilian prince and contemporary of Tocqueville who became an American citizen. In his account of westward expansion, Murat portrayed the post office and the newspaper as essential elements in the development of the quintessential "American" town. The postmaster was a prominent citizen, and his was the first governmental post of importance. He was responsible for the mail, which carried letters from loved ones back East as well as the newspapers. "Everyone" received a newspaper or two, one from "the village from which he [had] emigrated" and one from "Washington, or from some Atlantic town." Murat boasted that Americans were remarkably well informed, receiving "reviews and magazines, literary journals, novelties of every sort, [which] come to us from New York, Philadelphia, and England, at a moderate price, and a month or two after their publication over the Atlantic."[54]

Murat's observations, made during the very year of British abolition, suggest a deep level of American engagement with the print culture of the Anglo-Atlantic world. While many Americans continued to read British periodicals, most Americans learned of world events through the newspapers. Editors throughout the country derived their news from the exchange papers that arrived in the mails, but the newspaper editors in the "Atlantic towns" were also responsible for spreading the news from the West Indies, which typically derived from one of three transatlantic routes: the testimony of the captain or a passenger from a ship recently arrived from the islands, a personal or official letter available to the editor, or a newspaper printed in a West Indian town.

The letters and people that provided American editors with so much of their news about the West Indies traveled such dizzying paths that misinformation was practically inevitable. An account of a slave rebellion in the West Indies, which appeared in both the *New York Commercial Advertiser* and the *Washington Daily National Intelligencer* in May 1816, reveals the exigencies of nineteenth-century communication. The papers' cited source was Captain Copeland of the schooner *Betsey,* which had arrived in Edenton, North Carolina, after sailing from St. Eustatius, a Dutch island

---

54. Achille Murat, *The United States of North America* (London: Effingham Wilson, 1833), 63. Contemporary literature often featured scenes or characters from the British West Indies; see, e.g., "Russell's Adventures" (n.p., 1813?), a broadside in the New York Historical Society. This development is fully explored in Sean X. Goudie, *Creole America: The West Indies and the Formation of Literature and Culture in the New Republic* (Philadelphia: University of Pennsylvania Press, 2006).

that served as an entrepot in the West Indian trade. Direct trade between the United States and the West Indies had just been banned during that year, and it seems probable that Copeland had shipped West Indian–bound American goods to St. Eustatius. While in St. Eustatius, Captain Copeland learned from someone on a British schooner, which had just arrived from Antigua, that the slaves of St. Vincent had revolted and had possession of most of the island. Copeland also reported that he had heard of an insurrection in Barbados, where "the Blacks had destroyed thirteen estates."[55]

In reality there had been only one rebellion—in Barbados. The *Commercial Advertiser* gleaned the captain's report from an exchange paper from North Carolina which the editor did not cite. Copeland's information was in turn derived from hearsay. One can imagine the many conversations among seamen in the ports of the Caribbean during slave insurrections, and it is not surprising that St. Vincent's replaced Barbados as the scene of insurrection. The islands are right next to each other—indistinguishable, perhaps, with the right amount of rum—and if location could be mistaken, more significant details could as well. The casual talk among sailors became the "facts" in news stories that found their way into the West Indian press and then were reprinted verbatim in papers exchanged throughout the United States.

But there is more at stake here than the misrepresentation of distant events (a reality we still live with despite vast technological advance). The effort made by American editors to procure news of West Indian events is clear, but what was the effect of this news in American society? Michael Schudson has suggested that the societal role played by the newspaper can be understood according to two models. The first is to see the newspaper as a vehicle of information—a transmitter—that carries news or an idea from one place to another. The second is to see the newspaper as an instrument within the "ritual" of communication through which an entire community becomes connected and defined by the newspaper. Both models of communication can be usefully employed in describing the nineteenth-century Anglo-Atlantic world. When one sees that a newspaper in Boston printed the price of flour in the Jamaican market, for example, the transmission model is perfectly sufficient for understanding the newspaper's historical

55. *New York Commercial Advertiser,* May 20, 1816; *Washington (DC) Daily National Intelligencer,* May 25, 1816.

role. Merchants needed the newspapers to help them make decisions on their personal involvement with the West Indian trade. At this level of communication, little beyond economic interest connected the merchants in these ports. But for recognizing the implications of a denominational paper printing an account of the conversion of slaves in the West Indies, the transmission model no longer seems adequate. The believing reader in Boston might have felt inspired by the addition of souls to his or her spiritual world. A pious slaveholder in Virginia might have been moved to consider the religious instruction of his or her own slaves. These readers would have been reminded of their connection to a community of faith, linked for a moment by the newspaper.[56]

The ritual model of understanding the newspaper is critical to understanding Americans' relation to the Anglo-Atlantic world of the nineteenth century, especially with respect to the debate over slavery. When America was a young republic, most West Indian planters—and editors— were militantly opposed to abolition, and news from the West Indies— especially the way it was reported by American editors—helped to form the opposed communities in the American struggle over slavery.[57] There was a broad spectrum of opinion on slavery in the early nineteenth century, but the groups within this spectrum clearly transcended political boundaries. Southern slaveholders had much more in common with the slaveholders in the West Indies than with New England abolitionists, who in turn shared more with their British counterparts than with planters in South Carolina. An underlying premise in the chapters to come is that news from the West Indies played a critical role in the formation of American public opinions on slavery, as well as on the movement to abolish it.

Contemporaries and historians alike have recognized the critical role of public opinion in the history of the United States. Richard Brown has described public opinion as "powerful and unruly" during the Revolution, when pamphlets articulated the rhetoric of independence, and newspapers organized resistance to the Stamp Act and applauded boycotts of British

56. Michael Schudson, "Preparing the Minds of the People: Three Hundred Years of the American Newspaper," in *Three Hundred Years of the American Newspaper,* ed. John B. Hench (Worcester: American Antiquarian Society, 1991), 426. Schudson is applying the ideas of the communications scholar James W. Carey; see Carey's *Communication as Culture: Essays in Media and Society* (1989; reprint, New York: Routledge, 1992), 13–23.

57. Andrew Lewis, "'An Incendiary Press': British West Indian Newspapers During the Struggle for Abolition," *Slavery and Abolition* 16 (December, 1995), 353–55.

imports.[58] With independence "the people" were theoretically sovereign, and, as James Madison warned, "public opinion must be obeyed by the government." This sounds like a lofty ideal, and as Pasley has shown, Madison's statement arose from his personal opposition to the John Adams administration. His unsigned essay appeared in the *National Gazette*, which was formed for the purpose of swaying "public opinion" toward Madison and Jefferson's view of proper governance. Madison believed that public opinion was a powerful but malleable entity that should be carefully formed by enlightened men and regularly leavened by the *"circulation of newspapers through the entire body of the people."*[59] But, as the venue for his essay shows, newspapers were never mere sources of objective information, they were instruments of opinion formation that had particular agendas.

As the second party system of Democrats and Whigs emerged from the vibrant presidential campaigns of 1828, the number of political newspapers available to American readers vastly increased. Jacksonians and Adamsites made enormous investments in time and capital to create opposing systems of newspapers throughout the country, which they hoped would create political constituencies that could vote their parties into power. Martin Van Buren, an architect of the Democratic Party, reportedly claimed in 1832 that he could influence public opinion by speaking "through fifty presses in a fortnight." Papers such as the *Richmond Enquirer*, the *Charleston Mercury*, the *Baltimore Niles' Register*, and the *New York Evening Post* had enormous influence, as they were widely read and became the most important exchange papers along the vast network of information that both molded and reflected American public opinion.[60]

Significantly, both parties required national constituencies in order to gain power, and both parties therefore needed southern support. Neither system of party papers would ever completely embrace antislavery until the formation of the Republican Party in the late 1850s. In September 1834,

58. Richard D. Brown, *The Strength of a People: The Idea of an Informed Citizenry in America, 1650–1870* (Chapel Hill: University of North Carolina Press, 1996), 61.

59. [James Madison], "Public Opinion," *National Gazette*, December 19, 1791, in *The Papers of James Madison*, ed. Robert A Rutland et al. (Charlottesville: University Press of Virginia, 1983), 14:170. On the creation of the *National Gazette*, see Pasley, "*Tyranny of Printers*," 60–66. See also Colleen Sheehan, "Madison and the French Enlightenment: The Authority of Public Opinion," *William and Mary Quarterly*, 3d ser., 59 (October 2002): 925–56.

60. Robert V. Remini, *The Election of Andrew Jackson* (Westport, CT: Greenwood, 1963), 80–86, 128; *Baltimore Freeman's Banner*, February 11, 1832.

for example, J. Z. Goodrich, a little-known Whig editor who published the *Massachusetts Eagle* in Lenox in the Berkshire mountains, noted the emergence of an "overturning radicalism" and a group of agitators who lived for "experimenting on the public mind." Several months later, under the heading "PUBLIC OPINION," Goodrich printed his assessment of emancipation in the British West Indies. The islands were in an "unsettled state," he reported, providing a "lesson of caution" to the United States. Goodrich advised prudence on the question of abolition and deplored the "rashness which would make it a subject of party bitterness." The politics of slavery worked on either side of the Mason-Dixon line, and as the slavery debate rose in intensity and national importance, public opinion on slavery and abolition would not be shaped by benevolent elites; rather, it would be fiercely contested in the newspapers.[61]

The emergence of a national struggle over slavery speaks to the failure of political elites to monopolize the formation of opinion through their newspapers. The Evangelical press, for example, worked to form a moral constituency. By the 1830s there were about fifty religious newspapers in the United States, all of which were connected to the same network of exchange papers employed by the political press.[62] Papers such as the Methodist *Christian Advocate and Herald and Zion's Journal,* published in New York, had a national readership that transcended sectional lines.[63] Others such as the Baptist *Christian Watchman,* published in Boston, and the Congregationalist *Boston Recorder* also aspired to inform broad readerships. As a writer for the *Christian Herald* asserted, "The press is as necessary to the pulpit, as agriculture and the arts are to commerce."[64]

American abolitionists worked within the same system of public opinion. Benjamin Lundy's *Genius of Universal Emancipation,* William Lloyd

61. *Lenox Massachusetts Eagle,* September 11 and December 4, 1834; William J. Cooper Jr., *The South and the Politics of Slavery, 1828–1856* (Baton Rouge: Louisiana State University Press, 1978); Leonard Richards, *The Slave Power: The Free North and Southern Domination, 1780–1860* (Baton Rouge: Louisiana State University Press, 2000).

62. Daniel Dorchester, *Christianity in the United States from the First Settlement down to the Present Time* (New York: Hunt and Eaton, 1890), 425; Simon Dexter North, *History and Present Condition of the Newspaper and Periodical Press of the United States* (Washington: Government Printing Office, 1884), 119–20.

63. John H. Wigger, *Taking Heaven by Storm: Methodism and the Rise of Popular Christianity in America* (New York: Oxford University Press, 1998), 179–80. The *New York Christian Advocate and Zion's Herald* was the most popular weekly in the country by 1831.

64. Quoted in *Hartford Christian Secretary,* June 7, 1823; see also April 5, 1823.

Garrison's *Liberator,* Gamaliel Bailey's *National Era,* and Frederick Douglass's *North Star* were all intent upon guiding the moral consciousness of the American people. They too had learned from the example of Great Britain, where abolitionists established what Seymour Dresher has called a "structure of opinion" that made the abolition of slavery seem almost inevitable.[65] During that same period, and extending throughout the antebellum decades, a similar process took place in the United States. The results, of course, were starkly different. Slavery was the most divisive issue in American society, and hundreds of careers were dedicated to the formation of a "structure of opinion" that would either sustain slavery or destroy it. At the cutting edges of this struggle, abolitionists and proslavery activists wrote pamphlets and published newspapers that explicitly addressed the problems of slavery and abolitionism. In the political papers and the religious press, the issue of slavery became increasingly prominent, and Americans were consistently challenged with the place of slavery in the national life. In all of these constituencies, emancipation in the British West Indies became a topic of frequent comment. The lasting connections between the British West Indies and the United States made the abolition of slavery in the West Indies an easily accessible example of what emancipation entailed, and Americans paid attention.

65. Seymour Drescher, *Capitalism and Antislavery: British Mobilization in Comparative Perspective* (New York: Oxford University Press, 1987), 166.

2

Abolitionists and Insurrections

On August 22, 1791, a group of slaves in the French colony of Saint-Domingue launched an insurrection that reverberated throughout the Atlantic World. Insurrection developed into the revolution led by Toussaint L'Ouverture, and by 1804 the black state of Haiti had been forged through a bloody defense of freedom against French, Spanish, and British armies, all sent to reimpose slavery and restore the eighteenth-century world of black and white, slave and free. As long as black slavery existed, Haiti framed the background of every discussion about slavery and its abolition.[1]

The rebellion in Saint-Domingue affected the United States almost immediately. White colonists fleeing for their lives landed in every mainland port from Boston to Charleston, and many brought their slaves. Over the next ten years, the stance of the federal government shifted in accordance with the president's views on slavery. The Washington administration allotted money to assist the refugee slaveholders, even while American merchants traded with the black rebels. The policy of the Adams administration, led by the antislavery New Englander Timothy Pickering, was quite favorable to the rebels. American merchants supplied Toussaint's regime with much needed provisions and materiel. In 1800 the U.S. frigate *General Greene* even participated in Toussaint's defeat of the forces of Andre Rigaud, the free colored general who controlled the colony's

1. The classic account is C. L. R. James, *The Black Jacobins: Toussaint L'Ouverture and the San Domingo Revolution* (1938; New York: Vintage, 1989); important recent studies include two books by Laurent Dubois, *Avengers of the New World: The Story of the Haitian Revolution* (Cambridge: Harvard University Press, 2004), and *A Colony of Citizens: Revolution and Slave Emancipation in the French Caribbean, 1787–1804* (Chapel Hill: University of North Carolina Press, 2004).

southern province. But as Jefferson replaced Adams in the executive office, the slaveholders' view of black insurrectionists returned. Jefferson did not participate in Toussaint's demise, but he did cut off commerce with independent Haiti in 1806, and the United States did not formally recognize Haiti until the Radical Republicans controlled Congress in 1863. The official nonrecognition spoke volumes, and the example of Haiti had a profound influence upon Americans as their own struggle over slavery and its abolition grew with an intensity that could only end in war.[2]

The most durable effect of Haiti's revolution in the United States was that of its history or, rather, the dominant interpretation of its history according to Anglo-Atlantic presses. The Haitian Revolution could have been rendered into any number of narratives (as eventually it was), but during the U.S. struggle over slavery, Bryan Edwards's *Historical Survey of the French Colony of St. Domingo* had the most powerful influence. As a West Indian planter, Member of Parliament, and historian of the Caribbean, Edwards stood at the center of the struggle between slaveholders and abolitionists in the Anglo-Atlantic world of the late eighteenth century. When the insurrection of the slaves in Saint-Domingue broke out, Edwards was in Jamaica, and he visited the stricken island on behalf of the British government. As an eyewitness and the most prominent historian of the West Indies, his account became the standard proslavery interpretation of the Haitian Revolution throughout the antebellum period.[3]

2. Donald Hickey, "America's Response to the Slave Revolt in Haiti, 1791–1806," *Journal of the Early Republic* 2 (Winter 1982): 364–71; Stanley Elkins and Eric McKitrick, *The Age of Federalism* (New York: Oxford University Press, 1993), 656–62. See also Tim Matthewson, *A Proslavery Foreign Policy: Haitian American Relations during the Early Republic* (Westport, CT: Praeger, 2003); Rayford W. Logan, *The Diplomatic Relations of the United States with Haiti, 1776–1891* (Chapel Hill: University of North Carolina Press, 1941); Alfred Hunt, *Haiti's Influence on Antebellum America: Slumbering Volcano in the Caribbean* (Baton Rouge: Louisiana State University Press, 1988).

3. Edwards's account of the Haitian Revolution was first published as a single volume: *An Historical Survey of the French Colony in the Island of St. Domingo: Comprehending an Account of the Revolt of the Negroes in the Year 1791, and a Detail of the Military Transactions of the British Army in the Years 1793 & 1794* (London: John Stockdale, 1797). Later, it was reprinted as volume four in several later editions of *The History, Civil and Commercial, of the British Colonies in the West Indies*, 4 vols. The references that follow are from the first edition to be printed in Philadelphia in 1806 by James Humphreys. Edwards's lasting influence can be seen in the reappearance of his argument in later discussions of the Haitian revolution. Some examples include: Brutus [Robert J. Turnbull], *The Crisis: or, Essays on the Usurpations of the Federal Government* (Charleston, 1827), 133; James Franklin, *The Present State of Hayti* (London, 1828), 60; Thomas R. Dew, "Abolition of Negro Slavery," in *The Ideology*

Edwards argued that the *Amis des Noirs,* the French abolitionist society, was entirely responsible for the insurrection in Saint-Domingue. Over time, Edwards's interpretation translated into a general theory of insurrection that implicated abolitionist agitation in the origins of slave rebellion. As the movement to abolish slavery became increasingly radical in Britain and then the United States, a series of rebellions or plots in the West Indies and the American South demonstrated to slaveholders that Edwards's thesis was correct. Abolitionists denied the charge, arguing that insurrections arose from the injustice and brutality of slavery and that rebellions were punishments for the sin of slaveholding. Both sides were intransigent and the debate over slavery grew more and more divisive.

But the planters had a point. In 1816 the absentee planter and gothic novelist "Monk" Lewis traveled to Jamaica to visit the sugar plantations he had recently inherited. In the journal he kept during his travels, published in 1834, Lewis recorded the following song, which an overseer had found upon the mysterious "King of the Eboes," who was arrested for plotting a rebellion.

> Oh me good friend, Mr. Wilberforce, make we free!
> God Almighty thank ye! God Almighty thank ye!
> God Almighty make we free!
> Buckra in this country no make we free!
> What negro for to do? What negro for to do?
> Take force with force! Take force with force![4]

---

of Slavery: Proslavery Thought in the Antebellum South, 1830–1860, ed. Drew Gilpin Faust (Baton Rouge: Louisiana State University Press, 1981), 68–69; Louis Schade, *A Book for the "Impending Crisis!". . . "Helperism" Annihilated! The "Irrepressible Conflict" and its Consequences!* (Washington, 1860), 8–14. It was not inevitable that Edwards's interpretation became dominant. The Charleston (S.C.) Library Society, e.g., listed Marcus Rainsford's work on the rebellion in its 1811 catalog. Rainsford quoted an anonymous French writer who cast doubt upon the authenticity of Edwards's account, and offered a nuanced discussion of the revolution that found its origins in the brutality of French colonial slavery. Edwards's reading of the revolution, however, was much more useful to political leaders in the South. See Marcus Rainsford, *An Historical Account of the Black Empire of Hayti: Comprehending a View of the Principal Transactions in the Revolution in Saint Domingo with its Antient and Modern State* ([London], 1805), xiii, 100–101; *A Catalogue of the Books Belonging to the Charleston Library Society, January, 1811* (Charleston, 1811), 20. On the multiple narratives of the Haitian Revolution, see Michel-Rolph Trouillot, *Silencing the Past: Power and Production of History* (Boston: Beacon Press, 1995), 70–107.

4. Mathew Gregory Lewis, *Journal of a West Indian Proprietor, Kept during a Residence in the Island of Jamaica,* ed. Judith Terry (1834; New York: Oxford University Press, 1999), 139.

The famous British abolitionist William Wilberforce, albeit unwittingly, had traversed the Atlantic and imbedded himself in the consciousness of this rebellious bard. Wilberforce believed that slavery was a sin, and he said so in Parliament. Jamaican slaves now had an ally. While Wilberforce employed moral suasion and parliamentary maneuvering, West Indian rebels opted for force. Edwards's thesis on the origins of insurrection became a self-fulfilling prophecy. While his interpretation of the Haitian Revolution was a politically motivated, self-serving narrative, the response he drew from abolitionists made waves across the ocean. Slaves, whose lives were grounded in resistance, felt empowered to take the often fatal step of rebellion. Slaves had always rebelled, but they did so with increasing frequency in the early nineteenth century. The radicalization of Atlantic abolitionism played a critical role in that process.

THE GENESIS OF AN ACCUSATION:
BRYAN EDWARDS AND THE HAITIAN REVOLUTION

When Edwards's account of the Haitian Revolution appeared, he had already authored the popular *The History, Civil and Commercial, of the British Colonies of the West Indies* and had served in the Jamaican House of Assembly since 1765. He had supported the mainland colonies during their struggle for independence and wrote in his *History* that Parliament had provoked the American conflict, echoing the mainland patriots who argued that colonies should govern themselves. Furthermore, as Parliament attempted to stifle the newly independent United States, Edwards led the West Indian struggle to open commercial relations with the young republic. But Edwards was more prominently involved in the West Indian planters' fight against the abolitionists in Britain, and both his *History* and the *Historical Survey* were designed as foils to the British reformers, led by William Wilberforce, who had begun to move against the transatlantic slave trade.[5]

Antislavery thought was rarely articulated until the mid-eighteenth century, and only in the 1770s did some begin to transform thought into action.[6] The first antislavery movements against slavery transpired in the

5. Olwyn M. Blouet, "Bryan Edwards and the Haitian Revolution" in *The Impact of the Haitian Revolution in the Atlantic World*, ed. David Geggus (Columbia: University of South Carolina Press, 2001), 44–45.

6. David Brion Davis, *The Problem of Slavery in the Age of Revolution, 1770–1823* (1975; New York: Oxford University Press, 1999); Christopher L. Brown, *Moral Capital: Foundations of British Abolitionism* (Chapel Hill: University of North Carolina, 2006).

Old World and did not touch upon the more entrenched slavery in the Americas. A black population in the British Isles had gradually emerged during the eighteenth century when Britain dominated the transatlantic slave trade with Africa. Although their legal status was ambiguous, many blacks in Britain were slaves and were abused as such. The humanitarian discovery of slavery within Britain led to the first efforts to challenge the legitimacy of slavery within a society that Britons celebrated as "free." The result was the famous Somerset case successfully pursued by Granville Sharp in 1772, when Judge Mansfield ruled (as most came to believe) that the very air of Britain was endowed with the power to liberate slaves.[7]

But only in the aftermath of the American Revolution did British reformers begin to agitate against colonial slavery, beginning with actions against the transatlantic slave trade. American revolutionaries invoked the rhetoric of liberty and portrayed the British Parliament as tyrannical. Colonial success in the war for independence appeared to validate American claims, and in a historically symbolic transfer of moral authority, the mantle of "freedom" passed from Britain to the United States. Yet a significant portion of American society were enslaved Africans, and, as Dr. Samuel Johnson memorably remarked, "the loudest *yelps* for liberty" had come from the "drivers of negroes." Britons celebrated freedom; they believed that they had invented it and Parliament protected it. In 1787, as Americans debated the Constitution that would uphold the right to own slaves, British abolitionists formed the Society for Effecting the Abolition of the Slave Trade. Abolitionist efforts began with a petition campaign that in 1788 sent to Parliament more than one hundred petitions calling for the abolition of the slave trade, a clear sign that public opinion had begun to shift. They found modest success in 1792, when Parliament agreed to a toothless resolution introduced by Wilberforce that the slave trade "ought to be abolished" within four years. Parliament's moral legitimacy was strengthened, and the colonial interests in slavery were warned. These events led Edwards to publish *The History, Civil and Commercial, of the British Colonies of the West Indies*, an erudite defense of the colonies and of slavery.[8]

7. Mansfield's ruling was actually quite narrow, and it did not make slavery illegal in Britain, though many came to believe this. See Ruth Paley, "After Somerset: Mansfield, Slavery and the Law in England, 1772–1830," in *Law, Crime and English Society, 1660–1830,* ed. Norma Landau (Cambridge: Oxford University Press, 2002), 165–84.

8. Davis, *The Problem of Slavery in the Age of Revolution,* 403–30; Brown, *Moral Capital,*

Edwards's *History* appeared after he had witnessed the insurrection in Saint-Domingue but well before it was clear that the slaves would be victorious in their struggles against the European armies. The book contains barely a mention of the insurrection in Saint-Domingue, referring to it only in passing in a discussion on the likely impetus that the collapse of Saint-Domingue's economy would provide for Jamaican coffee planters.[9] Instead, Edwards lovingly described the British West Indies as the most sophisticated arm of the British Empire, a source of great wealth and the training ground for soldiers, sailors, and administrators. It was a portrait designed to "remove those wild and ill founded notions" about slavery disseminated by abolitionists. Edwards cleverly adopted the same philanthropic voice cultivated by abolitionists. He claimed to be "no friend to slavery," yet he could not accept the dire visions aroused by the "misinformed writers" of the Abolition Society. Edwards acknowledged that slaveholders were "invested with powers" that might seem "odious" to the British sense of freedom. But these powers were never abused, he claimed, and West Indian slaves were only required to perform "moderate labour" that paled in comparison to the "wretched anxiety to which the poor of England are subject." Indeed, the West Indian slave lived a life of "comparative felicity." The abolitionists were badly informed. Amelioration might be needed, but this should be carried out by the slaveholders in the colonies; the abolitionists should direct their energies elsewhere. Slaveholders in the American South would adopt similar arguments.[10]

One suspects that Edwards was merely setting up his audience for the attack that was to come, but the events unfolding in Haiti were unexpected, and they gave a special urgency to his agenda. Rebellion spread to Jamaica in 1795, when the Maroons made war on the plantations, and by the end of 1796 the newly forged Haitian army had defeated Spanish forces that had attempted to reestablish slavery. In the summer of 1797 Britain's own attempt to conquer Hispaniola failed, with tremendous losses in British troops.[11]

105–206; Linda Colley, *Britons: Forging the Nation, 1707–1837* (New Haven: Yale University Press, 1992), 352–54; Seymour Drescher, *Capitalism and Antislavery: British Mobilization in Comparative Perspective* (New York: Oxford University Press, 1987), 67–88; Samuel Johnson is quoted in Davis, *The Problem of Slavery in the Age of Revolution*, 275.

9. Blouet, "Bryan Edwards," 48.

10. Edwards, *History*, 2:363, 236.

11. Michael Craton, *Testing the Chains: Resistance to Slavery in the British West Indies*

The violence caused concern among some abolitionists, but others, such as Thomas Clarkson, believed that the revolution bolstered their cause. When the West Indian lobby in Britain translated and printed the Dominguan planters' account of the rebellion, which blamed the *Amis des Noirs,* Clarkson responded with his own pamphlet indicting the slave trade and slavery itself. Clarkson agreed that the French Revolution had created serious divisions between Dominguan whites and the wealthy *gens de couleur,* the free-colored class. But where the planters argued that the *Amis des Noirs* had taken bloody advantage of the split, Clarkson pointed to the inhumanity of the slave trade, which had placed on the island thousands who were "fraudulently and forcibly deprived of the Rights of Men." Such oppression made rebellion practically inevitable. Clarkson argued that the Haitian Revolution must not end trade agitation—quite the contrary—it must give the movement more urgency as the only means of securing the safety of the colonies. To abolish the slave trade was the best means of preventing future insurrections.[12] Edwards's *Historical Survey of the French Colony,* which first appeared in 1797, must be seen in the context of transatlantic struggle between the property rights of slaveholders and the human rights of slaves. The interpretation of the fundamental origins of the insurrection in Saint-Domingue posed a serious question that shaped this struggle for more than half a century: Did abolitionist agitation endanger slaveholding societies?

One only needed to peruse the introduction to Edwards's *Historical Survey* to grasp his intent. "The rebellion of the negroes in St. Domingo," Edwards claimed, "had one ... origin. It was not the strong and irresistible impulse of human nature, groaning under oppression, that excited [the slaves] to plunge their daggers into the bosoms of unoffending women and helpless infants. They were driven into those excesses—reluctantly

(Ithaca: Cornell University Press, 1982), ch. 17; David Geggus, *Slavery, War, and Revolution: The British Occupation of Saint Domingue, 1793–1798* (New York: Oxford University Press, 1982), 199, 379.

12. *A Particular Account of the Commencement and Progress of the Insurrection of the Negroes in St. Domingo, which began in August, 1791: Being a Translation of the Speech made to the National Assembly, the 3d of November, 1791 by the Deputies from the General Assembly of the French Part of St. Domingo,* 2d ed. (London, 1792); Thomas Clarkson, *The True State of the Case, Respecting the Insurrection at St. Domingo* (Ipswich, 1792); David Geggus, "British Opinion and the Emergence of Haiti, 1791–1805," in *Slavery and British Society, 1776–1846,* ed. James Walvin (Baton Rouge: Louisiana State University Press, 1982), 123–27; Blouet, "Bryan Edwards," 46–49.

driven—by the vile machinations of men calling themselves philosophers." Edwards aimed "to instruct" his audience as to how the world had changed in the aftermath of Haiti's revolution. He alleged a causal relationship between the agitation and writings of the *Amis des Noirs* and the slave insurrection that had caused so much carnage. The only solution, of course, was to silence abolitionism.[13]

The trouble had begun among the *gens de couleur*, who had suffered, Edwards acknowledged, under the civil disabilities of a prejudiced society. After revolution broke out in France, representatives of this group led by Vincent Ogé had traveled to Paris in 1790 to seek recognition of their rights as citizens. According to Edwards, once in Paris, Ogé came under the malevolent influence of the *Amis des Noirs,* who "initiated [him] into the popular doctrine of equality, and the rights of man." From the *Amis des Noirs* Ogé "learnt the miseries of his condition" and was led to believe that all the free coloreds would join him against the whites if only he would lead them. The *Amis des Noirs* were fanatics who sought only to destroy the French Empire. Ogé was the "tool" of their ambition.[14]

Ogé could not find money and arms in France to carry out his plans, so he ventured to New England, where he procured the materiel for his rebellion (a disturbing thought for southern slaveholders.) He established a camp near Cape Francois and began to raise support. He found little, according to Edwards, and those who joined him were "raw and ignorant youths." Their actions hardly matched the rhetoric of philanthropy, as "the first white man that fell in their way they murdered on the spot." A second white man met the same fate, and when they came upon a free colored man of moderate wealth, they demanded that he join them. The man declined, pleading his responsibility for his wife and six children, but Ogé's men were ruthless; they slaughtered the entire family. Such were the actions of black men inflamed with fanatical ideas of freedom.[15]

The depredations of Ogé's rebels aroused the fury of the *petit-blancs*, the poor whites in Saint-Domingue who sought above all to maintain white supremacy. They began to attack the free coloreds, who defended themselves, gathered in camps and threatened civil war. Despite a few small skirmishes, war was averted, and Ogé and his band were captured and tried. Twenty were hung, and their leader was sentenced to be broken on the

13. Edwards, *History,* 4:xv–xvi, 9, 65–69.
14. Ibid., 4:46–47.
15. Ibid., 4:48–50.

wheel. While some went to their deaths with honor, Ogé "implored mercy with many tears and an abject spirit" and claimed to know "an important secret" that he would disclose if only his life were spared. The colonial authorities gave him one day, and at the time, Edwards claimed, "it was not made known ... that he had divulged anything of importance." But nine months later "it was discovered that [Ogé] had made a full confession ... of the dreadful plot ... to excite the negro slaves into rebellion." Edwards suggested that he was privy to the facts of Ogé's confession and clearly implied that the subsequent insurrection stemmed from the plot of the free coloreds. Ogé had been the "ambassador" for the *Amis des Noirs;* he had introduced their fanatical ideas and plotted rebellion with the slaves.[16]

The timing of Ogé's death could not have been worse for the planters of Saint-Domingue. Ogé had been popular in Paris, and the news of his brutal death arrived when the *Amis des Noirs* were proposing to extend the rights of the *gens de couleur.* The news raised a "storm of indignation" among Parisians. His tragic end was made the subject of a pantomime and aired in the "public theatres." The *Amis des Noirs* took advantage of the moment and successfully pushed through the decree of May 15, 1791, which granted all the rights of citizenship to free coloreds in the colonies. The planters had "predicted the utter destruction of the colonies," but the *Amis des Noirs* were heartless. "Perish the colonies," said Robespierre, "rather than sacrifice one iota of our principles." The planters were right, of course, for the decree of May 15 was the catalyst for insurrection, "the brand by which the flames were lighted."[17]

Thus began the "horrors of St. Domingo," which would become so powerful in the discourse over slavery and its abolition in the Anglo-Atlantic world. Edwards spared no details in his account of the insurrection, vividly portraying the slaughter so as to cease the reckless talk of those who would free black slaves. He told of a "general massacre of the whites"; a band of rebels with the standard of an impaled white infant; white women violated "on the dead bodies of their husbands and fathers"; a planter nailed alive to a tree, his limbs chopped off one by one and a carpenter caught sawing wood, who was bound between two boards and "sawed asunder." These were the visions that would haunt slaveholders for most of the nineteenth century.[18]

16. Ibid., 4:xv, 51–53.
17. Ibid., 4:xv, 69.
18. Ibid., 4:74–75, 79; and it goes on like this for another seven pages.

In addition to denouncing abolitionism, Edwards's narrative of the Haitian Revolution described a transformation in the nature of slave rebellions that made the silencing of the abolitionists all the more important. Slave insurrections were nothing new to the Caribbean, as Edwards himself had related. He had first arrived in Jamaica in 1759 on the eve of "Tacky's Revolt," one of the largest slave rebellions of the eighteenth century. Edwards's account is one of the most detailed to survive, and his guardian in Jamaica, Zachary Bayley, was an eyewitness. Tacky's Revolt was organized by Africans (identified by Edwards as "Koromantyn"), and between thirty and forty whites were killed. The 1760 revolt epitomized earlier rebellions, as they had "originated among the newly-imported negroes only." Edwards speculated that the Africans who had organized past rebellions had done so to regain the "state of freedom" they had enjoyed in Africa. These slaves had probably been "fraudulently, or forcibly sold by their chiefs," and rebellions were the "natural consequence" of such actions.[19] Edwards and most slaveholders of the Americas did not believe that black slaves harbored a natural desire for freedom. Their contentment in servitude, slaveholders said, arose from the rise in living standards that Africans experienced in their transatlantic journey to a "benign" American slavery.

Saint-Domingue was different because so many of the slaves involved in the rebellion were "Creoles, or natives" like Toussaint L'Ouverture. They led the revolt, and for Edwards their prominence revealed another nexus between the abolitionists and the slave population at large. Foolish whites had taught some of their favorite slaves to read, which enabled them to "imbibe and . . . to promulgate, those principles and doctrines" that inspired the slaves to destroy France's wealthiest colony. From the slaveholding perspective, the problem with Creole slaves lay in the loss of their "natural" contentment, a change that abolitionists had exploited. The lessons to be learned from Haiti could not be clearer: slaves must not learn how to read, and abolitionists must be silenced.[20]

Edwards made the connection between print and rebellion even clearer as he impugned British abolitionists for engaging in the same radical tactics. The British Antislavery Society had disseminated throughout the colo-

19. Ibid., 4:xv.

20. Ibid., 4:xvi. In fact, modern historians have found that nearly two-thirds of the black population in Saint-Domingue was African born, and as in eighteenth-century rebellions, allegiances among particular African ethnicities were an important organizational factor during the Haitian Revolution. See Dubois, *Avengers*, 5, 108–9.

nies "tracts and pamphlets without number" which made the planters "odious and contemptible" in their slaves' eyes. Planters in the British West Indies now faced the likelihood of horrible vengeance, as reckless abolitionists had endowed the slaves with "ideas of their own natural rights and equality of condition, as should lead them to a general struggle for freedom through rebellion and bloodshed." Indeed, he expressed surprise that British slaves had not set the example for those of Saint-Domingue. The Haitian Revolution was a seminal event, and through his broadly influential narrative Edwards fixed in the slaveholding mind the idea that abolitionists caused slave insurrections. For several generations to come, the "horrors of St. Domingo" would mean reckless abolitionists, crazed slave rebels, and slaughtered white people. It was a narrative that pushed far beyond Edwards's initial intentions to stymie the abolitionists of the 1790s.[21]

Not only was Edwards's narrative powerful, it was also broadly disseminated. American printers often reprinted popular British works, and by the turn of the century Edwards's *History* had already gone through three editions published in London, Edinburgh, and Dublin. (The *History* was now a four-volume set, with the *Historical Survey of the French Colony* reprinted as the fourth volume.) The *History* sat on many an American bookshelf, but in 1805 James Humphreys, a Philadelphia printer, collected subscriptions for a fourth edition to be published in four volumes in the United States. Subscriptions came from Massachusetts, New York, New Jersey, Maryland, Virginia, Georgia, South Carolina, and Pennsylvania, and the list was headed by President Thomas Jefferson. Following in his wake were some of the most influential Americans of his day, including prominent Jeffersonians such as Senator Pierce Butler of South Carolina, Governor Thomas McKean of Pennsylvania, former governor James Jackson of Georgia, and John Bacon of Massachusetts, as well as leading Federalists like Joseph Hopkinson of Philadelphia, Thomas Pinckney of South Carolina, and the influential editor Joseph Dennie. Most subscribers were lawyers, but there were also powerful clergymen such as William White, Bishop of the Protestant Episcopal Church, and the physicians Benjamin Barton and Caspar Wistar, both professors at the University of Pennsylvania. Booksellers B.& J. Homans of Boston ordered six copies; James Kennedy of Alexandria, Virginia, ordered twelve; George Hill of Baltimore, Maryland, ordered three; and the young Thomas Ritchie of Richmond, Virginia, ordered six.[22]

21. Ibid., 4:89.
22. There were 186 subscribers in all. Thirty-eight self-identified as lawyers, five as medical doctors, and four as ministers. Institutional subscribers included the Insurance Co.

The 1805 edition rapidly sold out, paving the way for another printing in 1806, this time with a separate atlas. But even this next printing did not satiate American demand; the volumes were reissued in 1810 by three different printers, Levis and Weaver of Philadelphia, E. Morford, Willington & Co. of Charleston, and Coale and Thomas of Baltimore. There is little question that Edwards was well known in the United States, and when news of West Indian rebellions began to arrive in the spring of 1816 and again in the fall of 1823, it would be filtered through an Edwardsian lens.

PROVIDING SUBSTANCE FOR THE ACCUSATION:
BARBADOS, 1816

Bryan Edwards was only a little premature in speculating that British slaves would be influenced by abolitionist agitation, and his assertion of the connection between dangerous thoughts and wicked deeds was borne out by a series of rebellions that wracked the West Indies and the American South between 1816 and British abolition in 1833. The two we discuss here—the 1816 Easter Rebellion in Barbados and the 1823 Demerara Rebellion—should be understood as Atlantic rebellions in their origins and their effects. They stemmed in part from the challenges to slavery posed by the abolitionists in Britain and had broad ramifications throughout the Anglo-Atlantic world. Slaves in the West Indies, especially those privileged with access to knowledge of political events in Britain, chose to interpret abolitionist achievements as blows to their masters' power. Through print, the abolitionists appeared as powerful allies to the slaves, who perhaps believed them capable of more than was possible. Edwards may have exaggerated the evidence in drawing too direct a line between the decree of May 15, 1791, and the insurrection in Saint-Domingue, but his suggestion of the link between print and rebellion was absolutely correct.[23]

The first Atlantic rebellion after the French Revolutionary decade took

---

of the State of Pennsylvania, the Philadelphia Insurance Co., the Phenix Insurance Co., the Delaware Insurance Co., and the Haddonfield (N.J.) Library Co. See "Subscriber's Names" in Bryan Edwards, *The History, Civil and Commercial, of the British Colonies in the West Indies,* 4 vols. (Philadelphia: James Humphreys, 1805), 4:unpaginated appendix.

23. My interpretation of these rebellions builds upon Emilia da Costa's brilliant inquiry into the Demerara revolt of 1823. Da Costa's work focuses only on Demerara, but she draws from the opposed arguments of Eugene Genovese and Michael Craton, which were developed with respect to the nineteenth-century rebellions as a whole. Both Genovese and Craton point to the qualitative differences between the localized revolts of the eighteenth

place in Barbados on Easter Monday, 1816. During the previous year British abolitionists had proposed the Registry Bill, intended to monitor the ban on the transatlantic slave trade. Abolitionists had believed that once the slave trade was abolished, slavery itself would gradually wither, but as early as 1813 some British abolitionists had begun to investigate the real effects of the ban and found that slavery had expanded.[24] Saint-Domingue had been the single largest producer of sugar before the revolution, but Haiti's production was insignificant. Sugar production spread in Cuba, Puerto Rico, Brazil, and Louisiana, as well as in Britain's new Caribbean possessions in the lesser Antilles and the southern mainland colonies of Demerara, Essequibo, and Berbice (later combined into British Guiana). As sugar production expanded so did the slave trade wherever it was still legal, and British abolitionists could not believe that planters were respecting the ban. In 1816 abolitionists mounted a pamphlet campaign to impose on the West Indian colonies a registration system to impede the illegal purchase of slaves from transatlantic slavers. While not initially successful, antislavery agitation enraged West Indian planters, who organized public meetings throughout the islands and in London to protest any attempt at

---

century and the more extensive rebellions of the nineteenth. Genovese, following C. L. R. James's classic interpretation of the Haitian Revolution, links this shift to the hemispheric "Age of Revolution" and its stirring ethos of human freedom. Craton downplays the role of the transatlantic milieu. Instead, he argues that the rebellion must be seen as the ultimate manifestation of the resistance to slavery intrinsic to the slaves' worldview. Thus, the nineteenth-century rebellions were different because of the "creolisation" of the slave populations in the British West Indies after the cessation of the transatlantic slave trade. According to Craton, the eighteenth-century rebellions were localized because they sprung from ethnic alliances transplanted from Africa. Those of the nineteenth century were more extensive because most of the population was American born, with a shared language and culture that allowed for extensive organization and a shared ideology. Missionaries and abolitionists were "mere allies." DaCosta resolves this historiographical conflict by paying careful attention to the "contradictory worlds" of slaves whose lives were grounded in their resistance to slavery, and to the masters, whose rights to own people as chattel were under attack. But, as I argue, this insight can be broadened for all of the nineteenth-century rebellions. See da Costa, *Crowns of Glory, Tears of Blood: The Demerara Slave Rebellion of 1823* (New York: Oxford University Press, 1994), chaps. 1 and 2; Eugene Genovese, *From Rebellion to Revolution: Afro-American Slave Revolts in the Making of the Modern World* (Baton Rouge: Louisiana State University Press, 1979), 101–4; James, *Black Jacobins;* Craton, *Testing the Chains,* 13–14, 241–242 (quote on 242).

24. James Walvin, *England, Slaves and Freedom, 1776–1838* (Jackson: University of Mississippi Press, 1986), 125.

parliamentary interference with colonial concerns. The planters' arguments echoed the mainland revolutionaries of 1776, and they were not discreet, which provided the slaves with more than enough information about a group in Britain who agitated for their liberation.[25]

Evidence abounds that the Barbados rebellion was fueled by abolitionist agitation communicated to the slaves through the newspapers. An anonymous writer recalled that in the months before the insurrection, Barbadian newspapers had printed the vitriolic resolutions of the colonial House of Assembly which denounced the Registry Bill as a "plan for the emancipation of the slaves."[26] While such language may have been conscious exaggeration by the planters, printed statements of such revolutionary potential could be powerful. According to Robert, a slave on Simmon's plantation, sometime during 1815 it became the general expectation among the slaves that they would be freed on New Year's Day. The rumor had been spread by Nanny Grigg, an old slave women also at Simmon's who claimed that she had read it in the newspapers and that her master was "very uneasy" about the news. When the new year came, Grigg changed her prediction and "said the Negroes were to be freed on Easter Monday, and the only way to get it was to fight for it . . . as that was the way they did it in St. Domingo." Grigg had either read or heard about the successes of the abolitionists and knew that her master worried about these developments. The precedent of Haiti was clearly well known, and the combination was enough to convince Grigg that the abolitionists were valuable allies. Many were emboldened to rise in rebellion.[27]

The prevalence of such beliefs among the slaves was reinforced by the testimony of the planter Joseph Belgrave, who stated before the Barbadian

25. For example, the Society of West India Merchants and Planters of London argued that the imposition of registration "would be destructive of the constitutional Rights and Interests of the Colonial Legislatures, destructive of the private Right and Interests of Individuals, and aim a deadly Blow at the whole Tenure of West India Property." Minutes of the Society of West India Planters and Merchants, June 13, 1815, quoted in Lowell B. Ragatz, *The Fall of the Planter Class in the British Caribbean, 1763–1833: A Study in Social and Economic History* (1928; reprint, New York: Octagon, 1971), 391.

26. Anon., *Remarks on the Insurrection in Barbados, and the Bill for the Registration of the Slaves* (London, 1816) 5, quoted in Craton, *Testing the Chains*, 259.

27. Confession of Robert, *The Report of the Select Committee of the House of Assembly appointed to inquire into the Origin, Causes, and Progress of the Late Insurrection* (Barbados, 1818) quoted in Hilary M. Beckles, *Natural Rebels: A Social History of Enslaved Black Women in Barbados* (New Brunswick: Rutgers University Press, 1989), 172.

House of Assembly that he had been attacked by a slave woman who accused him of wrongly holding black people in slavery. The woman claimed that freedom "had been sent out for them, and they would have it."[28] Cuffee Ned, another enslaved witness, revealed that "previous to the Insurrection he had heard several negroes say, they had heard it read in the Papers that they were to be free . . . That a man named Sampson (Mr. Brathwaite's butler) came home from Town on the Saturday evening previous to the Insurrection and said to the negroes 'Well, this day's Newspaper has done our business—for the Packet has arrived, and brought our Freedom.'"[29] Like Nanny Grigg, Sampson seems to have assumed that abolitionist agitation portended emancipation. It is likely that a butler such as Sampson had relative freedom of movement about the island. Early in 1816, white Barbadians were incensed by what they saw as parliamentary meddling with what was traditionally the responsibility of the colonial House of Assembly. Slaveholders were notorious for speaking freely, if naively, in front of their slaves, and Sampson could have easily listened in on a planters' conversation on the "fanatics" in Britain. Sampson's reference to a newspaper would have enhanced his credibility, for in the world of the enslaved only knowledgeable men read the newspapers, and these would have been particularly interesting during times of abolitionist ferment.

On April 14, 1816, the insurrection began with fires that signaled to the rebels in surrounding plantations that rebellion had begun. The colonial government declared martial law early the next morning, and four days of fighting ensued between the slaves, who divided themselves into guerilla bands, and British troops supported by local militias. While only two soldiers were killed during the rebellion, the white response in its aftermath was extreme; more than 200 slaves, women and men, were killed.[30]

The slaves of Barbados would never again rise in violent rebellion. But in the Atlantic world of masters and slaves, the revolt in Barbados had important ramifications; it appeared to demonstrate the nexus between abolitionist agitation and slave insurrection alleged by the Edwards thesis. Predictably, West Indian planters quickly blamed the rebellion on the abolitionists in Britain. For one member of the Barbadian House of Assem-

---

28. *The Report of the Select Committee of the House of Assembly appointed to inquire into the Origin, Causes, and Progress of the Late Insurrection* (Barbados, 1818), quoted in Beckles, *Natural Rebels*, 171.

29. *The Report of the Select Committee . . .* , quoted in Craton, *Testing the Chains*, 260.

30. Craton, *Testing the Chains*, 262–64.

bly, it was not enough that the insurrection had been suppressed. Greater danger lay in the fact that "the spirit [of insurrection] is not subdued, nor will it ever be subdued whilst these dangerous doctrines which have been spread abroad continue to be propagated among the Slaves."[31]

MORE SUBSTANCE FOR THE ACCUSATION: DEMERARA, 1823

Situated on the northeast coast of the South American mainland, the colony of Demerara (now Guyana) was acquired by the British after the wars with Napoleon. Between 1816 and 1823, when the Demerara rebellion took place, British abolitionists had been emboldened by their successes to agitate for legal measures for the amelioration of slavery. In 1822, James Cropper, a Quaker merchant and reformer, began to promote the development of East Indian sugar produced by "free" labor as a means to challenge the dominance of the slave-grown West Indian product.[32] In May 1823, Thomas Fowell Buxton opened the assault on colonial slavery by asserting, "the state of slavery is repugnant to the principles of the British Constitution and of the Christian religion."[33] Another petition campaign followed, and again agitation proved effective. The tangible results were a series of dispatches issued from the colonial office of Earl Bathurst to the governors of the West Indian colonies that mandated the amelioration of the colonial slave codes. There were several reforms that limited the power of slaveholders and intended to reduce the physical oppression of slavery, but the most significant reform for the future of West Indian slavery was the support given to the Evangelical missions to the slaves. The colonial office endowed religious instruction with the protection of imperial law, requiring planters to allow their slaves to attend religious services.[34]

To white West Indians, the missionaries were immediately associated with the antislavery movement. This was a logical conclusion, as most British abolitionists were religiously motivated and active in their churches. Since the mid-eighteenth century many planters had seen the missionaries

31. Minutes of the Barbados Assembly, August 6, 1816 quoted in Craton, *Testing the Chains*, 266.

32. Davis, *The Problem of Slavery in the Age of Revolution*, 62–63.

33. Quoted in William Law Mathieson, *British Slavery and Its Abolition, 1823–1838* (London: Longmans, 1926), 119.

34. Drescher, *Capitalism and Antislavery*, 59, 91; Mathieson, *British Slavery*, 131–33.

as a serious threat to the status quo, and they repeatedly acted to eradicate their influence from the colonies. When revolution swept Saint-Domingue in 1791, mobs of "respectable whites" in Kingston, Jamaica, disrupted the missionaries' services and threatened to destroy their chapel. In 1802 Sir Simon Taylor, proprietor of a large sugar plantation in St. Thomas in the East, Jamaica, took advantage of the panic induced by the proximity of French ships to propose an act to curtail the Evangelicals' missions to the slaves. The Jamaican Assembly agreed with Taylor and passed the bill. Much to the chagrin of Jamaican whites, the colonial office rejected the act, setting a pattern of government support for missionaries to the West Indies that would continue. Jamaica was not alone among the West Indian colonies to obstruct the work of the missionaries; colonists in Bermuda, Anguilla, Tobago, and St. Vincent all used legislative power to infringe upon the missions to the slaves.[35]

Demerara also received the attention of missionaries, and Le Resouvenir, the plantation where the rebellion began, had been a missionary station since 1808, when John Wray, a Methodist minister assigned by the London Missionary Society (LMS), had arrived in Demerara at the invitation of Hermanus Hilbertus Post. Post's decision to bring in Wray was rather unpopular with his fellow planters, and as soon as Wray showed some success in attracting a congregation (about 600 slaves and a few whites attended the opening of the mission's chapel), the word spread that the Court of Policy intended to send Wray back to England. Wray wrote his superiors in London about planter opposition. The LMS contacted William Wilberforce, who secured for them an interview with Henry Bentinck, the new governor for the colony who had yet to leave England. Bentinck would arrive in the colony with the society's entreaties still fresh in his mind. Wray's early support from abolitionists in Parliament extended the pattern already evident in Jamaica of government support for the missions to the slaves. It is not so surprising, then, that the planters saw the missionaries as proxies of the abolitionists, sent to turn their contented slaves into rebellious malcontents.[36]

Wray's struggles with the planters of Demerara did not end with Wilberforce's intervention in 1808. When an overseer abused slaves in his con-

---

35. Da Costa, *Crowns of Glory, Tears of Blood*, 12; Mary Turner, *Slaves and Missionaries: The Disintegration of Jamaican Slave Society, 1787–1834* (Urbana: University of Illinois Press, 1982), 13–16.

36. Da Costa, *Crowns of Glory*, 87–90.

gregation, Wray protested and received support from the government in Britain, and when the planters sought to obstruct his mission, he again received support. Resulting from these conflicts was the correct perception among the slaves that they had white allies in the colony as well as in Britain, an unprecedented development. Conflict also intensified white colonial distrust of the imperial government, assuring heightened outrage on the occasion of further refoms.[37]

In 1817 Wray was replaced by John Smith, a young working-class seminarian from Coventry. Smith encountered the same resistance from the planters but was so powerfully moved by his work that their harassment only reinforced his dedication to the mission. As Emilia da Costa has observed, Smith's experiences at Le Resouvenir "converted" him to the cause of human rights for slaves. Smith was particularly affected by the sound of the whip, recording in his diary one morning soon after arriving in the colony: "The first thing as usual which I heard was the whip. From ½ past 6 until ½ past 9 my ears were pained by the whip. Surely these things will awaken the vengeance of a merciful God." Writings such as these would eventually condemn Smith, for when insurrection struck, the planters used Smith's words to demonstrate his sympathy for rebel slaves.[38]

The missionary agenda lay in the conversion of the slaves to a Christianity that would bring them salvation in heaven. Missionaries taught slaves not to be concerned with "worldly" matters, namely their bondage, and that faith in God and living a moral life were the only means to salvation. An important component of this moral life entailed the acceptance of their lot and silent submission to their "worldly" master. The Christianity taught to slaves also called for the converted to live a life free from sin, efficiently defined as sins against the master—lying, stealing, and disobeying. The missionaries assured slaves that the rewards beyond the grave were too wonderful for comprehension if life on earth were lived this way. The missionaries taught through rote memorization exemplified by John Shipman's *Instructions for Children*, a catechism for slaves with seven basic lessons, five of which were concerned with the Christian life. Of these five, three emphasized the importance of obedience and submission.[39]

37. Ibid., 125.
38. John Smith, journal, September 14, 1817, quoted in da Costa, *Crowns of Glory*, 153, n. 91.
39. On Shipman, see Turner, *Slaves and Missionaries*, 72–76. See also da Costa's discussion of Smith's instructions from the LMS, *Crowns of Glory*, 131–32.

Emerging from this theology were the contradictory tenets of first, obedience and submission that demanded conformity to slavery, and second, the mandate for critical reflection upon one's actions and the acceptance of personal responsibility to change those actions that were sinful. Regardless of the emphasis on obedience and submission, critical reflection and personal responsibility were a potentially subversive combination among people who lived under the oppressions of slavery. Reflection might lead slaves to question the rectitude of their own behavior, as well as the mores and pastimes of their communities, but it was not illogical for some to begin questioning the morality of the institutions, especially slavery, that governed their entire society.[40]

Compounding the contradiction inherent in missionary theology was the central message of the missionaries that all men were equal in the eyes of God. This was a radical notion in a slave society where gross inequality in wealth and power underlay every relation between white and black, free and slave. Despite missionary attempts to use conversion as another way to create docile slaves, the linkage between the Evangelical missionaries and the rebellions in Demerara and Jamaica (discussed in chapter 4) suggests that slaves took the process of introspection much further than the missionaries intended.

One missionary practice that encouraged slave autonomy was the use of slave deacons to broaden the mission's influence. As we have seen, this practice was not new, but in Demerara and Jamaica slave deacons became major leaders of insurrection. Empowering individual slaves with religious authority raised their stature in the eyes of their community and affirmed their own ability to interpret the lessons of conversion. In the British West Indies, especially as Evangelicals in Britain agitated for the abolition of slavery, such a practice undermined the planters' need to maintain the status quo as well as the missionary agenda to cultivate pliant, Christian slaves.

The testimony of Bristol, a slave deacon at Smith's mission, elucidates the process. Bristol recalled that Smith had once spoken of "the time, when the children of Israel were with king Pharaoh, that Moses went to deliver them from the hands of Pharaoh, and carried them to the promised land . . . Moses went to deliver the children of Israel because they were slaves under Pharaoh." It is not clear from the testimony whether or not

40. Turner, *Slaves and Missionaries*, 78–79.

Smith preached on Moses and the Israelites, or simply read from the Bible, but the story itself lends easily to a radical interpretation, especially from the perspective of slaves.[41]

Later in his testimony, Bristol showed how this indeed had happened:

I have heard some of the boys who read the bible speak about the Israelites and the Jews, about the fighting of the Israelites when they go to war; when the prisoner [Smith] read about the fighting of the Israelites, after they went home and read it again, I heard them speak of it; they said the people of Israel used to go warring against the enemies, and then I explained the meaning of the enemy and told them it was the people who would not believe the word of God when Moses used to preach to them; the people applied the story of the Israelites and the Jews, and put it on themselves; when they read it then they begin to discourse about it; they said that this thing in the bible applied to us just as well as the people of Israel; I cannot tell what made the negroes apply it to themselves."[42]

Planters were right to fear the missionaries working among their slaves. Conversion empowered slaves with a certain amount of knowledge of the dominant religion of their world, which enabled them to formulate a Christian argument defending their right to free themselves, by force if necessary. After all, God's chosen ones from the Bible had done so; why should not black slaves?

The worldview encouraged by Evangelical theology created an ideological bond that united a large enough group of slaves in Demerara to act as a whole against slavery. The mission provided the means by which the slave leaders could organize their plan and provided an autonomous space for slaves to gather and disseminate news. Smith was quite popular among the slaves, and his services were known to attract as many as 600 blacks from plantations all over the colony. The Bethel Chapel at Le Resouvenir was well known, and there was sure to be a slave from every plantation who either attended Smith's services or knew someone who did. For Smith,

41. [Testimony of] Bristol, *Proceedings of a Court Martial in Demerara, on Trial of John Smith, A Missionary* in *Slave Trade*, vol. 66 of *Irish University Press Series of British Parliamentary Papers*, 95 vols. (Shannon: Irish University Press, 1969), 64–65. More evidence for Smith's reading of the story of Moses can be found in [Testimony of] Manuel, *Proceedings*, 61.

42. Ibid.

such a network enhanced the spread of Christianity. For the leaders of the rebellion, the network disseminated the news that freedom had come and spread the plan by which the people would seize it.[43]

Smith had no part in organizing the revolt, but members of his mission clearly did.[44] As had occurred in Barbados six years before with the announcement of the Registry Bill, the seeds for rebellion arrived on the mail boat with Bathurst's dispatch on the amelioration of the colonial slave codes. The orders from the colonial office enraged West Indian planters throughout the Caribbean, and many argued heatedly and publicly about the "fanatics" back home. Overheard by interested slaves, these conversations inspired rumors of imminent freedom to circulate among the slave communities. Particularly interested in these rumors were Quamina and his son Jack, both of Success plantation. Father and son were artisans and like Sampson (the butler in Barbados) had relative freedom of movement in the colony and access to better information than most slaves. Quamina had been involved in the mission at Le Resouvenir since Wray's arrival in 1808. He was a carpenter and the head deacon of Smith's congregation. Jack, sometimes known as Jack Gladstone, was not a deacon but was a member of Smith's congregation and was known to teach as well.[45]

The men sought out Daniel, one of the governor's domestic slaves who had access to the governor's papers, which confirmed the arrival of the important "paper." Jack also learned that a driver on Mr. Post's plantation had flogged a slave, saying, "because you are to be free, you will not do any work."[46] Gilles, a slave from the western region of the colony, told Jack that his master had read to the slaves a paper that said women could no longer be flogged; another slave told him that he had heard his overseer complain that the king was "foolish" for giving the slaves freedom.[47]

43. Da Costa, *Crowns of Glory*, 183–92.

44. The preponderance of slave testimony makes it clear that Smith had no part in planning the revolt and that he attempted to dissuade the leaders from carrying out their plans when he discovered them. See, e.g., [Testimony of] Manuel, *Proceedings*, 61; [Testimony of] Bristol, *Proceedings*, 64.

45. [Testimony of] Manuel, *Proceedings*, 61.

46. Examination of Jacky, *Further Papers Relating to Insurrection of Slaves in Demerara* in *Slave Trade*, vol. 66 of *Irish University Press Series of British Parliamentary Papers*, 95 vols. (Shannon: Irish University Press, 1969), 173; da Costa, *Crowns of Glory*, 180.

47. Da Costa, *Crowns of Glory*, 182–83. The colony was split into East/West by the Demerara River. The rebellion was concentrated on the East Coast, which was significantly more developed.

The accretion of so much evidence convinced Quamina and his son that their people had been freed and that the planters acted illegally in keeping them enslaved. It is hard to say just when Quamina and Jack began to form plans to seize their freedom. Estimates range from a year to three months.[48] Regardless of when the plans emerged, Jack actively spread the news in the black community that "the paper" had come that proclaimed their freedom. The slaves Manuel, Sandy, Jacky, Hanover, and Barson all stated that Jack had told them about "the paper."[49] Hanover, of Paradise plantation, testified that one Sunday after chapel services a group of slaves gathered around Jack, who read to them from a newspaper that stated that the king had freed them, that the whites refused to allow it, and "that it was now high time to seek for it."[50] The scene described by Hanover suggests that Jack not only read from the newspaper but "explained" its contents in his own words. Such habits had been developed through Smith's mission where Jack was known to teach. The Bible, as it turned out, was not the only text worthy of interpretation.

The evidence also suggests that the plan set by at least some of the slave leaders bore closer resemblance to a labor strike than an insurrection. Bristol, a deacon at Smith's chapel, testified that Quamina had told the slaves to "lay down their tools, and not work."[51] Sandy, of Non-Pareil, stated that "Paris" had suggested putting the whites in the stocks, as they would think the slaves were rising if they refused to work and would shoot them.[52] Demeraran slaves knew of "the Barbadoes plan," especially its bloody repression, and hoped to avoid the same fate.[53]

The rebellion began on the evening of August 17 with conch shells and drums spreading the word to those in the know that the uprising had begun. The rebellion ultimately involved between nine and twelve thousand slaves from at least sixty plantations in the East Coast region of the

48. Examination of Paris, *Further Papers;* Examination of Joe, *Further Papers,* 190.

49. [Testimony of] Manuel, *Proceedings,* 61; Sandy's deposition to the governor, *Further Papers,* 61; Sandy's deposition to the governor, *Further Papers,* 168; Examination of Jacky, *Further Papers,* 173; Examination of Hanover, *Further Papers,* 175; Deposition of Barson, *Further Papers,* 177.

50. Examination of Hanover, *Further Papers,* 175; see also Deposition of Barson, *Further Papers,* 177.

51. [Testimony of] Bristol, *Proceedings,* 65; Sandy's deposition to the governor, *Further Papers,* 168.

52. Sandy's deposition to the governor, *Further Papers,* 168.

53. Deposition of Sandy, *Further Papers,* 171; Evidence of Jack, *Further Papers,* 186.

colony.[54] The governor ordered martial law the next day and organized an army of the king's troops supported by the local militia. Fighting continued for several days, but only two or three whites were killed. It seems likely that the missionaries were influential in this, humanizing whites despite the brutalities of slavery. Colonial forces, however, did not exercise such restraint, and suppression, which quickly devolved into summary executions of slaves by the militiamen and soldiers, was ruthless. During the rebellion itself, 255 slaves were killed, and during the trials, which lasted until January 1824, thirty-three more were killed, ten of them decapitated, their heads impaled on poles by the roadside.[55]

Smith's trouble began when the rebellion was well under way. He had heard about the uprising and was writing his superiors in England when Lieut. Thomas Nurse of the militia came to his door, angry that Smith had not responded to the call for all whites to join the militia. When Smith refused to comply with the order to enroll in the militia, Nurse returned with a full guard to arrest Smith (as well as his wife) and seize his papers.[56]

The planters' court-martial of Smith followed shortly after their bloody repression of the rebellion. In trying Smith the Demeraran planters followed in the tradition of Bryan Edwards and the Barbadian planters, asserting before the world that it was not their contented slaves but meddling philanthropists, this time a missionary, who had caused their slaves to rebel. The trial lasted twenty-seven days and featured an array of instructed slave witnesses and angry planters. Smith's diary, complete with his anti-slavery musings, was read aloud, and selections were reprinted in the local press. On November 24, Smith was found guilty and sentenced to be hung, with an appeal to the king for mercy. The king did grant Smith a reprieve, but the news arrived too late, as Smith had already died in prison.[57]

White Barbadians were terrified by news of another rebellion, and repression proved just as contagious as insurrection. A Barbadian newspaper denounced the missionaries for disseminating "principles entirely subversive" of West Indian society,[58] and in solidarity with their Demeraran cousins, a white mob razed the Methodist Chapel in Barbados, nearly

54. Da Costa, *Crowns of Glory*, 197.

55. Craton, *Testing the Chains*, 280–88; David Brion Davis, *Inhuman Bondage: The Rise and Fall of Slavery in the New World* (New York: Oxford University Press, 2006), 217.

56. Da Costa, *Crowns of Glory*, 212–15.

57. Ibid., 251–54, 273–74.

58. Ibid., 278.

destroying the Reverend Shewsbury's library and causing him and his wife to flee for their lives.[59] The Barbadian mob shared with other white West Indians the opinion that insurrections resulted from the dangerous ideas of the abolitionists, this time spread by Evangelical missionaries.

But West Indian planters made a crucial mistake when they condemned John Smith to death and destroyed the chapel in Barbados. Many of Smith's co-religionists believed that his death made him a martyr in the great cause of abolition, and this lasting belief was perpetuated through many writings on Smith and paralleled by the reaction of New England transcendentalists to the execution of John Brown thirty-five years later.[60] The events in Demerara mobilized several interested constituencies in Britain. The London Missionary Society and the Evangelical press generally took up the postmortem defense of John Smith and the mission to the slaves. Abolitionist and antiabolitionist forces were also reinvigorated. The Demerara rebellion became a polarizing issue that fueled the debates on slavery and abolition. Antiabolitionists pointed to the destruction of colonial property and blamed the revolt on the misguided philanthropy of abolitionists and missionaries. Abolitionists pointed to the martyrdom of John Smith and decried the corruption of colonial institutions, rotted to their core by slavery. While the abolitionists did not achieve their goals at this point, the creation of a martyr in John Smith brought valuable and beneficial publicity to their cause, leaving them in a stronger position for future battles.[61]

59. *Bermuda Gazette*, November 15, 1823, in William Smith papers, Perkins Library, Duke University, Durham, NC; *Hartford Christian Secretary*, March 2, 1824.

60. Edwin Angel Wallbridge, *The Demerara Martyr: Memoirs of the Reverend John Smith, Missionary to Demerara* (London: Charles Gilpin, 1848). Wallbridge was a missionary in Demerara who reported that Smith and, by extension, the whole missionary project was still tainted by the insurrection more than twenty years after the fact. He hoped to counter this prejudice with this work.

61. See, e.g., the pamphlets *Riot in Barbadoes, and Destruction of the Wesleyan Chapel and Mission House*, [1823]; *The Late Insurrection in Demerara, and Riot in Barbadoes*, [Wesleyan Methodist Missionary Society, 1824] both in William Smith papers; da Costa, *Crowns of Glory*, 278–90.

❧ 3 ❧

Conflicting Impressions

By the end of 1823, most American readers had learned of two rebellions in the West Indies attributed to the agitation of the abolitionists in Britain or their missionary proxies in the colonies. In between these two rebellions came the rise of the American Colonization Society (ACS) and its rejection by the black community in the North; the Missouri Crisis; the white terror of slave conspiracy in Charleston, South Carolina; and the bloody repression meted out by slaveholders against Charleston blacks. Any investigation into the development of the slavery debate in the United States requires discerning the particular factors that influenced American opinions on slavery and abolitionism. News from the West Indies was one of those factors, especially in the South, as slaveholders witnessed the gradual erosion of support in the Atlantic world for the right to own slaves.

By the end of the 1820s, well before the rise of radical abolitionism in the North, many white Americans had been introduced to Bryan Edwards's thesis that there was a direct, causal relationship between abolitionist agitation and slave rebellion. Southern leaders feared that even the slightest agitation of antislavery belief would cause slave insurrections, and beginning in South Carolina, they acted to forestall the abolitionism that caused such mayhem in the British West Indies. The fear of rebellion that came to prominence in the early nineteenth century must be distinguished from the general fear of slave insurrection that has characterized the slaveholding mind across time and space. Slaveholders throughout the Americas expressed fear of rebellion well before the rise of abolitionism, but in the nineteenth century slaveholders began to attribute plots and insurrections among slaves to the activity of the abolitionists. Limited by the geographic boundaries of the United States, most historians of the American South have failed to appreciate that southern fears of abolitionism were genuine and rooted in the lessons of Bryan Edwards, the Easter rebellion in Barbados in 1816, the conspiracy in Charleston, South Carolina, in 1822, and the Demerara rebellion of 1823. Each of these episodes of slave violence or its threat was preceded by a public discussion of slavery, which demonstrated to slaveholders that abolitionist agitation served as a catalyst for rebellion. These disruptions of the Anglo-Atlantic slave regimes reinforced Edwards's theory and inspired a southern rearticulation of it by the South Carolinian Robert Turnbull. They also enabled the American argument that slavery was a "positive good." Threats to the tranquility of slave societies, slaveholders alleged, came only from the outside, never from discontented slaves.

NEWS FROM BARBADOS, MAY 1816

Reports on the insurrection in Barbados began to appear in American newspapers in the middle of May 1816, first in New York where the commercial links with the West Indies were the strongest, and then spreading throughout the country through exchange papers. On May 11 the *New York Evening Post* learned from one Captain Thompson that "insurrection had broken out among the blacks of Barbadoes." Forty plantations had been set afire, and troops were on the way.[1] The reports linked the rebellion to British abolitionists. On May 27, for example, the *New York Commercial Advertiser* disclosed the rebellion's cause as well as its bloody end. The rebels had been "deluded" into believing "that their *friends* in England, had obtained their freedom." They had "demanded ... payment for their labour," and when this was refused, they set fire to the estates, destroying eighty. In the end two thousand slaves had been killed in the suppression, along with "two whites who were ringleaders."[2] For those who had read Edwards, the pattern was remarkably similar to what had happened in Saint-Domingue.

The fullest account of the rebellion to appear in American newspapers was copied whole cloth from the *Bridgetown Mercury* of Barbados. On April 30, the *Mercury* published for the first time since the thirteenth of that month. The Barbadian editor realized that readers on the island would

1. *New York Evening Post,* May 11, 1816.
2. *New York Commercial Advertiser,* May 27, 1816.

understand the long silence, as they were "painfully impressed" by the horrors they had witnessed. "But those of our subscribers who reside in the neighbouring settlements," he added, were surely interested in further information, and a long article thick with details of the prowess of several Barbadian colonels described the suppression of the revolt. As for the rebels, the editor left no doubt that "designing persons" had misled the slaves through "misrepresentations." Within the context of a revived abolitionism, there was no mistaking the target of blame.[3]

Both the *Richmond Enquirer* and the *Commercial Advertiser* of New York reprinted the *Mercury's* narrative along with the text of Governor James Leith's "Address to the Slave Population of the Island of Barbados" as their final reports on the insurrection in 1816. According to the governor, the insurrection had been caused "by the misrepresentation and instigation of ill disposed persons" who deceived the slaves into believing they had been freed and were wrongly kept in slavery. While explicitly addressed to the slaves, who were blithely asked to "return with cheerfulness to your duties," the address also responded to abolitionist arguments voiced in Britain. Much of the governor's address involved a defense of slavery coupled with praise for Britain's solitary efforts in the naval suppression of the slave trade. He reminded his listeners that African traders had been the "joint-authors" of slavery in the West Indies and only Great Britain worked to humanize the bondage of those already enslaved. As for emancipation, at present it was impractical, as it foreboded "the absolute subversion of public order and tranquility," which the rebellion had clearly demonstrated.[4]

American editors, especially Virginians, did not let Governor Leith have the final say on the meaning of the rebellion in Barbados. In a widely reprinted article, Thomas Ritchie, editor of the *Richmond Enquirer,* employed the familiar trope of British tyranny to expound upon the meaning of the rebellion. Ritchie was an influential player in southern politics, and his opinions had clout. "The insurrection of the slaves in Barbadoes is distressing to every generous heart," he wrote, "but is it possible to forget that the butchered planters are only the victims of those misfortunes which their countrymen would have brought upon us?" The rebellion in Barbados was a lesson in the benefits of independence. The horrors faced by Barbadian planters were the responsibility of their own "countrymen" in Britain,

3. *New York Commercial Advertiser,* May 31, 1816; *Richmond Enquirer,* June 8, 1816.
4. Ibid.

and had the South still been a part of the British Empire, they too would now suffer. To elaborate the metaphor, Ritchie compared Parliament's antislavery meddling in the West Indies to Lord Dunmore's emancipatory proclamation during the Revolutionary War: "It was they who would have taught our slaves to rebel, to desert, and to massacre their masters—it was they who wove them into regiments, landed them upon our shores, and taught them to lure away their fellows."[5] Pauline Maier has observed that during these same years Americans began to emphasize the preservation of the Revolution's history.[6] Ritchie's allusion to the Revolution bears this out, but with an agenda for his own time. British tyranny linked West Indian planters with the Revolutionary generation, and abolitionism was the equivalent of Lord Dunmore's proclamation. Both were threats to the lives of slaveholders, and both had originated in the British Parliament.

An editorial that first appeared in the *Norfolk Ledger* and was later picked up by the *Washington Daily National Intelligencer,* the *New York Commercial Advertiser,* and Ritchie's *Enquirer* made the parallel with the American Revolution even more explicit. The *Ledger* reprinted selections from the proceedings of a meeting the General Assembly of Barbados held to protest the Registry Bill. Barbadian speakers were quoted opposing Parliament's intentions to raise taxes without colonial assent, as well as its inclination to "openly attack the character of the Island," a reference to metropolitan criticism of slavery. The *Ledger* commented that the Barbadians evinced "a degree of firmness not inferior to what the American people displayed in a similar situation and under similar grievances." Moreover, if Great Britain decided to force the doctrine of "taxation without representation," the colonial relationship might devolve into a "rooted and perpetual animosity" that could transform "the state of things." Not only did the writer see a parallel between the American Revolution and West Indian reactions to parliamentary interference with slavery, but it was also

5. Quoted in the *Baltimore Niles' Register,* June 1, 1816, and the *Washington (DC) Daily National Intelligencer,* May 31, 1816. Both papers cite the *Richmond Enquirer,* but the particular issue in which this writing appeared has not survived. For more on Dunmore's Proclamation, see Benjamin Quarles, *The Negro in the American Revolution* (1961; New York: W. W. Norton, 1973), 19–32. It is also possible that Ritchie alluded to the War of 1812, when Britain again protected runaway slaves and made some into soldiers in the West Indian regiments. See Frank A. Cassell, "Slaves of the Chesapeake Bay Area and the War of 1812," *Journal of Negro History* 57 (April 1972): 144–55.

6. Pauline Maier, *American Scripture: Making the Declaration of Independence* (New York: Knopf, 1997), 177.

clearly implied that the British West Indies might follow the course of the rebellious colonies that became the United States.[7]

Even more disturbing were the comments of James Bovell, a Barbados assemblyman who directed his ire at the African Institution, a new organization of British abolitionists which had successfully campaigned for the Registry Bill. The Institution claimed philanthropy for its inspiration, said Bovell. It alleged to have the moral well-being of the colonies in mind; they merely sought the "amelioration" of the slaves' condition. But such advocacy displayed a dangerous ignorance of history, for the *Amis des Noirs* had also been philanthropists. Had Britons forgotten the horrors of Saint-Domingue? Bovell had not: "We who have been enlightened by the history of the Antilles know too well the confidence that is due to these lofty pretensions." The Easter Rebellion recalled the "example of St. Domingo," and Bovell accused the African Institution of dangerously treading where history taught men not to go. Edwards clearly influenced Bovell's argument, and for American readers who also knew Edwards, it was no wonder that West Indians protested these incursions of Parliament with the same spirit of '76. Their very lives were in danger.[8]

News of the Barbados rebellion also contributed to the American understanding of the nature of slave rebellion. Reports from the West Indies on the threat of rebellions continued to appear in American newspapers well into November, conveying the impression that the Barbados revolt was contagious and that only a swift and overwhelming military response had stifled its spread throughout the islands. Several papers reprinted false reports that the rebellion had spread to the neighboring colony of St. Vincent.[9] The *Enquirer* printed an excerpt from a letter from Barbados, lifted from the *Philadelphia Advocate*, which described the imposition of martial law throughout "all the neighboring islands." This course of action was es-

7. Citation of the "*Norfolk Ledger* of June 19" appears in *New York Commercial Advertiser*, June 26, 1816. See also *Washington (DC) Daily National Intelligencer*, June 24, 1816, and *Richmond Enquirer*, July 16, 1816. Similar assertions were made in *Baltimore Niles' Register*, June 5, 1816, *Washington (DC) Daily National Intelligencer*, June 5, 1816.

8. *New York Commercial Advertiser*, June 26, 1816; *Washington (DC) Daily National Intelligencer*, June 24, 1816; *Richmond Enquirer*, July 16, 1816. Thomas Ritchie later printed another attack on the African Institution, including an account of Wilberforce offering a toast to Henri Christophe, then the King of Haiti. See *Richmond Enquirer*, September 16, 1816.

9. *New York Commercial Advertiser*, May 20, 1816; *Baltimore Niles' Weekly Register*, May 25, 1816; *Washington (DC) Daily National Intelligencer*, May 25, 1816.

sential because "the slaves in those islands, and in Demerara, were secretly apprized of the plan of ours, and were only waiting to hear of its success, to follow the example."[10] In September, well after the suppression of the rebellion in Barbados, Ritchie reprinted a notice that "the females and children of some of the most respectable families in [Jamaica] have come for security to the U. States." And in November, Hezekiah Niles reprinted news from a Jamaican newspaper that two regiments were en route to the island due to "fears entertained of an insurrection of the negroes."[11] The American reader who followed these events had learned much by the end of 1816. The African Institution was the new abolitionist society in Britain and its agitation had caused another rebellion in the islands. The warnings of Bryan Edwards had come to pass—the British West Indies were threatened.

FROM COLONIZATION TO CHARLESTON: THE UNITED STATES AND SLAVERY, 1816–1822

The African Institution in England was not offensive to all southerners, for this society of reformers was also identified with Sierra Leone, Britain's colony for freed slaves in West Africa and the model for the American Colonization Society. The colony at Sierra Leone had been the project of the first generation of British abolitionists, Granville Sharp and company, who brought the Somerset case and began to agitate for the abolition of the slave trade.[12] The idea of colonizing black Americans in some distant locale had been voiced in the United States as well, and in December 1816, soon after Americans learned of the rebellion in Barbados, the first meeting of the ACS took place. According to Douglas Egerton, credit for the push to give institutional form to the idea of colonization belongs to Charles Fenton Mercer, a Federalist member of the Virginia state legislature, who discovered the idea while investigating a tale told in a drunken conversation

10. *Richmond Enquirer,* June 12, 1816. For evidence that Atlantic slaveholders were right to be concerned, see Julius S. Scott, "The Common Wind: Currents of Afro-American Communication in the Era of the Haitian Revolution" (Ph.D. diss., Duke University, 1986), chap. 2.

11. *Richmond Enquirer,* September 21, 1816; *Baltimore Niles' Register,* November 23, 1816.

12. P. J. Staudenraus, *The African Colonization Movement, 1816–1865* (New York: Columbia University Press, 1961), 20, 28; James Walvin, *England, Slaves and Freedom, 1776–1838* (Jackson: University Press of Mississippi, 1986), 63–65.

one winter evening. Philip Doddridge, another Federalist who sat in the Virginia legislature, had called Thomas Jefferson a hypocrite for advocating colonization and then failing to support the idea when it arose in the fearful atmosphere that followed the Gabriel plot of 1800. Mercer looked at the old journals that contained the correspondence between Jefferson and then governor James Monroe, discovered the claim to be correct, and became intrigued with the idea.[13]

Over the next several months, Mercer talked about colonization with his friends and small groups of would-be supporters. Like many white Virginians, Mercer was greatly concerned with the rising population of free blacks in Virginia, which, he believed, could be severely disruptive in a slave society. A project along the lines of the colony in Sierra Leone could relieve white America of this dangerous population, and Mercer believed that the Virginia legislature should inaugurate this effort. The British example was far from perfect, however, for during the same months that Mercer began to advance his cause, news of the rebellion in Barbados began to appear in American newspapers. This news, especially the way the newspapers said the rebellion had started, would have aggravated Mercer's conservatism. Reform might be good, but it must be controlled, and in Britain it appeared that the voices of reform had gone too far. Americans would approach reform in their own stable manner. Mercer's idea of colonization rejected any change to the institution of slavery.[14]

One of the people Mercer convinced was the Reverend Robert Finley of Somerset County, New Jersey, who seized upon the idea of colonization as a benevolent project that fulfilled his spiritual needs. Finley was driven more by Christian benevolence than anything else. There were more free blacks in his county than anywhere in New Jersey, and as he sought to pastor to them, he became frustrated that so many did not know the Bible and could not read the religious tracts that he disseminated. Finley rightly attributed the deprived condition of the African American population to slavery and white racism, not to an inherent racial disability. He differed from racists like Mercer not in the perception that blacks were inferior but in his belief about the origins of that inferiority and the solutions to it. Finley believed that "Africans" (as he called all peoples of African descent) were capable of improvement through education and the acceptance

13. Douglas R. Egerton, "Its Origin Is Not A Little Curious": A New Look at the American Colonization Society," *Journal of the Early Republic* 5 (Winter 1985): 466.
14. Egerton, "Its Origin Is Not A Little Curious," 469–75.

of Christianity. He also believed that slavery was morally wrong, a burden upon American society, and he made clear that his goals for any colonization society included the gradual end of slavery, not through its abolition from above but through generous manumission by a new generation of Christian slaveholders. Colonization was the best, perhaps the only, way of accomplishing this feat, for Finley understood the depth of white racism.[15]

Mercer and Finley revived the idea of colonization at a moment when American elites were in the midst of a great movement to reform their society and make it an example of Christian benevolence for the civilized world. These years saw a fusion of religious enthusiasm and nationalism that was reflected in the names of the many reforming societies that were organized. The decade that saw the formation of the ACS also saw the organization of the American Education Society, the American Bible Society, and the American Temperance Society. The consistent choice of "American" in the nomenclature of reform groups drew from the intense nationalism in the years following the War of 1812, especially the defeat of Britain in the battle of New Orleans. Building on the lingering animosities of the Revolution and British travel writers' acid critiques of American society, the War of 1812 fostered a strong dose of Anglophobia in early American nationalism. As all of these reforming societies had British precedents, the formation of separate American societies revealed a desire to compete in benevolence on the international stage.[16] But if they were going to truly compete, Americans had to take on the problem of the enslaved African, the subject of much discussion in the British journals that American elites still read. For the southern elites who supported the ACS, African colonization was the only safe means of participating in this particular benevolent cause. It allowed many to think that Americans could be just as benevolent and Christian as any other nation, yet maintain the right to own slaves. After all, they argued, the guilt in slavery lay in its origins in North America and that was the responsibility of the British. Americans merely inherited their slaves; they were not personally responsible for the fact of enslavement. Supporting African colonization allowed many northern elites to act upon genuine antislavery views without offending

15. Staudenraus, *African Colonization,* 15–22.

16. George M. Fredrickson, *The Black Image in the White Mind: The Debate on Afro-American Character and Destiny, 1817–1914* (Hanover, NH: Wesleyan University Press, 1971), 6; Staudenraus, *African Colonization,* 255, n. 3.

their fellow citizens in the South. The ACS seemed the perfect organization for the nationalism and benevolence of the times, a singular moment
in this era of good feelings.

While Mercer and Finley agreed on much, they disagreed on one crucial point, which made the ACS an ineffective institution almost immediately. They disagreed on slavery. While Finley hoped that slavery would
gradually wither with colonization in Africa assisting the process, Mercer saw no connection between colonization and slavery, a view laid out
in no uncertain terms by Henry Clay in the society's first meeting on December 21, 1816. The "delicate question" of slavery would not be raised in
discussions among colonizationists. Colonization was for black Americans
who were already free, not for those still legally enslaved. One suspects that
an ample majority of the great names in attendance at the first meeting
were pleased to hear such cautious words. Men like Bushrod Washington,
Andrew Jackson, and John Randolph of Roanoke were all slaveholders of
considerable wealth with political futures to consider. They were not interested in discussing the end of slavery, but they did want their names attached to a benevolent cause, especially if it worked toward ridding society
of freed blacks who threatened the stability of their world.[17]

The founders of the ACS also presumed the cooperation of African
Americans. Finley had corresponded with the prominent black merchant
and New England ship owner Paul Cuffe, who had long shown an interest
in the British colony of Sierra Leone. Cuffe had discussed with British
philanthropists the possibility of African American settlement there and
in 1810 traveled to the colony to establish trading contacts. Two of his crew
members (Samuel Hicks and Primrose Edwards) decided to settle in the
colony. The War of 1812 with Britain interrupted these efforts, but in 1815
Cuffe launched another voyage to Sierra Leone, this time accompanied by
thirty-four settlers, some of them Africans who wished to return home.
While Cuffe himself was more interested in adding a branch of West African commerce to his already extensive trading ventures, those who went
with him likely sought the opportunity to start anew, free of American
racism.[18]

---

17. *Washington (DC) National Intelligencer,* December 24, 1816, quoted in Staudenraus, *African Colonization,* 28. For more on the social position of the men who attended this
meeting, see Staudenraus, *African Colonization,* 25–30.

18. James Oliver Horton and Lois E. Horton, *In Hope of Liberty: Culture, Community
and Protest Among Northern Free Blacks, 1700–1860* (New York: Oxford University Press,
1997), 181–86.

When the ACS was formed, black leaders in the North such as James Forten and Richard Allen of Philadelphia supported the idea, no doubt inspired by the example of Cuffe. But in January 1817, when Forten and Allen called a general meeting of the black community at Allen's Bethel Church to cultivate support for the society, three thousand attended, and their overwhelming response was "No." More clearly than their leaders, the black Americans in attendance saw the racism and the defense of slavery at the core of the colonizationist project. Some had personally escaped from slavery, more still had family members in slavery, and this public rejection of colonization and the advice of their leaders demonstrated the growing realization among African Americans that their own status was intrinsically linked to the future of American slavery. Moreover, white reformers in Philadelphia were at the forefront of antislavery activism, and while most supported the ACS, it seems likely that their established dedication to black freedom offered a better hope than emigration. Another mass meeting held in August spoke directly to this group, asking that "the humane and benevolent Inhabitants of . . . Philadelphia" reject any organization that worked to "stay the cause of the entire abolition of slavery in the United States."[19]

The African American response to the early colonizationist project indicated a transnational orientation receptive to British humanitarian efforts but deeply resentful when that effort was joined to a proslavery agenda. It also revealed a profound ambiguity about emigration that would persist. On the one hand, Paul Cuffee and those who accompanied him embraced the British humanitarian effort, and in the African American community this position would flourish as British abolitionism matured over the following decades. Moreover, the intensity of white racism sustained the African American impulse to leave the United States well into the twenty-first century. On the other hand, American blacks were now five generations rooted in the soil of the United States. Most took that birthright seriously and sought to manifest in their own lives and the lives of their children, the rhetoric of "freedom" that was so fundamental to American political life. While it was not yet clear in 1817, opposition to colonization would be the formative experience in the radicalization of American abo-

19. Quoted in Gary Nash, *Forging Freedom: The Formation of Philadelphia's Black Community, 1720–1840* (Cambridge: Harvard University Press, 1988), 240. On early abolitionism in Philadelphia, see Richard S. Newman, *The Transformation of American Abolitionism: Fighting Slavery in the Early Republic* (Chapel Hill: University of North Carolina Press, 2002).

litionism in the next decade. Thus, while the slaveholding leaders of the ACS thought they had discovered the safe alternative to British antislavery, enabling them to participate in transatlantic benevolence while retaining their slaves, they had in fact awakened the passion of those they sought to export. The overwhelming majority of African Americans opted to stay and fight.[20]

Despite the clear rejection of northern blacks, the outpouring of prominent white support encouraged the organizers of the ACS. They established headquarters in Washington, and appeals went out to prominent Americans in every state to raise funds for the new society and to investigate conditions in Africa for a colony. The ACS staged annual Fourth of July celebrations to drum up financial support and spread word of the cause. This approach was fairly effective. Colonization societies began to form all over the country and by 1820 the parent society had received the endorsement of the state legislatures of Virginia, Georgia, Maryland, Tennessee, and Vermont. It would prove very difficult, however, to maintain such support in the age of British abolition.[21]

The ACS rested upon a compromise that was impossible to maintain. Transatlantic antislavery was becoming more radical, which caught the attention of many northerners. One of them was James Tallmadge, the New York congressman who in December 1819 pushed an amendment to bar the spread of slavery into the proposed state of Missouri. The political crisis that developed out of Tallmadge's proposed amendment has been recognized by contemporaries and historians as a watershed in American history. The heated debate over the extension of slavery into Missouri brought the nation dangerously close to disunion, yet the political compromise that resulted from these debates maintained sectional peace—with slavery—for the next forty years. The United States expanded into a continental power as a slaveholding nation. For old antislavery Federalists like James Tallmadge, to allow the further spread of slavery into the lands of the Louisiana Purchase would be another concession to the South and the prolonged ac-

20. Sandra Sandiford Young, "John Brown Russwurm's Dilemma: Citizenship or Emigration," in Timothy Patrick McCarthy and John Stauffer, eds., *Prophets of Protest: Reconsidering the History of American Abolitionism* (New York: New Press, 2006): 90–113; James T. Campbell, *Middle Passages: African American Journeys to Africa, 1987–2005* (NY: Penguin Press, 2006).

21. Lawrence J. Friedman, "Purifying the White Man's Country: The American Colonization Society Reconsidered, 1816–1840," *Societas* 6 (Winter 1976): 6–7.

ceptance of slavery's moral weight. Tallmadge intended to provoke the debate. He believed that slavery was a moral abomination incompatible with the values of a republican nation. He also believed that the time had come to halt the expansion of slavery on the southern bank of the Missouri river. The United States was on the cusp of expansion, an "extended empire," in Tallmadge's words, which he hoped to see "inhabited by the hardy sons of American freemen." His vision dissipated when he considered that his opponents wanted to "people this fair dominion with the slaves of your planters." Slavery was an "abomination of heaven" that would forever taint the young republic, and northerners like Tallmadge had decided that colonizationist claims of gradual emancipation were fictions. If slavery were to be stopped, it would take more than patient persuasion.[22]

Tallmadge's imperial vision drew from the reigning nationalism, whose power the colonizationists had attempted to harness, and it allowed him to bring world opinion to bear upon American slavery. He reminded his audience that "the eyes of Europe are turned upon you" and told them of a British cartoon that he had seen. It portrayed America "as holding in one hand the Declaration of Independence, and with the other brandishing a whip over our affrighted slaves." Britain mocked America. She pointed to the "inconsistencies" of a nation that claimed the mantle of freedom while expanding the geography of slavery. "I felt for my country," he told his audience, when he realized the charge was true.[23]

As had happened in Britain, slavery was being challenged in the halls of government, and the fear of a resulting insurrection was a common theme in the speeches that followed Tallmadge. Many present would have read Edwards and had probably followed the news of the insurrection in Barbados. One Mr. Colston, of Virginia, accused a proponent of the amendment of "speaking to the galleries, and, by his language, endeavoring to excite a servile war."[24] Colston's accusation was a clear rearticulation of Edwards's thesis on the origin of rebellion—if Congress discussed the question of slavery, Colston expected the slaves to rebel. Mr. Barbour, also of Virginia, used the threat of insurrections in a different manner. Barbour asked his audience to imagine a future time "when we shall be engaged

22. *Annals of Congress,* 15th Cong., 2d sess., 33:1206; Robert Forbes, *The Missouri Compromise and Its Aftermath: Slavery and the Meaning of America* (Chapel Hill: University of North Carolina Press, 2007), 35–36.

23. *Annals of Congress,* 15th Cong., 2d sess., 33:1211; Forbes, *Missouri Compromise,* 44.

24. *Annals of Congress,* 15th Cong., 2d sess., 33:1205.

in war." Were that to happen, he warned, the strength of the South would only be equal to the difference in population between the white men and the black. Slaves would surely rebel during a war, and white men of the South would be called to defend their very homes, weakening their contribution in the struggle against the national enemy. The solution to this potential weakness was to allow the geography of slavery to expand. Let masters move into Missouri with their slaves, and the slave populations would be less dense. They would pose less of a risk in the event of war, and the nation would be stronger. Barbour articulated an early version of the "safety valve" theory of slave expansion, which as we shall see, became quite prominent in the next struggle over the expansion of slavery, in Texas.[25]

Tallmadge responded directly to Barbour's argument. He agreed that a slave rebellion endangered the nation's security, but like Clarkson in 1792, Tallmadge argued that the cause would not lie in the discussion of slavery but in slavery itself. Tallmadge addressed slaveholders directly. By continuing to allow slavery to expand, he told them, American slaveholders "whet the dagger and place it in the hands" of slaves, whose "envious contrast between your liberty and their slavery, must constantly prompt them to accomplish your destruction."[26] To rebel violently against slavery was only natural to human nature, and Tallmadge fully expected that as long as there was slavery there would be rebellions. Southerners, of course, saw things differently. As Edwards had said in the early years of their century, the abolitionists must be silenced, or the horrors of Saint-Domingue would be repeated. And as the rebellion in Barbados had shown, Edwards was right. Southerners fought the Tallmadge amendment in both houses of Congress in a raging debate that terrified the living founders. Robert Forbes reminds us that for as much as the South decried the Missouri compromise in the 1850s, they had the best side of Clay's first compromise in 1820. Slavery was allowed into Missouri—and even more importantly—the discussion of slavery was stopped, or so they thought.[27]

Only months after the tense debate over Missouri had closed, Charlestonians discovered what they believed was a rebellious plot among their slaves. The first arrests were made in late May. By June 16, 1822, more than ten slaves had been arrested, and by the afternoon of July 2 the bodies of Denmark Vesey and five of his accused co-conspirators hung from a gal-

25. Ibid., 1189–90. See below, chap. 7.
26. Ibid., 1206.
27. Forbes, *Missouri Compromise,* 3–4.

lows recently erected on the outskirts of town. They had been executed by the authority of the Charleston Court of Magistrates and Freeholders, which first met on June 19 to deal with the ten men who had just been arrested on suspicion of being involved with a conspiracy. The court sat until July 26 and heard 131 cases during that short time. Of the defendants in these cases, thirty-five were executed, thirty-one were transported, and the remaining sixty-five were ultimately released. The fearful, bloody episode was over by the middle of August.[28]

Some were not convinced by the court's proceedings. Judge William Johnson was South Carolina's senior jurist at the time, having served as a Supreme Court justice since 1804 when he was appointed by Thomas Jefferson. The new court's actions seemed hurried to Johnson, and on June 21—just two days after the court began its interrogations—the *Charleston Courier* printed a story entitled "Melancholy Effect of Popular Excitement," written by Johnson, which told of the overreaction about fifteen years earlier in Edgefield, South Carolina, to the rumor of a slave rebellion. The cavalry had been alerted, but though no threat materialized, a bored, half-drunken trumpeter sounded his horn, alerting a group of cavalry who galloped off to crush the rebellion. They found only an old slave crossing a field and promptly arrested him. The man said he knew nothing, but after a whipping and the measured sharpening of a sabre, the old man "now recollected" that a slave named Billy owned a horn. The cavalry found Billy asleep at home, but with him there was a "terrific horn," still in its cover and filled with cobwebs. Despite the paucity of evidence, a rapidly convened court found Billy guilty of a plot to incite insurrection, and though his master tried to intervene, Billy was hung.[29]

<hr />

28. The slave conspiracy in Charleston in the summer of 1822 has recently become the subject of a heated historiographical debate as to whether the conspiracy was real or a figment of white paranoia. See Michael P. Johnson, "Denmark Vesey and His Co-conspirators," *William and Mary Quarterly,* 3d ser., 58 (October 2002): 933–71, as well as the responses to Johnson's article by Edward A. Pearson et al. in "The Making of a Slave Conspiracy, part 2," *William and Mary Quarterly,* 3d ser., 58 (October 2002): 135–92. The debate continues in Robert L. Paquette and Douglas R. Egerton, "Of Facts and Fables: New Light on the Denmark Vesey Affair," *South Carolina Historical Magazine* 105 (January 2004): 8–48; Robert L. Paquette, "From Rebellion to Revisionism: The Continuing Debate about the Denmark Vesey Affair," *Journal of the Historical Society* 4 (Fall 2004): 291–334.

29. Johnson, "Denmark Vesey and His Co-conspirators," 935; Donald G. Morgan, *Justice William Johnson, the First Dissenter: The Career and Constitutional Philosophy of a Jeffersonian Judge* (Columbia: University of South Carolina Press, 1954), 130–31.

Judge Johnson later wrote that he had hoped readers might take "a moral" from the story, which might slow the actions of the Court of Magistrates and Freeholders, but as the historian Michael Johnson has argued, the judge's subtle critique stung the court deep. Seven prominent Charlestonians sat on the court, and they took the didactic fable as an admonition. They saw it as an insult to the court's honor and proceeded to demonstrate with the power of the court just how great a threat the conspiracy had posed. The interrogations and hangings continued into August, and in November the court published the *Official Report of the Trials of Sundry Negroes,* an account replete with all of the horrible images that rebellion brought to the slaveholding mind.[30]

Michael Johnson has suggested that the *Official Report* be read as a text created by a powerful body that had just abused its power and sought to defend its actions. Robert Paquette and Douglas Egerton have found complementary evidence of conspiracy that suggests the *Official Report* may not be as flawed as Johnson believes in revealing the intentions of the rebels.[31] But as Johnson insists, the *Official Report* also sheds light on the fears and assumptions of the white officials who wrote it. The *Official Report* told readers that Charleston had been threatened by a massive conspiracy of slaves led by Denmark Vesey; some of the conspirators were members of the newly formed African Methodist Episcopal Church. The alleged plan was to kill all the white inhabitants and escape by ship to Haiti, where they would be welcomed. Vesey himself had lived in Haiti for a time and had imbibed the dangerous spirit of rebellion from an early age. Moreover, he had used the arguments of James Tallmadge and Rufus King—the abolitionist leaders in the Missouri struggle—to convince the poor, deluded slaves who fell under his wing that Congress had granted them their freedom. The pattern of agitation and revolt that Charlestonians had read about in Edwards, that they had heard about in Barbados, and that they had feared might happen during those irresponsible debates over Missouri, had now been repeated in their own city.

30. Johnson, "Denmark Vesey and His Co-conspirators," 936. For a different interpretation of Johnson's motives in publishing the story, see Paquette, "From Rebellion to Revisionism," 296–301.

31. In particular consider the evidence from the records of the Charleston Bible Society and the papers of Mary Lamboll Thomas Beach; see Paquette and Egerton, "Of Facts and Fables," 12–15, 23, 33, 36–48. The *Official Report* has been reprinted in John Oliver Killens, ed., *The Trial Record of Denmark Vesey* (Boston: Beacon, 1970).

Other Charlestonians emphasized elements of the report which were clearly drawn from Edward's *Historical Survey*. "A Columbian" spoke of the "madness" of the French Convention when it "emancipated the slaves of St. Domingo." In their ignorance, they did not know that "this decree would produce the extermination of the whites." The same "would be the case for the southern states," he argued, if Congress were to abolish slavery here.[32] Thomas Pinckney (who had subscribed to the Philadelphia edition of Edwards's *History*) wrote of three explanations for the plot they had just averted: the example of Haiti, the "indiscreet zeal" of northern abolitionists, and the presence of a large population of free blacks in Charleston. He paid particular attention to the connection between free blacks and abolitionists, the same connection that Edwards had focused on almost twenty years earlier. The central problem with free blacks, Pinckney argued, was "their being taught to read and write," which allowed "the powerful operation of the Press to act upon their uninformed and easily deluded minds." Another problem with free blacks was that they could access money, which enabled them to carry out plans for the rebellion. And, finally, there were just too many of them. Pinckney estimated that the ratio of blacks, including slaves, to whites in Charleston was twenty-two to fourteen. White Charleston was not safe.[33]

The South Carolina legislature did not react lightly to the threat of slave rebellion. Most representatives were slaveholders themselves, so in December 1822 they passed the infamous Negro Seamen Act, which mandated that every black sailor who entered the port of Charleston could be imprisoned for the duration of his stay, and had to leave with his ship when it departed. One of the key authors of the law was the low-country planter Robert J. Turnbull, "the cosmopolitan product of a cosmopolitan marriage" in the words of William Freehling. Turnbull was born in Spanish Florida; his father was Scottish, a doctor trained in England, and his mother was Greek. Dr. Turnbull established a successful practice in Charleston, and Robert, the second son, trained in Philadelphia for a career in the law. By 1810 Robert Turnbull had earned enough from his Charleston law practice to buy land and slaves in the sea islands and become a planter. He main-

32. [A Columbian], *A Series of Numbers Addressed to the Public, on the Subject of the Slaves and Free People of Color: First Published in the South Carolina State Gazette, in the Months of September and October, 1822* (Columbia: State Gazette Office, 1822), 18.

33. [Thomas Pinckney], *Reflections, Occassioned by the late Disturbances in Charleston. By Achates* (Charleston: A. E. Miller, 1822), 6, 10.

tained a residence in Charleston, though, and when the city was gripped with fright at the discovery of the Vesey conspiracy, Turnbull served on the Court of Magistrates and Freeholders.[34]

The Negro Seamen Act represented Turnbull's solution to Charleston's apparent weakness against slave insurrection. He had learned from recent history. The agitation of the abolitionists in Britain was followed by rebellion in Barbados; the Missouri debates were followed by the Vesey conspiracy. Clearly, abolitionism was on the rise, and white populations were in danger. And because free blacks who could read—like Denmark Vesey—were the most common vehicle for slaves to learn of abolitionism, they must not be allowed to speak to Charleston's slaves, for those conversations could lead to devastation. The example of Haiti had loomed for twenty years, but the British now spoke of abolitionism, and even fellow northerners were raising this dangerous issue. Words had power, and Negro seamen were particularly dangerous because they were so mobile. A free black sailor could pick up these subversive ideas in any Atlantic port, but if the legislature could enforce its power, he would not spread those ideas in Charleston.[35]

The Negro Seamen Act was tested in the courts almost immediately, but when American ship captains sued, South Carolina courts supported the law. In January 1823, however, the mate and four black seamen of a British ship were arrested, and the British ambassador in Washington, Stratford Canning, protested to Secretary of State John Quincy Adams against this clear violation of international law. Adams apparently agreed, and he corresponded with South Carolina officials who seem to have assured him that the law would not be enforced. In June Adams wrote back to Canning that his concerns had been addressed, a situation that lasted until July, when a free black Jamaican named Henry Elkison was arrested according to the new law. The British consul in Charleston protested to Judge William Johnson and sought a writ of habeas corpus. The consul also carried with him a copy of Adams's letter to Canning. On August 7, Judge Johnson delivered his opinion to a packed courtroom. He was ob-

34. William Freehling, *Prelude to Civil War: The Nullification Controversy in South Carolina, 1816–1836* (New York: Harper and Row, 1965), 126; Philip M. Hamer, "Great Britain, the United States, and the Negro Seamen's Act Acts, 1822–1848," *Journal of Southern History* 1 (February 1935), 3–4.

35. Jeffrey Bolster, *Black Jacks: African American Seamen in the Age of Sail* (Cambridge: Harvard University Press, 1997), 190–214.

liged to dismiss the request on a technicality. The act under question was a state law; Johnson was a federal judge and had no jurisdiction. But he used the occasion to deliver an obiter dictum that the law was unconstitutional; it violated the federal government's right to regulate commerce, and all arrests under its authority should be considered void. Johnson not only read his opinion but also had it published as a pamphlet, sold, and disseminated, and by the next week it was answered by Robert J. Turnbull.[36]

Turnbull had been alarmed by his experience on the Court of Magistrates and Freemen. He clearly believed that a conspiracy had been contemplated and serious measures were necessary. He had pushed the law against black seamen as a security measure, and he probably assisted with the crafting of the *Official Report*. And he noticed when South Carolina officials, under Adams's direction, declined to enforce his law. Turnbull and a group of prominent citizens formed the South Carolina Association to make sure the law was enforced, and it was they who had arrested Henry Elkison. And now Judge William Johnson had condemned his law in public and in print.[37]

Beginning in late August 1823, Turnbull published in the *Charleston Mercury* a series of essays above the pseudonym "Caroliniensis," which became the title of a pamphlet. Turnbull leveled sharp, personal criticism at Judge Johnson for publishing his opinion on the Negro Seamen laws and at the same time made a powerful argument for the political rights of states which would be refined during the nullification crisis of the next decade. These essays are significant, for they reveal the influence of Edwards on Turnbull's thought and the fear of insurrection as the emotional root of states rights theory.

Edwards's influence appears at several moments, the first one almost comical and revealing of Charleston's reading culture in the early 1820s. In one of the first *Caroliniensis* essays, Turnbull cited Edwards's discussion of the races of the West Indies and drew from it that Elkison, because he was black, would not have had access to a court even in Jamaica. But Turnbull was wrong. He had misread Edwards, and "Amicus" left a note with the *Mercury*'s editors. In fact, wrote "Amicus" (who referred to Edwards on

36. Hamer, "Great Britain, the United States, and the Negro Seamen's Act Acts," 4–7; Alan F. January, "The South Carolina Association: An Agency for Race Control in Antebellum Charleston," *South Carolina Historical Magazine* 78 (July 1977): 194–97; Morgan, *Justice William Johnson,* 192–97.

37. January, "The South Carolina Association," 193.

his or her own), free blacks did have rights to the courts in Jamaica, though they were under other disabilities. Turnbull conceded; he thanked "Amicus" for the careful reading and assured readers that the slight change in facts did not compromise his arguments. He explained that he had gotten the Edwards quotation from a "literary friend," whose notes he had used when he wrote the essays. The exchange reveals the care with which Carolinians read and one fascinating way in which ideas traveled. Edwards was known well enough for Amicus to catch the mistake and respond, and Edwards was an important enough authority for the editors of the *Mercury* to print the correction. Ideas circulated not only through published works but also through the notes on various subjects that planter gentlemen shared with each other in fashioning their essays.[38]

More central to Turnbull's argument was the Edwards thesis on slave rebellion, particularly the alleged nexus between print and insurrection. This connection was Turnbull's fundamental reason for challenging Judge Johnson's decision to publish his opinion. It was not just the opinion itself that Turnbull critiqued (although he did that too), he worried about the effect that the airing of ideas such as Johnson's would have in Charleston, a city of blacks. In light of the "occurrences of the past summer," Turnbull argued, wouldn't it have been better for Johnson not to publish his opinion? Writers in a slave society must be wary of ideas that were "liable from the very nature of [their] subject, to be misunderstood by one class of our population." This was particularly true for their own moment in history, when the careful observer could see "the progress of opinions in other countries on this subject ... societies, and plans ... striking at the vital interests of the States of the South." The danger was nowhere more apparent than in the West Indies, where "the colonial interests of the British Empire [were] about to be immolated on the altars of folly ... surrendered to the fanaticism of a thousand Wilberforces." And was Johnson not aware that this "self same spirit" was abroad in his own country? "Go over the sections of this confederacy," Turnbull suggested, and Johnson would realize that "fanaticism, false charity, fashionable humanity ... are in dreadful operation, and array against the State, which gave him birth."[39]

Turnbull accused Johnson of risking insurrection in Charleston by printing his pamphlet. He conceded that the framers of South Carolina's

38. *Charleston Mercury*, August 19 and 20, 1823.

39. [Robert J. Turnbull and Isaac Edward Holmes], *Caroliniensis* (Charleston: A. E. Miller, [1824]), 20, 24, 40.

constitution had not excluded free black seamen but argued that developments over the last twenty years had transformed the slaveholding world. The fundamental issue was not a matter of legal precedent; it was a matter of the safety of the white population. At the moment of independence "there were then afloat no doctrines of African emancipation . . . the *Abolition Society* of Philadelphia, the *British Association* in London, and the *Amis des Noirs* in Paris, had not yet formed . . . and the Abbe Gregoire had not written that celebrated letter, which was afterwards the torch, which lighted up the insurrection of St. Domingo."[40] Turnbull warned his readership that South Carolina must keep in mind the recent past and not forget the lessons of former generations. His account came straight from Edwards's *Historical Survey,* but Turnbull blended this familiar history with remarks about the recent organization of the Pennsylvania Abolition Society to warn his readers of the current threats that faced South Carolina. The parallels were profoundly disturbing. French Saint-Domingue had been sacrificed by the abolitionists in Paris, the British West Indies were under mortal threat from abolitionists in London, and abolitionists were on the move in Philadelphia. Fanatical abolitionism had emerged on both sides of the Atlantic, and the South was threatened by potential insurrections.[41]

Turnbull's answer was to develop the rationale by which South Carolina could exert power in its own right as a sovereign state in order to protect its interests, despite the possibility that this action might conflict with the policy or law of the federal government. The threat was clear enough. Abolitionist ideas were afloat, free blacks were known to disseminate abolitionist ideas, and slave rebellions were known to result. As a sovereign state, South Carolina had the right to "self-preservation," a political truth attested by the great political philosophers, of whom Turnbull cited Vattel, Grotius, and Pufendorf, who had all defended slavery as well. He quoted specifically from Vattel: "A nation or state has a right to every thing which can secure it *from threatening danger,* and *to keep at a distance whatever is capable of causing its ruin.*" The emphasis alluded to free black seamen, of course, and the Negro Seamen Act that kept them "at a distance," beyond the earshot of South Carolina's slaves. But the political concept at the heart

40. *Caroliniensis,* 45. Turnbull used Edwards's metaphor; see chap. 2.

41. On the activities of the Pennsylvania Abolition Society to which Turnbull referred, see Richard S. Newman, *The Transformation of American Abolitionism: Fighting Slavery in the Early Republic* (Chapel Hill: University of North Carolina Press, 2002), 39–59.

of this law, and Turnbull's argument, was that South Carolina could act in any way it wished on the question of slavery and abolitionism. This same concept reappeared during the nullification movement and again during southern secession.[42]

NEWS FROM DEMERARA, SEPTEMBER 1823

About a week after the publication of the last *Caroliniensis* essay in the *Mercury,* the newspapers from Richmond, Baltimore, and New York began to print the first reports on the insurrection in Demerara. There had been a "general uprising" in the interior; troops were on the way from Barbados; martial law had been proclaimed. By mid-October readers of the *Baltimore Niles' Weekly Register* and the *Richmond Enquirer* had learned that "a fanatic preacher, a white man" had caused the revolt by misleading the slaves into believing they had been freed by Parliament. Ritchie's comment that "this is one of the unhappy fruits of the misdirected zeal of the British philan-thropists" reinforced the links between the abolitionist agitation in Britain and the insurrection in Demerara.[43]

As the story of the rebellion continued to unfold, the connection be-tween the rebellion and the abolitionist movement appeared repeatedly in American newspapers. In mid-October a widely disseminated excerpt from the *Demerara Royal Gazette* reported that "evidence and confessions" demonstrated that the organization of the rebellion was too complex to have been developed by black slaves. There was little "doubt that a supe-rior order of people" had planned the insurrection. "Perhaps the intriguing Saints at home had a hand in it—if so, they will hear with disappointment and pain that a superintending and just Providence has frustrated their diabolical intentions ... to make Demerara a second St. Domingo!" The accusation was direct. While Governor Leith of Barbados had referenced abolitionist agitation in his remarks to the slaves of that colony in 1816, the writer for the *Royal Gazette* suggested that the "intriguing Saints" had played a direct role in the insurrection in Demerara. Moreover, by making the historical allusion to the Haitian Revolution, the Demeraran writer heightened the moral opprobrium to be cast upon the abolitionists.[44]

42. *Caroliniensis,* 40.

43. *Baltimore Niles' Register,* October 11, 1823; *Richmond Enquirer,* October 7, 1823.

44. *Baltimore American & Commercial Advertiser,* October 16, 1823; *New York Albion,* October 18, 1823.

In November, Baltimore editor Hezekiah Niles returned to the news from the West Indies in an article entitled "The Curse.""The people of one of the southern states," he observed, "have hardly recovered from their agitation at the discovery of a plot among the slaves to effect a general rising . . . [and] we now hear of fearful apprehensions in another quarter on a similar account." Niles reported unrest in nearly all of the West Indian colonies, especially Barbados, where it appeared that some colonists believed the Methodists intended to raise another insurrection. The belief proved so pervasive that a white mob destroyed the Methodist Chapel in town and forced the minister to flee for his life. In Jamaica a meeting of colonists resolved that abolitionism was nothing less than "MEDITATED ROBBERY." Echoing American colonizationists, white Jamaicans protested that slavery was a "curse entailed on the people of her American colonies, on the continent and in the West Indies" by Britain, and that pure hypocrisy moved British writers to "blame us because we have slaves!" These Jamaicans admitted slavery was a curse—upon themselves and upon their cousins in the United States. Not only had it brought upon them unfair moral censure by their countrymen in Britain, but that very censure had threatened their lives by instigating their slaves to rebel.[45]

In December 1823, Thomas Ritchie reprinted a piece from the *Charleston Patriot*. West Indian whites "from Barbados to Jamaica" had roundly protested Parliament's measures to ameliorate colonial slavery. As he had during his coverage of the rebellion in Barbados in 1816, Ritchie turned to the familiar parallels of the West Indian experience with the American Revolution. He reported that the language of writers in the islands' newspapers was "precisely the tone and character of that used in this country previous to the revolution."[46] Ritchie also reprinted the *Bermuda Gazette*'s accounts of West Indian planters who were "all in arms against the regulations which the Saints of the African Institution have induced Ministers to propose, relative to the future treatment of the slave population."[47] The sarcastic nickname "Saints" had been applied to the abolitionists by their conservative critics in Britain and the West Indies. The anecdote suggested an analogy between British abolitionists and the oppressions of an odious, meddling Parliament on the eve of the American Revolution. The British West Indian colonial struggle against the abolitionists in Parliament

45. *Baltimore Niles' Register*, November 29, 1823.
46. *Richmond Enquirer*, December 16, 1823 (reprinted from the *Charleston Patriot*).
47. *Richmond Enquirer*, December 20, 1823.

was to be understood as a just cause reminiscent of the American Revolution.

As colonization, the Missouri Crisis, and the conspiracy scare in Charleston fueled the debate over slavery in the United States, American newspaper coverage of West Indian rebellions changed in a manner that reveals the growth of slavery as a national issue, as well as some of the regional distinctions that already portended a threat to national stability. In 1816 news of the rebellion in Barbados appeared in the American political press through twenty-two reports. These reports spread around the country through thirteen identifiable exchange papers and were based upon six letters, five ear-witnesses, and five West Indian newspapers. News from Demerara reached American readers through thirty-one reports, and these were based upon five letters, five ear witnesses, and nine West Indian newspapers. Information on the Demerara rebellion spread through fourteen identifiable exchanges of American newspapers. The infrastructure of the information network did not develop all that much in the seven years between rebellions, but the coverage became more prolonged. In 1816 American editors discussed the events in Barbados for as long as thirty-eight days (*Baltimore Niles Register*) to as few as twelve days (*Charleston Mercury*) with an average news cycle of twenty-six days. But in 1823 U.S. newspapermen followed the rebellion for an average of ninety-seven days, more than three times as long. The *New York Evening Post* kept up coverage for 165 days, a stark contrast to the one lonely report offered by Henry Pinckney of the *Charleston Mercury*.[48]

The *Mercury*'s unique approach is not surprising. South Carolina was the only state whose racial composition approximated that of the West Indies, and in the lowcountry parishes that produced the mentality of a

48. Few newspapers in the early republican United States enjoyed any sort of longevity, making systematic analysis of the change in press coverage between 1816 and 1823 difficult. The newspapers chosen to analyze American press coverage of the rebellions represent influential regions or editors of the United States during this period. For the rebellion in Barbados, the following newspapers were thoroughly investigated from May 1, 1816, to the end of that year: *Baltimore Niles' Register, Charleston City Gazette and Commercial Advertiser, New York Evening Post, Richmond Enquirer, Washington (DC) Daily National Intelligencer*. For the rebellion in Demerara, the following newspapers were thoroughly investigated from July 1, 1823, to the end of that year: *Baltimore Niles' Register, Baltimore American and Commercial Daily Advertiser, Charleston Mercury, New York Evening Post, Richmond Enquirer*.

Robert J. Turnbull, blacks could exceed 90 percent of the population.[49] Turnbull had warned against printing anything that might inspire thoughts of black freedom, and the news of the rebellion in Demerara was kept to a minimum. The *Mercury's* sole report on the 1823 rebellion conveyed that a "Preacher" had been arrested and would probably be hung, but there was no discussion of the "saints." The report ended on a sobering note for any slave or free black who harbored subversive ideas: "Many of the Negroes had been killed by the troops sent against them, and several executions had taken place." The *Mercury's* coverage indicates the exception of South Carolina nationally as well as within the South. The incredible reaction to the conspiracy of 1822 made Carolinians remarkably sensitive to any news of rebellion during the next summer. By contrast, the *Richmond Enquirer* printed eight reports on the Demerara rebellion, some complete with analysis that likened the situation to that in the United States. It was a significant change from news coverage of Barbados in 1816, before Denmark Vesey and when the ACS was just being formed. The *Enquirer* had only printed four reports of the rebellion, and the *Charleston City Gazette* had printed only two. Now Richmond and Charleston had gone in opposite directions.

The news from Demerara that an Evangelical missionary had instigated the rebellion was alarming and provocative, and as we have seen, American Evangelicals were deeply interested in the Christian missions to the slaves. A survey of the religious press in the North indicates that Evangelical editors chose to ignore the news from Demerara as it first began to reach the United States in October 1823. But by February 1824, religious newspapers and journals began to reprint the defenses of John Smith that had already appeared in British Evangelical publications. The *Christian Herald and Seaman's Magazine,* for example, reprinted an article from the January edition of the London Missionary Society's *Chronicle,* which defended Smith against the charges of Demerara's planters. The article gave a short account of the rebellion and focused upon Smith's whereabouts as the rebellion spread. According to the LMS, the rebellion began far to the east of Smith's residence. It only spread to his mission's plantation at Le Resouvenir when the colonial authorities arrested two inno-

---

49. Lacy Ford, *Origins of Southern Radicalism: The South Carolina Upcountry, 1800–1860* (New York: Oxford University Press, 1988), 123.

cent slaves, prompting the forceful demand by the community that these two be released. At this point Smith had intervened and "successfully used his endeavors ... to rescue the Manager from the Negroes, and continued his exertions to induce them to return to their duty." The charges against Smith were based upon "the false assertions" of convicted rebels, and the LMS claimed to have information that these charges were coerced. Some of the condemned slaves had later stated "in the most solemn manner" that they had been induced to lie about Smith. For the London Society, the evidence suggested that Smith was innocent, and in choosing to reprint their opinion, the editors of the *Christian Herald* agreed.[50]

In April and May, the *Religious Intelligencer,* a Congregationalist paper in New Haven, and the Presbyterian *Christian Advocate* of Philadelphia devoted considerable attention to the trial and death of John Smith. Both papers drew from the *London Evangelical Magazine,* which had only heard of Smith's death in March 1824 and promptly began an effort to clear his name.[51] Short notices in April were followed by detailed articles in May, informing American readers of the innocence of John Smith, the gross abuses of the Demeraran planters, and the "true" causes of the rebellion.[52] The papers attempted to demonstrate Smith's innocence by reprinting his original instructions as a missionary, which were dated to 1816. Missionaries were to remain silent on the political aspect of slavery and attend only to the spiritual needs of their community. Neither paper saw any evidence that Smith had violated his instructions. Moreover, the court that condemned him was itself suspect. The only evidence against Smith had been the testimony of slaves, which, according to the laws of the colony, should not even be admissible in a civil case, much less against a charge of instigating rebellion. And Smith's treatment by the court in Demerara had been atrocious. He was imprisoned in horrible conditions for the duration of the trials, even though his health was already poor. His private quarters at the mission had been ransacked, and his personal musings in his private journal had been "tortured to support the imputations" that had been coerced

50. "South America.—Demerara," *Christian Herald and Seaman's Magazine* 11 (February 1824): 113–15.

51. Emilia Viotti da Costa, *Crowns of Glory, Tears of Blood: The Demerara Slave Rebellion of 1823* (New York: Oxford University Press, 1994), 279.

52. "Demerara," *Religious Intelligencer ... Containing the Principal Transactions of the Various Bible and Missionary Societies, with Particular Accounts of Revivals of Religion* 8 (April 1824): 730; *Christian Advocate* (April 1824): 185–86.

from the captured rebels. His death in prison, despite the royal commuta-
tion of the sentence, made Smith a "martyr" in the words of the *Advocate*,
an "unmerited sufferer" for the *Intelligencer*. Editors on both sides of the
Atlantic shifted their focus from rebellion to repression; they appealed to
Evangelical sentiment, and they fostered antislavery opinion.[53]

The most important issue, however, was how the insurrection had really
begun, and it is highly significant that the religious papers addressed this
question. Readers of the political press would have come away convinced
that yet again the agitation of the abolitionists had caused a slave rebellion.
But the *Advocate* and the *Intelligencer* had a different interpretation of the
cause. The *Intelligencer* listed the "causes of the revolt" as: "*immoderate labour, severity of treatment, opposition on the part of the planters to religious instruction, and withholding from the slaves certain instructions of the English
government, which* [the slaves] *supposed to be in their favour.*" Simply put, the
abuses of slavery had led to the rebellion, not the machinations of the abolitionists and the missionary John Smith. This was a direct refutation of the
Edwards thesis rearticulated by the political papers and Robert J. Turnbull.
Smith had only been involved because he provided the religious instruction that the slaves had rightfully wanted. And while the violence of the
rebellion could not be denied, the fault lay with the planters, who abused
their slaves and then refused to end these abuses when requested to by
their own government. Slavery, not abolitionism, lay at the root of insurrection.[54]

REFORMULATING THE ACCUSATION: ROBERT TURNBULL AND *THE CRISIS*

Turnbull likely noticed and was concerned by the editorial slant taken by
the northern religious press toward Smith. According to Turnbull's expressed opinions in *Caroliniensis*, it was good that the most southern papers had ignored the more disturbing news from Demerara. Slaveholders
needed to be warned of their rights, their power, in a very careful manner,
one that did not introduce similar ideas among the slaves. Turnbull had

53. "Rev. John Smith—Missionary to Demerara," *Religious Intelligencer* 8 (May 1824):
775–77; "Demerara," *Christian Advocate* 2 (May 1824), 237–38.

54. "Rev. John Smith," 775; "Demerara," 237–38, emphasis in the original. See also
"Case of the late Rev. John Smith, Missionary at Demerara," *Religious Monitor and Evangelical Repository* 1 (September 1824), 197–98.

warned of ruinous events in the West Indies, and the rebellion in Demerara demonstrated his prescience.

The news of another rebellion in the West Indies instigated by abolitionism simply confirmed a recognized pattern. More disturbing to Turnbull and his ilk were developments in the North and in Washington, D.C., which hinted not only at the growth of antislavery sentiment but also at its influence on national policy. The election of 1824 had brought the "corrupt bargain" and the presidency of John Quincy Adams, who was known by Carolinians to be soft on slavery. As secretary of state, Adams had interfered with the operation of the Negro Seamen Act, and when he became president, he sent Rufus King—of abolitionist repute during the Missouri discussion—as the U.S. ambassador to Great Britain. King was the worst possible choice for Turnbull's Carolina, especially in light of the bloody successes that British abolitionists had wreaked upon West Indian planters. The co-conspirator in the "corrupt bargain" was the equally unacceptable Henry Clay, the president of the ACS and a very ambitious man.

The advance of these two potentially antislavery forces prompted Turnbull in 1827 to write (under the pseudonym "Brutus") *The Crisis* essays, an elaboration of the same themes he had set forth in the *Caroliniensis* essays several years before. Contemporaries and historians have long recognized *The Crisis* as one of the founding documents of the nullification movement that brought South Carolina close to rebellion in 1831.[55] President Adams set the stage in 1826 with his proposed agenda to participate in the Panama National Congress, which had been called by the newly independent Republic of Columbia. Adams had wanted to engage in an inter-American congress for quite some time, and he pressed Congress for support.[56]

But in Congress lay the problem. Participation in the Panama Congress meant discussing the slave trade and slavery in an international forum, which was unacceptable to Carolinians sensitized to the menace of hazardous discussions. Participation also meant rubbing shoulders with the representatives of Haiti, the second oldest independent republic in the Americas and the most potent symbol of insurrection in the Atlantic world. This prospect was too much for Senator Robert Hayne of South Carolina. Hayne had been a member of the South Carolina Association and he had

55. Freehling, *Prelude to Civil War,* 126.

56. Samuel Flagg Bemis, *John Quincy Adams and the Foundations of American Foreign Policy* (New York: Knopf, 1949), 545–49.

supported the Negro Seamen Act. The senator declared that "the question of slavery" must not be discussed in Congress. Moreover, the United States could not "treat with other nations" on the subject of slavery and must never consider the "independence of Hayti ... whose own history affords an example scarcely less fatal to our repose." He warned his colleagues of the North that this was no light matter: "To touch it at all, is to violate our most sacred rights—to put in jeopardy our dearest interests—the peace of our country—the safety of our families, our altars, and our firesides." Hayne's was a stern warning that the South would "never permit" federal interference with their "domestic concerns." If such were attempted, the southern States would "consider ourselves as driven from the Union." This was no paranoid response. Hayne's response reflected the lessons of the Edwards thesis, deeply embedded in his belief in a threat posed by the likely topics of discussion at the Panama Congress. Another Missouri-like discussion might lead to another conspiracy of rebellion.[57]

The second worrisome development took place in 1827, when Clay supported a petition to Congress from the ACS. The society was struggling. They had only been able to send 572 black migrants to Africa, and Liberia was hardly prosperous, besieged as it was by disease and hostile neighbors. Organizers had known from the beginning that the project would need federal assistance, and the petition of 1827 was one of several.[58] But from Turnbull's perspective, the petition was a dangerous advancement for the colonization cause. It is important to remember that among the colonizationists there were many who participated out of genuine antislavery sentiments. For Turnbull, Clay advancing colonization in the Senate paralleled Thomas Fowell Buxton's advocacy of antislavery measures in the British Parliament in 1823. And Turnbull knew that Buxton's agitation had spawned the insurrection in Demerara.

But too many in the South did not feel his alarm, and Turnbull's comments on the timing of his "Brutus" essays offer important clues to the genesis of the nullification movement and the proslavery argument of the early 1830s. Turnbull wrote when he did because of the "delightful and comparatively calm state of the public feeling ... when we are in the full enjoyment of the blessings of peace." His purpose was to unsettle minds, "to arouse [the southern people] to a just and lively sense of the dangers

57. [Speech of Robert Hayne], quoted in Freehling, *Prelude to Civil War,* 141.
58. Staudenraus, *African Colonization,* 169–75, 251.

that threaten your temporal prosperity and your domestic quiet." Turn-bull's dissonant contrast between "the blessings of peace" and "the dangers that threaten" invites consideration. Why did he feel such urgency to warn the South during a time of peace and security? He accepted the Edwards thesis, and he saw it substantiated by the events in Barbados, Demerara, and Charleston. Clay's petition in Congress represented the potential catalyst for someone's insurrectionary doom.[59]

With rhetoric that inspired the fire-eaters of later decades, Turnbull warned the South that one potential future of their section of the country was visible in the ruins of the British West Indian colonies. In his estimation the abolitionism manifested in the ACS posed the direst threat to the South. Internal improvements were enriching the North at the South's expense, and tariffs were an unjust burden, but the ACS was "an insidious attack meditated at the domestic tranquility of the South," more serious than the prospect of a foreign invading army. Turnbull wrote of the "vituperation and constant vulgar abuse of Southern institutions, which now prevails." He mentioned by name Benjamin Lundy's *Genius of Universal Emancipation*, which he mistakenly located in New York, and an unnamed paper recently established in Philadelphia. "Sooner or later," he predicted, emancipation would be discussed in the halls of Congress, giving Congress the opportunity "officially to express its opinion against slavery as an evil, and the profession of a desire to eradicate it from the land." This would be disastrous, as it would deter investment in the southern economy and "fill us all with the DEEPEST apprehensions . . . on account of the discontent and uneasiness which might thereby be produced in the minds of those, who are now contented and happy."[60]

Any discussion of slavery in Congress would cause "DEATH and DE-STRUCTION" in the South. Turnbull made an ominous prediction: "Discussion will be equivalent to an act of emancipation, for it will universally inspire [that hope] amongst the slaves. It will be to teach the slave, that for a gradual amelioration of his condition, he is not to look to his master . . . but . . . to Congress alone." After all, it had been "the discussions in the British Parliament, which have caused from time to time, the insurrectionary movements in the West Indies, and brought the colonists from wealth to despondence, and from despondence almost to despair; and it will be

59. *Charleston Mercury*, August 17, 1827, [Robert J. Turnbull], *The Crisis: Or, Essays on the Usurpations of the Federal Government. By Brutus* (Charleston: A. E. Miller, 1827), 6.

60. [Robert Turnbull], *The Crisis*, 13, 121, 129. Lundy's paper was printed in Baltimore.

discussion of the subject by Congress, which will bring us, one and all, to complete ruin."[61] Repeating the lesson that had appeared in newspaper reports of the rebellions of 1816 and 1823, Turnbull endowed mere "discussion" with the ability to *cause* an insurrection of the slaves.

Turnbull was unconvinced by southern leaders such as George McDuffie, who placated his constituents with the argument that the colonizationists in both houses of the Congress numbered less than twenty men. In the 1780s the West Indian colonists had enjoyed the same security, only to be on the verge of ruin forty years later. Turnbull found it "most alarming" that there should even be found "five members with such sentiments" in Congress. Wilberforce, after all, had been "even *more cautious* than the Colonization Society" in his early agitations against the slave trade in the 1780s. And just as Wilberforce masked his intentions to end slavery once and for all by focusing on the slave trade, so too did the ACS deceive the South with their pronouncements on colonization.[62]

Turnbull compared the colonial relationship between the West Indies and Parliament to the relation between the southern states and the federal government. The "unfortunate fate of the people of the West Indies may be our lot," he wrote, if the southern states did not assert their power as "Sovereign and Independent States." If southerners remained "patient and submissive before Congress," their similarities with the "weak colonists" in the British Caribbean would become painfully evident. This was the heart of the "crisis" that Turnbull saw in 1827. The remedy lay in the nullification doctrines for which he is better known.[63]

As Bryan Edwards's assertions of the abolitionist genesis of the Haitian Revolution were seemingly confirmed by the rebellions in Barbados and Demerara, so too would Turnbull's premonitions be confirmed by the rebellions of 1831. From August 1831 through the first half of 1832, American readers were confronted with news of two more slave insurrections, one in Southampton, Virginia, and one in Montego Bay, Jamaica, both of which were widely attributed to the agitation of abolitionists. The Southampton rebellion led to the consideration and rejection of gradual emancipation by the Virginia legislature, but Jamaica's led to the abolition of West Indian slavery by the British Parliament in 1833.

61. Ibid., 132.
62. Ibid., 128, 132.
63. Ibid., 128–29.

The Rebellions of 1831

In 1831 slave rebellions in Virginia and Jamaica brought the transatlantic struggle over slavery to a tipping point. The aftermath of insurrection left Great Britain on the verge of becoming an abolitionist empire, while slaveholders in the United States deepened their power in the governance of the republic. In August the black preacher Nat Turner led a band of rebels through Southampton County, Virginia. They wreaked havoc and killed more than sixty whites; the white backlash killed several hundred blacks. In the following months the Virginia legislature debated a bill that proposed the gradual abolition of slavery with the mandatory colonization of those freed, which inspired Professor Thomas Roderick Dew, the president of the University of Virginia, to move beyond defensive rationalizations of slavery to a bold argument that asserted a positive role for slavery in southern society. Nat Turner was "a demented fanatic," Dew argued, an anomaly among American slaves; insurrection was unlikely to recur. Dew calmly reminded his audience that even "the Parliament of Great Britain, with all its philanthropic zeal ... has never yet agitated this question, in regard to her West India possessions." Dew won the debate. Insurrection had threatened, colonization was proposed but rejected, and, ideologically, Virginia's slaveholders moved closer to South Carolina.[1]

As Americans throughout the country read of the debates in Virginia, news of another rebellion arrived daily on ships that hailed from West In-

1. Thomas Roderick Dew, "Review of the Debate in the Virginia Legislature of 1831–1832" reprinted in *The Ideology of Slavery: Proslavery Thought in the Antebellum South, 1830–1860*, ed. Drew Gilpin Faust (Baton Rouge: Louisiana University Press, 1981), 24, 68. For the Virginia debate, see Alison Freehling, *Drift Toward Dissolution: The Virginia Slavery Debate of 1831–1832* (Baton Rouge: Louisiana University Press, 1982).

dian ports. Jamaica's rebellion seemed an echo of Southampton, and for those with longer memories it had clear similarities with the Demerara uprising in 1823. A black preacher named Sam Sharpe led the Jamaican rebels, and white planters on the island blamed the missionaries in the Caribbean and the abolitionists at home. There was retaliation, as there had been against Nat Turner and John Smith. More than 500 blacks were killed, whether they had rebelled or not; missionaries were arrested, some were tarred and feathered, and chapels were torn down all over the island. But this time rebellion and retaliation led straight to Britain's abolition of colonial slavery. The persecuted missionaries returned to Britain as heroes in the abolitionist cause. They condemned West Indian slavery for its assaults on Christianity, and the abolitionists in Parliament began to demand immediate abolition, not the gradual measures they had demanded in the past. British abolitionism now drew from the movement to reform the British Parliament, and, in an act that demonstrated its moral legitimacy, the reformed Parliament abolished colonial slavery in August 1833.[2]

Historians have long argued that the early 1830s were a pivotal moment in the American struggle over slavery, but only recently have scholars begun to construct a narrative that places British abolition squarely within the coming of the Civil War. Past generations have offered plenty of hints. While he is rightly condemned for his dismissive view of William Lloyd Garrison, Gilbert Barnes's path-breaking 1933 study of abolitionism devoted an entire chapter to "The British Example." Benjamin Quarles's equally seminal *Black Abolitionists* (1969) contains a chapter, "Duet with John Bull," which argues that Great Britain played a crucial role in the support of black abolitionism. In his landmark *Prelude to Civil War,* William Freehling suggests (in a footnote) that "the English Emancipation Bill was, I think, one of the more important reasons for the intensity of the Great Reaction" of 1835. Freehling shows in that book that the explosion of southern rage at northern abolitionism had been developing for quite some time, but he has only recently followed up on his tantalizing suspicion with regard to British Abolition. But such hints in the historiography only scratch the surface of Great Britain's impact upon the American

2. Gelien Matthews, *Caribbean Slave Revolts and the British Abolitionist Movement* (Baton Rouge: Louisiana State University Press, 2006), 164–65; David Brion Davis, *Slavery and Human Progress* (New York: Oxford University Press, 1984), 118–19, 210; Seymour Drescher, *From Slavery to Freedom: Comparative Studies in the Rise and Fall of Atlantic Slavery* (New York: New York University Press, 1990), 79–80.

struggle over slavery at this pivotal moment in Atlantic history. British abolition, the political accomplishment of West Indian rebels and British abolitionists, had a profound impact upon the nascent struggle over slavery in the United States that would only end with civil war.[3]

BLACK RADICALIZATION IN THE 1820S

The rebellions of 1831 marked the pinnacle of a radicalization of the English-speaking Black Atlantic which had first become evident through three separate developments that had all crystallized by 1829. First, two pamphlets were published in New York and Boston during that year expressing a northern black militancy that had arisen from more than ten years resistance to the American Colonization Society. Robert Young's *Ethiopian Manifesto* and David Walker's *Appeal to the Coloured Citizens of the World* denounced slavery and racism and proclaimed a new era of resistance to white oppression. Both men saw the African peoples of the Caribbean as organically linked to the black American struggle, and their works signaled the budding of a transnational black imagination that would blossom with British abolition in 1834 and mature throughout the antebellum decades. During that same year—1829—between one and two thousand free African Americans from Cincinnati, Ohio, marched north, emigrating to British Canada West. They were refugees of the racial violence of their white neighbors, whose forebears had passed laws (1804–7) that made blacks pay $500 bonds to live in the city. City authorities decided to enforce these laws in 1829, and when they met with resistance from the black community, white mobs leveled black neighborhoods and businesses. The

3. Gilbert Hobbes Barnes, *The Anti-Slavery Impulse, 1830–1844* (New York: Harcourt, Brace and World, 1933), chap. 3; Benjamin Quarles, *Black Abolitionists* (London: Oxford University Press, 1969), chap. 6; William Freehling, *Prelude to Civil War: The Nullification Controversy in South Carolina, 1816–1836* (New York: Harper and Row, 1965), 307, n. 10; William Freehling, *The Road to Disunion: Secessionists at Bay, 1776–1854* (New York: Oxford University Press, 1990), 160–61, 254, 290. Important exceptions to scholarly neglect of British influence include Joe Bassette Wilkins, "Window on Freedom: The South's Response to the Emancipation of the Slaves in the British West Indies, 1833–1861" (Ph.D. diss., University of South Carolina, 1977), which followed up on William Freehling's suggestive footnote, and, more recently, Steven Heath Mitton, "The Free World Confronted: The Problem of Slavery and Progress in American Foreign Relations, 1833–1844" (Ph.D. diss., Louisiana State University, 2005). For an important narrative of American history in global context during the Civil War era, see Thomas Bender, *A Nation Among Nations: America's Place in World History* (New York: Hill and Wang, 2006), chap. 3.

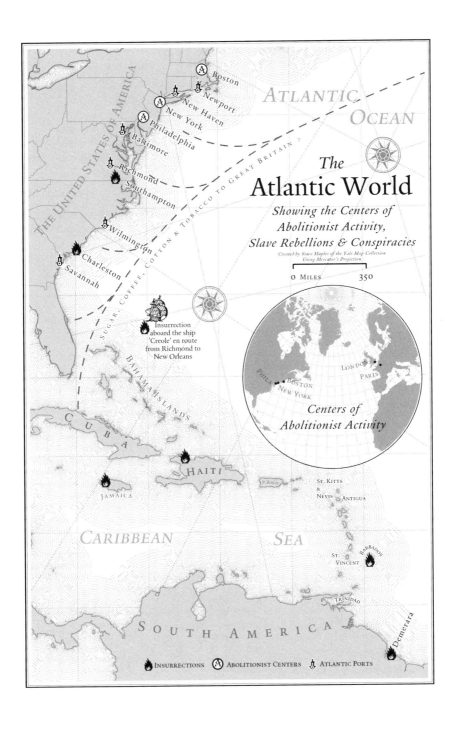

The Atlantic World

Showing the Centers of
Abolitionist Activity,
Slave Rebellions & Conspiracies

Created by Stace Maples of the Yale Map Collection
Using Mercator's Projection

0   MILES   350

Centers of
Abolitionist Activity

Insurrection
aboard the ship
'Creole' en route
from Richmond to
New Orleans

INSURRECTIONS   ABOLITIONIST CENTERS   ATLANTIC PORTS

governor of Canada welcomed the exiles with a diplomatic flourish, advising their leaders to "tell the Republicans on your side of the line, that we royalists do not know men by their color." He also made a significant offer, that "should you come to us you will be entitled to all the privileges of His Majesty's subjects." That was important in an era when the British Empire was the greatest power among states.[4] And third, in the British West Indies, the agitation of the free colored populations for the expansion of their civil rights brought the first concession from the British government, which in 1829 ordered that the free coloreds of the crown colonies of St. Lucia and Trinidad be considered the "legal equals" of whites. By the next year free coloreds in the older colonies such as Jamaica had also gained their civil rights, cracking the structure of white supremacy, paving the way for the abolition of slavery.

These events in 1829 set the stage for a geography of freedom within the Atlantic world that would expand enormously with British abolition in 1834. This liberated space became increasingly useful to African Americans and white abolitionists as they continued the struggle against American slavery. The works of Young and especially Walker pushed white reformers like William Lloyd Garrison away from the ACS, broadening radical abolitionism. The pamphlets were also direct statements of the black militancy against slavery that would find more tangible expression two years later in Southampton, Virginia, and western Jamaica. The African American emigrants from Ohio named their new community after William Wilberforce. Their settlement brought abolitionism to Canada and founded the core of a community that became the final depot in the Underground Railroad. Thousands of African Americans moved there over the next thirty years.[5] Moreover, in 1832, the Wilberforce settlement sent Nathaniel Paul to raise funds for the settlement among British philanthropists. Paul not only raised funds but also battled ACS agent Elliot Cresson for the support of British public opinion. As Richard Blackett has shown, this struggle between Cresson and Paul put the American struggle over slavery on the international stage, and Paul's speaking tour had a "decided impact" upon the success of British abolitionism during the next year. The experience of listening to a personal representative of American blacks repeatedly de-

4. Quoted in Leon F. Litwack, *North of Slavery: The Negro in the Free States, 1790–1860* (Chicago: University of Chicago Press, 1961), 73.

5. Robin Winks, *The Blacks in Canada: A History* (Montreal: McGill-Queens University Press, 1971), chap. 6.

nounce the gradualism of the ACS convinced the majority of Britons that the immediate abolition of West Indian slavery was the only moral choice.[6] Finally, the emancipation of West Indian free coloreds revealed the political weakness of the planter class, and, in the island of Jamaica, slaves coined the phrase: "Brown already free, black soon," a prescient slogan with far more potency than their masters understood.[7]

West Indian free coloreds descended from mixed European and African ancestry and were generally known as "browns." While many were educated and some acquired wealth, West Indian free coloreds were everywhere ostracized by white society and by law were prohibited from government office, a variety of professions, and even from acquiring substantial levels of property. By the late eighteenth century, free coloreds had formed a critical population mass in all of the islands, and as early as 1792, a group of them presented a petition to the Jamaica Assembly demanding a relaxation of the oppressive laws. The war against Napoleonic France slowed the free colored movement for reform, as it did the abolitionist movement in Britain, but in the 1820s communities in several West Indian colonies again began to petition the colonial governments, as well as the colonial office in London, for the abolition of prejudicial laws.[8] The 1820s also saw a proliferation of newspapers that introduced free colored voices into the public discourse. Henry Loving of Antigua founded the *Weekly Register,* Edward Jordan and Robert Osborn began publication of *The* [Jamaica] *Watchman* in 1827, William Baker operated the *Grenada Chronicle,* and in St. Kitts, Richard Cable's *Advertiser* had been advancing free colored interests since 1806.[9]

It was probably these newspapers that caught the eye of British abolitionists, who adopted the free colored cause as part of the movement to ameliorate West Indian slavery. Abolitionist M.P. William Smith brought the petitions of free colored West Indians to Parliament as early as 1815, but it was the notorious case of the Jamaican free coloreds Louis Celeste Lecesne and Edward Escoffery in 1823 that brought the full force of Brit-

6. Richard Blackett, *Building an Antislavery Wall: Black Americans in the Atlantic Abolitionist Movement* (Ithaca: Cornell University Press, 1983), 66.

7. Henry Bleby, *Death Struggles of Slavery* (London: Hamilton, Adams, and Co., 1853), 119.

8. Gad Heuman, *Between Black and White: Race, Politics, and the Free Coloreds in Jamaica, 1792–1865* (Westport, CT: Greenwood, 1981), 23–24, 33–34.

9. Andrew Lewis, "'An Incendiary Press': British West Indian Newspapers During the Struggle for Abolition," *Slavery and Abolition* 16 (December, 1995), 354–56.

ish abolitionism behind the free colored cause. Lecesne and Escoffery descended from free colored fathers who had fled Saint-Domingue during the Haitian Revolution, and both had gained substantial wealth and become leaders of the agitation for free colored rights. They were imprisoned on specious charges of conspiracy; colonial authorities alleged that the pair had corresponded with Haitian authorities with the intention to spark an insurrection of the slaves and to overthrow the island. Upon conviction their property was seized and they were exiled. The case attracted the attention of the abolitionist M.P. Stephen Lushington, who brought the case before Parliament as an example of the injustice endemic in the slave societies of the West Indies. Wilberforce argued before Parliament that the case demonstrated the intransigence of West Indian racism, which undermined any hope that the colonial leadership was capable of ameliorating slavery. As Gad Heuman has shown, British abolitionists employed the case of Lecesne and Escoffery as a tool in the resurgence of the movement then underway. The plight of these men became a cause célèbre, and the agitation that stemmed from their case led to the landmark legislation of 1829.[10]

Activist newspapers and community leaders engaged the public authorities with formal petitions, a move that found notice in *Freedom's Journal,* the first black-owned and edited newspaper in the United States. In August 1827, for example, the *Journal* reported on the parliamentary debate on the condition of West Indian free coloreds (in response to a petition), noting the size and wealth of the community, as well as the "grievous legal oppression" under which it suffered. Nothing came of the debate, but over the next two years *Freedom's Journal* devoted extensive coverage to Britain's movement to abolish West Indian slavery, and as Patrick Rael has argued, northern African Americans embraced the identity of "free people of color," in part from the example of the brown classes of the West Indies. It was a moment of transatlantic black politicization that would reshape the Atlantic world.[11]

First published in March 1827, *Freedom's Journal* represented the political maturation of the African American community in the North, which had parallels to the social process then transforming the British West Indies. Like West Indian free coloreds, northern African Americans were

10. Heuman, *Between Black and White,* 38.

11. *Freedom's Journal,* August 10, 1827; Patrick Rael, *Black Identity and Black Protest in the Antebellum North* (Chapel Hill: University of North Carolina Press, 2002), 106.

free of slavery yet subject to racial discrimination. As we have seen in the response of Philadelphia blacks to the formation of the American Colonization Society, African American communities in the North had been growing in size and political sophistication since the first emancipations in the northern states in the late eighteenth century. A network of independent churches, schools, and benevolent societies had developed that gave African Americans a powerful sense of community and self-worth, and at the same time cultivated a leadership that actively pursued black rights. *Freedom's Journal* was the project of two men who epitomized this moment of black political ferment, the Reverend Samuel Cornish and John Brown Russwurm. Both men were born free—Cornish in Delaware, Russwurm in Jamaica—and both were involved with African American education early in their public careers. Cornish was the senior editor, having the experience of a twelve-year ministry with the Colored Presbyterian Church. Russwurm had recently become the second African American college graduate and had raised eyebrows during his Bowdoin commencement speech, a laudatory treatment of the Haitian Revolution.[12]

Freedom's Journal was specifically targeted toward blacks in the United States, but in its distribution and subject matter the paper engaged the entire English-speaking black Atlantic. Its subscription agents were concentrated in the northern states, but there were also agents in Haiti and England, and as black seamen regularly appeared in port cities throughout the Atlantic, it is probable that copies of the paper found their way to the British West Indies.[13] The paper focused on the condition and everyday happenings of African American life, including the West Indies, and became a political forum for attacks on the American Colonization Society and a steady source of news from Britain's movement to abolish slavery. Connections between the West Indies and the black community in the North could be as simple as death notices, such as those of John H. Smith, a native of Jamaica who died in New York; the Reverend Charles Corr of Philadelphia, whose early ministerial career was in his native Jamaica; and the remarkable Flora Gardner of Lynn, Massachusetts, who had been a slave in the West Indies and lived to be 115 years old.[14] Readers were also kept

---

12. Floyd Miller, *The Search for a Black Nationality: Black Emigration and Colonization, 1787–1863* (Urbana: University of Illinois Press, 1975), 82–85.

13. *Freedom's Journal*, April 4, 1828; W. Jeffrey Bolster, *Black Jacks: African American Seamen in the Age of Sail* (Cambridge: Harvard University Press, 1997), chap. 7.

14. *Freedom's Journal*, November 16 and December 7, 1827, October 10, 1828.

informed of black life in the West Indies, such as the slave laws in the colonies Dominica and St. Vincent, the most recent estimate of the slave population in the islands, and the escalating persecution of the Evangelical missionaries who ministered to the slaves of Jamaica. Most importantly, *Freedom's Journal* frequently used its columns to disseminate the news of Britain's abolitionist movement. Readers were treated with now historic anecdotes such as the case of James Somerset, freed from slavery by Chief Justice Mansfield, and the infamous slave ship *Zong*, whose captain jettisoned his human cargo to collect the insurance. The *Journal* also reprinted British abolitionist literature such as "What Does Your Sugar Cost?" And the eloquent speeches of parliamentarians Brougham, Wilberforce, and Buxton could be regularly found. As early as 1827, one anonymous author predicted, "British slaves will soon be free citizens." Moreover, the writer pointed out, black West Indians lived "in the immediate neighborhood of our own. They speak the same language. The intercourse is easy, constant, and unavoidable." Caribbean emancipation mattered.[15]

The transatlantic scope of *Freedom's Journal* prompts inquiry into those remarkable pamphlets of 1829, Young's *Ethiopian Manifesto* and Walker's *Appeal to the Coloured Citizens of the World*. In the winter of that year, Robert Alexander Young used his own funds to print *The Ethiopian Manifesto, Issued in Defence of the Black Man's Rights in the Scale of Universal Freedom*. Scholars have found too little material to explore the life of Robert Young, but from his pamphlet we know he was well educated, perhaps trained as a minister, and perceptive of the transatlantic dimensions of African America. His short *Manifesto* spoke to "the Ethiopian, or African people." He challenged them to "know . . . your present state of standing . . . in any nation within which you reside," and protest the unjust fact that blacks did not enjoy the "rights of government." Young denounced the racism of white society and spoke in apocalyptic terms: "the time is at hand when many signs shall appear to you." Young likened himself to John the Baptist and proclaimed the imminent arrival of "a leader" who would "prove thy liberator from the infernal state of bondage." That man had already been born, said Young, on Grand Anta Estate on the island of Grenada, where "the church books of St. Georgestown . . . can truly prove his birth." The Ethiopian liberator was "in appearance, a white man," for his father was the owner of the estate, but he had "been born of a black woman, his mother."

15. Quote is from *Freedom's Journal*, March 23, 1827. See also *Freedom's Journal*, April 6, September 14, November 30, and December 7, 1827, July 4 and 11, 1828, March 7, August 29, September 19, November 21, 1829.

Young did not portend a violent rapture at emancipation, on the contrary, he advised "the degraded sons of Africa to submit with fortitude to your present state of suffering," and to trust in themselves and in the justice of God that the "the time is at hand, when, with but the power of words and divine will of our God, the vile shackles of slavery shall be broken asunder from you, and no man known who shall dare to own or proclaim you his bondsman." Speaking in the scriptural language of five generations of black Christian reflection, Young predicted nothing less than the abolition of chattel slavery, and significantly, the abolitionist Christ-figure he invoked was to emerge from the British West Indies.[16]

In the fall of 1829, as readers pondered Young's *Manifesto*, the first edition of Walker's stirring *Appeal* appeared in Boston and spread. Walker addressed the same transnational audience, and he too envisioned an abolitionist messiah—"a Hannibal"—sent by a just God to crush slavery. Thanks to the scholarship of Peter Hinks, we know much more of the life and activities of David Walker than of Robert Young. Born free, probably around the turn of the century near Wilmington, North Carolina, Walker traveled extensively throughout the United States, north and south, before he settled in Boston by 1825. He quickly became involved in the black community, joined the African Lodge of Freemasons, worshipped in a black Methodist church, and started a business as a dealer in second-hand clothing. Walker emerged as a leader, serving as a subscription agent for *Freedom's Journal*, and addressing the first meeting of the Massachusetts General Colored Association in 1828. Walker conceptualized Black America in the same geographic terms as had Young. He admired the British abolitionists Granville Sharp and Wilberforce, who had gone to "all lengths for our good." Walker's use of the plural recognized the commonality of the black struggle in the United States and the British Caribbean. Black Americans must "unite the colored population" of the Atlantic world and lead the effort against slavery and racial oppression.[17]

The *Appeal* was a full elaboration of this argument. Displaying im-

16. Robert Alexander Young, *The Ethiopian Manifesto, Issued in Defence of the Black Man's Rights in the scale of Universal Freedom* (New York, 1829), reprinted in Sterling Stuckey *The Ideological Origins of Black Nationalism* (Boston: Beacon, 1972), 31–37.

17. "Address, Delivered before the General Colored Association at Boston, by David Walker," *Freedom's Journal*, December 19, 1828, reprinted in Peter P. Hinks, ed., *David Walker's Appeal to the Coloured Citizens of the World* (University Park: Pennsylvania State University Press, 2000), 88. For a brilliant exploration of Walker's life and times, see Hinks's *To Awaken My Afflicted Brethren: David Walker and the Problem of Antebellum Slave Resistance* (University Park: Pennsylvania State University Press, 1997).

pressive erudition, Walker argued from classical and contemporary comparisons that African American life under the whites in the Americas, whether slave or free, was the most dire experience of racial oppression in recorded history. American slavery was a harsher oppression than the reign of Pharaoh over the Israelites, worse than the enslavement of the Helots by the heathen Spartans, worse than the slavery of ancient Rome. These ancient experiences of slavery were miserable, Walker acknowledged, but on no "page of history" could anyone find slaveholders making the "*insupportable insult . . .* that [the slaves] were not of the *human family.*"Yet this is what white Americans had done, and Walker cited a no less distinguished American than Thomas Jefferson, who had justified slavery with this very argument. Walker observed that the great man had already gone "to answer at the bar of God," and he challenged his audience to go out and purchase a copy of Jefferson's *Notes on Virginia,* and "put it in the hands" of their children. The next generation must be educated in the depth of oppression they faced, and it must be people of color who answered this challenge to justice. Walker acknowledged the "white friends" who had rejected Jeffersonian racism, but he emphasized that "We, and the world wish to see the charges of Mr. Jefferson refuted by the *blacks* themselves." The just, Christian God in whom Walker and his audience believed would not allow slavery forever. "Every dog must have its day," he dryly noted, "the American's is coming to an end."[18]

When Walker named "the American," he meant the generations of white men, beginning with the Spaniards in the Caribbean, who had established and maintained African slavery in the new world to satisfy their "sordid avarice."[19] African American suffering in the United States had emerged from this larger history, and Walker further defined slaveholders as the "Americans of North and of South America, including the West India Islands." God had "blessed" these people with all the "comforts of life," yet they continued to hold slaves, and the day was "fast approaching, when there will be a greater time on the continent of America, than ever was witness upon this earth."Walker thus envisioned a broad Atlantic stage for the contest between two racial antagonists—the "Coloured Citizens of the World" and the "Americans."[20]

18. Hinks, *David Walker's Appeal,* 12, 16–17; Thomas Jefferson, *Notes on the State of Virginia,* ed. William Peden (Chapel Hill: University of North Carolina Press, 1982), 143.

19. Hinks, *David Walker's Appeal,* 37–38, 41.

20. Ibid., 51.

Walker's transnational definition of the "American" as slaveholder further defined his scope of vision for the black abolitionist project. The colored citizens of the United States could only achieve greatness through *"the entire emancipation of your enslaved brethren all over the world."* The black American struggle was interwoven with that of enslaved peoples everywhere, and as in his address the year before, Walker took special notice of the British. They were "the best friends the coloured people have upon earth" and had already done "one hundred times more for the melioration of our condition, than all the other nations of the earth put together." Though he did not go into detail, Walker clearly referred to British abolitionism, and his language alluded to the reforms of the colonial slave codes, as well as the relaxation of civil disabilities imposed on West Indian free coloreds, enacted only months before. Yet there was ambiguity in Walker's praise for the English, for he did not forget the "colonies now in the West Indies, which oppress us sorely." And he called particular attention to Jamaica, where the abject results of three hundred years of slavery were painfully evident. On that island there were 15,000 whites "ruling and tyrannizing over 335,000 persons!!!!!!!!" How could this happen? No wonder "the white tyrants of the world . . . say we are not men, but were made to be slaves." Walker must not have known the rebellious history of Jamaica's slaves, who rebelled more than any West Indian people, but in 1829 there had been more than thirty years of peace since the Maroon war of 1795, and without a closer look, the island's demographic imbalance suggested acquiescence to slavery. This could not be, Walker cried. Black peoples must "take possession" of their lands; they must emancipate themselves.[21]

Although Walker came quite close to endorsing violent rebellion as the means of emancipation, he was careful, framing his endorsement with the histories of Haiti and ancient Carthage. Both histories were well known to African Americans; they were frequently discussed in essays and orations, and at an emancipation day celebration in Brooklyn, New York, in 1828, celebrants had painted a "representation of Hannibal and his hardy legions" on a banner and processed behind it.[22] Hannibal of Carthage had led an army from North Africa against the Roman Empire in the second Punic War in the second century B.C.E, only to be defeated. While we cannot be sure of the physical appearance of the historic Hannibal, Af-

21. Ibid., 43, 66. Emphasis in the original.
22. *New York Freedom's Journal,* July 18 and 25, April 4, December 12, 1828.

rican Americans celebrated him as a black African. "Remember the divisions and consequent sufferings of Carthage and of Hayti," Walker counseled, and "read the history particularly of Hayti, and see how they were butchered by the whites." The Haitian Revolution may have represented "the glory of blacks and the terror of tyrants," but like Carthage, it also taught the lessons of division. Haiti's ten-year revolution had seen massive loss of life, much of it during the long civil war between the slaves and the *gens de couleur.* And Haiti's postrevolutionary history had been fraught with division and civil unrest. Walker's central argument of black unity was therefore grounded in both the hopes and warnings that stemmed from Caribbean experience, and with Walker's words in mind, black Americans looked to the 1830s.[23]

RADICAL ABOLITIONISM AND THE REBELLIONS OF 1831

By January of 1831 David Walker's pamphlet had been found throughout the South, rousing southern legislatures to enact more stringent laws curtailing the movements of black sailors and criminalizing the literacy of slaves. Walker had made every effort to circulate his pamphlet, hopeful that its message of black unity might bear fruit. In the North, the militancy of black Americans like Walker convinced William Lloyd Garrison, then an abolition-minded colonizationist, to denounce the ACS. Garrison signaled his conversion to the world with the publication in Boston of the *Liberator,* the first newspaper in the United States to call for the immediate abolition of slavery. While evidence directly linking the abolitionist activities of Walker and Garrison to the rebel leader Nat Turner has not surfaced, historians Vincent Harding and Peter Hinks have argued that it is implausible to remove the rebellion in Southampton from the national context of an increasingly radicalized black community. And in light of the pattern of agitation and rebellion clearly evident in the British West Indies, I think it probable that a similar connection between abolitionism and insurrection existed in Virginia. Either way, in the politicized milieu created by Walker and Garrison, white Virginians could only see Turner's rebellion as a clear recurrence of the West Indian pattern of abolitionist agitation and slave rebellion. They had learned from West Indian precedent.[24]

23. Hinks, *David Walker's Appeal,* 22.

24. Clement Eaton, "A Dangerous Pamphlet in the Old South," *Journal of Southern History* 2 (August 1936): 328–32; Paul Goodman, *Of One Blood: Abolitionism and the Origins of*

As we have seen, Bryan Edwards's account of the insurrection in Saint-Domingue paid careful attention to the role of free blacks in instigating rebellion, as well as the disruptive connections between print, slave literacy, and insurrection. Accounts of the rebellion in Southampton articulated precisely the same argument. An early report that appeared in the *Richmond Enquirer* and the *Richmond Constitutional Whig* highlighted Turner's ability to read and write, implying the influence of abolitionist literature.[25] A letter written to the editor of the *Constitutional Whig* reminded his audience that in Saint-Domingue it had not been "the *slaves* alone," but the "march of intellect among the free blacks" that had caused the insurrection. It had been the same in Southampton.[26]

The influence of the Edwards thesis can also be seen in Governor John Floyd's understanding of the rebellion. Some of his constituents had sent him copies of Garrison's *Liberator* (indicating their suspicion of abolitionist culpability), and Floyd noted in his diary that the Boston newspaper had "the express intention of inciting the slaves and free negroes . . . to rebellion." As he explained to Governor James Hamilton of South Carolina, the rebellion had originated from a convergence of "Yankee" influences. First, northern preachers had taught the slaves that "God was no respecter of persons—the black man was as good as the white—that all men were born free and equal—that they cannot serve two masters—that the white people rebelled against England to obtain freedom, so have the blacks a right to do." This dangerous message had been compounded by the naïve religiosity of women who had taught "the negroes to read and write" in order to comprehend the scriptures for themselves. Literate slaves had then come upon "the incendiary publications of Walker, Garrison and Knapp of Boston" brought by "Yankee peddlers." Rebellion had been the inevitable result. The time, place, and persons involved were all different,

Racial Equality (Berkeley and Los Angeles: University of California Press, 1998), chap. 4; Vincent Harding, "Symptoms of Liberty and Blackhead Signposts, David Walker and Nat Turner," in *Nat Turner: A Slave Rebellion in History and Memory,* ed. Kenneth S. Greenberg (Oxford: Oxford University Press, 2003): 79–102; Hinks, *To Awaken My Afflicted Brethren,* 160.

25. *Richmond Enquirer,* August 30, 1831; *Richmond Constitutional Whig,* September 3, 1831, both reprinted in Kenneth S. Greenberg, ed., *The Confessions of Nat Turner and Related Documents* (Boston: Bedford, 1996), 67, 76.

26. *Richmond Constitutional Whig,* September 26, 1831, reprinted in Greenberg, *The Confessions,* 80.

but Floyd's argument simply echoed what Edwards had written, and what newspaper accounts of the rebellions in Barbados and Demerara had reaffirmed.[27]

As Governor Hamilton worriedly perused the thoughts of his Virginia counterpart, another black preacher, Sam Sharpe of Montego Bay, Jamaica, was building support for the rebellion that would lead to the end of British colonial slavery. Sharpe's life as a slave had been singularly humane. By his own account he had never been flogged, and his master had always been kind to him. He could read, he could probably write, and he had risen to head deacon at the mission founded by the Baptist missionary Thomas Burchell. But like all slaves Sam Sharpe had a deep hatred for slavery, and 1831 had brought a series of developments that emboldened him to lead a rebellion that would break the chains of slavery once and for all. British abolitionists had waged a massive public campaign to move Parliament toward the immediate abolition of slavery. Public meetings had been held, nearly half a million tracts had been disseminated, and more than five thousand petitions demanding immediate abolition had been sent to Parliament. Moreover, in December 1830 the Jamaica House of Assembly had legislated equal rights for Jamaican free coloreds, a victory in their long struggle to overcome the civil disabilities that colonial law had forced upon them.[28]

Slaves and masters were deeply interested in the political ferment in Britain. "Brown already free, black soon" had become a mantra for the slaves, and some said that the king had made them free and the planters wrongly kept them enslaved. Some even said that the king's soldiers would not fight against the slaves or that they would join with them if the slaves were to fight for their freedom. Sam Sharpe added to these rumors that Burchell, who had left several months before for England, was coming back for Christmas and would bring the "freedom paper" with him.

27. Excerpts from the Diary of John Floyd, 1831–1832; John Floyd to James Hamilton, Jr., November 19, 1831, both reprinted in Greenberg, *The Confessions*, 107, 110. Isaac Knapp was the publisher of the *Liberator*.

28. James Walvin, *England, Slaves and Freedom, 1776–1838* (Jackson: University Press of Mississippi, 1986), 160, Seymour Drescher, *Capitalism and Antislavery: British Mobilization in Comparative Perspective* (New York: Oxford University Press, 1987), 59; Mary Turner, *Slaves and Missionaries: The Disintegration of Jamaican Slave Society, 1781–1834* (Urbana: University of Illinois Press, 1982), 149–50; Heuman, *Between Black and White*, 50.

Burchell had started the mission in Montego Bay seven years before. He was popular among the slaves and well known in the region, which fostered the validity of the rumor.[29]

From July through November of 1831, Jamaican planters held a series of public meetings during which they decried the abolitionists in Britain, verbally abused the missionaries, called for representation in Parliament, and even threatened to seek annexation to the United States. The missionary William Knibb recalled that the planters engaged in "free and passionate conversation," oblivious to the curious ears of their slaves. One slaveholder purportedly said "that freedom was come from England but that he would shoot every d—d black rascal before he should get it." The island's newspapers printed resolutions from the protest meetings, accounts of the parliamentary debates, and angry editorials by planters.[30]

On December 27, 1831, the inhabitants of Montego Bay saw in the surrounding hills the glow of a great fire burning. Rebels had torched the cane-trash house of Kensington Estate, marking the onset of insurrection. To white Jamaicans the fire confirmed the terrible fear that had always lurked in their minds; to Samuel Sharpe, also in Montego Bay, it was a sign that his plans were doomed to failure. Sharpe had not intended to raise a violent rebellion. He was an intelligent leader, well aware of the brutal repression a violent rebellion would unleash. The missionary Henry Bleby interviewed Sharpe several times while he was in prison and left a noble portrait of the slave leader in *Death Struggles of Slavery*. Sharpe claimed to have planned an organized sit-down after the Christmas holiday. The slaves were to refuse to work unless they received wages. Sharpe believed, perhaps naively, that such collective action would force the planters into ameliorative measures. He was tragically wrong.[31]

The rebellion took nearly a month to suppress and, just as Demeraran planters had blamed John Smith in 1823, Jamaican whites quickly labeled the rebellion the "Baptist War," a reference to Sharpe, Burchell, and the

29. Michael Craton, *Testing the Chains: Resistance to Slavery in the British West Indies* (Ithaca: Cornell University Press, 1982), 295, 299.

30. John Howard Hinton, *Memoir of William Knibb, Missionary in Jamaica* (London: Houlston and Stoneman, 1847), 112–14; Craton, *Testing the Chains*, 294–95.

31. Bleby, *Death Struggles of Slavery*, 113–15. The evidence suggests that while Sharpe's plan was followed by some, others rebelled violently almost immediately. See, e.g., *Kingston Watchman*, and *Jamaica Free Press*, January 4, 1832.

many Baptist slaves who were involved. Only fourteen whites were killed in Jamaica, and as in the backlash in Southampton, Jamaican whites exacted a terrible vengeance. About 200 black Jamaicans were killed during the suppression of the rebellion, and 340 more were hung during the trials, which one historian has rightly called "judicial murder."[32]

White missionaries also felt the wrath of planter vengeance. White mobs destroyed more than a dozen chapels, and when Burchell returned from England, he was greeted by a seething crowd, which he likened to "the savage hordes" of Africa. His was an ironic transformation of the racial order in which the planters, not the slaves, were the savages, yet Africa remained the symbol of savagery. Bleby, who left a stirring account of the rebellion and its aftermath, was tarred and feathered by a white mob. Reverend George Bridges, the Anglican spokesman for the planters, acidly observed in the *Jamaica Courant:* "Shooting is too honourable a death for men whose conduct has occasioned so much bloodshed, and the loss of so much property. There are fine hanging woods in St. James and Trelawny, and we do sincerely hope, that the bodies of all the Methodist preachers who may be convicted of sedition may diversify the scene."[33] Knibb, Burchell, and Francis Gardener, who had been Burchell's replacement, were all imprisoned for a time and indicted for inciting the rebellion. All were acquitted, and all escaped in fear for their lives.[34]

The rebellion's origins can be traced to the cosmopolitan center of Montego Bay. In addition to being Burchell's base for his mission, the bay was Jamaica's second most important port and had a deep hinterland. In this freewheeling city more than 2,000 slaves mingled easily with almost 6,000

32. Craton, *Testing the Chains*, 313. As in Barbados and Demerara, the low number of whites killed in Jamaica is striking. Turner's rampage in Virginia involved far fewer slaves but killed four times as many whites. This qualitative difference in these near-contemporaneous rebellions speaks to the profound demographic differences between slave societies in the Caribbean and the South. Whites in the British West Indies were ten percent or less of the population, while whites in the American South were a dominant, armed majority everywhere except some of the low-country counties of South Carolina and Georgia. The demographics of the South also explain the absence of Caribbean-scale insurrections in the United States from 1832 until the Civil War. See Eugene Genovese, *Roll Jordan Roll: The World the Slaves Made* (New York: Vintage, 1976), 591, 594.

33. Quoted in Lowell Ragatz, *The Fall of the Planter Class in the British Caribbean, 1763–1833* (New York: The Century Co., 1928), 444.

34. Craton, *Testing the Chains*, 317–18; Turner, *Slaves and Missionaries*, 166–70; Philip Wright, *Knibb "the Notorious": Slaves' Missionary 1803–1845* (London: Sidgwick and Jackson Ltd., 1973), 93–111.

free blacks. Furthermore, about 10 percent of the island's import trade, most of it from Britain, entered through Montego Bay, making it the most important port in northwestern Jamaica.[35]

For slaves in the age of the abolitionists, the most important items to come in on the ships to Montego Bay were the newspapers. In the aftermath of the rebellion, slaves and planters alike pointed to the influence of the newspapers as a cause in the rebellion. Samuel Carson, the overseer of Whitney Estate in Clarendon Parish believed the revolt had arisen from the "discussions" of slavery in Britain. Slaves were exposed through the "public prints" to "the most violent of the writings of the Anti-slavery society," and rebellion had been the result.[36] Henry G. Groves, quartermaster in the militia and the overseer of the Hazelymph estate, believed that the slaves were motivated by their "general knowledge" of the abolitionists, who they knew worked toward "obtaining their freedom." Groves also testified that the Baptists had gained "influence" over the slaves and that he considered the Baptists to be "emissaries of the party in England."[37] Linton, a slave held at the Savanna-la-Mar jail, testified that "we all believed this freedom business, from what we were told and from what we heard in the newspapers, that the people in England were speaking up very bold for us; we thought the King was on our side." When further pressed as to how he had "heard" from the newspapers, Linton said, "Those who cannot read always give 5d to those who can to read the papers to them when they hear they contain good news for them."[38] Linton's testimony opens an important window into the mind of Jamaican slaves. He tells us that slaves were acutely interested in the progress of their allies in Britain; slaves were not only influenced by the broader intellectual patterns of the Atlantic World, they were abreast of the latest developments in Britain and actively engaged in the transatlantic struggle for their freedom.

35. B. W. Higman, "Jamaican Port Towns in the Early Nineteenth Century" in Franklin W. Knight and Peggy K. Liss, eds., *Atlantic Port Cities: Economy, Culture, and Society in the Atlantic World, 1650–1850* (Knoxville: University of Tennessee Press, 1991), 117–37.

36. "Examination ... of *Samuel Carson*," *Jamaica: Slave Insurrection* in *Irish University Press Series of British Parliamentary Papers. Slave Trade*, vol. 80 of 95 vols. (Shannon: Irish University Press, 1969), 197. See also "Examination ... of *George Codrington* [planter]," 193.

37. Ibid., "Examination ... of *Henry G. Groves*," 202. See also "Examination ... of *Anthony Whitelock* [overseer]," 204.

38. Ibid., "Voluntary Confession of *Linton*," 217. See also [Confession of Robert Gardener], 224; "Confession of *McKinley*," 225.

THE AMERICAN POLITICAL PRESS,
THE BAPTIST WAR, AND BRITISH ABOLITION

The Baptist War and the subsequent parliamentary debates on abolition coincided with a period of transition in American politics. The old party system of Federalists and Democratic-Republicans was dead, killed by the Jackson machine of an ascendant democracy that had little interest in anti-slavery and little organized opposition. In the Deep South, the nullification movement in South Carolina attempted to act on the warnings of Robert J. Turnbull that the federal government posed a threat to southern civilization. Nullifiers battled Unionists in the elite politics of South Carolina, and in the aftermath of the rebellions of 1831 they seized power over the state government in the elections of 1832. The Committee on Nullification announced its intentions "to redeem ourselves from the state of Colonial vassalage" to the federal government, and warned that "the time must come when the people . . . will rise up in their might and release themselves from this thraldom, by one of those violent convulsions, whereby society is uprooted from its foundations, and the edict of Reform is written in Blood." David Walker could not have said it better. While the rhetoric echoed 1776, West Indian tumult fueled Carolinian fire.[39]

But the nullifiers could not nullify the news. American newspapers thoroughly discussed the events in Jamaica and the parliamentary debates on abolition that followed. The portrayal of imperial upheaval, however, differed radically according to section and editorial perspective. As we shall see, events in the British Empire exposed northern Evangelical readers to more and more antislavery sentiment, but in the political press, northern Democrats as well as the emerging Whig opposition sympathized with West Indian planters and, by extension, their slaveholding cousins in the American South.

In October 1831 the *Newport Mercury* of Rhode Island reported on the public meetings of island whites and the resolutions "of a strong character" that were passed to protest the interference of Parliament in the governance of slaves. Echoing the commentary from 1816 and 1823, the *Mercury* opined that the attitude of the Jamaicans closely resembled the resolu-

---

39. "Report of a Committee of the Convention, to whom was referred an Act to provide for calling a Convention of the People of South Carolina" in *State Papers on Nullification* (Boston, 1834), 17, 21. For more on Nullification, see Freehling, *Prelude to Civil* War, 219–97.

tion of the American colonies in the years leading up to the Revolution. In December, just before the outbreak of the rebellion, *Niles' Register* of Baltimore believed a "great crisis" appeared imminent in the British West Indies, an inference drawn from the "fearful apprehensions" of slave uprisings reported in Jamaica, Grenada, Tortola, and Barbados.[40]

Americans learned that the slaves had risen in Jamaica just as the news of Nat Turner began to subside and Virginia's debate on slavery began. Most newspapers began coverage of the Jamaican revolt in late January, apprising readers of an "insurrection among the slaves of the island" that had resulted in the establishment of martial law. By the next month the whole island was reported "in confusion," and the next weeks' papers saw Jamaica's plight as serious indeed. While "the leaders in the late insurrection ha[d] principally been taken, and great numbers executed . . . more than five hundred had fled to the mountains, and were still in a state of rebellion." The rebellion at its peak, Americans learned, had involved "thirty thousand [armed] negroes . . . two thousand [of whom] had been killed [and] who had destroyed the entire stock of one hundred and fifty plantations . . . valued at *fifteen millions of dollars.*"[41]

American editors devoted much more attention to the insurrection in Jamaica than they had to those in Barbados and Demerara. Thirty-nine reports of the insurrection appeared in the newspapers studied, and editors followed the news from Jamaica for a significantly longer period of time, averaging 148 days, almost two months longer than the Demerara rebellion had been covered in 1823. Some of the increase can be attributed to improvements within the transatlantic network of information. Ships engaged in trade were still the main conveyors of information, but with the development of the West Indian press, American editors depended far less on the personal letters and earwitnesses upon which earlier coverage had been based. Only nine reports came from these sources, while West In-

40. *Newport Mercury*, October 1, 1831; *Baltimore Niles' Register*, December 3, 1831.

41. Quotes are from some of the earliest reports of the insurrection, several of which were widely reprinted in the United States. See, e.g., *New York Albion*, January 21, 1832, February 18 and 25, 1832; *Boston Recorder*, February 15, 1832; *Boston Statesman*, January 28, February 25, 1832; *Charleston Mercury*, February 14, 1832; *New York Christian Advocate and Journal and Zion's Herald*, February 17, 1832; *Boston Christian Watchman*, January 27, February 17 and 24, 1832; *Hartford Connecticut Courant*, January 24, 1832; February 14, 21, 28, 1832; *Richmond Enquirer*, February 24, 1832; *Newport Mercury*, February 18, 1832; *Baltimore Nile's Register*, February 11, 18, 25, 1832; *Maryland Gazette*, January 26, 1832; *Bennington Vermont Gazette*, February 29, 1832.

dian newspapers provided the basis for twenty-five reports. Whereas ear-witnesses and letters were cited in 50 percent of the reports in 1816, and 33 percent in 1823; by 1832 only 23 percent of the reports had such foundations.[42]

While the structures through which information flowed were important, the comparative neglect of the rebellion in southern papers and the prolonged attention to the aftermath of the rebellion throughout the country demonstrate that Americans were powerfully affected by news of the struggle over slavery in the British Caribbean. Sectional difference in American coverage of West Indian rebellions had been evident in 1823 with the exceptionally sparse coverage of the *Charleston Mercury*. In 1832, as the South still reeled from the reports from Southampton, the sectional distinction was far deeper. Southern papers *began* with the news that "tranquility" had been restored and Ritchie's *Richmond Enquirer* and the *Annapolis Maryland Gazette* each printed only one report on the rebellion. While Ritchie simply cataloged the destruction of property and slaves, the *Gazette* noted the similarity to the rebellion in Southampton, reporting that "a negro preacher was at the head of the whole plot." The *Charleston Mercury* dismissed the rebellion as "local disturbances" in its first report in February and only returned to the story in April to report on the Jamaican Assembly's determination to resist "any measure tending to ameliorate the condition of the slaves." Such limited coverage was certainly due to fear of the possible spread of rebellious tendencies by word of mouth, via the newspapers.[43]

As the Baptist War inflamed the British public and led to the final round of parliamentary debates on the abolition of West Indian slavery, American papers South and North paid close attention. In August 1832, Hezekiah Niles of Baltimore provided his readers with a short "sketch" of the debates in Parliament and predicted abolitionist success. Britons were taken with "an enthusiasm" over West Indian slavery that promised "fearful events," wrote Niles, a clear allusion to the rebellion he expected abolition to ignite. Niles observed that these were developments of "deep in-

42. These figures are based on thorough investigations of the following papers for all of 1832: *Baltimore Niles' Register, Charleston Mercury, New York Evening Post, Richmond Enquirer*, and the *Baltimore Patriot and Mercantile Advertiser*.

43. *Richmond Enquirer*, February 24, 1832; *Annapolis Maryland Gazette*, January 26, 1832; *Charleston Mercury*, February 14, 1832; April 2, 1832.

terest to the United States," reflecting the increased importance of slavery within the nation's political discourse. Niles's coverage of the beginnings of the abolition debates preceded the rest of the country by several months, but his announcement set a precedent, as newspaper editors prepared their readers for the first legislated emancipation of a numerically predominant slave population in the history of the Atlantic world.[44]

In April 1833, the *New Orleans Bee* copied an article from the *London Globe* that reported the "intention of the Ministers to introduce a bill into the new Parliament for the immediate emancipation of the slaves in the West Indies." The British government was prepared to send "an imposing force" of 15,000 troops to protect the white colonists from the "probable consequence" in the West Indies if the intentions of Parliament were "prematurely announced." The assumption that slaves would rise up gave ammunition to the defenders of slavery in their attempts to forestall the progress of the emancipation bill. For proslavery editors in the American South, the assumption of inevitable rebellion created foreboding of the likely results of Britain's "experiment" with emancipation.[45]

As the debates in Parliament progressed, the *Bee* returned to this same worrisome theme. Following coverage of the abolition debates, the *Bee* opined that Britain's ministers, "in agitating the question of emancipation ... must have forgotten the consequences to a neighboring nation produced by similar measures adopted with equal imprudence," a clear allusion to the Haitian Revolution. The Edwards thesis was implicit in the *Bee*'s analysis.[46]

In support of such a terrifying reference, the *Bee* reprinted a letter from a worried Barbadian planter, who warned that the colonies neared a crisis of unprecedented magnitude. The planter could only hope that "Providence" would protect the islands from "the scenes of horror" that had devastated Saint-Domingue. Even more disturbing to southern readers, the writer argued that the proximity and shared interest in slavery doomed the United States to "participate ... in the deep and fatal results" of the colonies' imminent destruction. Indeed, the writer warned southerners to

44. *Baltimore Niles' Register*, August 18, 1832. Niles's assertion of the likely abolitionist impact of reform was supported in later articles: September 1 and 8, 1832.

45. *New Orleans Bee*, April 3, 1833. The same news with the same emphasis appeared in the *Baltimore Niles' Register*, April 6, 1833.

46. *New Orleans Bee*, July 24, 1833.

take "serious considerations" in the coming months with respect to their own "safety and repose."[47] West Indian planters fully expected slave rebellions to erupt as Parliament debated the abolition of slavery and emancipation itself grew near. White southerners shared the mentality of their West Indian cousins. They reprinted their fears and learned from their experience.

Britain's consideration of abolition also worked to revive the nullification debates among southern Democrats. Leading the charge to revive the nullifying sentiment were Duff Green's *United States Telegraph* and the *Charleston Mercury*, edited by John Stuart. The *Mercury* was the leading nullification paper in South Carolina, and Green's paper acted as the Washington news organ for John C. Calhoun, who had resigned in 1832 as Andrew Jackson's vice president only to return to Washington the next year as senator from South Carolina and the most influential southern statesman. Calhoun worked for his entire political career to unify the South on the question of slavery, and in 1833 when the British began to debate the immediate emancipation of their West Indian slaves, his editor worked to alert southern readers to the threat such actions posed to their interests.

Like most newspaper editors in the early American republic, Green was actively engaged in swaying public opinion. As the British Parliament debated the abolition of colonial slavery from June through August 1833, Green published a series of articles linking the nascent abolitionist movement in the North with the campaign in Britain. On June 4 Green printed in the *Telegraph* a letter written by a "Spy from New York" who claimed to have attended meetings of the American Colonization Society and witnessed "a great and fearful movement making at the north" that threatened to split the nation. "Spy" reported that "the latest news from England" had the abolitionists in "extasies." They believed that British abolition would have "a very great influence at the south," and overwhelm the "strong barriers" that protected slavery in the United States. The correspondent warned that the "fanatics" might be right, if the South allowed itself to be "lulled" into complacency by party politicians such as Daniel Webster. Spy did not trust the influence of such men when "gladiators" like William Lloyd Garrison were free to disseminate their theories and influence minds. They

47. Ibid., August 6, 1833.

were reckless men indeed who dared to "call George Washington a *thief,* because he held slaves."[48]

Early in July both the *Telegraph* and the *Mercury* ran an article reminiscent of Robert Turnbull's *The Crisis.* Under the heading "SLAVERY.—WEST INDIES. STATE RIGHTS" Green reprinted an editorial comment from Richmond. Thomas Ritchie had edited the *Enquirer* from 1804 and had become one of the most influential figures in Virginia politics. He had lambasted states rights advocates during the nullification crisis and was a rival of both Green and the *Mercury.*[49] Ritchie's original piece printed extracts from the parliamentary debates on emancipation in the West Indies and concluded that the fundamental dilemma of West Indian planters lay in their complete lack of "political control over those persons who can control their very lives and fortunes. The whole of the British W. Indies has no representative in Parliament," a plight the South had avoided through American independence and the Constitution. Green, however, considered Ritchie's opinions to be the "contradictions of a weak and trammeled judgment" that fell short of the measures needed to protect the South from abolitionism. As Turnbull had pointed out six years before, the West Indians' plight was entirely too similar to that of the southern states in relation to the federal government. In an imaginary dialogue between Ritchie and a representative nullifier, South Carolina's spokesmen explored the scenario that would occur if Turnbull's crisis were to come to pass. "Suppose," they asked, "the Federal Government, should do as the British Parliament has done, and bring out its scheme of Emancipation?" What was the South to do? "Remonstrate," s[aid] Mr. Ritchie." But what if remonstration were to fail, as it failed the slaveholders in the West Indies? Then we "rush into revolution," said Mr. Ritchie, like the patriots of 1776. And you'll "be hanged like dogs," thundered "A. Jackson, Esquire," echoing the thrust of the Force Bill. For Duff Green and the *Mercury,* the dialogue portrayed the lessons to be learned from the failure of the South to unite be-

48. *Washington (DC) United States Telegraph,* July 6, 1833. This same letter was reprinted in the *Charleston Mercury,* July 23, 1833. See also *Washington (DC) United States Telegraph,* June 1, 1833.

49. Jeffrey L. Pasley, *"The Tyranny of Printers": Newspaper Politics in the Early American Republic* (Charlottesville: University Press of Virginia), 260–61; Richard Ellis, *The Union at Risk: Jacksonian Democracy, States' Rights, and the Nullification Crisis* (New York: Oxford University Press, 1987), 128–32.

hind South Carolina during the nullification crisis. The imminent demise of West Indian slavery was "calculated to open the eyes of the people" to the tyrannical powers of the federal government.[50]

The dialogue reveals a continued and active interest in British abolition, and the editors' scuffle showed that divisions among the "various Souths" could be expressed in differing opinions on the lessons to be learned.[51] While Ritchie believed slavery was protected within the constitutional fold, Green and the *Mercury* saw a lesson for the South, whose rights were in the hands of a hostile majority. All of these papers had commented on how the West Indian situation reflected recent events in the United States, but Green and the *Mercury* had returned to Turnbull's message, showing that Carolinians continued to be peculiarly sensitive to West Indian events. Throughout July, both papers covered the progress of the emancipation bill in the British Parliament. For white Carolinians, the news was bleak, and coverage ranged from the worried letters of West Indian planters to re-printed parliamentary debates on the details of emancipation.[52] "Fanatical" abolitionists in the North would soon have the British precedent to bolster their movement, a precedent that would have to be countered.

The imminence of abolition in the British West Indies led southern editors to grossly exaggerate the influence enjoyed by abolitionists in the North. The *Mercury* printed a long letter written by a "Charlestonian" that made sweeping claims about abolitionist intentions. The writer described a "determined system of operations against the slave institutions of the South" and claimed that "almost every newspaper, pamphlet, book, or other publication, which comes from the North" had attacked the institution of slavery. The Charlestonian named a slew of northern papers that printed "earnest exhortations to rid the country" of slavery and "violent and abu-sive articles in relation to the treatment and condition of our slaves." Re-markably, this accusation came as the northern abolitionist movement was only beginning to radicalize. Garrison had begun publication of the *Lib-erator*, but his influence was still quite small. The American Anti-Slavery Society had not yet been formed, the "Declaration of Sentiments" had not been written, and the New England Anti-Slavery Society had not even published its second *Annual Report*. The great majority of abolitionist sen-

50. *Washington (DC) United States Telegraph,* July 3, 1833; *Charleston Mercury,* July 6, 1833.
51. William Freehling, *The Road to Disunion,* 1:16–19.
52. *Charleston Mercury,* July 10, 16, 22, 23, 27, 30, 1833; *Washington (DC) United States Telegraph,* July 10, 11, 1833.

timent printed in these papers during this period would have emanated from Britain. British abolition had begun to influence the American debate before a single West Indian was freed.[53]

While their rhetoric was perhaps more shrill, South Carolina editors did not stand alone in their view. Late in July, Ritchie's *Enquirer* quoted a selection from the *North American Review* and expressed "alarm" at the "disposition ... shown by some persons of intelligence and high respectability ... to encourage projects having the view to *the immediate abolition of slavery*." Ritchie called upon his "editorial brethren" in the North to respond as to "*how far*" this statement was correct. The *Boston Courier*, a voice of the emerging Whigs, was quick to answer Ritchie's query, asserting that they "were not aware until reading the article in the *North American Review*, that any number of persons of intelligence, sufficient to create alarm, entertained the project of immediate emancipation." The *Courier* went on to state that most respectable opinion in the North "repudiated" the program of the abolitionists and affirmed that "the general sentiment of New England" was with Senator Daniel Webster, who maintained that the Constitution protected the right to own slaves. Most northerners, the *Courier* promised, had no interest in interfering with this right and supported this stance by reprinting the following warning from the *Enquirer* with unqualified assent:

> We must again warn our Eastern brethren upon this solemn subject. Why should one be so infatuated in the North, as to touch it? *Laissez nous-faire.* We beg you to let us alone. We know the evil. We alone understand whether there be a remedy. You cannot be aware of what is best adapted to our situation. You can scarcely be aware of the sensibility of the South, upon the question. What matter too is so well calculated to be used by agitators, on either side of Mason and Dixon's line, as this most delicate and difficult subject? Depend on it, if this Union is ever to be split, *this is the rock.*[54]

Such sentiment is particularly striking from the pen of Thomas Ritchie, who had printed the debates on gradual abolition in the Virginia legis-

---

53. *Charleston Mercury*, July 31, 1833. The letter named the *Hartford Review*, the *Boston Transcript*, the *Boston Courier*, the *Pennsylvanian*, the *Pittsburg Statesman*, "Boulson's paper in Philadelphia," the *New York Advocate and Journal*, the *New York Daily Advertiser*, the *New York Commercial*, and the *Pennsylvania Advocate*.

54. *Boston Courier*, August 1, 1833.

lature.[55] Moreover, its endorsement by the *Boston Courier* illuminates the antiabolitionist sentiment that transcended the political divisions of Jacksonian America. British abolition had forced onto the pages of mainstream northern papers sentiments that were deeply offensive to the South, raising the level of sensitivity on the slavery question. The southern response to the expression of antislavery opinion pushed northern editors towards an antiabolitionist stance.

The racist, antiabolitionist, Whig James Watson Webb, editor of the *New York Courier and Enquirer*, joined with his counterpart in Boston to condemn abolitionism. In an article simply entitled "The South," the *Courier* expressed disbelief at southern assertions of any plan among the "sober, rational people of the non-slaveholding States" to interfere with slavery. At the same time, the *Courier* castigated northerners who had unjustly "stigmatized" slaveholders for "tyranny, and cruelty" and affirmed that southerners had "ample cause for apprehension on the subject of slavery." The writer's concerns were firmly grounded in the transatlantic influence of British abolition: "We see it in the force of the example presented by England in relation to her West India possessions, in the language of newspapers, pamphlets, public meetings, and in the organization of new societies for the purpose of influencing public opinion, *and public action*, on this most momentous subject."[56] When these words were written, and read by thousands, slavery was on the cusp of abolition in the British West Indian colonies, and as papers throughout the United States had reported, public action had followed the shift in public opinion. Southerners feared the same sequence of events could take place in the North, destroying the protection of their property, for as the writer in the *New York Courier* argued, "the laws and the Constitution are but the creatures of the people's will" and could be easily altered.[57]

As Britain passed the abolition bill in August, Duff Green reprinted from the *Boston Advertiser* a letter from Robert Monroe Harrison, the U.S. consul in Kingston, Jamaica, and an important figure later in our story. Harrison wrote that the white population of Jamaica lived in fear for their lives, as the slaves were dissatisfied with the plan of emancipation contemplated by Parliament and threatened to "emancipate themselves, the effect of which would be the destruction of every white inhabitant." Har-

55. Freehling, *Prelude to Civil War*, 82.
56. Quoted in the *Charleston Mercury*, August 5, 1833.
57. Ibid.

rison recommended that the United States station a "vessel of war" near the island to protect the white inhabitants should an uprising occur, as he thought likely. Significantly, Green found this information in a Boston paper, which indicates sentiment in the North that agreed with the southern interpretation of the probable ramifications of slave emancipation in the West Indies.[58]

Understandably, papers speaking for southern Democrats and the nullifiers were far more sensitive to British abolition than their northern counterparts, but once the debates began, excerpts from the London papers were widely reprinted in the North. Editors generally introduced the debates with reference to the "interest" they had to the people of the United States and reprinted excerpts from the speeches of opposing members of Parliament. The *Boston Courier* first announced Britain's intention to debate immediate emancipation in May 1833 and in July published extensive excerpts. Significantly, many of these presented arguments sympathetic with proslavery thought. Furthermore, antiabolitionist arguments appeared first, and only the persevering reader would arrive at the arguments of the abolitionists, buried, as they were, in the bottom half of the column. The opinions of Sir Richard Vyvyan proved popular among editors on either side of the Mason-Dixon. Vyvyan spoke against abolition with an array of arguments already popularized by Carolinian nullifiers. Vyvyan asserted that Parliament had no right to legislate upon the "internal affairs" of the West India colonies, as their own laws concerning the slaves functioned perfectly well. Furthermore, he warned Parliament that the struggle with the West Indian colonies might invite the same "foreign interference" that had robbed the empire of the mainland colonies nearly sixty years before.[59]

One Colonel Hay warned Parliament that their proceedings threatened to destroy the West Indian colonies through insurrection. He argued that the "negroes were not fitted for freedom" and that only a "moral education," as yet unfinished, could prepare them. Hay claimed to speak from experience. He had lived in Barbados for eighteen years, which proved to him that even the best-treated slaves were incapable of self-control. As evidence he cited the insurrection that had seized the island in 1816, when Parliament had engaged in similar debates. He claimed that the insurrection

58. *Washington (DC) United States Telegraph,* August 8, 1833.

59. *Boston Courier,* July 15, 1833. For other reprintings of Vyvyan's speeches, see *Charleston Mercury,* July 22, 1833; *Washington (DC) United States Telegraph,* July 10, 1833.

began on the estates of one of the island's "kindest" masters, proof that the time was not yet right to entertain such a measure. Mr. P. M. Stewart also spoke against abolition, contending as had Vyvyan that Parliament had no right to impose its will upon the colonial legislatures. Stewart voiced arguments, which southerners would repeat throughout the antebellum period, that only slaveholders had the knowledge or the right to take any measures effecting the emancipation of their property.[60]

The abolitionist voices recorded by the *Courier* were those of Edward Stanley, the colonial secretary, and Thomas Buxton, the leader of the abolitionists in Parliament. Buxton and Stanley both proclaimed that they had initially been in favor of a gradual emancipation and had hoped that this would be carried out by the colonies themselves. But the resistance of the colonies to the ameliorative measures encouraged by Parliament had left them with few options. Furthermore, Stanley knew of no limitation that had been placed upon the powers of Parliament to legislate for the colonies. Buxton supported the abolitionist stance with an anecdote that portrayed the cruel, anti-Christian character of West Indian slavery, which was reprinted by the *Courier* in very small print at the bottom of the column. Buxton related the story of Henry Willis, who had been brutally flogged by his owner for going to chapel. When a magistrate had sought to investigate the case, a jury of planters decided that the slave's owner had violated no law. For Buxton the tale proved that "cruelty was inseparable from a system of slavery" and would lead to a "servile war" if emancipation were postponed. Overall, these were hardly the strongest arguments that British abolitionists had employed in Parliament. The *Courier* gave only a nod to balance in its portrayal of the debates; editorial sentiment was clearly against Britain's "Great Experiment."[61]

FROM PERSECUTION TO IMMEDIATISM: THE NORTHERN RELIGIOUS PRESS AND JAMAICA'S MISSIONARIES

Historians of American reform have demonstrated the critical links between Evangelical Christianity and northern abolitionism.[62] While the political press tried to dampen the influence of British abolition, Evan-

60. *Boston Courier,* July 15, 1833.
61. Ibid.
62. John McKivigan, *The War Against Proslavery Religion: Abolitionism and the Northern Churches, 1830–1865* (Ithaca: Cornell University Press, 1984).

gelical editors in the North could not divert their attention from the stirring plight of Jamaica's missionaries, despite the concerns of their southern
counterparts. For this to have occurred, northern Evangelicals had to privilege their antislavery beliefs over the national communities of believers that
the Second Great Awakening had created. The rebellions of 1831 marked
a turning point for the northern Evangelical press and a critical step in the
formation of an antislavery public opinion that would eventually play a
critical role in the politics of the North.[63]

In February 1832 James Loring, the editor of the *Christian Watchman*,
faced the challenge of introducing his readers to the debate over slavery
then taking place in Virginia. In previous years, he wrote, it had been "difficult for Northern men to speak their sentiments publicly on this subject without giving offense." Those who had expressed their opinions on
the slave trade had been "severely denounced," but Loring believed that
most Baptists thought that the days of slavery were drawing to an end.
The prophet's call that "every yoke should be broken, and the oppressed
go free" would become manifest in their world. The South did not stand
alone in guilt. Loring argued that the North also participated in the sin of
slavery, but that now white southerners were "learning from facts before
their eyes . . . that slavery is a curse on our whole country."[64]

Loring's choice of words is important. That it had "hitherto been difficult for Northern men to speak" on slavery reveals an unbridling of language; the northern religious press, out of respect for its southern readers,
had kept its distance from Garrisonian extremes. But with Virginia's debate, clearly interpreted as southern permission for a broader discussion of
slavery, Loring felt license to express the views in which he "[had] long believed." James Loring's commentary on Virginia's slavery debate in 1832
offers the historian another view of the "broken seal" identified by Thomas
Dew. While Dew argued that the Virginia debate opened the doors for
slaveholders to offer an intellectual defense to the abolitionists, Loring's
careful phrases show that northerners milder than Garrison in their antislavery views now felt comfortable with a public discussion. This meant
that readers of the religious press in the North could now be exposed to
news and commentary critical of human bondage.[65]

63. Leonard Richards, *The Slave Power: The Free North and Southern Domination, 1780–
1860* (Baton Rouge: Louisiana State University Press, 2000), 136–41.

64. *Boston Christian Watchman*, February 10, 1832.

65. Dew, "Review of the Debate," 28.

Five months later, the Reverend J. Liefchild, editor of the Congregationalist *Boston Recorder*, marked a similar moment of hesitation when
confronted by the news of the persecuted missionaries in Jamaica. "I have
been called to touch a pensive theme; I have to move a vote of sympathy
to our brethren of the Baptist and Wesleyan missionary Societies, on their
present sufferings in the West [Indies] ... Though prudence leads me to
abstain from inflammatory topics, shall we be prevented from offering a
tribute of sympathy to our brethren?"[66] The question was rhetorical; not
only would the Reverend offer prayers for Jamaica's persecuted missionaries, but his and other religious papers of the North kept their readers
abreast of the events in Jamaica as they unfolded and spread awareness of
the struggle over slavery within the British Empire.

The Baptist *Christian Watchman* of Boston described the violence against
the missionaries: "It is with regret we perceive the feeling excited by these
disturbances has vented itself in an improper channel; and that the dreadful lesson seems to have done little good. The Baptist meeting houses at
Falmouth and Montego Bay were demolished, and the Methodist Church
[at Falmouth], much injured by the infatuated mob, who ascribed to the
best means for remedying a great evil, the unhappy consequences growing
out of the nature of that evil itself."[67] Though the prose was rather opaque,
it appeared that the whites of the island blamed the missionaries for the
revolt, and alert readers would have been reminded of the death of John
Smith. But the *Watchman* was going further than simple reporting on these
persecutions. The *Watchman* endowed the rebellion with didactic content;
it was a "dreadful lesson," the "unhappy consequence" that grew out of the
nature of slavery itself. The missions to Christianize the slaves were "the
best means for remedying a great evil," and the *Watchman* left it entirely
unclear as to whether the "great evil" was slavery itself, or the violation of
Christian principles that resulted from slavery. These were abolitionist sentiments shrouded in unclear writing. Loring's decision to report and to
teach reveals the introspection encouraged by observance of the events in
the West Indies.

As the persecution continued, the religious press in the North filled its
pages with anecdotes that portrayed Jamaican slaveholders as cruel oppressors preying upon the innocent missionaries. In April 1832, the *Christian
Advocate and Journal and Zion's Herald* and the *Christian Index* reprinted the
proslavery Anglican reverend George Bridges's hope to "diversify" Jamai-

66. *Boston Recorder*, July 11, 1832.
67. *Boston Christian Watchman*, March 16, 1832.

can forests with the swinging corpses of missionaries.[68] Methodist readers would have been outraged. Equally disturbing were the letters of Reverend Box that were reprinted in May. Box was a Methodist missionary who was "as comfortable as possible among the felons" in the Common Jail in Spanish Town. Box wrote that despite his attempts to prevent his congregation from joining the rebellion, the "base periodicals" of the island had wrongly portrayed him as "deeply implicated."[69] When Box made it out of prison he came first to New York, where sympathetic ministers invited him to preach from their pulpits. Box informed his fellow Methodists of the destruction of eighteen chapels, including those belonging to the Baptists, and lamented the fate of Jamaica's Christians who had been left "without a shepherd."[70] In September readers were again shocked by the "tarring [of] a Wesleyan Missionary," an account of the mob's treatment of the missionary Henry Bleby.[71]

Baptist readers had to confront the destruction of their chapels, as well as the experiences of William Knibb, the Baptist missionary, whose letters were reprinted by Joshua Leavitt's *New York Evangelist* and the *Boston Christian Watchman*. Knibb described his arrest: "Commanding two black men to take me prisoner, [the officer] paraded before me in all the pomp of petty power with a drawn sword, and had me conveyed to the guard room ... The most horrid oaths that men or devils could devise, were poured upon us, with the most vulgar allusions that depraved nature could invent ... No fault had I committed, with none was I charged. But I was a Missionary, and that was enough."[72] These were scenes reminiscent of Christ's arrest and humiliation by Roman soldiers, and religious readers would have recognized them as such. Rome's slave society had attacked and imprisoned Jesus Christ; Jamaica's slave society attacked Knibb and his fellow missioners. Readers had to ponder their own salvation as citizens of yet another slave society.[73]

But what if there was some truth in the lawless fury of Jamaica's whites?

68. *New York Christian Advocate and Journal and Zion's Herald,* April 20, 1832; *New York Christian Index,* April 14, 1832.

69. *New York Christian Advocate and Journal and Zion's Herald,* May 18, 1832.

70. Ibid., May 25, 1832.

71. *New York Christian Index,* September 22, 1832; *Boston Christian Watchman,* September 14, 1832.

72. *Boston Christian Watchman,* April 20, 1832.

73. In 1830 William Lloyd Garrison used his own prison experience in Baltimore in precisely the same manner. See James Brewer Stewart, *William Lloyd Garrison and the Challenge of Emancipation* (Arlington Heights, IL: Harlan Davidson, 1992), 46.

After all, Nat Turner was a preacher who had used Christian theology and his influence to justify and organize a bloody rebellion. It must have occurred to some readers that the same thing could have happened in Jamaica. Had the missionaries in Jamaica crossed the line between religious and civil concerns? If so, violence, although unfortunate, might be expected against men who had endangered the very lives of those who now attacked them.

As soon as the jailed missionaries were released, they formulated a defense of their mission which was disseminated first through Jamaica's opposition press and reprinted in British papers and religious periodicals in the North. The missionaries denied the charges that they had taught principles that encouraged "disobedience and insubordination" among the slaves and asserted their adherence to the doctrines of the "established Church."[74] More effective, however, were the anecdotes of slaves who were docile in the face of rebellion. Both the *New York Evangelist* and the *Boston Christian Watchman* published William Knibb's description of his own sermon to the slaves when rumors were rife that freedom had been granted and resistance was necessary. Knibb reported that he had told his people that the rumors were "false," the work of "wicked persons." "I love your souls!" Knibb had cried, and he reminded them of God's command "to be obedient!"[75] These were encouraging words for the dubious reader. Knibb showed that the missionary preacher to the slaves could marshal the authority of religion in the face of the disturbing rumors. Even more encouraging was the evidence from Knibb's diary, which revealed the impact of religious instruction on a potentially violent slave population. He recorded that on January 1, early in the rebellion, he held a prayer meeting attended by many slaves from the surrounding country. Those who could not come had "sent word that they should have come, but tarried at home to prevent the burning of the property of their masters. No estate, where the Baptists had members . . . had been burnt."[76] Testimony from both planters and slaves would prove the latter part of Knibb's statement clearly untrue, but to readers in the United States it showed that Christian slaves not only de-

74. *Boston Christian Watchman,* March 30, 1832; *Boston Recorder,* April 4, 1832; *New York Christian Index,* April 14, 1832. The missionaries' defense had first been printed in the *Kingston Chronicle,* February 25, 1832.

75. *Boston Christian Watchman,* April 20, 1832 (reprinted from the New York *Evangelist*).

76. Ibid.

clined to participate in rebellions but also protected the property of their masters. Jamaica's whites were surely misguided in their anger. The Evangelical mission to their slaves did not endanger their property; on the contrary, the mission had served as protection. These stories were pervasive in the northern religious press, endowing the missionaries with a legitimacy that upheld their mission and the immediatist stance that they would adopt.

Other religious periodicals teemed with news in the same vein. The *Boston Recorder* reported with pleasure that Jamaica's colonial assembly had recently passed an act that commended "the orderly and obedient conduct" of Presbyterian slaves. The Methodist *New York Christian Advocate* reported the satisfaction of the Wesleyan Missionary Society, which rejoiced in the knowledge "that there was no proof that any of the converted slaves had taken any active part" in the rebellion, and that "many . . . had risked, and some had lost their lives in defense of the property of their masters." The Moravian *Missionary Intelligencer* affirmed that slaves in their missions had exemplified the "fidelity and obedience worthy of their Christian profession." The judgment of the religious press was concentrated in the defense of the missionaries and their work. To readers of the religious press, the news emanating from Jamaica revealed that the missions had created peaceful pockets of Christianity within a slave society that was unstable as a result of its own contradictions.[77]

If northern editors of the religious press were trying to convince their southern brethren of the innocence of the Jamaican missionaries and the calming influence of the missions in the midst of a slave insurrection, they could have stopped at this point, with the evidence of peaceful, converted slaves. But stories of the persecuted missionaries were compelling, and some editors followed them to Britain. The missionaries returned to Britain in the midst of a tense election year infused with the struggle to reform Parliament. British abolitionists had capitalized on the movement for reform and demanded that candidates pledge for immediate abolition in order to receive the votes of antislavery-minded Britons. The persecuted missionaries became especially powerful speakers to a British public that was ready to abolish slavery in its Caribbean colonies.[78] Knibb "the Notorious" played

77. *Boston Recorder*, June 6, 1832; *New York Christian Advocate and Journal and Zion's Herald*, July 6, 1832; "From the West Indies," *United Brethren's Missionary Intelligencer and Religious Miscellany*, 4th Quarter (1832). See also *Boston Recorder*, November 14, 1832.

78. Walvin, *England, Slaves and Freedom*, 164.

a dual role, testifying in the Parliament's investigation of rebellion and delivering public harangues against West Indian slave owners. Bleby, the tarred and feathered missionary, was an equally potent presence, holding up his own bloodied and tarred nightshirt as a prop in his public attacks upon the West Indian slaveholders' power.[79]

The Baptist *Christian Watchman* and the Congregationalist *Recorder,* both Boston papers, followed the missionaries in their activities in Britain; the Methodist *Christian Advocate and Journal and Zion's Herald* of New York did not. The divergence indicates structural differences among the denominations and points toward the schisms that would split the Baptist and Methodist churches in 1844. The Congregationalists had little following in the South, so there were no boundaries for the *Recorder* to cross in its coverage of Jamaica's persecuted missionaries. And while American Baptists had a large following in the South, they adhered to a looser national structure than the Methodists, which cultivated regional autonomy. The *Watchman* spoke to the antislavery leanings of Boston Evangelicals and probably lost any southern readership it had. The Methodist *Advocate,* however, was clearly more aware of its southern readers, and when the missionaries went to Britain, the *Advocate* did not follow.[80]

In July 1832 the British Anti-Slavery Society had its anniversary meeting at which the rebellion at Jamaica and its aftermath received a full discussion. The *Christian Watchman* reprinted for its readers the following editorial comments of the *London World.*

[The West Indian planters'] open expressions of hostility to every effort made to instruct the negroes, and their wanton and reckless persecution of those who are engaged in the benevolent enterprise, proclaim to the public their hypocrisy and real intentions, and the incontrovertible fact, that Christianity is a system in its origin, principles, and results so totally diverse from Slavery, that they cannot co-exist in the same locality ... They have now declared their convictions, and the only course left for the friends of Emancipation,

79. Betty Fladeland, *Men and Brothers: Anglo-American Antislavery Cooperation* (Urbana: University of Illinois Press, 1972), 202–3; Philip Wright, *Knibb "the Notorious" Slaves' Missionary, 1803–1845* (London: Sidgwick and Jackson, 1973), 112–14, 126.

80. Mitchell Snay, *Gospel of Disunion: Religion and Separatism in the Antebellum South* (Chapel Hill: University of North Carolina Press, 1997), 134–35.

is one of direct opposition to Slavery, in order that the negroes may have at the same time the blessings of liberty and Christianity.[81]

Excepting remarks in Garrison's *Liberator*, this was as strong a statement against slavery as was ever made in the United States in 1832. To print "that Christianity is a system in its origin, principles, and results so totally diverse from Slavery, that they cannot co-exist in the same locality" was an idea barely acceptable to many Boston readers. That such a statement was printed at all in 1832 attests to the budding radicalism that existed in Boston's religious community. While it is difficult to say how many readers accepted the *World*'s portrayal of slavery, it would ultimately become a central component of antislavery doctrine.

The *World* began with a powerful condemnation of slave owners on grounds upon which every religious reader could identify, the righteous outrage at the persecution of missionaries who sought only to win the souls of the slaves for God. Persecution has great power in the Christian tradition. It is a sanctifying experience that bestows upon its sufferers an almost immortal quality enriched with stories of the ancient Jews, Christ's apostles, the disciples of Paul, and the colonial pilgrims, all persecuted and blessed for their works in the name of God. The *Watchman* presented to its Christian readers the argument that slavery produced yet another form of godless persecution incompatible with their own faith. To turn a blind eye to the persecuted was to ignore Christ himself. The logic was clear; only if American Christians became "friends of Emancipation" could they be true to their Christianity.

The commentary of an abolitionist newspaper might not have been convincing to more conservative religious readers, but the personal conversion of Knibb to immediatism was surely influential. Noting that "changes in the British West Indies must of necessity influence ... our own colored population," the *Boston Recorder* printed a speech Knibb delivered at the fortieth annual meeting of the London Baptist Missionary Society. He took his audience (and American readers) through his own conversion from a missionary to the slaves willing to "[maintain] the silence" on his congregants' civil condition, to an "undaunted advocate for immediate abolition." Knibb completely omitted the rebellion from his address and focused instead upon "the musket at [his] breast" through which he at-

81. *Boston Christian Watchman*, July 13, 1832.

tained that special authority that came with having suffered for Christ. What believer could doubt Knibb's authenticity as he denied his thirst for revenge and demanded the right to practice Christ's commandment to preach among all nations. Indeed, Knibb portrayed slavery as an impenetrable wall between the "oppressed slave" and the Christian faith he held so dear. Even more, he argued that "30,000 Christian slaves, of the same faith as yourselves" were barred from the "liberty to worship God" by the institution of slavery. By drawing clear lines of identification that connected his audience to the converted slaves, Knibb held out his own experience of conversion to advocating "immediate emancipation" as a Christian duty.[82]

As the year closed it was clear that the persecution of the missionaries had serious implications for the fate of British West Indian slavery. In November 1832 the *Boston Recorder* reported that "the [British] religious newspapers and magazines that we receive are unanimous in favor of the immediate adoption of measures by Parliament . . . the treatment of the Jamaica Missionaries . . . has awakened a spirit throughout the kingdom, that will not soon sleep."[83] The persecution of the missionaries had moved the British Evangelical public to the condemnation of slavery. American Evangelicals, in contrast to their co-religionists across the sea, were citizens of a nation and members of churches that condoned slavery—a wall against conversion, a violation of Christian practice.

AMERICAN ABOLITIONISTS AND BRITISH ABOLITION

As Parliament drew nearer to ending colonial slavery, American abolitionists paid close attention and believed that British success would bolster their cause. William Lloyd Garrison followed Nathaniel Paul on his transatlantic voyage in 1833 in order to witness firsthand slavery's defeat, and in the months preceding his departure, letters from his supporters expressed the belief that British abolition would have a profound influence upon the United States. Josiah Cassell, an agent for the *Liberator* in Philadelphia, wrote to Garrison of the "glorious news" about the British successes. Henry Benson reported that the news from Britain had "awaken[ed] some feeling" in Providence, Rhode Island, and was sure that it would prove a "blow to American slavery." James Otis sent his blessings from Portland, Maine,

---

82. *Boston Recorder,* August 22, 1832; *Boston Christian Watchman,* September 7, 1832.
83. *Boston Recorder,* November 14, 1832.

lauding Garrison for embarking "on a holier mission" than a man could ever undertake.[84]

The enthusiasm of Garrison's correspondents demonstrates the heightened awareness among American abolitionists during this momentous period. Apologists had long protested that if slavery were wrong, the responsibility lay with the British because they had planted slavery in the colonies. The United States had merely inherited it. If Britain abolished slavery in its own colonies, this argument would be severely weakened. As Garrison toured Britain in April 1833, the *Liberator* informed its readers that emancipation was the likely result of the recent reform of Parliament. Abolition would "wipe the stain from the British government," but, more importantly, it would "expose in its naked deformity, our guilt in the patient sufferance of so great an evil" as slavery. The writer believed that the "public mind" was ready for "a calm discussion" and likened the spirit of abolition to a "contagion" that would begin in the islands and "spread over our country with a rapidity that cannot be arrested."[85]

Such optimism seems naïve in light of the harsh rhetoric that already spilled forth from southern papers during the parliamentary debates. But abolitionists understood that the struggle over slavery in the American democracy was fundamentally a struggle for public opinion. Their own attitudes toward slavery and its abolition had gone through an intellectual transformation rooted in their political commitment to the human rights of African Americans. They also knew that American opinion was shaped through the printed word—the books, pamphlets, and newspaper essays that had been central to American politics since the Revolution. Abolitionist faith in the ultimate end of American slavery was always joined to a rigorous dedication to argument and the printed word.

The first major publication to draw strength from the imminence of British abolition was Lydia Maria Child's *An Appeal in Favor of that Class of Americans Called Africans*. Already an established author and "a paragon of feminine virtue," Child attracted as much, perhaps more, attention to

---

84. Jos[iah] Cassell to William Lloyd Garrison, March 23, 1833; Henry E. Benson to William Lloyd Garrison, March 23, 1833; James L. Otis to William Lloyd Garrison, March 19, 1823, Antislavery Manuscripts, Boston Public Library. My interpretation of Garrison's motivations to visit Britain differs from John L. Thomas but is consistent with that of Henry Mayer and James Brewer Stewart. See Thomas, *The Liberator*, 155–58; Henry Mayer, *All on Fire: William Lloyd Garrison and the Abolition of Slavery* (New York: St. Martin's Griffin, 1998), 153; Stewart, *William Lloyd Garrison*, 64.

85. *Boston Liberator*, April 27, 1833.

the abolitionist cause than the inauguration of William Lloyd Garrison's *Liberator*. In the 1820s she had advocated colonization, but beginning in 1830 Garrison worked to enlist her into radical abolitionism. Her husband David was an early recruit of Garrison's and became a founding member of the New England Antislavery Society. But Lydia Maria was not one to simply follow the men. She was intrigued by radicalism yet still found many colonizationist arguments convincing. So she researched the question. For the next three years she read widely on slavery and its abolition. By the end of her studies she was firmly dedicated to immediate abolition and the fight against racial prejudice; she had also authored a powerful new work.[86]

Child's *Appeal* appeared in August 1833, the very month that the British Parliament passed the Act of Abolition. This could not have been mere coincidence. Her book approached the problem of American slavery from its deeply rooted history in the Atlantic world. She began her account with the Portuguese explorations of the West African coast, the beginnings of the transatlantic slave trade, and the migration of black slavery to the Spanish Caribbean and, ultimately, the North American mainland in the seventeenth century. She compared the "modern" slavery of her time with the ancient slavery of Greece and Rome and declared the modern version harsher. As several generations of modern historians have done, Child also compared the institution of slavery in various nations to the slave codes of the Americas. And like twentieth-century researches, she concluded that the Dutch, the French, the Spanish, and the Portuguese operated milder forms of slavery than the English-speaking peoples. Child was sad to say that the American slave code was harsher than that of the British West Indies. The codes were originally almost precisely the same, but they had diverged since the independence of the United States. The British, she argued, had "long ago dared to describe the monster as it is" and were now "grappling" with the question of abolition while Americans had yet to honestly face the issue.[87]

86. Carolyn L. Karcher, *The First Woman in the Republic: A Cultural Biography of Lydia Maria Child* (Durham: Duke University Press, 1994), 174–94 (quote on 191).

87. Lydia Maria Child, *An Appeal in Favor of that Class of Americans Called Africans*, ed. Carolyn L. Karcher (1833; reprint, Amherst: University of Massachusetts Press, 1996), 36–37. Modern studies that have taken the same approach include Frank Tannenbaum, *Slave and Citizen: The Negro in the Americas* (New York: Vintage, 1946); Elsa Goveia, "The West Indian Slave Laws of the Eighteenth Century" in *Caribbean Slave Society and Economy: A Student Reader*, ed. Hilary Beckles and Verene Shepherd (New York: New Press, 1991), 346–62.

While the core of her argument against slavery and racism was essentially moral, Child employed this historical and comparative base of research to demonstrate the safety and practicality of immediate abolition. In choosing this approach she set the course for a critical theme of abolitionist argument which later writers would elaborate throughout the antebellum period. Having suffered the blame for the rebellion in Virginia, abolitionists were keenly aware of the potency of the Edwards thesis in American society, what Child called the "grand argument" of the slaveholder. Slaveholders emphasized the threat of insurrections because they thought that it might halt discussion, but Child took the charge head on, arguing that "slavery causes insurrections, while emancipation prevents them." The Antislavery Society aspired to prevent insurrections—not to cause them—and the only way to prevent insurrections was to abolish slavery. Child cited British abolitionists' struggles against the same charges from West Indian planters when insurrections struck Barbados and Demerara. She noted that missionaries were blamed for both insurrections but that in Barbados there had been no missionaries and in Demerara "only *two*" converted slaves had joined the rebellion. Child may have tweaked the evidence, or she may not have had access to the trial transcripts, but recent history had become the stuff of the slavery debate, and she skillfully presented an interpretation that advanced her cause. Wisely, she declined to discuss the rebellion in Jamaica.[88]

The taproot of the Edwards thesis was the revolution in Haiti, and Child proposed a history that challenged the dominant interpretation that Edwards and his followers had so thoroughly spread. Child drew her argument almost entirely from a pamphlet Clarkson had published in 1823.[89] She acknowledged that most Americans believed that "sudden freedom had occasioned the horrible massacres of St. Domingo" but declared that this was untrue and that no problems had arisen "until Bonaparte made his atrocious attempt *to restore slavery* in the island." The violence that occasioned freedom had resulted from civil war, and emancipation had actually brought peace. Child also cited Haiti as evidence against the argument that freed blacks would not work and that emancipation would lead to economic decay. She maintained that Haiti also made for "a strong argument" against the alleged "necessity of slavery." She cited an 1819 work

88. Child, *An Appeal*, 80, 134–37.

89. T[homas] Clarkson, *Thoughts on the Necessity of Improving the Condition of the Slaves in the British Colonies, with a view to their Ultimate Emancipation; and on the Practicality, the Safety, and the Advantages of the Later Measure* (London: Richard Taylor, 1823), 22–27.

by the planter Malenfant, an eyewitness to the revolution who testified that after emancipation the freed people had "continued to work upon all the plantations." She cited General Lacroix's "Memoirs for a History of St. Domingo" to the same effect, and quoted from W. W. Harvey's *Sketches of Haiti* (1827), to describe the "habits of industry and activity" that characterized the next generation of free Haitians. Haiti was not the bugbear for abolitionists to avoid; it was the best example of the good policy of immediate emancipation.[90]

Emancipations elsewhere in the Atlantic world further demonstrated that immediate liberation was a "safe and practical" policy that made immediate abolition a moral "duty." Child had read widely, and she described the process of emancipation in Columbia under Bolivar and in Bolivia, Argentina, and Mexico in the 1820s. Child did not acknowledge that slavery was peripheral to the economies in all of these regions; more important was that insurrections had nowhere accompanied the transition from slavery to freedom, as the Edwards thesis would have predicted. The British West Indies, of course, would be an even better precedent for the abolition of slavery in the American South. At the time of her writing, emancipation had only been proposed, but she could confidently predict that the British "were on the eve of entire, unqualified emancipation in all their colonies." She and other abolitionists would be disappointed by the gradualist elements of British abolition, but before the facts were known, American abolitionists looked hopefully to Britain to set the perfect moral precedent that could undermine the arguments of their detractors.[91]

AMERICA THROUGH THE PRISM OF AUGUST 1, 1834

When Britain's Act of Abolition came into effect on August 1, 1834, abolitionists perceived the dawning of a new age. The New England Anti-Slavery

---

90. Child, *An Appeal*, 80–81. Child cited the following works: [Colonel] Malenfant, *Des Colonies, Particuliérement de celle de Saint-Domingue; Mémoire Historique et Politique* (Paris, Audibert, 1814); Pamphile de Lacroix, *Mémoir pour servir á l'histoire de la Révolucion de Saint-Domingue* (Paris, 1819); W. W. Harvey, *Sketches of Hayti: From the Expulsion of the French to the Death of Christophe* (London: L. B. Seeley and Son, 1827). Unlike Bryan Edwards's *History*, none of these works were reprinted in the United States. Harvey's positive portrayal of Haiti after emancipation was never reprinted in the United States, but it was influential among abolitionists. See Theodore Weld to James Birney, January 5, 1836, in Dwight L. Dumond, ed., *Letters of James Gillespie Birney, 1835–1857*, 2 vols. (New York: D. Appleton-Century, 1938), 292.

91. Child, *An Appeal*, 88–89, 137.

Society celebrated the end of West Indian slavery with church services in the morning and a public meeting in South Reading, Massachusetts, which featured an oration by David Child and a performance by an African American children's choir. Garrison described the occasion as "The Great Jubilee" and proclaimed Britain's abolition of colonial slavery "one of the most signal and glorious events in the history of the world." African Americans in New York held a celebration in the Philomathean Hall which featured an address by David Ruggles and ceremonial readings of the Declaration of Independence as well as Britain's Act of Abolition. They cheered the emancipation "of more than *eight hundred thousand* of our brethren in the British Colonies" and called for the day when "boasted 'free America'" would follow the British example. These celebrations inaugurated a tradition of annual celebrations of the First of August that sustained black and white abolitionists who struggled in the face of terrible odds for the rest of the antebellum period.[92]

Despite this moment of hope, the political situation in the United States differed radically from that in Britain. In 1833 the West Indian interest, while not at its weakest point, had lost much influence as a result of parliamentary reform. The South had significant representation in Congress and most southerners there interpreted the Constitution as protecting the right to own slaves. The president was a slaveholder, and in the entire history of the republic all its presidents but the Adamses had been slaveholders.[93] Even if American abolitionists knew all the details of the back-room concessions that resulted in the passage of Britain's emancipation act, they could never attempt such tactics in Washington. They could only attempt to influence popular opinion, and as important as political maneuvering undoubtedly was in the passage of the Act of Abolition, British public opinion influenced the political complexion of parliament and the social milieu in which lawmakers worked. Abolitionists succeeded in convincing a large portion of the people that slavery was wrong, offensive to British liberty and incompatible with their identity as "Britons."[94] American abo-

92. *Boston Liberator,* August 9 and 30, 1834. First of August celebrations continued into the 1880s in the United States, and, in Canada, where the black population is predominantly of West Indian descent, the tradition lives on. I thank Afua Cooper for this information.

93. Kathleen Mary Butler, *The Economics of Emancipation: Jamaica and Barbados, 1823–1843* (Chapel Hill: University of North Carolina Press, 1995), 7–24; Leonard Richards, *The Slave Power: The Free North and Southern Domination, 1780–1860* (Baton Rouge: Louisiana State University Press, 2000).

94. Davis, *Slavery and Human Progress,* 119.

litionists realized this, and faced with more intractable opposition, they read in the story of British abolition the primary role of public opinion.

Such a reading was evident in David Child's address at the celebration in Boston. He saw the day as "an occasion of self examination ... of serious and humble preparation for following ... a noble example." British abolition had been the culmination of the near-flawless extension of the "free spirit of England" in seven identifiable "epochs" over the past two and a half centuries. While rather selective, Child's address reflected his wife's emphasis on the long history of the movement to which they were committed. He paid particular attention to the transatlantic slave trade. His only reference to Britain's role in the growth and spread of slavery was in describing the long-forgotten first epoch, when, ironically, England's first emancipation took place under the same sovereign, Elizabeth, under whom the slave trade began. Child explained this apparent anomaly by placing the entire responsibility for the slave trade upon "individual adventurers, actuated by love of gain." He thus created a clever opposition between the sins of the first epoch and the "free spirit" manifested during the fourth. While "love of gain" inaugurated the slave trade, "individual and voluntary movements ... effected by the operations of the press and public opinion" abolished it. Child's schema brings to light the dueling forces that occupied the world of the abolitionist imagination. History proved to him that greed stood against the true "spirit of freedom," and only when that spirit was spread throughout society through "the operation of the press and public opinion" could truth prevail. Britain's history with slavery and abolition had didactic import for American abolitionists; only through the force of public opinion could greed be overwhelmed.[95]

As David Brion Davis has argued, British and American abolitionists such as Child saw the end of West Indian slavery as a sure sign of moral progress. This interpretation saw in British abolition a manifestation of God's grace in the world which exemplified the wisdom of the reformed Parliament and the moral power of British public opinion.[96] Many were aware that this reading of abolition overlooked the reality of political bargaining that played such an important role in the passage of the bill, but they did not voice such knowledge openly. Garrison, for example, reported having daily breakfasts with British abolitionists "where the interchange

95. David Child, *Oration in Honor of Universal Emancipation in the British Empire, Delivered at South Reading, August First, 1834* (Boston: Garrison and Knapp, 1834), 3–15.

96. Davis, *Slavery and Human Progress,* 119–22, 177–79, 224–25.

of opinions in relation to the state of affairs, has been open and free."[97] It is hard to believe that along with opinions, the details of negotiations did not also circulate. But American abolitionists had an ambitious agenda and significant obstacles, and only an optimistic interpretation of British abolition suited their cause at that moment. They needed to seize upon every significant event that could broaden their influence within the American public. Disdain for racism may have radicalized white liberals in the North, but the predominance of racial prejudice in the rest of the white population and the influence of slaveholders in national politics demanded a broader attack that moved beyond demands for the human rights of African Americans. British abolition could and did prove quite valuable in strengthening and broadening abolitionist influence.

Black Americans were more sanguine. As we will see in chapter 7, celebrations of British abolition on the first of August became central events in African American life. But in 1834 there were only two, and these were not repeated annually until full British emancipation in 1838. Moreover, the National Conventions of the Free People of Color of 1833 and 1834 did not even mention Britain's abolition of slavery. They had endorsed Garrison's transatlantic venture in 1833, and in 1834 the conventioneers thanked the British abolitionists Charles Stewart and George Thompson for coming to the United States and assisting the abolitionist cause, but the strictures of Parliament's Act of Abolition, which required financial compensation to slaveholders and the continued enforcement of forced labor for former slaves, did not inspire the convention to the lofty heights imagined by David Child.[98]

For white Americans outside of abolitionist circles, the first news of emancipation in the British West Indies seemed to confirm the worst fears of the planters, who had predicted in strident tones that the slave populations, when released from the protective bonds of slavery, would unleash rebellion, fire, and bloodshed that would ultimately destroy the colonies.[99]

97. William L. Garrison to the Board of Managers of the New England Anti-Slavery Society, June 20, 1833, in Walter M. Merrill, ed., *The Letters of William Lloyd Garrison, 1822–1835*, vol. 1 (Cambridge: Harvard University Press, 1971), 237.

98. *Minutes and Proceedings of the Third Annual Convention* (New York, 1833), 9; *Minutes of the Fourth Annual Convention* (New York, 1834), 36, both reprinted in Howard Holman Bell, ed., *Minutes of the Proceedings of the National Negro Conventions, 1830–1864* (New York: Arno Press, 1969).

99. *Charleston Mercury*, July 10, September 21, 1833; *Washington (DC) United States Telegraph*, August 8 and 14, 1833.

The first report on emancipation to receive wide circulation in U.S. news-papers appeared in the *New Haven Herald* early in August and was later reprinted in Newport, Rhode Island; New York; Richmond, Virginia; and Charleston, South Carolina. The anonymous writer styled abolition the "beginning of the end," clearly indicating his or her expectations. The news hailed from "one of the Islands (Antigua or St. Kitts)" and told of the gov-ernor's announcement to the slaves of the conditions of emancipation. Ac-cording to the report, "a spirit of revolt was immediately manifested, and martial law was about to be proclaimed for the protection of the whites."[100] This report created for thousands of American readers their first impres-sion of the workings of a legislated emancipation of a large population of black slaves. It was a story of momentous import.

Despite its confident tone, several vague details called to question the accuracy of the report. The unclear identity of the island, for example, "An-tigua or St. Kitts," indicated a weak factual base. Moreover, the statement that "martial law was about to be proclaimed" gives the story the feel of a rumor, something heard by a sailor passing through the Leewards. Despite the report's doubtful authenticity, editors did not hesitate to offer their opinions on the future. The *Morning Courier and New York Enquirer*, for example, promised to "hope for the best" in the West Indies but expressed "serious apprehensions" that the British would have to either "re-subject the negroes to slavery—annihilate them by military force, or see their own citizens annihilated."[101]

If we glimpse into 1835, we see the impact of British abolition in the South and in the federal government. American abolitionists, influenced by the model of the successful movement that had swayed public opinion and cleansed Great Britain of the sins of slavery, made lists of southern ministers, whose names and addresses they gleaned from the membership rolls of a host of church and reform organizations. Southern men of God, they believed, would be moved by the antislavery literature that had con-verted Britons and some northerners to the abolitionist cause. They printed massive quantities of antislavery newspapers, pamphlets, children's litera-ture, and sent it all southward in the post.[102]

100. *Newport Mercury*, August 16, 1834; *Charleston Mercury*, August 21, 1834; *New York Courier and Enquirer*, August 23, 1834; *Richmond Enquirer*, September 5, 1834.

101. *New York Morning Courier and Enquirer*, August 23, 1834.

102. Bertram Wyatt-Brown, *Lewis Tappan and the Evangelical War Against Slavery* (New York: Athenaeum, 1971), 149–50; Richard John, *Spreading the News: The American Postal System from Franklin to Morse* (Cambridge: Harvard University Press, 1995), ch. 7.

On July 29, 1835, a mob of citizens stormed the post office in Charleston, South Carolina, and seized and burned the mail from New York. Rumors had circulated that the shipment contained abolitionist publications, and white Charlestonians were concerned about their potential revolutionary effect among the slaves. The next evening, three thousand whites gathered around the effigies of William Lloyd Garrison and Arthur Tappan, which were swinging from a gallows erected for the symbolic silencing of the abolitionists. A meeting of citizens labeled the abolitionists "INCENDIARIES" and accused them of attempting "to undermine our Institutions, regardless of the fatal consequences which must inevitably result from the prosecution of their nefarious plans." President Andrew Jackson pronounced that to receive an abolitionist publication was to "subscribe to this wicked plan of exciting the negroes to insurrection," a sentiment he repeated in his State of the Union address of that year.

Similar vigilante censorship took place in communities throughout the South, where as Susan Wyly-Jones has shown, slaves were most concentrated and the postal system was most full developed. These were also the regions where slaveholders expressed the unequivocal feeling in the white South that the agitation of the abolitionists would not be tolerated. It was a preemptive application of the lessons learned from the West Indies and the Edwards thesis.[103]

In December of that same year, the freshman congressman James Henry Hammond of South Carolina moved that the House should reject the petition of William Jackson of Massachusetts for the abolition of slavery in the District of Columbia. This was a significant departure from past precedent, when such petitions were accepted into committee only to be quietly silenced. But the events of the past summer made southern representatives such as Hammond quite concerned with the emboldened movement in the North. Hammond accused the abolitionists and their congressional supporters of attempting to "excite a servile insurrection [through] their meetings, publications, lectures, and missions," and his motion represented

---

103. Proceedings of the Citizens of Charleston on the Incendiary Machinations, Now in Progress Against the Peace and Welfare of the Southern States (Charleston: A. E. Miller, 1835), 8; Andrew Jackson to Amos Kendall, August 9, 1835 in John Spencer Bassett, ed., *Correspondence of Andrew Jackson*, 6 vols. (Washington, DC: Carnegie, 1926–33), 5:360–61 quoted in Clement Eaton, *The Freedom of Thought Struggle in the Old South*, rev. ed. (1940; New York: Harper, 1964), 201; Susan Wyly-Jones, "The 1835 Anti-Abolition Meetings in the South: A New Look at the Controversy over the Abolition Postal Campaign" *Civil War History* 47 (2001): 300–302.

the first step in the establishment of the "gag rule" that stifled most discussions of slavery, at least in the halls of Congress, until the late 1840s.[104]

The insurrections of 1831 brought the Anglo-Atlantic world to a moment of divergence. The rebellion in Jamaica moved British abolitionists toward immediate emancipation, and within the next year they had ended West Indian slavery. For American abolitionists, British abolition was a tremendous inspiration. It gave them clear evidence that the path of moral suasion could work, and they immediately stepped up their efforts to persuade the American people that slavery was a great national sin that demanded abolition. The British success also alerted white southerners to the perils that abolitionism posed. Professor Dew had spoken too soon. Not only had abolitionism caused another insurrection, it had also led the British Parliament to act on its "philanthropic zeal." Slaveholders had a far larger hand in American politics than the nascent abolitionist movement, though, and after witnessing William Lloyd Garrison and Nat Turner, and then Sam Sharpe and British abolition, they were more motivated than ever before to exert their power and quash the discussion of slavery.

104. Remarks of Mr. Hammond of South Carolina on the Question of Receiving Petitions for the Abolition of Slavery in the District of Columbia (Washington, [DC]: Duff Green, 1836), 12; William Lee Miller, *Arguing About Slavery: The Great Battle in the United States Congress* (New York: Knopf, 1996), 27–35.

PART II

The Lessons of Abolition

5

The Conversion of
William Ellery Channing

The reformers who created the American Antislavery Society waited for the news of British abolition before calling their first meeting in August 1833. William Lloyd Garrison had just returned from London, crowned by his presence at the blessed act, to write in stirring cadences the "Declaration of Sentiments" that boldly announced plans to agitate for immediate abolition. American antislavery proponents hoped to seize the momentum as their audience would read this provocative news from Britain and ponder the future of slavery in the United States. It seemed to be the ideal moment to embark upon the great project of convincing the American people that slavery was wrong and that it should be abolished.[1]

The second half of the 1830s saw important publications on West Indian emancipation by American abolitionists such as William Jay, James Thome, and Horace Kimball, which built upon the work of Lydia Maria Child. These authors offered an optimistic portrayal of the postemancipation West Indies which complemented the immediatist agenda of American abolitionism. But for most white Americans, the question of slavery was fraught with difficulty, and some did not give the issue much thought until the 1850s. Beyond those willing to engage in violence to stymie abolitionist agitation, those sympathetic to antislavery opinion exhibited a broad

---

1. Gilbert H. Barnes, *The Anti-Slavery Impulse, 1830–1844* (New York: Harcourt, Brace and World, 1933), 48; James Brewer Stewart, *Holy Warriors: The Abolitionists and American Slavery,* rev. ed. (New York: Hill and Wang, 1997), 51. For an important analysis of the transnational dimensions of American abolitionism, see William Caleb McDaniel, "Our Country is the World: Radical American Abolitionists Abroad" (Ph.D. diss., Johns Hopkins University, 2006).

spectrum of attitudes, and most disagreed with radicals like Garrison. The *Lenox Massachusetts Eagle,* for example, a Whig paper published in the Berkshires, acknowledged the immorality of slavery but refused to endorse the immediatism of radical abolitionists.[2] Representative of this group was William Ellery Channing, the Unitarian minister from Rhode Island recognized by his contemporaries and historians as one of the seminal Christian thinkers of his time. Channing's first contribution to the slavery debate in 1835 illuminated the ambiguity of conservative northerners who admired antislavery principles but disliked abolitionist tactics. In less than a decade, however, the example of British West Indian emancipation convinced Channing that the abolition of slavery was entirely safe and essential to the moral stature of the United States. Moreover, his conversion to abolitionism was well publicized through seven pamphlets he wrote on the slavery question from 1835 until his last public address at a First of August celebration in Lenox in 1842. Antislavery sentiment in the North became an increasingly important factor in American politics during these years, especially within the northern Whig party in which Channing was influential, and while it is difficult to chart with precision the sources of this change, this chapter argues that emancipation in the British West Indies was an important factor, evident in Channing's conversion and those who he, in turn, converted.[3]

WILLIAM ELLERY CHANNING, THE WEST INDIES, AND THE PROBLEM OF EMANCIPATION

Born in 1780 in Newport, Rhode Island, William Ellery Channing made his first mark upon the American public in 1819 with his famous explication of "Unitarian Christianity" at the ordination of Jared Sparks in Baltimore. New England Unitarians such as Channing had been quietly challenging Calvinistic doctrines like predestination and the trinity, and Baltimore was a bastion of Protestant orthodoxy. Channing embraced the

---

2. *Lenox Massachusetts Eagle,* June 4, 1835.

3. While occasionally noted, Channing's role in American abolitionism remains largely unexplored. His biographers include Arthur W. Brown, *Always Young for Liberty: A Biography of William Ellery Channing* (Syracuse: Syracuse University Press, 1956); Jack Mendolsohn, *Channing: The Reluctant Radical* (Westport, CT: Greenwood, 1971); and Andrew Delbanco, *William Ellery Channing: An Essay on the Liberal Spirit in America* (Cambridge: Harvard University Press, 1981).

opportunity of Sparks's ordination to put forth his New England faith to the entire nation. He rejected belief in the trinity and asserted the power of human reason to interpret the scriptures and God's revelation. Orthodox ministers responded to Channing's "Baltimore sermon," as it came to be known, with a slew of pamphlets that bolstered his reputation throughout the country. As Calvinism was generally on the wane, Channing grew to be considered a leading moral philosopher.[4]

While prolific, Channing wrote nothing on the problem of slavery until 1835. But he had seen slavery firsthand, and he had pondered its moral implications. As a young graduate of Harvard in 1794, he had worked as a tutor in Richmond, Virginia, for the children of David Randolph, a prominent slaveholder and U.S. Marshal for Virginia. With the Randolphs Channing was exposed to the Virginia aristocracy; he met national figures such as Chief Justice John Marshall and for the first time moved in Jeffersonian circles. He enjoyed Richmond, and he was charmed by southern society. It intrigued him that Virginia men addressed each other by their Christian names. He was impressed by their "familiarity and frankness" and attributed its absence in the North to the "avarice and ceremony" that fostered the "cold" and "unfeeling" New England character. To be sure, he found "great vices" in Richmond but "greater virtues" than he had left in New England.[5]

In Channing's mind the greatest of Virginia's vices was slavery. Like many northern visitors, he was curious about slavery. He participated in the distribution of the slaves' weekly rations; he visited the Randolph's slave quarters and was once left in charge of the domestic slaves when the Randolphs were away. It was not the physical suffering of slavery that appalled Channing but its moral dimensions. He believed that as a slave, the laborer was forced "to substitute" the master's "will" for his or her own, which robbed the individual of moral agency. Slavery thus violated the essential human right "of exerting the powers which nature has given us in the pursuit of . . . good." Slaves had no power to exert their own gifts in the com-

4. Brown, *Always Young,* 38–39; Daniel Walker Howe, *The Unitarian Conscience: Harvard Moral Philosophy, 1805–1861* (Cambridge: Harvard University Press, 1970), 17–20; David Brion Davis, *Challenging the Boundaries of Slavery* (Cambridge: Harvard University Press, 2003), 49–54.

5. William Henry Channing, ed., *Memoir of William Ellery Channing, with Extracts from his Correspondence and Manuscripts,* 2 vols. (Boston: W. Crosby and H. P. Nichols; London: J. Chapman, 1848), 60.

mon human effort to achieve good. The results of slavery could be seen in the "situation and character of the negroes of Virginia," which was so "degrading to humanity" that Channing felt pained to even write of it.[6]

Channing's experience in Virginia left dueling impressions of slave society which would long prohibit him from openly condemning the South even as its leaders defended slavery. On the one hand, slavery disgusted him, but, on the other, he found that he enjoyed the company of slaveholders. Channing left Richmond in 1800 when illness induced him to return home for rest. For a few years he maintained his ties to Virginia through a correspondence with Molly Randolph (David's wife), who was not at all happy to live among masters and slaves. When Gabriel's conspiracy terrified slaveholders soon after Channing had left, she sarcastically referred to "our boasted land of freedom," and expressed "great desire to quit the land of slavery altogether."[7] It seems likely that Channing often encountered such views as a young man in polite Virginian society. Robert McColley has demonstrated that the "gentlemen" of Jeffersonian Virginia often expressed antislavery views in the earshot of outsiders, while never actually considering abolition in conversation among themselves. In Virginia at the turn of the nineteenth century, slavery was a "necessary evil," not yet a "positive good." Jefferson himself had once considered plans for a gradual emancipation but never formally proposed them.[8] Channing with his Rhode Island accent was an outsider, and he later remembered that when he was in Virginia, many acknowledged slavery to be a "great evil," and that it was commonly spoke of "with abhorrence."[9] As he seldom returned in his writing to the subject of slavery until before the early 1830s, it seems likely that his time in Virginia left him with the hope that slavery would die a slow death. It did not, and when Channing again showed interest in slavery, British abolitionists had revived their movement in the West Indian colonies.

Channing's interest was renewed during a visit with his wife Ruth to

6. Ibid., 60–62.

7. Ibid., 61.

8. Robert McColley, *Slavery and Jeffersonian Virginia*, 2d ed. (Chicago: University of Illinois Press, 1973), 114–40. See also Paul Finkelman, *Slavery and the Founders: Race and Liberty in the Age of Jefferson* (Armonk, NY: M. E. Sharpe, 1996), 124–27; William W. Freehling, *The Road to Disunion: Secessionists at Bay, 1776–1854* (New York: Oxford University Press, 1990), 124–27.

9. William E. Channing, *A Letter to the Hon. Henry Clay, On the Annexation of Texas to the United States* in *The Works of William Ellery Channing, D.D.* (Boston: American Unitarian Association, 1878), 770.

the Danish island of St. Croix in the winter of 1831. He had always been sickly, and Ruth suffered from "rheumatic complaints" that year.[10] Like many other Americans then and now, the Channings decided that a vacation in the Caribbean might restore their health; those tropical breezes and the all-important escape from New England's winter might work to cure what ailed them. They stayed at Clifton Hall estate, a sugar plantation in a verdant valley in the center of the island. Channing brought along a fresh, empty journal, and he looked forward to some distance from the "noisy & busy world," as well as time away from his responsibilities as pastor to the Federal Street congregation in Boston. He reflected on the beauty of the Caribbean, where he "saw in the oceans & heavens, expressions & emblems of [God's] infinity." He found great pleasure in "the waving of the palms" and the "many new vegetables in the midst of winter." He "wanted no books and hardly needed thought to fill up the time." One does not expect such a discourse of relaxed contemplation to simply stop. But after one more entry on the second page describing the "universal, uniform growth of cane," the journal ends, the remaining pages left entirely blank.[11]

I suspect that at this moment Channing discovered the slaves whose labor made possible those fields of cane that dominated the St. Croix landscape. As had been true in Virginia, he felt a deep revulsion at encountering slavery again, and his analysis of its problems in the early 1830s shows remarkable consistency with what he thought as a young man at the turn of the century. The slaves' physical suffering did not appall him. To the contrary, he felt that the slaves' lives were "of a better quality than the peasantry of Europe generally enjoy" and he saw "no marks of the emaciation so often produced by care & toil in our own country." The degradation of the enslaved grew from living under a system that "generation after generation" doomed them to an animal existence that "extinguish[ed] their intellectual and moral nature."[12]

But Channing maintained hope. He saw in Danish St. Croix "a new

10. William E. Channing to Lucy Aikin, June 22, 1831, in Anna Letitia Le Breton, ed., *Correspondence of William Ellery Channing, D.D. and Lucy Aikin, from 1826 to 1842* (Boston, 1874), 71.

11. Santa Cruz Journal, William Ellery Channing Papers, Massachusetts Historical Society, Boston; *New York Antislavery Standard,* August 4, 1855. On nineteenth-century tourism in the Caribbean, see Frank Taylor, *To Hell with Paradise: A History of the Jamaican Tourist Industry* (Pittsburgh: University of Pittsburgh Press, 1993), 27–30.

12. Quotes are from William Ellery Channing to Rev. Dr. [Joseph] Tuckerman, January 15, 1831, Channing Papers. See also Channing to Ezra Gannett, May 5, 1831, Channing Papers; Channing to Lucy Aikin, December 29, 1831, Le Breton, *Correspondence,* 113.

spirit of humanity" that he ascribed to the abolitionist movement in Britain. For him, the awakening of British antislavery went beyond its tangible influence in the colonies. British actions had ramifications throughout the globe, and Channing believed he saw these changes as he observed the lives of slaves in St. Croix. He hoped the British influence would be felt in the United States.[13]

Channing's visit to St. Croix inspired a desire to act. He did not "blame the slaveholders alone" for the injustice of slavery. He implicated "the prosperous classes of society everywhere," in which he included himself. The wealthy ignored the poor, and left them to "live & die in a darkness and vice little inferior to the Slave's." This oppression of the many by the few was a condition of society that went beyond the boundaries of slave and free. If humanity were to progress, and he believed that it would, all people must be free to exercise the gifts God had granted them. "I should not shrink," he wrote, "from many of the toils which give one suffering in the cause of the *multitude* of our race." The "cause" reached well beyond the plight of America's slaves, but few in the nineteenth century envisioned such a broad scope of reform. Channing returned to a country on the cusp of long and bitter debate over slavery; fortunately for the cause, America's most prominent minister had recently awakened to the evils of slavery, ready to "toil" in the movement for its abolition.[14]

Channing returned from his winter in St. Croix to news of the revived agitation in Britain, and he was disturbed by the state of the "public mind" in the United States. "*You* are far in advance of us on this subject of slavery," he wrote his English friend Lucy Aikin, adding that when he pondered this state of affairs his "national pride die[d] within." Like many other Americans with antislavery leanings, Channing felt that the continuance of slavery in the United States placed the "foulest blot" upon the national character.[15]

Between his awakening in St. Croix and his first published contribution to the slavery debate in 1835, developments in the United States and

13. William E. Channing to Mrs. Kinder, [1831], Channing Papers. On slavery in St. Croix, see Neville A. T. Hall, *Slave Society in the Danish West Indies, St. Thomas, St. John, and St. Croix* (Baltimore: Johns Hopkins University Press, 1992).

14. Channing to Tuckerman, January 15, 1831; for Channing's belief in human progress see W. E. Channing to Henry Channing (his uncle), July 28, 1832, Channing Papers.

15. Channing to Lucy Aikin, August 27, 1831, Le Breton, *Correspondence*, 84. For more of the same sentiments, see Channing to Mrs. Sedgewick, February 11, 1832, Channing Papers.

Britain continued to grate upon his sense that the country needed moral regeneration. He considered the gradual abolition debates of 1831 in the Virginia legislature "the most interesting & important event in the history of our country."[16] But the nullification movement that followed threatened "civil war," and while he expressed relief at its closure, he feared that the "danger of disunion" had not been removed. Channing saw too much difference between the North and the South for the union to be maintained. "Our southern brethren," he lamented, felt no dishonor in being "taskmasters to slaves" and held northerners in contempt as "heirs to the vices of the roundheads." Abolitionist agitation continued in Britain, however, and Channing found hope in its transatlantic influence. "Perhaps you are to give us emancipation," he prodded Aikin in May 1833. "Set up an African empire in the West Indies, & you will break the chain here."[17] While such a prediction was surely exaggeration, it indicates the possibilities he placed in the British example.

Hope did not salve Channing's conscience. The news of Britain's imminent abolition in August 1833 came less than two years after his winter in St. Croix and moved him to reflect upon the state of the slavery question in the United States. "I have long seen & lamented the want of moral feeling with us on this greatest evil in our country," he wrote his friend and fellow minister Ezra Gannett from his summer home in Newport. But with British abolition, Channing felt "more ashamed of our country, & more alive to its deep guilt, than I have ever been before." He drew no comfort from American reform movements. He regarded the American Colonization Society with "suspicion," fearing it never intended to abolish slavery and that its only real effect was to suppress "true moral feeling" on slavery. He had no personal connection to the abolitionist movement, and he believed that its leaders were "rash men," who lacked "calmness and wisdom." Nevertheless, the abolitionists had adopted "great principles" and Channing argued that it was the responsibility of "enlightened & respectable" men such as himself and Gannett to support their efforts. If this were to occur, Channing believed that Christians in the South would be awakened to the wrongs of slavery. British abolition would contribute to a "resurrection of the [Christian] spirit on this subject," but he feared that it would first cross the Atlantic "in the form of fanaticism." All the more

16. Ibid.
17. Channing to Lucy Aikin, May 30, 1833, Channing Papers.

reason, Channing argued, for respected men to support the abolitionist cause.[18]

Gannett's thoughtful response offered Channing little room for optimism. Gannett had long supported the Colonization Society, and he argued that any censure the society passed upon the abolitionists must be seen as a response to their "unscrupulous warfare." Garrison was "the most dangerous" person in the country, and Gannett warned his friend that in light of the nullification movement, "plain language" would divide the union, leaving northern men utterly powerless to influence opinion in the South. As for the British example, Gannett felt it hardly mattered. He reminded Channing that Parliament's relation to the colonies had little in common with the relation between the North and the South. While Britons could agitate and demand that Parliament abolish slavery in the West Indian colonies, it would be practically impossible for northerners to overcome slaveholding interests in Congress. If New England Christians were to do any good, Gannett argued, "they must be prudent, slow, & solicitous not to provoke the slave-holders." Abolitionist tactics were counterproductive. Southerners would not listen.[19]

Channing's *Slavery* did not appear until the autumn of 1835, and it seems probable that Gannett's advice slowed his inclination to write. The summers of 1834 and 1835, however, had seen a rash of antiabolitionist violence that moved Channing to lend his qualified support to the "persecuted" abolitionists. In his introduction to the book, he cited the "bewildering excitement" of the times. The country was "convulsed by the question of slavery," a state of affairs that required the assertion of "great principles" by the leaders of society.[20]

Channing hoped to bridge the gap between antislavery-minded Christians throughout the country and the radical abolitionists. The early chap-

18. William Ellery Channing to Ezra Gannett, August 6, 1833, Channing Papers. See Channing to Lucy Aikin, August 30, 1833, Le Breton, *Correspondence*, 181, for Channing's hope for British influence.

19. Ezra Gannett to William Ellery Channing, August 21, 1833, Channing Papers. Gannett stayed true to this opinion for the next twenty years, changing his mind only in 1854 with the rendition of Anthony Burns. See Albert J. Von Frank, *The Trials of Anthony Burns: Freedom and Slavery in Emerson's Boston* (Cambridge: Harvard University Press, 1998), 270–276.

20. William E. Channing, *Slavery* (Boston: James Munroe, 1835), 143. For another account of the circumstances surrounding the publication of *Slavery*, see Brown, *Always Young*, 227–31.

ters laid out in clear, inspired prose his argument for the immorality of slavery as he had conceived it since his first experiences in Virginia. The great sin of slavery lay in its suppression of the human spirit, the violation of essential "human rights" that God bestowed on every individual. But unlike most abolitionist attacks on slavery, there were no vivid descriptions of cruelty or whipping, no analogies of the South to a great brothel, and no personal blame cast upon the slaveholder. Furthermore, Channing had harsh words for the abolitionists. While he rejected southern accusations that abolitionists would instigate "servile wars," he condemned the harsh rhetoric of abolitionist newspapers and the divisive enmity they inspired from the South. As Gannett had suggested, Channing's language was prudent and solicitous to the slaveholder, but he left no doubt that slavery violated God's will and must be abolished.[21]

Channing insisted, however, that the details of abolition be left to the slaveholders, a stance that set him apart from other opponents of slavery. Radical reformers such as Garrison never formulated any actual plans for abolition. Like Channing, they saw slavery as a sin, but they insisted on its immediate abolition with no West Indian–like apprenticeship and no financial compensation to slaveholders. To continue to own slaves, the immediatist argument went, violated God's will in a manner unacceptable to any Christian. Channing did not accept such logic, and he believed it necessary to look to the future peace of society in the consideration of emancipation. Channing argued that only slaveholders possessed the "intimate knowledge of the character and habits of the slaves" and that any plans of emancipation must take such knowledge into account. He denied any "right of interference" for nonslaveholders, arguing that the dangers of emancipation would be immeasurably heightened if the slaves were to perceive that their masters had been coerced to emancipate by a "foreign hand." Channing placed the greatest importance upon the relationship between the former masters and the former slaves, arguing that it was imperative for the freed slave to see his former master as his "benefactor and deliverer."[22]

The emancipation that had begun in the British West Indies in August of the previous year provided the context for Channing's argument. In his estimation, this "experiment" presented a worst-case scenario because it

21. Channing, *Slavery*, 8.
22. Ibid., 116. On the immediatist argument, see Stewart, *Holy Warriors*, 46–47.

had been imposed by Parliament, a "foreign hand," upon the planters who had protested "with a pertinaciousness bordering on insanity." Channing cautiously hoped for success in the West Indies, but he feared the outcome. The planters had done nothing to prepare the slaves for liberty, instead frustrating them with their unwillingness to concede immediate freedom. The planters' behavior taught the slaves to "look abroad" for relief and to see their masters as "obstacles" to emancipation instead of "benefactors." If emancipation were to fail, Channing wrote, the fault would lie with the planters.[23]

Despite his doubts about the prospect of West Indian emancipation, Channing advocated a plan clearly inspired by the British apprenticeship system. In an echo of British gradualism, he directly rejected the immediatist position, arguing that the slave should not "be immediately set free from his present restraints." Channing asserted that every individual was obligated to the community, which in turn, naturally sought to insure the safety and the well-being of all. In the event of a general slave emancipation, communities in the South would be justified in putting any "restraints" upon the freed people that they deemed necessary in order to insure the safety and well-being of all citizens. Furthermore, Channing argued that even while the relation of master and slave must cease, the obligation of the slave to work did not. He did not even alter the appellation of the people who were to be freed: "The slave should not . . . be allowed to wander at his will beyond the plantation on which he toils." By the same rationale that justified compelling the vagrant in other communities to work, former slaves should be forced to labor if "rational and natural motives" did not provide adequate inducement. Such obligations had to be monitored, and Channing suggested the creation of an "official authority," similar to the special magistrate of the apprenticeship system, who would be charged with preparing the freed people for "personal freedom."

The British act of emancipation had called for religious instruction; so too did Channing. He advised the establishment of schools for religious instruction that would enable the slave to feel his accountability to God, and thus make him "fit for freedom." Religious instruction would also cultivate a new "relation between the races" that would benefit southern society. Whites would be the teachers and thus the patrons of the black population. In closing his proposed plan of emancipation, Channing emphasized

23. Ibid., 117–18.

that he wanted no "violent changes" but asked only that the slaveholders employ their "intelligence, virtue and power" to end "this greatest of moral evils and wrongs." As the British plan of apprenticeship had been a compromise that pleased few, so too was Channing's plan a compromise that neither the abolitionists nor the nullifiers of 1835 would have accepted.[24]

Channing was one of the first public intellectuals to contribute to the slavery debate, and, according to the remembrances of the abolitionist Samuel J. May, his book "caused a great sensation." Garrison learned of *Slavery's* publication from an excerpt, printed in the *Christian Register,* that he considered "singularly weak." Still, he was anxious to read it. When he did, he was outraged and fired off to Henry Benson an angry note denigrating *Slavery* as an "inflated, inconsistent and slanderous production."[25] Not all agreed. Ellis Gray Loring told Garrison that he considered Channing's treatise the most articulate expression of the "philosophy of antislavery" that he had ever read. He considered Channing's censure of the abolitionists unfortunate but agreed with "19/20ths" of the book. Mary Clark of Concord thought Channing's work would do "immense good" for the antislavery cause.[26] The *Boston Recorder* opined that *Slavery* would become the "rallying point" for people throughout the country, excepting "ultra abolitionists" and the "fanatical" defenders of slavery.[27] At least four pamphlets were written in direct reply to Channing, and some of these received their own responses from his defenders.[28] Southern spokesmen cited Channing as part of the northern betrayal of the Constitution, and Thomas Cooper, the old radical of South Carolina, advised the young congressman James

24. Ibid., 116, 119, 126–27.

25. Samuel J. May, *Recollections of the Antislavery Conflict* (Boston: Fields and Osgood, 1869), 175; Garrison to Henry E. Benson, December 5 and 10, 1835. See also Garrison to Samuel J. May, December 5, 1835; Garrison to Amos Phelps, December 16, 1835; Garrison to Lewis Tappan, December 17, 1835, all in Merrill, ed., *Letters of Garrison,* 1:569, 572, 574, 577, 581.

26. Ellis Gray Loring to Garrison, December 5, 1835; Mary Clark to Francis Jackson, January 9, 1836, both in Garrison Papers, Antislavery Manuscripts, Boston Public Library, Boston, MA.

27. *Boston Recorder,* December 18, 1835.

28. [James Trecothick Austin], *Remarks on Dr. Channing's Slavery, by a Citizen of Massachusetts* (Boston: Russell and Shattuck, 1835); George Frederick Simmons, *Review of the Remarks on Dr. Channing's Slavery, by a citizen of Massachusetts* (Boston: J. Munroe, 1836); *Reply to the Reviewer of the Remarks on Dr. Channing's Slavery* (Boston: John Eastburn, 1836); Minot Pratt, *A Friend of the South in Answer to Remarks on Dr. Channing's Slavery* (Boston: Otis and Broaders, 1836).

Henry Hammond not to concern himself with Channing's stature and to borrow Calhoun's copy of James Austin's *Reply* as a valuable source for slavery's defense.[29] Channing made waves, and as reports on emancipation in the West Indies continued to change his thinking about abolition, he would keep the country informed and push the North to act on its "duty" to finally do something about the great sin of American slavery.

THE POLITICAL PRESS AND
THE POSTEMANCIPATION WEST INDIES

Channing's interest in emancipation in the British West Indies was part of a national phenomenon that cut across the partisan divide. In his second report on emancipation, Thomas Ritchie of the *Richmond Enquirer* reprinted without comment the opinion of the *Daily National Intelligencer,* a Whig organ, that West Indian emancipation "naturally renders that part of the world a scene of deep interest ... to every class of American citizens."[30] Virginians who had recently advocated gradual emancipation in their own state could now witness a similar process in the British Caribbean. American abolitionists and their sympathizers hoped to observe the fruits of abolitionist effort, while fiery nullifiers cynically awaited disaster. Americans of every political stripe looked to the West Indies, making press descriptions of emancipation an essential factor in the development of public opinions on slavery in the United States.

Readers of American newspapers in the summer and fall of 1834 would have believed that the nullifiers were confirmed in their expectations. Through the end of 1834, American newspapers continued to exaggerate accounts of violence in the West Indies. September saw riots in Trinidad and rebellion in Montserrat, St. Kitts, and Essequibo. In Barbados the planters formed a "strong rural police force" that waited anxiously for revolt, and one planter in Jamaica warned that the island would soon revert to "wilderness."[31] Early in October the *Charleston Mercury* reported "se-

29. Thomas Cooper to James Henry Hammond, January 8, 1836 and February 12, 1836, James Henry Hammond Papers, Library of Congress, Washington, DC, reel 2.

30. *Richmond Enquirer,* September 6, 1834; *Washington (DC) Daily National Intelligencer,* September 5, 1834.

31. *Lynchburg Virginian,* September 8, 1834; *Warren (RI) Northern Star and Constitutionalist,* September 6, 1834; *Richmond Enquirer,* September 5 and 6, 1834; *Newport Mercury,* September 6, 1834; *Boston Courier,* September 11, 1834; *New York Morning Courier and Enquirer,* September 5, 1834; *Baltimore Patriot and Mercantile Advertiser,* September 8, 19 and 24, 1834.

rious disturbances" in all the islands, the *Boston Courier* detailed a rash of arsons, and the *Baltimore Patriot* described the condition of Jamaica as "feverish and unsettled."[32] Toward the end of November, news of more riots hailed from Port of Spain, Trinidad, where a thousand apprentices had reportedly torn down the jail and rescued a prisoner. The mob was dispersed by British troops and the *Port of Spain Gazette* denounced emancipation as "ruinous to the planters."[33] The year closed with accounts of arson in Savannah-la-mar, Jamaica, several reprintings of the *Kingston Chronicle's* account of a rebellion on the north coast of Jamaica, and news that the violence might spread beyond the British West Indies. In the words of a worried Martinique planter, the Caribbean was a "part of the world [where] we live upon volcanoes."[34] These early accounts of the postemancipation West Indies appeared in newspapers that cut across sectional and party lines, cultivating a deep skepticism of black emancipation.

As the first months of freedom passed, there were no insurrections on the scale that had previously occurred in the Caribbean. Fear of bloody revenge however, was not the only obstacle that American abolitionists faced. Economic arguments supporting slavery had been the most obdurate barrier for abolitionists in Britain and had only been overcome through the compromise of financial compensation for the planters and the apprenticeship system. The predominant view on both sides of the Atlantic held that blacks were lazy, which substantiated for most whites the planters' defense of slavery. Abolitionists, however, predicted that societies emancipated from slavery were morally and economically superior. British abolitionists had assured West Indian planters that freedom would produce more sugar than slavery ever had, and, beginning in August 1834, their predictions would be tested in the great "laboratory of freedom."[35] The abolition of slavery in the British West Indies was a compelling story for American newspaper editors, and reports on the workings of gradual emancipation created for their readers a portrait of free black labor that would become increasingly important in the national debate over slavery.

32. *Charleston Mercury,* October 3, 1834; *Boston Courier,* October 30, 1834; *Baltimore Patriot and Mercantile Advertiser,* October 9, 1834.

33. *Baltimore Patriot and Mercantile Advertiser,* November 8, 14, 1834; *Charleston Mercury,* November 20, 1834.

34. *Newport Mercury,* December 27, 1834; *Lenox Massachusetts Eagle,* December 16, 1834, *Baltimore Patriot and Mercantile Advertiser,* December 23, 1834; *Boston Recorder,* January 2, 1835.

35. Seymour Drescher, *The Mighty Experiment: Free Labor versus Slavery in British Emancipation* (New York: Oxford University Press, 2002), 7.

On September 6, 1834, the *John W. Carter* arrived in New York's harbor with news from Jamaica about the first two weeks of emancipation. An unnamed New York paper assembled a report that the apprentices had been peaceful ever since the first of August but that recently in the parish of St. Ann's they had "refused . . . to perform their assigned labor."This report spread through the country, appearing in newspapers in Boston, Providence, and Lynchburg, Virginia. A few days later, the *Amulet* arrived in Alexandria, Virginia, from Barbados with news dating to the twenty-second of August. The *Alexandria Gazette* reported that while "everything remained as yet perfectly quiet . . . a considerable inclination to idleness" had been exhibited by the laborers of the island. This news spread to papers in Lynchburg, Richmond, and eventually New Orleans.[36]

The *Boston Courier* of September 29 reprinted an anonymous letter dated Antigua, August 30, which revealed the uncertainty among white West Indians after the fear of rebellion had passed. The writer was "happy to state" that the day of emancipation itself had been tranquil and that the island continued to be calm. The laborers, however, had not "worked so regularly as was confidently expected," and many were asking for wages that planters could not afford. This was worrisome, as the writer believed that the colony's wealth, even its "existence as a portion of the civilized world" depended on the success of free black labor. At present, however, everything was stable, and the writer believed that the experiment with black freedom would end "beneficially." It was the "least of two evils," he declared, between "six years of apprenticeship, or unconditional freedom, we have chosen the least."[37]

Many reports were not so hopeful. In October 1834 the *Charleston Mercury* and the *Boston Courier* carried a report gleaned from the *Norfolk Beacon*. The *Beacon* had obtained the *Cornwall Courier* of September 24 from the British brig *Victor*, which had recently arrived from Falmouth, Jamaica. The *Beacon* noted several accounts of arson and printed a letter from a frustrated planter in Montego Bay. The apprentices were only performing "one fourth of their former labor," and the special magistrates showed undue favor to the workers. This weakened the planters' control over their labor force and threatened the viability of sugar planting.[38] In December

36. *Boston Courier,* September 8, 1834; *Newport Mercury,* September 13, 1834; *Lynchburg Virginian,* September 15, 1834; *Richmond Enquirer,* September 19, 1834; *New Orleans Bee,* October 3, 1834.

37. *Boston Courier,* September 29, 1834.

38. *Charleston Mercury,* October 15, 1834; *Boston Courier,* October 30, 1834.

of 1834 the *Newport Mercury* printed a report from the *Kingston Chronicle,* which told of an estate with more than four hundred apprentices who had refused to work past six o'clock ever since emancipation. As a result, the estate's earlier yield of thirty hogsheads of sugar per week during the sugar harvest was now down to one.[39]

From New England to South Carolina, the dominant portrayal of the freed West Indies in the political press was overwhelmingly negative. Of the forty-six newspaper reports examined from the moment of emancipation through 1835, only seven characterized emancipation as a success.[40] The *Newport Mercury* reported in January 1835 that threats of arson caused the governor of Jamaica to deploy troops throughout the island. In April of that year the *Charleston Mercury* reviewed an article from the British journal *Blackwood's Magazine* that condemned the apprenticeship system. Black West Indians were now subject to "military flogging" that was no kinder than the whippings their masters had dispensed. In Jamaica there was the "incessant [sound] of insurrection," and the refusal of the apprentices to labor doomed the island to the "savage anarchy" of Haiti. In May both the *Boston Courier* and the *Charleston Mercury* copied a report from the *Norfolk Beacon,* which had taken its assessment from the *St. George's Chronicle* of Grenada. The apprenticeship system in Grenada appeared a total failure, with most estates producing only half of what they produced under slavery. The island's entire crop was expected to be two thousand hogsheads of sugar less than the average of the previous ten years. The news was the same in November when *Niles' Register* of Baltimore and the *Newport Mercury* carried accounts that the apprentices in Barbados were "lazy and insolent," while those of Jamaica were "becoming more licentious and corrupt" with every day of freedom.[41] By the end of 1835, the newspapers'

39. *Newport Mercury,* December 13, 1834. See also *Warren (RI) Northern Star and Constitutionalist,* December 13, 1834. Other reports portraying the "idleness" of the laborers include: *Lynchburg Virginian,* October 13, 1834; *Newport Mercury,* December 20, 1834; *Warren (RI) Northern Star and Constitutionalist,* December 6, 1834.

40. These reports were drawn from the following newspapers: *Baltimore Patriot and Mercantile Advertiser, Baltimore Niles' Register, Boston Courier, Boston Daily Evening Transcript, Charleston Mercury, Lenox Massachusetts Eagle, Lynchburg Virginian, New Orleans Bee, Newport Mercury, New York Morning Courier and Enquirer, Philadelphia Pennsylvanian, Richmond Enquirer, Richmond Whig and Public Advertiser, Warren (RI) Northern Star and Constitutionalist.* Positive reports of the postemancipation West Indies include: *Baltimore Patriot and Mercantile Advertiser,* August 28, 1834, and March 21, 1835; *Lenox Massachusetts Eagle,* September 11, 1834; *Newport Mercury,* January 31, March 21, and April 25, 1835; *Baltimore Niles' Register,* January 31, 1835.

41. *Newport Mercury,* January 24, 1835, November 28, 1835; *Charleston Mercury,* Feb-

vision of the postemancipation West Indies could never have convinced moderate northerners to abandon their fears of black emancipation. For the abolitionists, there was much to do.

AMERICAN ABOLITIONISTS AND
THE POSTEMANCIPATION WEST INDIES

On June 17, 1835, Elizur Wright, the corresponding secretary of the American Antislavery Society, asked the New York abolitionist judge William Jay to lend his assistance in challenging the negative portrayals of the emancipated British West Indies which permeated the American press. The society's annual meeting had resolved that agents should be employed to travel to "the British West Indian Islands & Hayti" in order to "collect & transmit to this country facts from official & unofficial sources relative to the condition of the colored population of those islands & the effect of the various systems of emancipation . . . upon the physical, agricultural, commercial, education & religious prosperity of the Inhabitants." As a prominent New York judge, a second-generation abolitionist, and the son of a founding father, the executive committee felt that Jay's stature in the nation would bestow a strong measure of authenticity to any report he produced. Where just two years before many abolitionists had been certain that British abolition would have a positive impact, it was now clear that the success of emancipation in the West Indies had yet to be demonstrated.[42]

But Jay demurred. He was an outspoken abolitionist and had already attracted the ire of white Americans who considered abolitionists to be little more than egotistical troublemakers. There was no question in Jay's mind that the information acquired on such a trip would be of great value

ruary 2, 1835, April 10, 1834, May 29, 1835; *Boston Courier,* May 28, 1835; *Baltimore Niles' Register,* November 28, 1835. Other negative portrayals include *Newport Mercury,* March 21, 1835, July 11 and 25, 1835; *Baltimore Niles' Register,* June 13, 1835, July 11, 1835; *New Orleans Bee,* May 18, 1835, July 20, 1835; *Charleston Mercury,* April 10, May 7, 1835; *Wilmington People's Press and Advocate,* January 7, 1835.

42. William Jay to Elizur Wright, July 2, 1835, Elizur Wright Papers, Library of Congress, Washington, DC. This shift in abolitionist tactics coincided with the nascent split within abolitionism between moderates and radicals that also stemmed from antiabolitionist violence. See James Brewer Stewart, "Peaceful Hopes and Violent Experiences: The Evolution of Reforming and Radical Abolitionism, 1831–1837," *Civil War History* 17 (December 1971): 305. For a similar request to write on the emancipated West Indies, see Robert H. Rose to James G. Birney, September 28, 1835, in Dwight L. Dumond, ed., *Let-*

to the abolitionist cause if it could be cogently argued and broadly disseminated. But he doubted that sending confirmed abolitionists to study emancipation would produce a report that would "be received with confidence
by the community." Jay believed that information of "a more official & au-
thentic character" could be acquired at less expense through the work of
British abolitionists and the official reports from Parliament.[43]

Jay envisioned a series of problems that would confront any American
abolitionist who sought to report on the postemancipation West Indies.
Being "strangers & foreigners," American abolitionists might find it difficult to acquire information, and if so, their report would be based entirely on "*hearsay* testimony." More importantly, the agents' identities as
abolitionists would hinder any report from achieving the avowed goal of
convincing American readers that emancipation in the West Indies was
successful. The report, Jay argued, "would be published by the A.A.S.S. &
would be presented to the public as an *abolition document* made by *abolition agents* paid for making it." Such a report "would be read by few
anti-abolitionists, & be believed by still fewer. The political newspapers
would not notice it, & the Southern post masters would suppress it." Jay
noted that British abolitionists were equally interested in the workings of
emancipation and had better access to intelligence from the West Indies,
which they would lay before Parliament as a part of their own program to
end the apprenticeship system. Jay argued that such information would
enter the United States in the traditional way, through the mainstream
newspapers. It would then become political news from Britain—not abolitionist propaganda—and would be "extensively circulated & read without
suspicion & prejudice."[44]

Jay's suggestions envisioned a more detailed study that could have
stemmed from what he himself had already done. His *Inquiry into the
Character and Tendency of the American Colonization Society, and American
Antislavery Societies* employed emancipation in the West Indies as a critical
element in his argument against gradualist approaches. As the title suggests, the *Inquiry* began with a lengthy discussion of what Jay saw as the
destructive hypocrisy of the ACS, grounded almost entirely in the society's
own publications. But the *Inquiry* was not simply an attack. Jay used the

---

ters of James Gillespie Birney, 1835–1857, 2 vols. (New York: D. Appleton-Century, 1938),
1:336–37.
    43. Jay to Wright, July 2, 1835.
    44. Ibid., emphasis in the original.

last seven chapters to demonstrate the safety, practicality, and good policy of the immediate abolition of slavery in the United States.[45]

Jay had read the early reports on West Indian emancipation, which demonstrated that the Edwardsian assumption of black emancipation as a chaotic process prone to violence was still predominant. He quoted the colonizationist Reverend Dr. Hawkes, who had argued that if the slaves were "let loose at once, they must of necessity . . . either beg or steal, or destroy and displace the whites." Employing the approach established by Lydia Maria Child, Jay arrayed evidence from throughout the Atlantic world to demonstrate the safety of emancipation. He cited the peaceful emancipations in Chile, Argentina, Colombia, Mexico, and the state of New York, but, as had Child, Jay understood that the "SCENES IN ST. DOMINGO" were still in the background of all discussions of slavery, and he expanded significantly on her argument against Edwards's pervasive views.[46]

While Child had avoided discussing the role of the free colored Ojé in the civil war that initiated the insurrection of the slaves in Saint-Domingue, Jay included this part of the story. He explained the origins of this war, which had been the starting point of Child's analysis and which Edwards had omitted entirely. Before the civil war, Ojé had led a delegation of Saint-Domingue's free coloreds to petition the National Assembly of Revolutionary France for the relaxation of the political disabilities imposed upon them. The National Assembly had responded with the ambiguously worded decree of March 8, 1791, which granted citizenship to "all free persons in the colonies" without specifying race. But as Jay pointed out, Ojé had specifically denied the intention to abolish slavery. In his letter to the Assembly of Saint-Domingue demanding the end of the legal strictures, Ojé had explicitly distinguished his demands from those who called for the abolition of slavery. He pledged that he "*would not have recourse to any raising of the slave gangs,*" and Jay noted that in his claims to the National Assembly, Ojé had never included the slaves in his demands for rights. The civil war had resulted from the refusal of Dominguan whites to acknowledge the rights of the free coloreds, and only with the war had the insurrection begun among the slaves. Emancipation had not *caused* the insurrection.[47]

45. William Jay, *Inquiry into the Character and Tendency of the American Colonization, and American Anti-Slavery Societies* in his *Miscellaneous Writings on Slavery* (1853; New York: Negro Universities Press, 1968), 167–206. *Inquiry* was first published in February 1835.

46. Ibid., 167–70.

47. Ibid., 172, italics in the original.

Moreover, Jay argued that the decree of May 15, 1791, which for Edwards had been the "brand by which the flames were lighted," had actually restored peace to the island in the wake of civil war. This decree had specifically granted rights to the free coloreds, and once this was done, "*the free blacks even assisted the planters in reducing to obedience their revolted slaves.*" The war quickly resumed, however, in consequence of an attempt on the part of the whites to disarm the free coloreds. Americans of Jay's generation would have remembered the next phase, when white refugees flooded American ports as the civil war widened and the revolt of the slaves intensified. But still, Jay noted, not a single slave had been freed—the chaos stemmed from the civil war. It was at this point that the British had invaded Saint-Domingue and tried to seize the island in the midst of the chaos and insurrection. Only now—and Jay quoted the eyewitness Bryan Edwards—did the French resort to "the desperate expedient of proclaiming all manner of slavery abolished." Just as Jay used the colonizationists' own words to expose their hypocrisy, he employed Edwards's own words to demolish the antiabolitionist argument of insurrection that Edwards had long ago constructed. The abolition of slavery in Saint-Domingue had been "an act of political expediency," not the result of abolitionist agitation and not the result of an insurrection of the slaves.[48]

Not only was abolition politically useful to Revolutionary France, it had also been highly beneficial for the peace and prosperity of Saint Domingue. Jay depended on the same voices as had Lydia Maria Child. He quoted from Malenfant, who had described the colony under Toussaint as a "flourishing" place where "the whites lived happily, and in peace upon their estates, and the negroes continued to work for them." He also cited Lacroix, James Barskett's *History of the Island of St. Domingo*, a "London periodical," testimony taken by the British Parliament in its investigations of the practicality of emancipation, and Haiti's exportation figures as reported in J. R. McCulloch's *Dictionary of Commerce and Commercial Navigation*, published in 1834.[49] All of these voices—official and publicly available—demonstrated that emancipation had been safe and beneficial for the former masters and the former slaves. Any violence had been the result of civil war, an unfortunate and misleading event in this highly contested history. From this broad evidential base, Jay argued that the "scenes of St. Domingo" should

48. Ibid., 172–74, italics in the original.
49. Jay's sources included: [Colonel] Malenfant, *Des Colonies, Particuliérement de celle de Saint-Domingue; Mémoire Historique et Politique* (Paris, Audibert, 1814); Pamphile de Lacroix, *Mémoir pour servir á l'histoire de la Révolucion de Saint-Domingue* (Paris, 1819); [James

not be recited by slaveholders but by abolitionists. They should be "constantly kept before the public as an awful and affecting memento of the justice due to the free blacks, and as a glorious demonstration of the perfect safety of immediate and unconditional emancipation." The Edwards thesis was a fraud.[50]

Jay then turned his attention to emancipation in the British West Indies. He did not approve of the gradualist apprenticeship system and attributed its inadequacy to two sources. First, he considered Parliament's desire to "conciliate the West India proprietors" morally unwarranted, and, secondly, his history of Saint-Domingue demonstrated that "apprehension of the danger of immediate emancipation" was based on historical fictions. Fortunately, Jay argued, the example of emancipation in the British West Indies and the dissimilarity between the politics of the United States and the British Empire nullified both of these obstacles to immediate emancipation in the United States.[51]

In the British West Indies, Jay argued, the divergent experiences of those colonies that chose immediate emancipation compared with those who adopted the apprenticeship system demonstrated the clear superiority of immediate emancipation. Despite the injustice of the apprenticeship, there was no violence in those colonies that chose to enforce it, which was especially encouraging because the black populations so far outnumbered the whites. The problem with the apprenticeship system was that "some have either refused to work, or accomplish much less than their appointed tasks." But this arose from the inability of the apprentice to fully enjoy "the fruits of his labor." While Jay did not cite Adam Smith, he was invoking the classic free labor argument against slavery that would become a central component of Republican ideology in the late 1850s. The lash had been abolished, but wages had not replaced it. Who could be surprised that this system did not work?[52]

In Bermuda and Antigua, where immediate emancipation was granted, the transition to free labor was far smoother than in places using the apprenticeship system. Jay quoted papers from both colonies which reported the "perfect regularity and quiet" in Bermuda and "the solemn and deco-

Barskett], *History of the Island of St. Domingo, from its First Discovery by Columbus to the Present Period* (London: Archibald Constable, 1818).

50. Jay, *Inquiry into the Character,* 176–86, quote on 177.

51. Ibid., 186.

52. Ibid., 187. Jay specifically mentioned the population statistics of Jamaica to emphasize the numerical preponderance of the black populations in the West Indies. There were

rous tranquility" in Antigua. Moreover, in the sugar island of Antigua, immediate emancipation had been a boon to the economy which boded well
for the staple economies of the South. He quoted entirely from Antiguan
sources. One Antiguan paper "[knew] of . . . *no gang of laborers in the island, which has not returned to its accustomed employment.*" Jay also quoted
from a letter from Antigua that appeared in "a Norfolk, [Virginia] paper,"
which reported the encouraging news that "*two sugar plantations have recently leased for as much as they were worth with the negroes included prior to
emancipation.*" It seemed "as if Providence had provided facts to refute every argument against abolition."[53]

   While Jay's analysis was probably convincing to some, the desire per-
sisted among American abolitionists to actually visit the West Indies and
offer an eyewitness report. In November 1836, the American Antislavery Society again resolved to send agents to the West Indies, and this time
there were volunteers—James Thome and Horace Kimball. Despite their
absence from most discussions of American abolitionism, Thome and Kimball hold a prominent place in the history of American reform as the first to
investigate the facts of emancipation.[54] Like the Channings in the winter
of 1831, Thome and Kimball had recently been ill, and they believed a visit
to the West Indies would be good for their health. But they had a higher
purpose as well, to bring home a report that would prove to the American
public that emancipation was safe, practical, and even profitable.

   We know little about Kimball. Before his journey to the West Indies,
he was the editor of the *Herald of Freedom,* an abolitionist newspaper published in Concord, New Hampshire. Kimball was really too sick for the
journey and died soon after he returned home, only twenty-five years old.
Thome was one of the first southerners to convert to abolitionism. He
hailed from a wealthy, slave-holding family in Kentucky and took part in
the antislavery debates at Lane Seminary in Ohio in the spring of 1834.
Thome joined the antislavery exodus to Oberlin College in the fall of 1835

331,000 slaves in Jamaica, and only 37,000 whites. On the free labor ideology of the Republican party, see Eric Foner, "The Idea of Free Labor in Nineteenth Century America," new
introduction to his *Free Soil, Free Labor, Free Men: The Ideology of the Republican Party Before
the Civil War* (1970; New York: Oxford University Press, 1995), ix–xxxix.

   53. Jay, *Inquiry into the Character,* 189–90, italics in the original.

   54. Exceptions are Barnes, *Anti-Slavery Impulse,* 138–39; Benjamin Quarles, *Black Abolitionists* (New York: Oxford University Press, 1969), 126; Louis Filler, *Crusade Against
Slavery: Friends, Foes, and Reforms, 1820–1860* (Algonac, MI: Reference Publications,
1986), 175.

and traveled the West as an antislavery agent during the summers. He lectured so often that he nearly lost his voice, and friends were concerned that if he were to continue speaking on the antislavery circuit the damage could be permanent. To study emancipation in the West Indies made good use of his prodigious energies.[55]

Thome and Kimball sailed from New York on November 31, 1836, and returned early in June the next year. The AAS published two versions of their *Emancipation in the West Indies,* both in 1838. A pamphlet version of 128 pages appeared as the seventh number of the *Anti-Slavery Examiner* and sold for twenty-five cents, while a much longer bound version sold for a dollar. Both read like travel literature, as the authors detailed the scenery, the ports, and the people they met. They structured their narrative in a manner clearly designed to advance the immediatist agenda of the society. The book discussed only three of the British West Indies: Antigua, Barbados, and Jamaica, with each island representing one of the "grand phases" of the "experiment" of emancipation. Antigua had foregone the apprenticeship system and represented "immediate emancipation" as radical abolitionists wished it to take place in the United States. Barbados represented the best working of the apprenticeship system, despite its injustice, while Jamaica represented the worst. Antigua led the narrative, and in the pamphlet version filled nearly half of the pages, while Barbados and Jamaica were given equal weight.[56]

Like much antislavery literature, *Emancipation in the West Indies* consisted primarily of testimony and description, substantiated with newspaper accounts and excerpts from official reports. The authors privileged evidence from whites, with planters, missionaries, special magistrates, and colonial governors supplying most of the testimony; they rarely interviewed the freed people. Such a choice is not surprising, as the authors hoped to show that emancipation did not result in the chaos described in so many American newspaper accounts. Readers such as Channing wanted to be assured that the social disruption of emancipation did not outweigh its positive consequences; the authors complied. They described, for example,

55. Barnes, *Anti-Slavery Impulse,* 45, 138–39, 263, n. 19; Barnes and Dumond, *Weld-Grimke Letters,* 1:149, n. 4; James A. Thome and J. Horace Kimball, *Emancipation in the West Indies. A Six Months' Tour in Antigua, Barbadoes, and Jamaica, in the Year 1837* (New York: American Anti-Slavery Society, 1838), 5.

56. Thome and Kimball, *Emancipation.* The title pages of both versions contain the same information.

a dinner they had with the governor and several resident planters in Antigua. One Colonel Jarvis declared that he had been in England when the Antiguan legislature had voted to forego the apprenticeship, but had he been in Antigua, he would have voted against the measure, believing then that the consequences of immediate emancipation would be disastrous. Now, however, he was happy the measure had prevailed, as "the evil consequences" that most had foreseen never materialized. Such testimony revealed the conversion of at least one former slaveholder that immediate emancipation had inaugurated.[57]

The most feared "evil consequence" was an insurrection, or a race war, that so many observers predicted would commence on August 1, 1834. Thome and Kimball addressed this problem by focusing on the moment of emancipation, the night of July 31. Their description of the eve of emancipation in Antigua became one of the most popular in abolitionist circles and was widely reprinted in newspapers and pamphlets until the Civil War. The Wesleyans throughout the island, they reported, kept a "watch-night" and assembled their congregations at their respective chapels.[58] According to the missionary at St. John's, the ceremony was planned so that the congregation would take to their knees when the clock began to strike. So it happened, that when the first bell tolled, the "immense" congregation "fell prostrate," and all was silent. When the twelfth bell tolled, lightning flashed in the sky, thunder roared, and the congregation "*burst*" into prayer and song. Calm followed, and the missionaries delivered addresses that explained "the nature of the freedom just received," exhorting the people to industry and obedience to the laws. The planters reported that when they went to the chapels where the people were assembled, "they shook hands with them, and exchanged the most hearty good wishes." Such a description emphasized the abolitionist conception of emancipation as an act of God by demonstrating that the freed people understood it as such, and that nature itself had signified the event with lightning and thunder. Attention to the hearty greetings among ex-masters and ex-slaves would have eased

57. Thome and Kimball, *Emancipation,* 10. Citations that follow refer to the more widely read pamphlet version.

58. The *watch-night* was an all-night prayer service held by Moravians and Methodists on special occasions, especially the New Year. The watch-night would have been deeply rooted in Antigua, as Moravian missionaries began to work there in 1756, followed by the Methodists who started a mission in the early 1760s. See chap. 1, 27–29, and Frank Baker, "Watch-Night," in *Historical Dictionary of Methodism,* ed. Charles Yrigoyen Jr. and Susan E. Warrick (Lanham, MD: Scarecrow Press, 1996), 220–21.

the concerns of the many who believed that slaves, when freed, would seek revenge upon masters who had oppressed them for so many generations. Also significant was the setting of this scene—in Antigua—where emancipation had been immediate. The authors did not include similar descriptions from Barbados or Jamaica, where emancipation had not been immediate and, presumably, God did not show such favor.[59]

Plantation tours further substantiated this vision of the calm transition to immediate freedom in Antigua. On their visit to "Millar's estate," which the previous year had produced the largest crop in the island, the authors were "kindly received" by a Mr. Bourne, the estate's manager, who led them on a tour of the plantation. At one point they came upon a group of laborers, women and men, who paused to greet them but immediately returned to their labor, "wielding their hoes with energy and effect." Bourne "kindly" addressed the laborers, telling them that the visitors came from America where there were still many slaves. Bourne appealed to the laborers to "be sober, industrious and diligent" so that American slaveholders could see the benefit of "freeing all their slaves." According to the authors, the laborers responded to each request with "Yes, massa" or "God bless de massas," and when the visitors prepared to leave, the laborers reportedly asked Thome and Kimball to comment on their "industry." The Americans replied that they were "much pleased," to which the people responded with a hearty "thankee, massa." Here was a scene of compliant, energetic, and polite black laborers at the command of a gentle white manager. The only difference between such a portrait of freedom and the slavery that had preceded it were the kindness of the manager and the absence of the whip. Blacks still labored in the fields, whites were still in command, emancipation had not turned the world upside down, but the sin of slavery was gone.[60]

In concluding their discussion of Antigua, Thome and Kimball argued not only that immediate emancipation had gone smoothly but also that this had occurred under extremely difficult circumstances that the South would not have to face. The South had "resident proprietors," while most

59. Ibid., 36–37. Examples of this scene reprinted include *Boston Recorder*, March 30, 1838, and *Providence Daily Journal*, August 1, 1838. At the First of August celebration in Troy, New York, in 1839 Daniel Payne read aloud to the audience this description of the moment of emancipation. See *New York Colored American*, September 28, 1839. These celebrations are discussed in greater detail in chapter 7.

60. Ibid., 9.

owners of Antiguan estates were absentees who lived in Britain. In the South there was a white majority, while in Antigua there were only 2,500 whites to 30,000 blacks. Perhaps most importantly, the South had the opportunity to choose emancipation while the "energies, the resources, the sympathies, and the prayers of the North, stand pledged to her assistance." To the contrary, white West Indians had been forced into emancipation by Parliament, a foreign power. For the authors and their abolitionist readers, the evidence from Antigua proved incontestably that immediate emancipation was safe and practicable.[61]

Thome and Kimball's discussions of Barbados and Jamaica aimed to show that the immediate emancipation in Antigua was superior to the gradual emancipation of apprenticeship and that the problems that arose in those islands came from the inconsistencies of the apprenticeship system. To be sure, gradual emancipation was better than slavery, and the transition had been just as peaceful in Barbados as in Antigua, with only slight disturbances in Jamaica.[62] Colonel Ashby of Barbados, for example, had felt only "unmingled hatred" for the abolitionists as they agitated for the abolition of colonial slavery, but the experience of emancipation had proved an "incalculable blessing." He personally had no problem in "managing his apprentices" and had only heard of difficulties when masters had been "intolerably passionate" in disciplining their laborers. Ashby professed not to fear "losing a single laborer" when full emancipation was scheduled to take place in 1840.[63] From the reformers' perspective, however, apprenticeship shared too much with slavery to be cause for celebration. The authors concluded that the system they witnessed in Barbadoes was only "something like freedom." The apprentice, after working nine hours of the day for his master, would be paid for any additional work he did. On receiving his pay, "he begins to have the feelings of a freeman." On Sunday, "he awakens . . . and is still free. He puts on his best clothes, goes to church, worships a free God, contemplates a free heaven, sees his free children around him . . . [and the] consciousness that he is a slave is quite lost in the thoughts of liberty . . . [but] *Monday morning he is startled from his dreams by the old 'shell blow' of slavery,* and he arises to endure another week of toil, alternated by the same tantalizing mockeries of freedom." Such back and forth between slavery and freedom made the apprenticeship system im-

61. Thome and Kimball, *Emancipation*, 6, 34.
62. Ibid., 55, 108.
63. Ibid., 62.

possible to endorse, especially when the shining example of Antiguan success was so clear.[64]

The antislavery response to *Emancipation in the West Indies* was ecstatic.
Governor Edward Everett of Massachusetts wrote that the "success" of
emancipation in the West Indies "*would seal the fate of slavery throughout
the civilized world.*" The Rev. Justin Edwards, president of the Andover
Theological Seminary, wrote that the "facts" in Thome and Kimball's work
showed that emancipation was "safe . . . [and] salutary to both classes of the
population," even when the "colored persons" outnumbered the whites ten
to one.[65] Neither of these men was an abolitionist, but both were opposed
to slavery in the abstract. Thome and Kimball's report on the safely emancipated West Indies bolstered their antislavery beliefs.

THE CONVERSION OF WILLIAM ELLERY CHANNING

William Ellery Channing paid close attention to the evolving portrait of
emancipation in the West Indies. He regarded Thome and Kimball's report as "the most important work" that had yet been published in the antislavery cause. He drew particular attention to the "trust-worthy" sources of
testimony from island elites and the fact that their names were included,
making the facts verifiable. As John Adams had observed, "facts are stub-
born things," and it was the facts, Channing wrote, that the South would
have to scrutinize, for they directly contradicted the impression of "many
well-disposed people, both North and South" that emancipation would result in "massacre and universal misrule."[66] Channing approved of Thome
and Kimball's work but did not yet change his own opinion on emancipation in the United States.

64. Ibid., 84, emphasis in original.
65. [Edward] Everett to Edmund Quincy, April 29, 1838 reprinted in *Correspondence
between the Hon. F. H. Elmore, One of the South Carolina Delegation in Congress and James G.
Birney, One of the Secretaries of the American Anti-Slavery Society* (New York: American
Anti-Slavery Society, 1838), 55. Justin Edwards to J. G. Birney, June 16, 1838 in Dumond,
ed., *Letters of Birney*, 407, n. 4. Another study of the Free West Indies to appear in 1838
was Sylvester Hovey, *Letters from the West Indies: Relating especially to the Danish Island of
St. Croix, and to the British Islands Antigua, Barbadoes and Jamaica* (New York: Gould and
Newman, 1838). For a positive, comparative review of the work of Thome and Kimball, and
of Hovey, which favors the latter, see "Emancipation in the West Indies," *Quarterly Christian Spectator* 10 (August 1838): 440–68.
66. Channing to the editor of the *Christian Register and Observer*, in *Correspondence between the Hon. F. H. Elmore*, 55.

The gradual shift in Channing's opinion can be seen in the final pamphlets of his long career, in which he declared West Indian emancipation a complete success and American slavery a national disgrace. On August 1, 1837, the third anniversary of West Indian emancipation, Channing published an open letter to Whig leader Henry Clay on the annexation of Texas. Citing Benjamin Lundy's *War in Texas*, Channing argued that the Texas revolution of 1835 was hardly the echo of 1776 that the supporters of annexation claimed it to be but was instead the project of slaveholders and land speculators. To annex Texas would bolster the influence of slavery in the United States, a result contrary to Channing's desire to rid his country of the "great evil." Channing agreed with Whigs such as John Quincy Adams who lambasted annexation as a rotten gift to the slave power, but Channing's concerns extended to the relationship between the United States and the rest of the "civilized world." He argued that Britain's various interests in the region militated against the expansion of the slaveholding United States. Britain's abolition of slavery demonstrated the "progress of civilization and a purer Christianity" that was utterly opposed to the ideas manifested in the Texan revolution. He argued that the position of the West Indian archipelago between the Atlantic and the Gulf of Mexico would lead to "cruel, ferocious conflicts" between the slaveholding South and the British West Indies if Texas were to be annexed to the United States. He believed that the islands were destined to be the "nurseries of civilization and freedom to the African race," a clear departure from the fears of emancipation he had expressed in 1835. Britain's empire of freedom, which had just begun to bear fruit, might soon clash with the American empire of slavery. Channing trembled at the thought.[67]

Two years later, Channing's *Remarks on the Slavery Question*, though addressed to his friend Jonathan Phillips, actually responded to a speech Clay had given in February 1839 on the reception of abolitionist petitions. Clay's speech was part of his canvas for the Whig presidential nomination, intended, no doubt, to shore up support in the Deep South. It was the second time that Channing had addressed Clay publicly. As national leader of the Whigs and long-time president of the American Colonization Society, it seems likely that Clay represented for Channing one of the last hopes of convincing southerners of the immorality of slavery. Most political abolitionists were Whigs, and the dedication to colonization of

67. William Ellery Channing, *A Letter to the Hon. Henry Clay, on the Annexation of Texas to the United States*, [1837], in *Works*, 763–65.

friends like Ezra Gannett showed Channing that perhaps there was some benevolence among colonizationists.[68] But in his 1839 address, Clay argued that American slavery would be perpetual. For him, the "principal" cause of U.S. abolitionist agitation had been British abolition. American abolitionists had mistaken the federal government for the British Parliament, and they were utterly deluded about the possibility of American abolition. Moreover, Clay had "fearful forebodings of a disastrous termination" of emancipation in the West Indies and warned that abolition in the South "would end in the extermination or subjugation of one race or the other." He had returned to the Edwards thesis. John Calhoun was overjoyed with Clay's speech, and Channing correctly recognized Clay's effort as a "herald of peace" between southern moderates and proslavery diehards like Calhoun. But for Channing, it was "a summons to new conflict," for *he* would now join with the abolitionists.[69]

Clay's assertions, Channing argued, should awaken the North to its moral responsibility as a part of a nation that supported slavery. He noted that the slave markets of Washington, D.C., were daily witnessed by "foreign ministers," whose "reports of us determine our rank in the civilized world." He discussed the 1793 fugitive slave clause in the Constitution which made citizens of the North partly guilty for the crime of slavery. Foreshadowing Thoreau's *On Civil Disobedience,* Channing argued that these realities demanded that conscientious Christians in the North "abstain" from constitutional duties if they interfered with the moral demands of faith. Southern slavery should be condemned. Clay's argument for the permanence of slavery flew in the face of the "civilized world," which had begun to abandon slavery. Furthermore, emancipation in the West Indies was undermining slaveholders' arguments that freedom would produce horrors greater than slavery. Channing now wrote that emancipation had been accomplished "without the least shock to property," and that in many parts of the West Indies, workers performed twice as much labor for wages as they had as slaves. Indeed, the situation in the islands was "teaching"

68. James Brewer Stewart, "Abolitionists, Insurgents, and Third Parties: Sectionalism and Partisan Politics in Northern Whiggery, 1836–1844" in *Crusaders and Compromisers: Essays on the Relationship of the Antislavery Struggle to the Antebellum Party System,* ed. Alan M. Kraut (Westport: Greenwood, 1983), 25–43.

69. Daniel Malloy, ed., *The Life and Speeches of Henry Clay,* 2 vols. (New York: Robert P. Bixby and Co., 1843), 2:360. On the context of Clay's speech, as well as Calhoun's joy, see Merrill D. Peterson, *The Great Triumvirate: Webster, Clay, and Calhoun* (New York: Oxford University Press, 1987), 286–88.

observers in the United States that "immediate emancipation, in the full sense of the words, is safer than a gradual loosening of the chain." Channing had turned full circle on the success of West Indian emancipation, and in the process he came to advocate immediate abolition.[70]

It was one thing for Channing to change his own mind, but as he had argued before, the responsibility of prominent men was to move public sentiment. He lamented that "the greatest part of our newspapers" had not reported on emancipation in the West Indies and that "the great majority of the people had forgotten it." He blamed the proslavery bias of the political press. He blamed the "all devouring passion for gain," which rendered Americans impervious to the higher law of human rights and blithely complacent about slavery. He also blamed racial prejudice, which blinded white Americans to the violation of the human rights of black slaves. Channing asked his readers to look to Europe, where racism was not predominant, and reflect upon the validity of their own racial beliefs. White Americans had much to overcome, he wrote: "*We have to conquer old and deep prejudices,* and to see a true man in one with whom we have associated ideas of degradation inconsistent with humanity." These were "painful truths" that Americans would have to face before they could see the glory of emancipation in the West Indies and work for the end of slavery in their own country.[71]

Channing's focus on the "passion for gain" and racial prejudice stemmed from characteristics he shared with other American reformers who embraced abolitionism, namely, distrust for the transformations wrought by the market revolution and a repugnance for racial prejudice.[72] His use of "we" indicates a personal aspect to his struggle. As the minister of a wealthy Boston congregation, Channing had lost many friends through his association with abolitionism, and it seems likely he attributed the wealth of his congregation to the ostracism he experienced.[73] Furthermore, his attack on racial prejudice reflected a strong dose of self-criticism. In an interview

70. William Ellery Channing, *Remarks on the Slavery Question, In a Letter to Jonathan Phillips, Esq.*, [1839] in *Works*, 783, 787, 788, 790, 799–802.

71. Ibid., 808–9, emphasis added.

72. Stewart, *Holy Warriors*, 36–37; 43–44; Paul Goodman, *Of One Blood: Abolitionism and the Origins of Racial Equality* (Berkeley and Los Angeles: University of California Press, 1998), 36–44; 69–80.

73. William F. Channing to Caroline H. Dall, October 7, 1883, Caroline H. Dall Papers, reel 12, Massachusetts Historical Society, Boston. William F. Channing was William Ellery's son to whom Dall had written about the relationship between Channing and Gar-

with the English traveler Edward Abdy published in 1835, Channing had clearly revealed his own racial prejudices, which he then considered an "invincible" element in white American culture that no one could "subdue."[74] His attack on racial prejudice six years later indicates a change in attitude, a realization that the prejudices in which he shared were powerful obstacles to the antislavery movement he supported.

It did not take long for Channing to act upon his conversion. In November 1840 he published *Emancipation,* in which he answered the doubts he had expressed five years before in *Slavery.*[75] He wrote that *Emancipation* had flowed "almost insensibly" from his reading of Joseph John Gurney's *A Winter in the West Indies,* which had been published earlier in the year.[76] Perhaps, but other motives were involved beyond sheer inspiration. Gurney was a British Quaker who, according to Channing, was not connected with American abolitionists and had in fact "shunned" them. While Channing had applauded the work of Thome and Kimball, he did not evince a change of position for about two years after reading their study. It is likely that Channing shared the opinion of most Americans that the convinced abolitionists Thome and Kimball had gone to the West Indies seeking evidence to match their foregone conclusions. Gurney was free of such a reputation, which in Channing's mind made his observations all the more credible.[77]

Gurney's book, Channing argued, would help to overcome the skepticism that hindered so many in the United States from believing the "good reports from the West Indies." He hoped that his own fame could dis-

---

rison. William F. wrote that "when [William E.] identified himself with the anti-slavery movement, he met the nearly solid censure of the Federal St. Church of Boston Society . . . For a year or two he was singularly isolated & cast out by all who had previously honored him."

74. Edward S. Abdy, *Journal of a Residence in the United States of North America, from April, 1833 to October, 1834,* 3 vols. (1835; reprint, New York: Negro Universities Press, 1969), 3:217–33; Goodman, *Of One Blood,* 240–43.

75. William E. Channing, *Emancipation,* [1841] in *Works,* 820–53.

76. We can follow Channing's reading of Gurney's book through a manuscript leaf of notes that has survived in his personal papers. Like any student, Channing noted the page numbers and the topics of interest, which align perfectly with the first edition of Gurney's work. See [undated manuscript], William E. Channing Papers, reel 4, Massachusetts Historical Society, Boston. Joseph John Gurney, *Familiar Letters to Henry Clay of Kentucky, Describing a Winter in the West Indies* (New York: Mahlon Day, 1840).

77. Channing, *Emancipation,* in *Works,* 821.

seminate Gurney's vision of the free West Indies through American society as an antidote to the "poison" southern slavery had injected into the
"opinions and feelings" of the northern mind. In his attempt to appeal to
the widest possible audience, Channing selected quotations from Gurney's
book that illustrated both the social and economic aspects of the successful emancipation in the West Indies. He told of Gurney's visit to Robert
Claxton, a planter in St. Kitts, who said that his estate had become worth
three times what it had been under slavery. He relayed the general conviction among Antiguan planters that labor costs had decreased by 30 percent since free labor had replaced slavery, and he noted that in Jamaica the
plough had replaced the hoe. But Channing devoted equal attention to the
social benefits that arose from emancipation. In Antigua there were now
seven thousand students in the schools begun by the missionaries, crime
had decreased significantly, and during the first year of full freedom in
1839 one missionary reported performing 185 marriages. In Jamaica, Gurney had seen the same "rapid diffusion of marriage," the Sabbath was regularly observed, and freeholders' villages with beautiful gardens flourished.
Channing argued (as had Gurney) that these social indicators were just as
important in evaluating the free West Indies as economic indices. He felt
it beneath Christian sensibility to privilege "pounds of sugar" above the restored rights of human beings and challenged Americans to engage his vision of the West Indies as a beacon to light the way to their own emancipation from the sin of slavery.[78]

With his now unqualified endorsement of emancipation in the West
Indies, Channing intensified his own position on slavery in the United
States through two more pamphlets that further disseminated his views.
The first appeared in March 1842 and was Channing's response to the
case of the slave ship *Creole*.[79] As we see in more detail below, the *Creole*
was involved in the coastal slave trade between Virginia and New Orleans.
In December 1841 a group of slaves led by a young man named Madison
Washington staged a rebellion, took control of the ship, and made their

78. Channing, *Emancipation*, in *Works*, 822–29.

79. William E. Channing, *The Duty of the Free States; Or, Remarks Suggested by the Case
of the "Creole,"* [March 1842], in *Works*, 853–907. The original was printed as two separate
pamphlets. Andrew Delbanco argues that *Duty of the Free States* demonstrated a transformation in Channing's social thought through which he abandoned the "pious conservatism"
that had kept him from embracing abolitionism in 1835. Delbanco, *William Ellery Channing*, 142–43.

way to the free West Indies where British authorities granted them refuge.[80] Secretary of State and Massachusetts Whig leader Daniel Webster demanded redress from Britain, arguing that the "comity of nations" required that Britain recognize the slave status of the African Americans aboard the *Creole* despite Britain's abolition of slavery.[81]

Channing was outraged, and he lent his pen in support of radical Whigs like Joshua Giddings, who protested the government's proslavery stance in Congress. Webster's letter poignantly revealed that national policy now catered to the interests of "the slave-power." Channing defended the rights of the rebellious slaves of the *Creole* to their freedom regardless of the manner in which they had achieved it. Freedom did not derive from differences in national jurisdiction but from the "rights of mankind" on which Channing believed the country had been founded. It had thus become the Christian "duty" of the free states of the North to "abstain" from any act that legitimated slavery, such as returning fugitive slaves, or assisting in the suppression of insurrection. Channing had voiced this argument for civil disobedience the year before, but only in relation to individuals. Now he argued that Christian "duty" called upon the northern legislatures to seek amendments to the Constitution that would absolve the northern states from any participation in the defense of slavery. He did not detail what these amendments should say, but at the very least they would have revoked the Fugitive Slave Act of 1793 and barred the northern militias from participating in the suppression of slave rebellion. Channing was surely aware that such proposals would roil the political waters, but he argued that "excessive deference" to stability had eviscerated the "individual responsibility" of citizens. Christian conscience had been deferred to the political needs of the country, especially on the issue of slavery. For Channing this was an untenable reality that demanded action at the highest levels of governance.[82]

Channing delivered his last public address on August 1, 1842, before an interracial audience in Lenox, Massachusetts, which had gathered for a celebration of West Indian emancipation. Channing was very ill and had

80. For more on the *Creole* and its effects in the United States, see Howard Jones and Donald A. Rakestraw, *Prologue to Manifest Destiny: Anglo-American Relations in the 1840s* (Wilmington, DE: Scholarly Resources, 1997), 81–89; James Brewer Stewart, *Joshua R. Giddings and the Tactics of Radical Politics* (Cleveland: Press of Case Western Reserve University, 1970), 70–74.

81. Channing, *The Duty of the Free States*, 854.

82. Ibid., 855, 863, 868, 885, 888, 880, 872.

not advertised his appearance at the event out of fear that he would not be able to attend. He did summon the strength to speak, however, and according to one observer "looked like one inspired."[83] Channing's conversion was complete, and this last address was his final opportunity to convey to his audience the important lesson for the United States that had transpired in the West Indies. He heralded British abolition as "one of the great events in modern times" and again lamented the lack of attention it had received in the United States. He recalled his visit to St. Croix in 1831, where "the volume on slavery opened" before his eyes. He read from Thome and Kimball of that moment of emancipation when it came to Antigua. He repeated his condemnation of "prejudice of color" and "the love of money" that hindered Americans from understanding the "progress of liberty" in the West Indies. And he again called for amendments to the Constitution, to remove the sanction given to slavery by the free states of the North.[84] His final address appeared as a pamphlet first in Lenox and then Boston and London, and so his celebration of West Indian emancipation, his attacks on greed and racial prejudice, and his call to amend the Constitution came before the broad audience he had cultivated for more than thirty years.[85]

Antislavery sentiment spread through several regions in the North during the 1830s, cultivated by the hard-working agents of the American Antislavery Society and the flood of literature that began to turn the northern mind against slavery. One favored subject was the great success of emancipation in the British West Indies, and if facts were wanted they could be found in Thome and Kimball's pamphlet, the antislavery press, the religious press, and Channing's pamphlets. For those who "knew" of emancipation's disastrous results through the poisoned pen of Bryan Edwards, the example of the free West Indies undermined expectations of insurrections and chaos. Channing's conversion was critical. He was a moderate, an acknowledged friend to the South, and a weighty public figure who could di-

83. Journal of Mrs. Charles Sedgewick, Charles Sedgewick Family Papers, Massachusetts Historical Society, Boston.

84. William Ellery Channing, *An Address Delivered at Lenox, On the First of August, 1842, being the Anniversary of Emancipation in the British West Indies* [1842] in *Works*, 907, 908, 914, 915, 921, 923.

85. [William Ellery Channing], *Dr. Channing's last address, delivered at Lenox, on the first of August, 1842, the anniversary of emancipation in the British West Indies* (Boston: Oliver Johnson, 1842); *An address delivered at Lenox, on the first of August 1842, the Anniversary of Emancipation in the British West Indies* (London: John Green, 1842).

rect his writings to some of the most prominent men in the country. Channing became convinced of emancipation's safety and painfully aware of the moral imperative to end slavery in the United States. As southern leaders grew more steadfast in the defense of their peculiar institution, they lost allies such as Channing who came to advocate changes in the Constitution which would have nullified slavery's national sanction.

Channing's conversion had been twofold. From a skeptical view of the possibilities of black freedom in the West Indies he had come to see British abolition as a lesson for the United States on the safety and blessings of immediate emancipation. From a critic of the abolitionists in 1835 he had come to presage one of their most radical stances—that the Constitution, in the words of Wendell Phillips, was a *"Proslavery Document"* that must be reformed.[86] And, most importantly, William Ellery Channing underwent this conversion publicly through a series of pamphlets directed at the Whig leadership, lending his formidable prestige to American abolitionism and reaching a broad spectrum of readers who may not have listened to the radicals. Charles Sumner was deeply influenced by Channing. The abolitionist Whig George Julian cited "the writings of Dr. Channing" as fundamental to his dedication to political abolitionism. In the words of Joshua Giddings, another abolitionist Whig, Channing's pamphlets "encourage[ed] the people of the free states to think and act for themselves . . . and to spurn all attempts to draw them to the support and aid of slavery in violation of our Constitution and of the natural rights of man."[87]

Six years after British abolition, antislavery sentiment had taken root in enough northern districts to have a tangible effect on American politics. The Whig party in the North had become the vehicle for many antislavery-minded people to express their interests in the halls of Congress. John Quincy Adams defended their right to petition against slavery, Giddings attacked the nation's stance toward the blacks freed from the *Creole,* and Webster would fall to abolitionist voters and Channing disciple Sumner in the aftermath of his compromises in 1850. Antislavery sentiment

86. James Brewer Stewart, *Wendell Phillips: Liberty's Hero* (Baton Rouge: Louisiana State University Press, 1986), 123–24.

87. David Herbert Donald, *Charles Sumner and the Coming of the Civil War* (Chicago: University of Chicago Press, 1960), 99–100, 133; George Julian, *Political Recollections, 1840 to 1872* (1884; New York: Negro Universities Press, 1970), 23, 29, 38 (quote); Joshua Giddings to William Ellery Channing, May 12, 1842, reprinted in Granville Hicks, "Dr. Channing and the Creole Case," *American Historical Review* 37 (April 1932): 523.

affected northern Democrats as well. In New York, Martin Van Buren's "Bucktail" faction gradually lost the capability to win the pro-southern votes they had been enjoying since the late 1820s. The same was true in parts of Massachusetts, New Hampshire, and northern Ohio, as too many constituents were no longer willing to vote for politicians who supported the "slave power." In 1840 the Liberty Party entered national politics on a strictly antislavery platform and placed James Birney on the presidential ballot. Soon, the Liberty Party held the "balance of power" in New York and Ohio.[88] Public opinion in the North was moving against slavery, cultivated in part by the antislavery vision of the postemancipation West Indies—evidence for citizens like Channing that proslavery argument was groundless froth that spewed from the mouth of the slave power.

88. Leonard Richards, *The Slave Power: The Free North and Southern Domination, 1780–1860* (Baton Rouge: Louisiana State University Press, 2000), 172; Jonathan Earle, *Jacksonian Antislavery and the Politics of Free Soil, 1824–1854* (Chapel Hill: University of North Carolina Press, 2004).

6

The Fears of Robert Monroe Harrison

Slaveholders' exercise of political power had worked in the South and in Congress to thwart a wide-ranging national debate on the future of American slavery, but British abolition and the rise of antislavery in the United States forced southern leaders to actively defend the institution. West Indian planters had also defended it, but the American argument that slavery was a "positive good" for human society was unique in world history. Southern planters did not see themselves as immoral or atavistic, and British abolition became the turning point in their effort to portray slavery as a modern institution in no way contrary to the progress of humanity. In chapter 8, I turn to the intellectual construction of proslavery argument as it related to emancipation in the British West Indies, but our subject here is the tangible impact of British abolition in the United States. Southern interpretations of British abolition led to a perception of the British that permanently altered the course of American history, as many white southerners came to see British abolition as part of a conspiracy designed to weaken the United States.[1]

Conspiracy theories have long been a part of American history, and the southern-led propaganda campaign to annex Texas in the spring of 1845 was one of the most significant. The arguments varied, but the administration's opinion makers agreed that if Texas remained independent, it would

1. The most recent assessment of proslavery thought can be found in Michael O'Brien, *Conjectures of Order: Intellectual Life and the American South, 1810–1860*, 2 vols. (Chapel Hill: University of North Carolina Press, 2004), vol. 2, chap. 18. For more on the historiography of proslavery, and particularly on the impact of British abolition, see Edward B. Rugemer, "The Southern Response to British Abolition: The Maturation of Proslavery Apologetics," *Journal of Southern History* 70 (May 2004): 221–48.

be overrun by the British, whose abolitionism would create an asylum for runaways and a staging ground for insurrection. It was the "domino theory" of the 1840s.

Historians have long pointed to the powerful Anglophobia that fueled Texas annexation, but there has been much disagreement on its sources and integrity. Further research shows that the genesis of a conspiratorial vision of British abolitionism began well before John Tyler's presidency and stemmed from a variety of sources. At the level of public opinion, this view appeared in some of the initial readings of West Indian emancipation and found more fuel in the transatlantic cooperation between British and American abolitionists. The belligerence of British abolitionism appeared even more threatening in a series of incidents in which British colonial agents freed enslaved African Americans from coastal slavers that wrecked in the Bahamas. The most prominent case was that of the *Creole* in 1842, where a group of slaves led by Madison Washington murdered the ship's captain, seized control of the ship, and headed for British Nassau and freedom. But the most significant contribution to the perception of British foreign policy as subversive to slavery was the official intelligence received by a series of Secretaries of State from Robert Monroe Harrison, the longest-serving American diplomat in the antebellum period and the consul to Jamaica from 1831 until his death in 1858. Harrison's regular dispatches made for compelling if not entirely believable reading, and through them he developed a portrait of a disastrous emancipation in Jamaica, which the British hoped to transform into an abolitionist *foco* that could spawn insurrection in the American South.[2]

THE CONSPIRATORIAL VISION OF BRITISH ABOLITION

British abolition kindled a deep Anglophobia in the South which gave the American struggle over slavery a transatlantic dimension. Rooted in the Edwards thesis and Robert Turnbull's warnings, southern Anglopho-

2. I have reviewed this historiography in Rugemer, "Robert Monroe Harrison, British Abolition, Southern Anglophobia, and the Annexation of Texas," *Slavery and Abolition* 28 (August 2007): 169–91. On conspiracy theories in American history, see Richard Hofstadter, *The Paranoid Style in American Politics and Other Essays* (New York: Knopf, 1965), 3–40; David Brion Davis, Introduction to *The Fear of Conspiracy: Images of Un-American Subversion from the Revolution to the Present*, ed. David Brion Davis (Ithaca: Cornell University Press, 1971), xiii–xxiv.

bia was further aroused by British abolitionist visitors to the United States in the early 1830s, George Thompson the first among them. The dominant proslavery view held that abolitionists intended to violate the constitutional right to own slaves and that they had now combined with British "fanatics" to do so. In these accusations, the lineaments of a conspiratorial vision of British abolition become evident. By portraying the abolitionists as tools of Britain—a foreign power with a recent belligerent history—southerners charged the abolitionists with treason and sought to undermine the Christian rhetoric that underpinned transatlantic antislavery. Even now, they said, as evidence damning the "experiment" in the West Indies flooded the country, northern abolitionists collaborated with the British to wreak havoc in the South. The atmosphere was perfect for the cry "Conspiracy!" to sound.[3]

Thompson had been a leading abolitionist in Britain's movement, and once abolition was accomplished there, he traversed the Atlantic to assist in the effort to abolish American slavery. Mobs greeted Thompson wherever he spoke in the North, and southerners considered him an incendiary.[4] The Harvard graduate and educator Thomas Sullivan of Boston considered Thompson a "noisy bully" who was attempting to "sow dissension."[5] In a speech against the reception of abolitionist petitions, James Henry Hammond of South Carolina neglected to mention either Garrison or Tappan but instead attacked the "miscreant Thompson," whom he accused of attempting to raise insurrections in the South.[6] Following Bryan Edwards, Hammond traced abolitionism across the Atlantic to the French Revolution, which for Hammond defined the "spirit of the age." In Europe, "hereditary institutions" such as those enjoyed by the French nobility were the

3. Interestingly, a similar Anglophobic argument was employed by French antiabolitionists during the same period. See Seymour Drescher, ed. and trans., *Tocqueville and Beaumont on Social Reform* (New York: Harper and Row, 1968), 149, n.19.

4. Leonard L. Richards, *"Gentlemen of Property and Standing": Anti-Abolition Mobs in Jacksonian America* (New York: Oxford University Press, 1970), 63–71.

5. T[homas] R. Sullivan, *Letters Against the Immediate Abolition of Slavery; Addressed to the Free Blacks of the Non-Slaveholding States. Comprising a Legal Opinion on the Power of Legislatures in Non-Slaveholding States to Prevent Measures Tending to Immediate and General Emancipation* (Boston: Hilliard and Gray, 1835), 11.

6. *Remarks of Mr. Hammond of South Carolina on the Question of Receiving Petitions for the Abolition of Slavery in the District of Columbia* (Washington City: Duff Green, 1836), 12. For other attacks on Thompson, see the remarks of James Garland of Virginia in *Congressional Globe*, 24th Cong., 1st sess. (December 23, 1835), 15.

first victims of this fell spirit, but its British counterpart appeared as "confiscation," Hammond's term for abolition, which he predicted would soon devastate the planters of the West Indies.[7]

In the same debate, Francis Pickens, also of South Carolina, directed his ire toward the "Irish demagogue" Daniel O'Connell. One of the most vocal abolitionist MPs in Parliament, O'Connell often directed his attacks on slavery across the Atlantic. Pickens saw British abolition as a violation of "the rights of property" and forcefully argued that the U.S. Constitution would never allow for such an act.[8] Abolition stemmed from a wicked combination of "stupid fanaticism" and the monopolistic impulses of the British East Indian Company, the old bête noir of Boston Tea Party fame. Pickens drew a parallel between the "capitalists" of the North and their counterparts in Britain, both of whom struggled to control the labor of the "*hungry* multitude" and required a "strong Federal Government" to do it. The planters of the South owned a "class of laborers" and therefore wanted no such government. Representatives of the North chose the sword, Pickens warned, if they discussed the abolition of slavery, as such talk would drive the South from the Union. Abolition provoked fighting words in Congress, and the British were never far from the debate.[9]

The same charges appeared in the newspapers, as southerners worked to undermine the abolitionist threat by tying the movement to foreign influence. In July 1835, for example, Thomas Ritchie declared that, regardless of the "interference of all the Fanatics and Foreigners," the South would never change its "civil institutions." Abolitionism was the product of foreign hands and was "calculated" to divide the Union.[10] A few years later the

7. *Remarks of Mr. Hammond,* 14–15. It was quite common for southerners to trace "fanaticism," as they styled abolitionism, to European origins. See, e.g., *Address to the People of Beaufort and Colleton Districts, upon the Subject of Abolition, by Robert Barnwell Rhett, January 15, 1838,* 6–7.

8. *Speech of Mr. Pickens, of South Carolina, in the House of Representatives, January 21, 1836, on the Abolition Question* (Washington: Gales and Seaton, 1836), 5–10, pamphlet at South Caroliniana Library. Other assertions that British abolition was a "robbery" can be found in Paulding, *Slavery in the United States,* 51.

9. *Speech of Mr. Pickens,* 14. To make an analogy between the United States and Britain was a common rhetorical thread in southern proslavery expression. See, e.g., Edmund Bellinger Jr., *A Speech on the Subject of Slavery; Delivered 7th Sept'r, 1835. At a Public Meeting of the Citizens of Barnwell District, South Carolina* (Charleston: Dan J. Dowling, 1835), 11. Bellinger lamented the "language" of abolitionism, which "echoed and re-echoed across the Atlantic, from the fanatics of the North to the fanatics of Europe."

10. *Richmond Enquirer,* July 24, 1835.

Raleigh Star and North Carolina Gazette followed the same line of argument with an article on that "Irish demagogue" O'Connell, whose insults received a "hearty response" in the North. The South must "know," the *Gazette* warned, of the "sentiments and designs" of their enemies on both sides of the Atlantic and guard its interests against them.[11]

The deep Anglophobia expressed in the broad antiabolitionist reaction of the 1830s lent itself to a conspiratorial vision of British abolition. While not yet accusing the British of martial intentions, an anonymous pamphlet entitled *An Appeal to the Good Sense of a Great People,* published in Charleston in 1835, offers one of the earliest glimpses of the conspiratorial vision of British abolition. The author believed that America found itself threatened with disunion over the issue of slavery, a situation he attributed to the "fell Machiavelli spirit of the British nation." Britain, the argument went, was an aristocratic nation that perceived its most dangerous threat as the "influence of American republicanism." The destruction of America would stifle reform in Britain, as the great beacon of republican freedom would be snuffed out. The writer alleged that Britain sought to dominate the globe and had concluded that only America stood in the way. British statesmen had seized upon the scheme of abolishing West Indian slavery as a means of driving the "wedge of disunion" into the United States. The loss of the West Indies was "trifling," as the gains made by the destruction of the United States surpassed any profits they would have produced. Abolition was primarily an antirepublican act.[12]

The *Appeal*'s argument was still rare in 1835 and did not frequently appear in the southern press until the early 1840s. During this time, however, a conspiratorial interpretation of British abolition developed in the mind of Robert Monroe Harrison, a career diplomat who had been deeply involved in U.S. diplomacy in the Caribbean since the early 1820s. The significance of Harrison's opinions lies in the form in which they arrived in the United States—as consular dispatches from Jamaica, the richest of Britain's sugar colonies and the predominant index used to assess the success or failure of West Indian slave emancipation.[13] Southern Anglophobia

11. *Raleigh Star and North Carolina Gazette,* March 7, 1838.

12. *An Appeal to the Good Sense of a Great People* (Charleston: Dan J. Dowling, 1835), 3–5, pamphlet at South Caroliniana Library. A similar argument appears in [A Slaveholder], *Remarks upon Slavery and the Slave-Trade, Addressed to the Hon. Henry Clay* (1839), 16, pamphlet at South Caroliniana Library.

13. Thomas Holt, *The Problem of Freedom: Race, Labor, and Politics in Jamaica and Britain* (Baltimore: Johns Hopkins University Press, 1992), 8.

would eventually manifest itself in the annexation of Texas to the United States in 1845, the project of a small group of dedicated southerners genuinely concerned with the potential threat of British abolitionism on the nation's southwestern frontier. Harrison's dispatches provided disturbing information that validated the concerns of this group.

ROBERT MONROE HARRISON

Harrison was one of many consuls who represented the interests of the United States and its merchants in the West Indies. In the final years of the eighteenth century, the United States began to place consuls in the various states and colonies of the Caribbean basin and Latin America where American merchants traditionally did business. With respect to the British West Indies, the United States had representatives in the sugar colonies of Jamaica, Barbados, Antigua, Trinidad, and Demerara, as well as the entrepots on Turks Island and Nassau in the Bahamas. In the early years of American diplomacy, consuls sent to the secretary of state occasional dispatches concerning particular cases, usually shipwrecks or litigation involving U.S. citizens. Eventually, they included quarterly reports that assessed the quantity of American commerce, a practice that was only gradually standardized during the 1830s. For most consuls, the quarterly report replaced the dispatch, which became a perfunctory note or at best a short anecdote of a shipwreck. Harrison's dispatches, however, were distinctively long and detailed, offering a peculiar perspective upon slave emancipation as it looked to a southerner transplanted to Jamaica.

Born in 1770 and proudly self-identified as a "native born Virginian," Harrison was probably the illegitimate son of Robert Hansen Harrison, a prominent planter and slaveholder who served in the Continental Army under George Washington and later became chief justice of Maryland. As a teen, family connections provided him with the opportunity of an education in England, but during a transatlantic crossing in the mid-1780s, Harrison was impressed into the British navy and served for seven years in the Mediterranean. In 1799 he joined the U.S. navy and served in the Quasi-War with France. In 1801 he left the navy and departed for Europe. He married his wife Margaret in Sweden, fought for Russia against Napoleon's army, and departed for the United States when the War of 1812 broke out. On his passage home Harrison was again captured at sea by the British and imprisoned in Cowes, England. After the war, Britain transported him and other American prisoners to the Danish island of St. Thomas, where he played an important role coordinating the connecting voyages home for his fellow prisoners. Harrison parlayed his efforts in St. Thomas into an appointment as U.S. consul there, beginning a diplomatic career that ended only with his death in 1858.[14]

Harrison's career took him to almost every major island in the Caribbean. Following his service in St. Thomas, Harrison held an appointment as consul in Swedish St. Bartholomew from 1821 to 1823, then was transferred to the same post for the British colonies Antigua and St. Kitts. He served there until the summer of 1827, when Secretary of State Henry Clay commissioned Harrison to travel throughout the Caribbean to investigate the trade between the United States and the British West Indies, which had been a source of diplomatic tension since the Peace of Paris in 1783.

In the spring of 1831, as the British Parliament debated abolition and Samuel Sharpe plotted rebellion, Harrison was appointed consul to Jamaica. He already had contacts in the island, and his first dispatch to Secretary of State Edward Livingston reported a "dreadful state of apprehension." One slave had made a dying confession of a planned rebellion, and mysterious fires had blazed throughout the island. The rebellion that ensued prohibited Harrison from traveling to his new post until April of the next year, when he reported that the insurgents had been suppressed. The island still lived under the "greatest distress imaginable," not due to the destruction of property during the insurrection but because of Britain's "extraordinary policy" with respect to slavery. Harrison believed the islands would be "ruined" and wrote that it might not be possible for him to remain at his post.[15]

14. This and the following paragraph are based on *New York Times*, June 17, 1858, and the research of Harrison descendant Derrick Phillips, who has kindly shared his unpublished genealogical work, and the historians Steven Heath Mitton, Fred A. Dellamura, and myself. Mitton's "The Free World Confronted: The Problem of Slavery and Progress in American Foreign Relations, 1833–1844" (Ph.D. diss., Louisiana State University, 2005), 141–43, contains the fullest account of Harrison's early life publicly available. Dellamura's "The Harrison Report and its Role in the British American Controversy over the West India Carrying Trade, 1827–1828" (M.A. thesis, University of Kentucky, 1972) details Harrison's 1827 West Indian tour and its context. Harrison's career has also been investigated in Joe Bassette Wilkins Jr., "Window on Freedom: The South's Response to the Emancipation of the Slaves in the British West Indies, 1833–1861" (Ph.D. dissertation, University of South Carolina, 1977). Harrison's self-identification is in R. M. Harrison to Louis McLane, June 14, 1834, *Despatches from U.S. Consuls in Kingston, Jamaica, 1796–1906*, Record Group 59, T 31, National Archives, College Park, MD.

15. R. M. Harrison to Daniel Brent, June 7, 1831, April 11, 1832, July 5, 1831, Au-

Once he got there, Harrison did not like Jamaica. The most disturbing aspect of society there was the black population known as the free coloreds. They were making "rapid progress," he informed Livingston, and already shared with their "*white brethren* an *equal proportion*" of lucrative positions in the colonial government. But they were not "satisfied" with these accomplishments. They were intent upon controlling the entire island, which they would do by first taking over the government, and then killing the whites by instigating rebellion among the slaves. In Harrison's mind the free coloreds were constantly plotting to "*poison* the minds of the *Slaves* by *seditious harangues and vile publications.*" And the slaves were always ready "to *execute* actions of the most *diabolical* nature against the white *Inhabitants!*"[16]

Abolitionist influence in Parliament and the supposed plotting of the free coloreds disturbed Harrison tremendously and he continually warned his superiors that Jamaica was in grave danger of another insurrection. On January 1, 1833, Harrison wrote that the colony was in a "most unsettled State," and reported the amassing of troops near districts where the authorities expected rebellions to break out.[17] In June he informed Livingston that a preliminary plan for emancipation had arrived and that all parties were appalled by its details. He again warned of a "general Insurrection" that would erupt as soon as the news had spread throughout the island. This time insurrection would be "fatal" to the island's white population, including Americans like himself, and he recommended that a "vessel of war" be instructed to hover nearby for their protection.[18]

Parliament's plan for emancipation, according to Harrison, promised little to the planters. The compensation money would go almost entirely to those who held West Indian debt, and most planters were convinced that sugar could "*never be raised by free labour!*" Due to the hostile atmosphere, plantation managers already faced tremendous difficulties in getting the

---

gust 22, 1831, and September 12, 1831, *Despatches from. . . Kingston, Jamaica* detail Harrison's difficulties with his appointment and the first news of "apprehension" in Jamaica. They are all written from Pensacola, Florida. R. M. Harrison to Edward Livingston, April 14, 1832, details his first impressions of the island.

16. R. M. Harrison to Edward Livingston, August 12, 1832, *Despatches from . . . Kingston, Jamaica.* Emphasis is in the original. In addition to frequently indulging in the triple exclamation point, Harrison liked to underline parts of his dispatches that seemed to particularly enrage him. All emphasis that follows is in the original.

17. R. M. Harrison to Edward Livingston, January 1, 1833, *Despatches from . . . Kingston, Jamaica.*

18. R. M. Harrison to Edward Livingston, June 30, 1833, *Despatches from . . . Kingston, Jamaica.*

slaves to work, and Harrison could not imagine their situation once the slaves became *"free apprentices."* Troops were already positioned throughout the island, and Harrison expected two more regiments to arrive before the first of August. When the insurrection came, Harrison predicted, the rebels would be driven into the mountains "as were the Negroes of St. Domingo." Then they would wage "La petite Guerre" in the same tradition. And just as the slaves of Saint-Domingue "met and conquered the best troops of Europe," so would Jamaican rebels defeat British regulars. Harrison had read his Bryan Edwards. Britain played with fire, and Harrison fully expected emancipation to devastate the colonies.[19]

Just as Robert J. Turnbull saw in British abolitionism a threat to American slaveholders, Harrison saw a great danger in Britain's actions in the West Indies. He reported that the planters in Jamaica and the British clearly perceived the "inevitable ruin" emancipation would bring, and were already anxious for other slaveholding nations to follow suit to reduce economic competition. The British government would soon attempt (under a philanthropic guise) to pressure other nations to abolish slavery, and when they found that "our Governments" would not listen to these suggestions, the British would take "measures that might lead to emancipation and of course insurrection!" Harrison was convinced that black "emissaries will go from hence to New York and find their way to our Slaveholding States" for that very purpose. "Witness their *intrigues* with the *Indians*," he explained, surely these had demonstrated Britain's *"medling* and *jealous dispostion."*[20] The British would use Jamaican free coloreds in the same way they had used the Indians during the war of American independence. In fact, prominent free colored leaders edited a newspaper (supported, he thought, by the Colonial Office in Britain), which already spoke "in terms not to be mistaken." Harrison advised that the United States adopt a policy of interdicting all black Jamaicans, as their only intention in traveling was to "poison the minds of the *Negroes* in the *Slaveholding States!"*[21] He added the threat of "secret emissaries" to the repertoire of subjects, like predic-

19. R. M. Harrison to Louis McLane, July 24, 1833, *Despatches from . . . Kingston, Jamaica.* Harrison makes similar references to St. Domingo in the dispatches of November 14, 1833 and January 10, 1834.

20. R. M. Harrison to Louis McLane, July 24, 1833, *Despatches from . . . Kingston, Jamaica.*

21. R. M. Harrison to Louis McLane, August 18, 1833, *Despatches from . . . Kingston, Jamaica.*

tions of insurrection and requests for naval protection, which he discussed in his regular dispatches home. After first making the charge in July 1833, he repeated it in August, twice during the next year, and several more times throughout his career.[22]

Harrison's perception of a British threat changed his opinion of the status of his own position. Jamaica was Britain's most important West Indian colony, he noted, and its proximity to the United States, combined with the possibility of abolitionist emissaries, made Jamaica important from "a political point of view."[23] Harrison took on this self-appointed responsibility with enthusiasm, taking care to detail for his superiors the disruptive effects the impending emancipation had already wrought upon the island. Several Jamaican whites already planned to escape to the "U States" (as they said it) with nothing to support them but "their old family plate." Harrison believed that the greater part of the white population would follow and wrote that all were disgusted with Parliament for bringing such a plague upon their fortunes. The most prominent Jamaicans, Harrison boasted, "think that our Government and institutions, are better adapted for the freedom and happiness of mankind, than any other under the Sun!!!"[24] The slaves were equally incensed with the government for not making them free immediately. As a consequence, slaves now offered nothing but resistance to their masters.[25] In December 1833—the second anniversary of the great insurrection—Harrison reported: "Every man in the Island considers he is standing on a Volcano and knows not when it will explode."[26]

BRITISH ABOLITION

The year 1834 found Harrison absolutely frantic. While insurrection had not come during the Christmas holidays as so many expected, he feared that the whites would be "lulled into fatal Security." He predicted that the

22. R. M. Harrison to Louis McLane, July 24 and August 18, 1833. Harrison repeated the charge in his dispatches to John Forsyth on August 11, 1834, September 6, 1834, and October 23, 1835, *Despatches from . . . Kingston, Jamaica*.

23. R. M. Harrison to Louis McLane, August 18, 1833, *Despatches from . . . Kingston, Jamaica*.

24. Ibid.

25. R. M. Harrison to Louis McLane, September 7, 1833. See also R. M. Harrison to Louis McLane, January 10, 1834, *Despatches from . . . Kingston, Jamaica*.

26. R. M. Harrison to Louis McLane, December 3, 1833, *Despatches from . . . Kingston, Jamaica*.

slaves would come down from the mountains and "sweep every thing like a *white or mulatto from the face of the Island.*" He sent his final plea for protection in June and warned his superiors that on August first all English merchant vessels planned to flee, as they feared emancipation. Whites in Kingston would therefore be left unprotected, with nowhere "to place our families, in the event of Insurrection." Harrison again begged his superiors to order war vessels to Kingston to save white Americans trapped in the city. It was the eighth time Harrison had made this request; he was petrified.[27]

To the relief of island whites there was no insurrection on the first of August 1834. Emancipation in the British West Indies was largely a peaceful affair. Harrison did not report on the state of the island until August 11, and while he noted that the first had come and gone quietly, he warned that insurrection still threatened at any moment. British troops marched throughout the island to protect the estates, and three companies had left for St. Ann's parish on the north coast. It was particularly regrettable, he continued, that no American war vessels had arrived, especially considering the "great many persons [who] expected them." Harrison made promises that turned out to be empty.[28]

Harrison also warned the new secretary of state John Forsyth that several black emissaries had already left the island "to poison the minds of the Slaves" of the South, and predicted that "difficulties" would soon arise between Britain and the United States.[29] He repeated the warning in September, now with more detail. At the "bottom" of it all were the free coloreds who, with their "writings in a paper called the 'Watchman' edited by one of them (who is a Magistrate and a Member of the Legislature!!!) keep the savage nature of the Negroe in a constant state of excitement." Moreover, the free coloreds were in cahoots with the missionaries, who exacerbated the discontent that threatened to spread to the South. Significantly, Harrison now saw imperial intent in Britain's act, as they had willingly "destroyed their own colonies" and now sought abolition throughout the Americas.[30]

---

27. R. M. Harrison to Louis McLane, January 10, and February 4, 1834. Dates of requests for naval protection include July 14, 1833; April 11, 1833; November 14, 1833; December 3, 1833; December 12, 1833; January 10, 1834; May 19, 1834; June 14, 1834, all in *Despatches from . . . Kingston, Jamaica.*

28. R. M. Harrison to John Forsyth, August 11, 1834, *Despatches from . . . Kingston, Jamaica.*

29. Ibid.

30. R. M. Harrison to John Forsyth, September 6, 1834, *Despatches from . . . Kingston,*

By October the island's apprentices had adopted "a kind of passive resistance" to their masters by refusing to work, a situation Harrison felt to be worse than rebellion, as it simply postponed the race war he believed was inevitable. He again warned that the American South would soon be "deluged in blood" if Britain's emissaries were not stopped. The dreaded insurrection had not arisen, but Harrison's imagination surely had.[31]

In November the missionaries William Knibb and Thomas Burchell returned to the island, reinforcing Harrison's belief in missionary complicity with Britain's abolitionist scheme. These men were the "authors of the late Insurrection," and Burchell had just come from New York, where the British Antislavery Society had sent him with the hopes that he could visit the South to spread his doctrines. Knibb had made the outrageous proposal that a statue should be erected in memory of Samuel Sharpe, the *"Negroe who planned the Insurrection."* The white colonists were horrified at the return of these men, especially "the friends and relations of those murdered husbands who *had their secret parts cut off and placed in the mouths of their wives and Daughters; and they themselves afterwards violated in the most cruel manner*!!!"[32] Such extraordinary detail of castrated masters and raped white women looked back to Bryan Edwards's descriptions of the "horrors" of Saint-Domingue. They also presaged the racist response exhibited by many southern whites during Reconstruction, as well as the lynchings that plagued black America well into the twentieth century. Whites' loss of the power of mastery was expressed through deeply felt sexual insecurities that reflected the abuses of generations as well as the fear of retribution. Most significantly in the case of Robert Harrison, these anxieties arrived in Washington in the form of official intelligence on Britain's experiment with emancipation, available to any future secretary of state who took interest.[33]

Jamaica. Harrison referred to Edward Jordan, editor of the *Kingston Watchman and Jamaica Free Press;* see Gad Heuman, *Between Black and White: Race, Politics, and the Free Coloreds in Jamaica, 1792–1865* (Westport, CT: Greenwood, 1981), 58–59.

31. R. M. Harrison to John Forsyth, October 8, 1834, *Despatches from . . . Kingston, Jamaica.*

32. R. M. Harrison to John Forsyth, November 14, 1834, *Despatches from . . . Kingston, Jamaica.*

33. In actuality most violence during the Baptist war was directed against property, not persons. See Mary Turner, *Slaves and Missionaries: The Disintegration of Jamaican Slave Society, 1787–1834* (Urbana: University of Illinois Press, 1982), 160. For more on similar responses during reconstruction and lynching scares, see Forrest G. Wood, *The Racist Response to Emancipation and Reconstruction* (Berkeley and Los Angeles: University of California

Harrison may have envisioned himself as a political agent protecting the rights of American slaveholders, but he was still a consul whose primary responsibilities were the American ships involved in the West Indian trade. The slaveholding attitudes that made him so sensitive to his political responsibilities with respect to emancipation made his more ordinary tasks unbearable and fed his paranoia. As consul, Harrison was required to appear in court on behalf of American captains whose sailors sued for discharge. These requests were frequent in the West Indies, as many seamen simply said they were English and applied to cooperative magistrates for discharges. Here lay Harrison's problem, as many of the magistrates were "Negroes, Mulattoes and Jews." Jamaican free coloreds had begun to hold such posts in the colonial government beginning with their liberation in 1830, and Harrison was "mortified beyond measure" that he was obliged to appear in an official capacity before such persons who were "ignorant of the courtesy and respect due to my official character." To his earlier charge that the free coloreds threatened to take over the island, Harrison added that the Jews, "a *cowardly* set of *wretches*," were so afraid of the free coloreds that they had combined with them politically. While it is hard to say if he had been anti-Semitic before his posting in Jamaica, only with emancipation did he begin to express such opinions in his dispatches.[34]

Harrison was embedded in a world that moved beyond his mental framework. Emancipation had instilled in the people a "haughty behavior," which resulted in various affronts. Jamaican blacks refused to "pull their hats off when coming into a gentleman's house." They always made "a white man give way to them" when walking in the street and habitually insulted whites.[35] Like most American whites of his time, "whiteness" and "blackness" had a fixed set of meanings for Harrison, all of which emancipation violated. Whites no longer had a monopoly on public deference, justice, or power, and, as Harrison revealed, black Jamaicans did not hesitate to assert their new freedoms. It was an adjustment that he found impossible.

In the fall of 1837, Harrison offered Secretary of State Forsyth a complete assessment of the first three years of emancipation. Jamaica was "rapidly declining in value" due to the blacks' laziness, and Harrison had no

Press, 1968), 64–65, 145–48; George Frederickson, *The Black Image in the White Mind: The Debate on Afro-American Character and Destiny, 1817–1914* (Hanover, NH: Wesleyan University Press, 1971), 275–82.

34. R. M. Harrison to Louis McLane, June 14, 1834, *Despatches from . . . Kingston, Jamaica.*

35. R. M. Harrison to John Forsyth, July 11, 1837, *Despatches from . . . Kingston, Jamaica.*

doubt that when the apprenticeship ceased the whites would abandon the island. While this laziness was in part congenital, he believed, it was exacerbated by "the fanatical wretches who daily arrive from the abolition societies in England and the U. States," whose agitation distracted the laborers from their duties on the plantations. Harrison emphasized the arrival of abolitionists from "the five New England States" who were "more zealous" than their English counterparts because they wished "to see the British flag once more waving over our happy land." He reported that he had gained possession of an abolitionist pamphlet from the United States, which he did not name, but described it as "striving hard to array the North against the South."[36]

A court case recounted in the same dispatch sheds light on the possible source of that pamphlet. Harrison had been called by an American captain to represent his appeal to a verdict that had freed two black seamen—a cook and a steward—from their responsibilities. The men had been "cobbed" by their fellow sailors, which Harrison described as a "common mode of punishment." When the abused men arrived in Jamaica, they brought complaint against the captain in a Kingston court. The magistrates judged in favor of the cobbed sailors, and on appeal did not accept Harrison's argument that these were disputes between *"foreigners at sea"* and therefore beyond the court's jurisdiction. Harrison vented his frustrations to Forsyth, calling one judge an "illiterate . . . *Jew peddler,*" and the other an "ugly Baboon of a Negroe." He found it "mortifying . . . to be adjudged interrogated and at times insulted" by black and Jewish judges. In addition to these personal affronts, Harrison argued that emancipation had turned justice itself on its head. Ever since abolition, punishment had been applied unfairly to whites. According to Harrison, when a white man committed a crime, he was administered the stiffest penalty, but if someone with "any *black blood in his veins*" committed a similar crime, he escaped with the "slightest punishment," and these were crimes that would *"hang a white man ten times over in England!"*[37] Harrison exhibited all the characteristics of ex-Confederates during Reconstruction whose world of black slavery and white freedom had been turned upside down.[38]

Harrison's misery was a black man's paradise, at least in comparison to

36. R. M. Harrison to John Forsyth, September 8, 1837, *Despatches from . . . Kingston, Jamaica.*

37. R. M. Harrison to John Forsyth, September 8, 1837. See also July 11, 1837, *Despatches from . . . Kingston, Jamaica.*

38. Eric Foner, *Reconstruction: America's Unfinished Revolution, 1863–1877* (New York:

the United States, and it is not at all surprising that black seamen tried their hand at equal justice in Jamaica. Black seamen had disseminated abolitionist materials since the days of David Walker, and there were growing connections between Jamaica and black abolitionists from the northern United States. James Barbadoes, a founding member of the American Antislavery Society, settled in Jamaica in the spring of 1840 with the hopes of getting started in silk production. Isaiah DeGrasse, an Episcopal missionary, settled in Jamaica in the fall of 1840. The *Colored American* of New York had a subscription agent in Kingston, the lawyer John Burger, and also received regular files of Edward Jordan's *Morning Journal,* the organ of the Jamaican free coloreds that Harrison feared. Black Jamaicans were also engaged with what Richard Blackett has called the "Caribbean arm of the abolitionist international." In June 1840, for example, the *Colored American* printed a letter from the Anti-Slavery Society of Brown's Town, Jamaica, which hoped that "the day is not far distant when America will be brought to repentance, and induced to restore to the Negro his long-withheld birthright." An avid reader of newspapers and particularly sensitive to threats to slavery, Harrison would have known about abolitionists in Jamaica. Harrison came to understand that Jamaican abolitionism, combined with the emergence of politically powerful blacks on the island, was becoming increasingly dangerous to the United States.[39]

The reality of free Jamaica enhanced Harrison's understanding of the political importance of his post.[40] He believed, and repeated time and again, that a dangerous connection existed between the West Indies and the United States. Britain planned war on America, which would be launched from Jamaica. In his elaborate dispatches to John Forsyth, Harrison developed a rather extensive conspiracy theory, which argued that Britain

---

Harper and Row, 1988), 128–35; Joel Williamson, *After Slavery: The Negro in South Carolina During Reconstruction* (1965; Hanover, NH: University Press of New England, 1990), 240–52.

39. *New York Colored American,* June 20, 1840; January 30, April 3, and November 13, 1841; Richard Blackett, "The Hamic Connection: African Americans and the Caribbean, 1820–1865" in *Before and After 1865: Education, Politics, and Regionalism in the Caribbean, in Honour of Sir Roy Augier,* ed. Roy Augier, Brian L. Moore, and Swithin R. Wilmot (Kingston, Jamaica: Ian Randle, 1998), 319.

40. After first asserting the "political" importance of his post to Louis McLane, Harrison repeated this claim to John Forsythe and later to John Calhoun. See R. M. Harrison to Louis McLane, August 18, 1833; R. M. Harrison to John Forsyth, June 5, 1838; R. M. Harrison to John Calhoun, June 5, 1844, all in *Despatches from . . . Kingston, Jamaica.*

had destroyed her own colonies in a fit of fanaticism and now sought to destroy the United States by raising an insurrection in the South. They would follow with an invasion launched from the West Indies by a vast army of "black regiments" recruited from the populations of freed slaves. One is tempted to dismiss such assertions as the mere delusions of a paranoid man, which they certainly were, but central components of Harrison's theory were eventually employed (although without his colorful language) by John C. Calhoun, the most influential leader of the antebellum South and, in 1844, the secretary of state.

Harrison's theory of a British conspiracy had begun previous to emancipation with the repeated warnings about secret abolitionist emissaries. He argued that the British would "zealously exert" themselves to effect abolition throughout the world, not out of humanitarianism but from an envy that arose from the prosperity of the slaveholding states. As evidence he cited the case of the Spanish in Cuba, who had recently appointed a consul in Jamaica to keep an eye on British activities. Harrison had befriended the Spanish consul, who was empowered to refuse passports to any one of questionable character who sought to visit Cuba. Harrison suggested that the United States adopt the same policy. The Spanish consul shared Harrison's conviction that the British sent emissaries to both the United States and Cuba to "unhinge the minds of the slaves" and cause insurrections. The Spanish consul encouraged Harrison in his suspicions and made the political importance of his post ever clearer.[41]

Military developments early in the next year pushed Harrison's theory to the next level. A rebellion of Canadian nationalists in the summer of 1837 was suppressed by British troops and Jamaica served as a depot in this effort. Harrison found the presence of troops in the island quite disturbing, and as he did not believe the Canadians to be a credible threat to British power, he deduced that the "machiavellian" British were taking advantage of the uprising for a more nefarious purpose. He had been informed by a source he trusted that the real purpose of British troops in Jamaica was to "settle" the dispute over the Maine boundary through military force. But Harrison suggested that it would not end there, as the British would "urge" Mexico to "commit aggressions" on the United States from the west and would send "incendiaries" into the South to encourage the slaves to "cut the throats" of all the whites. Harrison considered the U.S. armed forces to be

41. R. M. Harrison to John Forsyth, September 8, 1837, *Despatches from . . . Kingston, Jamaica.*

in lamentable condition and reported that British officers in Jamaica had a "contemptible opinion" of the American military arising from defeats in the war against the Seminoles in Florida. He feared the "humiliations" the country might suffer.[42]

In August 1838 Harrison reported two more developments in the island that seemed to illuminate Britain's Machiavellian designs. The apprenticeship system was abolished that year, and Harrison had spent the anniversary of emancipation in the countryside with his family and the Spanish consul, hiding from the insurrection he again supposed would take place.[43] Full emancipation left Harrison disgusted and terrified. Black Jamaicans were not only "unthankful" for their freedom, they also used "treasonable and seditious language" to describe their plans for the future. Some had even said, and he quoted, that "they would hang up all the whites, unite themselves with Hayti, and then attack Cuba, from whence with *three or four hundred thousand men* they would go to America." Moreover, the British were repairing all the island's fortifications, presumably for war with a *"foreign power."*[44]

Over the next two years Harrison came to believe that Britain's imperial strategy had become ever more apparent. In April 1839 he reported that "two Black regiments" were expected shortly in Jamaica from the Windward Islands and that two more regiments would soon arrive in Canada. Even more disturbing was the "recruiting of blackguard negroes" in Jamaica to serve in the British army. Harrison supposed that "these fellows will be excellent firebrands to be thrown ashore on our slaveholding states" in the case of a war between Britain and the United States.[45] By May of the next year, Harrison imagined a full-scale British assault upon the United States launched from Canada and the West Indies. British vessels would deliver munitions to various points in the South. These would be followed by "intelligent black officers in disguise" who would train the slaves in the use of arms and form a "powerful auxiliary Army" that would destroy the

42. R. M. Harrison to John Forsyth, January 25, 1838, *Despatches from . . . Kingston, Jamaica.*

43. R. M. Harrison to John Forsyth, August 8, 1838, *Despatches from . . . Kingston, Jamaica.*

44. R. M. Harrison to John Forsyth, August 27, 1838, *Despatches from . . . Kingston, Jamaica.*

45. R. M. Harrison to John Forsyth, April 2, 1839, *Despatches from . . . Kingston, Jamaica.*

South and sweep across the country toward British regulars advancing southward from Canada. Harrison understood from the newspapers that most Americans thought there would be no war. They were naïve. The British were "jealous of our rising greatness" and could never forget that that the United States had "once been their colonies." America was in great danger.[46]

SHIPWRECKED SLAVES AND BRITISH INTERFERENCE

One of the more remarkable aspects of this window into southern Anglophobia is the similarity in argument between Robert Monroe Harrison and that of the southern political establishment in their assessment of British abolition. Few white southerners before Reconstruction had ever personally experienced life in a predominantly black and free society, yet by 1844 southern leaders would publicly assert a conspiratorial interpretation of British abolition quite similar to Harrison's. Furthermore, the fear that Britain would attack the South using a black army from the West Indies was not uncommon. Even the New Yorker George Templeton Strong considered it possible that "England could land a wooly-headed and flat-nosed regiment on the shores of South Carolina from the West Indies . . . and proclaim emancipation, and the South would soon swim with blood."[47] While it is probable that some of Harrison's dispatches were leaked to the newspaper press, a series of confrontations between U.S. ships involved in the coastal slave trade and British colonial authorities created the impression in many minds that the British were intent on interfering with American slavery. These incidents fostered in the South an intense Anglophobia, which became the dominant factor in the push to annex Texas to the United States—a goal that was achieved in 1845.

British interference with the property rights of American slaveholders began well before West Indian emancipation in August 1834. When a storm hit on January 2, 1831, the brig *Comet* ran aground on a coral reef near the tiny island of Abaco, part of the archipelago of the Bahamas, a

46. R. M. Harrison to John Forsyth, May 23, 1840, *Despatches from . . . Kingston, Jamaica.*

47. Diary entry of March 9, 1839, in Allan Nevins and Milton Halsey Thomas, eds., *The Diary of George Templeton Strong: Young Man in New York, 1835–1875,* 4 vols. (1952; reprint, New York: Octagon, 1974), 1:100.

British colony. Captain Isaac Staples had begun his journey in Alexandria, Virginia, with a human cargo of 164 slaves. His destination was New Orleans, where Louisiana's burgeoning sugar industry created a seemingly unquenchable market for slaves.[48] Abaco residents assisted the *Comet*'s crew and slaves in reaching the main island of Nassau, where captain and crew intended to regroup and continue their journey. But the British customs authorities detained the slaves, arguing that the landing of slaves in a British colony violated the ban upon the transatlantic slave trade. John Storrs, the American consul in Nassau, protested the seizure, and in his dispatch to Secretary of State Martin Van Buren, expressed his belief that Britain's main object in seizing the slaves was "to deprive other States of their labourers." Storrs's next dispatch indicated his doubt that anything would come from his protest, and, presumably, the slaves of the *Comet* went free.[49]

In February 1834—six months before abolition was enacted in the West Indies—the brig *Encomium,* under the command of Paschal Sheffield, departed Charleston, South Carolina, with a cargo of forty-five slaves, rice, naval stores, and several millstones. The *Encomium* was also bound for New Orleans, but around midnight on the fourth, Captain Sheffield found his ship caught up in a maze of protruding rocks off Fish Key, just off the southern coast of Nassau. The crew succeeded in retrieving much of the cargo, including the slaves, and with the help of local wreckers made their way around to New Providence on the island's northern coast. As soon as the Americans entered Nassau's harbor, they were approached by a British customs officer, Alexander Mackey, who seized the slaves and informed the captain that the British crown was now responsible for them. Furthermore, Mackey commanded the Americans to remain on board the wreckers and to make no attempt to communicate with the shore. If they did so, they would be fired upon by the *Pearl,* a sloop of war then in New Providence harbor. The next day all were escorted to the police office in New Providence, where the slaves were interrogated by a magistrate. He asked their names, ages, places of birth, and, most importantly, if they wished to remain in Nassau and be free, or return to the United States and slavery.

48. On the coastal slave trade, see Michael Tadman, *Speculators and Slaves: Masters, Traders, and Slaves in the Old South* (Madison: University of Wisconsin Press, 1989), 79–81.

49. John Storrs to Martin Van Buren, January 17 and 24, 1831, *Despatches from U.S. Consuls in Nassau, West Indies, 1821–1906,* Record Group 59, T 475, National Archives, College Park, MD.

Despite the protests of the owners and the American consul, all but three chose to remain in Nassau.[50]

The actions taken by British colonial officials in 1831 and 1834—before abolition was enacted—probably stemmed from the antislavery tendencies of British customs officers, which became apparent during the controversy surrounding the rendition of a slave woman named Grace Jones. In 1822, one Mrs. Allen of Antigua brought her domestic slave Grace on a visit to England. They returned home in 1823. In August 1825, a customs officer seized Grace on the grounds that she had been unlawfully taken from Britain and was therefore wrongly being held as a slave in Antigua. The prosecutor from the customs house, one Mr. Wick, brought suit against Mrs. Allen in the Vice-Admiralty Court of Antigua, but the attorney general of the colony suspended the case, indicating white colonial sentiment. When Colonial Secretary Lord Bathurst directed the attorney general to pursue the case, he declined to fully present the information provided him by the customs house, resulting in a judgment for Mrs. Allen. Wick then brought an appeal to the High Court of Admiralty in London, where it came before Lord Stowell in the summer of 1827.[51]

With respect to the law, the attorney general of Antigua was correct not to prosecute; past judgments were clear, and he was doomed to lose. Wick and Bathurst apparently acted upon the antislavery understanding of the Somerset case of 1772. In this famous and often misunderstood case, the venerable Lord Mansfield ruled that a slave could not be forcibly removed from Great Britain to be returned to slavery in the Americas. He did not rule that slavery was illegal in Great Britain. Nevertheless, Wick argued that Jones, "being a free subject of his Majesty, was unlawfully imported as a slave from Great Britain into Antigua." But Grace Jones was never a "free subject," even when in Britain. The prosecution suggested that Grace Jones was in fact forced to return to Antigua, which would have freed her under the Somerset precedent, but they did not have evidence to convince Lord Stowell, and he disregarded the suggestion. Understandably, the case stimulated much excitement in Antigua and Britain, and when Stowell's

50. "Protest of Paschal Sheffield, Richard F. Evans, William Richardson, John Waddell, Amedie Garduane fils, Charles Allen" enclosed in George Huyler to Louis McLane, February 24, 1834, *Despatches from . . . Nassau*. See also George Huyler to Louis McLane, February 18, 1834, *Despatches from . . . Nassau*.

51. F. O. Shyllon, *Black Slaves in Britain* (London: Oxford University Press, 1974), 210–11.

decision affirming the judgment of the Vice-Admiralty Court emerged, British newspapers split according to their views on slavery, and the planter papers in Antigua were thrilled. The *Free Press* mocked the "harpies of office" in customs and celebrated the "justice" done for property and slaveholders. Customs house officers must have been humiliated, and when American slaves—unprotected by British law—landed within their jurisdiction, they did not hesitate to free them.[52]

About a year after the liberation of the *Encomium*, Elliot Smith, captain of the *Enterprise*, was caught in a storm that forced him into the port of Hamilton in the British colony of Bermuda. Smith was en route from Alexandria, Virginia, to Charleston, South Carolina, with a cargo of bricks, tobacco, seeds, and seventy-eight slaves. As soon as British customs officials heard that the distressed ship carried slaves, they seized it and declared the slaves free. Several days later a colonial court supported this action by serving Smith with a writ of habeas corpus for the slaves. The court declared all the slaves free, as they had arrived in a British colony where slavery had been abolished. When given the choice, seventy-two African Americans decided to stay in Bermuda, while six chose to continue on to Charleston.[53]

A series of Secretaries of State had protested the emancipatory actions of British colonial officials. In December 1831 after the wreck of the *Comet*, Secretary of State Edward Livingston had instructed Martin Van Buren, then the ambassador to England, to demand compensation for the liberated slaves, not only to reimburse the owners but also to support the 'principle involved.'[54] This initial demand was repeated after each case, but not until January 1837 did Lord Palmerston, the British foreign minister, convey his government's response to all three cases. Britain clearly hoped for a compromise, offering compensation for the slaves taken from the *Comet* and the *Encomium*. But compensation for those taken from the *Enterprise*

52. Ibid., 212–19, 224. On the antislavery understanding of Somerset, see Ruth Paley, "After Somerset: Mansfield, Slavery and the Law in England, 1772–1830," in Norma Landau, ed., *Law, Crime and English Society, 1660–1830* (Cambridge: Oxford University Press, 2002), 165–84.

53. W. Tudor Tucker to John Forsyth, March 2, 1835, *Despatches from United States Consuls in Bermuda, West Indies, 1818–1906*, Record Group 59, T 262, National Archives, College Park, MD.

54. Edward Livingston to Martin Van Buren, December 5, 1831, *Diplomatic Instructions of the Department of State, Great Britain, 1801–1906*, Record Group 59, M77, National Archives, College Park, MD.

was refused on the same grounds initially stated by the judge in Bermuda, that abolition in the British West Indies had nullified the legal status of slavery imposed on the seventy-eight African Americans.[55]

The most strident American response came from South Carolina senator John Calhoun. He was "perplexed" at Britain's long silence on the matter and chided Ambassador Van Buren for merely "tapping gently" at Lord Palmerston's door for the compensation due to slaveholders. The only possible explanation, he supposed, was that the present government in Britain depended on the support of that influential group who entertained "fanatical feelings" on the slavery question. Britain's stance on the matter was completely hypocritical, Calhoun argued, as the same government that condemned slavery in the Americas exercised "unlimited dominion" over more than a hundred million "slaves" in India. The British controlled the labor of Indian peasants "as effectually as our citizens do that of their slaves," which in Calhoun's opinion emptied Britain's antislavery stance of any moral authority.[56] Calhoun appealed to the doctrine of human rights, casting dark shadows on Britain's "philanthropy" in the West Indies by shining a harsh light on British oppression in Asia.

Britain did not offer compensation; nor did Her Majesty's government change its defense. So Calhoun returned to the subject in March 1840, this time sponsoring in the Senate four resolutions that demanded compensation for the slaves liberated from the *Enterprise*. He was concerned with the principle involved—that Britain should understand comity to include recognition of the chattel status of enslaved African Americans. He held that the "law of nations" provided for the protection of the vessels of peaceful nations driven into foreign ports by inclement weather. This included respect for the "municipal law" of the vessel's nation of origin while the vessel remained in port. Calhoun argued that it would be "cruel and inhuman, as well as unjust" to subject American slaveholders to the law of the British colonies which violated the sanctity of their property in slaves.[57]

Calhoun did not depend upon legal argument alone to sway the Sen-

55. Don E. Fehrenbacher, *The Slaveholding Republic: An Account of the United States Government's Relations to Slavery* (New York: Oxford University Press, 2001), 105.

56. John C. Calhoun, "Remarks on the Correspondence with Great Britain concerning the Brigs *Comet, Encomium,* and *Enterprise,*" March 2, 1837, in Robert L. Meriwether, W. Edwin Hemphill, and Clyde N. Wilson, eds., *The Papers of John Calhoun,* 21 vols. (Columbia: University of South Carolina Press, 1959–2001), 8:483–85.

57. John C. Calhoun, "Speech on the Case of the Brig Enterprise, [in the Senate, March 13, 1840]," *Calhoun Papers,* 15:142.

ate. Consistent with his earlier remarks, he observed that the abolitionists still controlled the present Whig ministry in Britain, which had therefore assumed an impossible position that required the adoption of one of two untenable propositions. Either Britain's municipal laws were "paramount" to international law, or slavery itself was a violation of international law. The first proposition would lead to war, which Calhoun did not believe the British desired. And the second ran contrary to the laws of most nations, including Britain. Here Calhoun launched into a veritable diatribe that looked to imperial history to demonstrate British hypocrisy. To deny slavery's legality would take "no small share of effrontery" from a nation that had been the "greatest slave dealer on earth" for generations past, and Britain continued to be, despite its alleged philanthropy, a slaveholder. He had an article entitled "Government of Slaves in Malabar" from the *Asiatic Journal* read into the public record and likened all of British India to "one magnificent plantation." Furthermore, he claimed, emancipation in the West Indies had only replaced the "mild and guardian authority" of the master with the power of the British state over an entire laboring population. It was a "mockery" to call this freedom. Similar instances could be found in the "starved, suffering condition" of the Irish peasantry, as well as in China, where the British reportedly forced on the Chinese the "use of opium, the product of her slaves on her Hindoo plantations." By the time Calhoun was finished, Britain was "making millions of slaves in one hemisphere—forcing, by fire and sword, the poisoning products of their labor on an old and civilized people, while, in another, interposing, in a flood of sympathy, in behalf of a band of barbarous slaves with hands imbrued with blood!" His colleagues were convinced, and Calhoun's resolutions sailed through the Senate. The resolutions, Calhoun's argument, and his diatribe on Britain's abolitionist hypocrisy were quickly published in a pamphlet and in newspapers throughout the country.[58]

As Calhoun's views spread, Americans learned the fate of the *Hermosa*, a brig carrying thirty-eight slaves from Richmond to New Orleans which had also wrecked on those liberating reefs of Abaco Island. Again, British

58. Calhoun, "Speech on the Case of the Brig Enterprise," *Calhoun Papers* 15:139–57. Calhoun's speech was reprinted as a pamphlet and also appeared in the *Washington Globe*, March 23, 1840; *Charleston Mercury*, March 28, 1840; *Edgefield (SC) Advertiser*, April 16 and 23, 1840; *Pendleton (SC) Messenger*, April 24 and May 1, 1840; *Baltimore Niles' Register*, May 2, 1840; *Richmond Enquirer*, December 1, 1840.

officials had freed the slaves.[59] But in November 1841 the pattern changed. One hundred and thirty slaves were bound from Richmond for New Orleans on the *Creole*, and nineteen of them organized a mutiny in which they killed one crew member and seized control of the ship. They were led by Madison Washington, the head cook, and Ben Johnstone, a blacksmith. Johnstone (and probably the others) knew about the *Hermosa*, and once in command the rebels directed the crew to point the ship toward the Bahamas and freedom.[60]

When they arrived in Nassau, a British vessel came alongside, and Zephaniah Gifford, the *Creole*'s first mate, informed the officers of the mutiny. The colonial governor ordered a guard of black soldiers commanded by a white officer to board the ship to prevent the escape of the mutineers while an investigation could proceed. The investigation lasted several days, during which time the people of Nassau learned of the revolt and determined to see the slaves liberated, forcibly if necessary. One morning, a number of small boats operated by local Bahamians armed with cudgels gathered in the harbor, while a crowd of people, black and white, assembled on shore. Violence was averted by the intercession of British troops, but at the end of the day those slaves not indicted for participation in the mutiny (about 110) were carried ashore and triumphantly accompanied by a crowd of "between one and two thousand people" to police headquarters where they were provided with food and shelter in the barracks.[61]

The *Creole* affair infuriated the South. Calhoun considered it an "atrocious and insulting outrage."[62] The *New Orleans Bee* called it "Mutiny and

---

59. For details on the *Hermosa*, see *Senate Documents*, 34th Cong., 1st sess., no. 102 (ser. 824), 238–40.

60. For accounts of the mutiny, see Edward D. Jervey and C. Harold Huber, "The Creole Affair," *Journal of Negro History* 65 (Summer 1980): 196–201; Howard Jones and Donald A. Rakestraw, *Prologue to Manifest Destiny: Anglo-American Relations in the 1840s* (Wilmington, DE: Scholarly Resources, 1997), 81–89; Phillip Troutman, "Grapevine in the Slave Market: African American Geopolitical Literacy and the 1841 Creole Revolt," in *The Chattel Principle: Internal Slave Trades in the Americas*, ed. Walter Johnson (New Haven: Yale University Press, 2004), 203–33.

61. Correspondence between American and British officials, as well as depositions of several crew members can be found in *Senate Documents*, 27th Cong., 2d sess., no. 51 (ser. 396): 1–46. Quote is from John F. Bacon (American consul to Nassau) to Daniel Webster, November 30, 1841.

62. "Remarks on British Seizures of Slaves [in the Senate, December 22, 1841]," *Calhoun Papers*, 16:14.

Murder" and reported that the British refused to give up the rebels for trial in their home state, adding to the "dark catalogue of outrages" Britain had committed against American slaveholders.[63] The *Lynchburg Virginian* offered its readers a short history of the *Comet*, the *Encomium*, and the *Enterprise* and argued that the United States "ought not only to demand, but to enforce reparation for this outrage," as it was now clear that British policy had encouraged a slave rebellion. The *Colored American* of New York considered the rebellion "another Amistad," paraphrased the famous line of the English poet William Cowper that "*on English soil slaves cannot breathe*," and advised "old Virginia to be careful how she ships her slaves to the South."[64] The rebellion on the *Creole* transformed the British presence in the West Indies. Knowledge of the liberating precedents set by the *Comet*, the *Encomium*, the *Enterprise*, and the *Hermosa* had spread among the enslaved of the American South. The hope of freedom steeled the will of Madison Washington and his fellow rebels, and while they had been captured, many more were freed and the punishment required by a slave society was thwarted. British abolitionism was more than an inspiring model for northern abolitionists; it was a real threat to American slavery.

ROBERT MONROE HARRISON AND
THE SOUTHERN DRIVE TO ANNEX TEXAS

In the spring of 1840, Harrison muddled along, miserable in free Jamaica and waiting hopelessly for the next insurrection. As the years passed, little changed except the recipients of his dire missives. Daniel Webster followed Forsyth, and Harrison did not spare the New Englander from his peculiar creativity. Britain was like "an unchaste female," he wrote Webster, who wished upon others the same destitute condition that emancipation wrought. Abolition had "ruined" the West Indies, and now Britain sought to deny the economic advantages of slave labor to other countries as well. To do this Britain would combine with Haiti to "throw up-

63. *New Orleans Bee*, December 3, 1841. See also December 2, 1842.

64. *Lynchburg Virginian*, January 6, 1842; *New York Colored American*, December 25, 1841. The *Creole* continued to be a source of diplomatic tension between Britain and the United States until 1853, when an umpire in an Anglo-American claims commission ruled in favor of U.S. slaveholders and ordered Britain to pay $110,330 in restitution. See David Brion Davis, *Inhuman Bondage: The Rise and Fall of Slavery in the New World* (Oxford: Oxford University Press, 2006), 269.

wards of 200,000 blacks" on the coasts of the South, a threat that required the country to unite not only to "resist *invasion*" but also to silence the abolitionists, as their agitations would lead inexorably to the "*separation of the states.*" He reminded Webster that Britain could never "forget that the United States were once her Colonies" and would always seek to "impede our rising greatness." Events throughout the British Empire made the moment all the more dangerous in Harrison's mind, as Britain had just "crushed Muhamet Ali, frightened 'John Chinaman' out of his wits and put down insurrection in her India possessions." Harrison suggested that these developments indicated a shift in Britain's imperial policy and that its next project would surely be to "clip the wings of that '*ambitious model republic,'*" as Britons in Jamaica were known to say.[65] But Webster was busy making peace with Great Britain, eventually manifested in the Webster-Ashburton treaty of 1842, and it seems unlikely that he took Harrison seriously.[66]

Evidence suggests, however, that President John Tyler *was* concerned with changes in British policies, for in the fall of 1841 he sent Duff Green to Great Britain as his unofficial representative to sound the waters of British policy. We have seen that in 1834 Green had been active in condemning British abolition as editor of the *United States Telegraph,* Calhoun's paper in Washington. In the election of 1840 Green departed from his usual alignment with Calhoun and supported the Whig ticket of William Henry Harrison and Tyler, establishing the *Baltimore Pilot* to advance their campaign. When Harrison's death brought Tyler to the presidency, Green became one of the "kitchen cabinet" of close advisers.[67]

In January of 1842, Green wrote to Tyler and to Abel Upshur (who was then secretary of the navy) that Britain actively sought to achieve commer-

65. R. M. Harrison to Daniel Webster, March 22, 1841, in *Despatches from . . . Kingston, Jamaica.* Harrison referred to Britain's actions in support of the Ottoman Empire against Muhammad Ali of Egypt, the Opium War with Qing China, and the First Afghan War, which turned out to be a disaster for the British. Harrison was fond of the "unchaste female" metaphor, repeating it for Secretary Abel Upshur. See R. M. Harrison to Abel Upshur, October 30, 1843, ibid.

66. Harrison's dispatches have not been included in Webster's published papers. For more on the Webster-Ashburton treaty, see Howard Jones, *To the Webster-Ashburton Treaty: A Study in Anglo-American Relations, 1783–1843* (Chapel Hill: University of North Carolina Press, 1977).

67. Fletcher M. Green, "Duff Green, Militant Journalist," *American Historical Review* 52 (January 1947): 258–59; Norma Lois Peterson, *The Presidencies of William Henry Harrison and John Tyler* (Lawrence: University Press of Kansas, 1989), 147.

cial supremacy throughout the world and that abolitionism was at the core of this imperial endeavor. British India produced the same tropical products as the slave-based economies of Cuba, Brazil, and the United States, and the British believed that without this competition, they would dominate the world market in all of these products. This could only be achieved if slavery was abolished, and Green believed that the British would use violent means to accomplish this end.[68]

It did not take long for Green's argument to enter the public sphere. In April 1842, the *Southern Quarterly Review* included an anonymous article entitled "East India Cotton," which posed as a review of four pamphlets written in the 1820s and 1830s. The author alleged a decades-long conspiracy between abolitionists and planters that was designed to defeat British India's economic rivals in the West Indies and the southern United States. In the 1820s and 1830s, East Indian interests had engineered the abolition of West Indian slavery to defeat their economic rivals in sugar production. To do this, they had created the abolitionist societies as humanitarian fronts, which successfully manipulated British public opinion and accomplished abolition. Now, the article claimed, this same conspiracy had set its sights upon dismantling American slavery in order to destroy cotton production in the South and thereby deliver the world cotton market to the English nabobs of the East.[69]

The alleged plot had begun with indigo, which in 1789 was primarily

68. Green to Tyler, January 24, 1842; Green to Upshur, January 24, 1842, both reprinted in Frederick Merk, *Slavery and the Annexation of Texas* (New York: Alfred A. Knopf, 1972), 187–92.

69. "East India Cotton," *Southern Quarterly Review* 1 (1842): 446–93. The works reviewed were: *Letters to Wilberforce, Recommending the Encouragement of the Cultivation of Sugar in our Dominions in the East Indies, As the Natural and Certain Means of Effecting the General and Total Abolition of the Slave Trade* (London, 1822); James Cropper, *Letters to the Liverpool Society for Promoting the Abolition of Slavery, on the Injurious Effects of High Prices of Produce, and the Beneficial Prospects of Low Prices on the Condition of Slaves* (London, 1823); *East and West India Sugar* (London, 1823); and John Phipps, *Treatise on the Principal Products of Bengal,- Indigo, Sugar, Cotton, Hemp, Silk and Opium* (Calcutta, 1832). The author of one of these essays, James Cropper, was an abolitionist and a wealthy East Indian merchant convinced that free trade and antislavery went hand-in-hand. Cropper faced similar criticism in the 1820s (and by later historians) that his economic interests, rather than his abolitionism, were his primary motivation. Ironically, Cropper also argued that American slavery was more benign than West Indian slavery because it was not protected by mercantilist policies. See David Brion Davis, *From Homicide to Slavery* (New York: Oxford University Press, 1986), 262, 272, 276.

grown in French Saint-Domingue.[70] "Swarms" of abolitionist emissaries traveled from London to Paris to spread "the same wild and spurious principles" that now pervaded the United States. British abolitionists created societies that sent "incendiary publications" throughout France and its West Indian colonies. Then the renowned abolitionist Thomas Clarkson had invited Vincent Ogé, the mulatto leader from Saint-Domingue, to London, and within a few months Ogé had "*sailed from London to the famous indigo island, with arms, ammunition and stores in abundance.*"[71] Readers of Bryan Edwards would have known Ojé as one of the prime instigators of the Haitian Revolution, which, as the author pointed out, had made British India the dominant producer of indigo.[72] Thus the template was formed, whereby East Indian planters profited from the schemes of British abolitionists who raised insurrections and abolished slavery.

A similar operation, the article stated, had destroyed slavery in the British West Indies in 1834. For this endeavor the East India Company created more abolitionist societies, now with the innovation of missionary societies as proxies. The author claimed to have evidence that the missionaries were the "political agents" of the abolitionist societies. They had gone to the West Indies under the cloak of a Christianizing mission but had instead "preached . . . incendiary doctrines, caused several insurrections, got the churches pulled down, [and] themselves mobbed" and returned home crying "persecution." The conniving missionaries had "stirred up all England in a blaze of abolition excitement," and the Emancipation Act of 1833 had been the result.[73] Southerners were quite familiar with the history of missionaries and insurrections in Demerara and Jamaica, and for those who had never believed that British abolition was philanthropic in any way, the story rang true.

British East Indian interests were now engaged in a similar plot, this time directed at their cotton rivals in the South. The writer purported to have evidence that the British abolitionist society that sent John Smith and William Knibb to start rebellions in the West Indies "was the identical society which sent the incendiary *George Thompson to the United States.*" Where Smith and Knibb had "incited" the rebellions that led to abolition in

70. "East India Cotton," 467.

71. Ibid., 470.

72. Bryan Edwards, *An Historical Survey of the French Colony of St. Domingo* (Philadelphia, 1806), 46–53.

73. "East India Cotton," 483–84.

the West Indies, Thompson had been instructed to turn the North against the South and let civil war destroy southern slavery. The result would be the same; the last competitors to British East Indian cotton planters would be destroyed.[74]

The arguments of Green's letters to Tyler and Upshur and his references to "East India Cotton" echoed Calhoun's use of India in his portrayal of British abolitionist hypocrisy in his 1840 speech about the *Enterprise.* Now, however, India appeared not as a demonstration of Britain's two-faced policy on "free" labor but as the economic rationale behind transatlantic abolitionism. This vision of Great Britain received further elaboration in a pamphlet written by the legal scholar Henry Wheaton, which appeared in the *Southern Literary Messenger* in June 1842. In July the *Messenger* followed Wheaton's piece with an anonymous article entitled "Speculations Upon the Consequences of a War with Great Britain" that accused Britain of contemplating an invasion of the South with a black army from Jamaica.[75]

Such propaganda complicated Webster's task of obtaining peace with Britain, but it aligned with the theory that Robert Harrison had been developing since British abolition. Webster's place in Tyler's cabinet had always been difficult, and soon after the treaty with Britain was passed in August 1842 Webster submitted his resignation. The next secretary of state was Abel Parker Upshur of Virginia.[76]

Upshur's view of the world shared much more with Calhoun's and Robert Harrison's than had Webster's. Born in 1790 to a wealthy planting family on the Eastern Shore Upshur pursued a career in law and in 1826 became a judge in Virginia's General Court. In the state's constitutional de-

74. Ibid., 489.

75. Henry Wheaton, "Our Relations with England," *Southern Literary Messenger* 8 (June 1842): 390–96; "Speculations Upon the Consequences of a War with Great Britain," *Southern Literary Messenger* 8 (July 1842): 444–47. Wheaton was an acknowledged expert on international law who was appointed minister to Prussia in 1835. He was also an associate of Duff Green's while Green was in Europe. See St. George L. Sioussat, "Duff Green's 'England and the United States': With an Introductory Study of American Opposition to the Quintuple Treaty of 1841," *Proceedings of the American Antiquarian Society* 40 (1930): 181; Rossiter Johnson, ed., "Henry Wheaton," *The Biographical Dictionary of America* (Boston: American Biographical Society, 1906), 10:unpaginated.

76. David Pletcher, *The Diplomacy of Annexation: Texas, Oregon, and the Mexican War* (Colombia: University of Missouri Press, 1973), 119.

bates of 1829, he aligned himself with John Tyler as a formidable champion of the eastern slaveholding elite, and a decade later he published "Domestic Slavery" in the *Southern Literary Messenger,* which advanced the "positive good" proslavery argument. Along with Thomas Dew and Edmund Burke, Upshur cited Bryan Edwards as one of his intellectual antecedents.[77] Upshur's friendship with Tyler brought him to Washington in 1841 as secretary of the navy and in July 1843 he became Tyler's secretary of state. Robert Harrison could not have asked for a more sympathetic correspondent.

One of the first consular dispatches Upshur received as secretary of state came from Harrison, who substantiated Green's allegations. His dispatch said that "partial insurrections" had become quite frequent in Cuba. His informants from Cuba had told him that "English emissaries," most notably David Turnbull, were responsible for the present state of the island, and Harrison feared the insurrections would spread to the United States.[78] Turnbull was a British abolitionist who had traveled extensively in the West Indies to document the continuance of the transatlantic slave trade despite British efforts to suppress it. Turnbull's *Travels in the West,* (1841), proposed an expansion of the powers of the mixed courts of commission that had been established by a treaty with Spain in order to prosecute slavers. Turnbull wanted to empower prosecutors to investigate Africans already landed in Cuba (beyond the present jurisdiction of the courts) in order to bring charges against their owners.[79] Harrison believed these courts were merely a "cloak" to facilitate British plans to bring about "emancipation of

77. William Freehling, *Road to Disunion,* 388–94; Randolph G. Adams, "Abel Parker Upshur" in *American Secretaries of State and Their Diplomacy,* 20 vols., ed. Samuel Flag Bemis et al., 6:67–77; Judge A. P. Upshur, "Domestic Slavery," *Southern Literary Messenger* 5 (October 1839): 677–87.

78. Robert Monroe Harrison to Daniel Webster, June 14, 1843, *Despatches from. . . Kingston, Jamaica.* Apparently, Harrison did not know that Webster had resigned on May 8, 1843. Hugh Legare replaced Webster but died soon after his appointment. Upshur became Secretary of State ad interim on June 23, 1843 and received his official commission on July 24, 1843. See Claude H. Hall, *Abel Upshur: Conservative Virginian, 1790–1844* (Madison: State Historical Society of Wisconsin, 1964), 190–91.

79. David Turnbull, *Travels in the West: Cuba with Notices of Porto Rico and the Slave Trade* (London, 1841), 340–60. For more on Turnbull and Britain's attempt to suppress the slave trade, see David R. Murry, *Odious Commerce: Britain, Spain and the Abolition of the Cuban Slave Trade* (Cambridge: Cambridge University Press, 1980), 134–36; David Eltis, *Economic Growth and the Ending of the Transatlantic Slave Trade* (New York: Oxford University Press, 1987), 118–19.

the Slaves in America and Cuba."[80] Turnbull was now in Jamaica, he reported, and Harrison was sure that he had been transferred in order to carry out his "villainous measures" in safety from the Spanish authorities in Cuba. In Jamaica Turnbull had access to a press, and Harrison predicted that Cuba would soon be "deluged" with pamphlets that would result in insurrection. Turnbull was "most intimate" with Henri Boyer, the former president of Haiti, and Harrison warned that in the event of an insurrection "a vast number of Haytiens" would combine with the "vagabonds of this Island" to create a formidable military force. Harrison ended his dispatch on a chilling note. He reminded the secretary that the slaveholding states were "only a stones throw from Cuba," and—as he had been saying for years—it would be wise for the South to be prepared.[81]

Harrison's dispatch would not have been the first time that Upshur had heard of the alleged intrigues of David Turnbull. The State Department had been warned of Turnbull's activities in Cuba early in 1843, and as secretary of the navy Upshur would have been made aware of this. The warning came from Alexander Everett, a former U.S. minister to Spain who had established a lasting correspondence with the Cuban planter Domingo Del Monte. Everett met Del Monte in 1840 when he visited Cuba on behalf of the Van Buren administration to investigate charges brought by British abolitionists against Nicholas Trist, the U.S. consul in Havana, for engaging in the transatlantic slave trade. In November 1842, Del Monte penned an anxious letter to Everett that described an extensive conspiracy wrought by British abolitionists to end slavery in Cuba through insurrection. Abolitionist agents had promised to support a movement for independence among Cuban Creoles on the condition that slavery would be abolished. Military assistance for the war with Spanish forces would come from Jamaica, where Santiago Marino, an exiled Venezuelan caudillo, would lead an invasion that would be followed by a general insurrection of the slaves.[82]

In January of 1843 Everett forwarded a copy of Del Monte's letter to

80. R. M. Harrison to Abel Upshur, November 24, 1843. See also R. M. Harrison to Daniel Webster, June 14, 1843; R. M. Harrison to Abel Upshur, October 3, 1843; R. M. Harrison to John Calhoun, June 5, 1844, August 23, 1844, all in *Despatches from . . . Kingston, Jamaica.*

81. Robert Monroe Harrison to Daniel Webster, June 14, 1843, *Despatches from . . . Kingston, Jamaica.*

82. Robert L. Paquette, "The Everett-Del Monte Connection: A Study in the International Politics of Slavery," *Diplomatic History* 11 (Winter 1987), 11.

Secretary of State Daniel Webster, who responded immediately by passing the information along to Robert Campbell, the U.S. consul in Havana, and to Washington Irving, the U.S. minister to Spain, asking both to investigate the allegations. Irving replied in March 1843 that the Spanish authorities were fully aware of the situation in Cuba but were not concerned, as the island's military capabilities were fully prepared to handle such threats. Any attempts at revolt would be "punish[ed] severely," which apparently satisfied Webster.[83] But Webster did not inform Everett of the steps he had taken, so Everett forwarded the information to John Calhoun. Calhoun deemed the information of the "highest importance" and assured Everett that he had written to President Tyler on the matter.[84] Everett's decision to inform Calhoun was critical, as it substantiated what Calhoun had suspected for quite some time—that Britain was acting to abolish slavery in the Americas and considered insurrection a viable tool.

Upshur responded to Harrison almost immediately and asked for more information on Britain's intrigues in Cuba. Harrison must have been exhilarated—someone had finally taken seriously the "political" dimension of his post![85] Upshur's concern with Britain's abolitionist intentions was soon confirmed. Within a month of his letter to Harrison, Upshur received another loaded missive from Green which shed new light on Harrison's accusations. Enclosed with Green's letter was another letter, which Green asked Upshur to read and forward to Calhoun. Green reported to both men that the British prime minister Sir Robert Peel had stated in Parliament that it was his government's intention to "promote the abolition of slavery in Brazil, Cuba, and the United States." Even more damning of British intent was the news that Foreign Minister Lord Aberdeen

83. Alexander Everett to Domingo Del Monte, May 20, 1843, in Joaquin Llaverias y Martinez, ed., *Centon Epistolario de Domingo Del Monte,* 7 vols. (Havana: Academia de la Historia Cuba, 1923–57), 5:101–2; Daniel Webster to Robert B. Campbell, January 14, 1843; Daniel Webster to Washington Irving, January 17, 1843; Washington Irving to Daniel Webster, March 10, 1843, all in William R. Manning, ed., *Diplomatic Correspondence of the United States: Inter-American Affairs, 1831–1860,* 12 vols. (Washington, DC: Carnegie Endowment for International Peace, 1936–39), 11:26–29, 331–32.

84. Everett to Del Monte, May 20, 1843 in Llaverias y Martinez, *Centon,* 5:102. Calhoun's response to Everett has apparently not survived. It is not included in the *Calhoun Papers.*

85. Upshur's letter has not survived, but Harrison's next dispatch was a response to Upshur's letter of July 8. See R. M. Harrison to Abel Upshur, October 3, 1843, *Despatches from . . . Kingston, Jamaica.*

did not want Texas annexed to the United States and would offer a loan to the Texan government that would secure the abolition of slavery in Texas if indeed this would prevent annexation. Green urged Upshur to advise the president to take a strong stand on the annexation of Texas on the grounds that a British-sponsored emancipation in Texas would create a "refuge" for runaway slaves and perhaps much worse.[86]

Britain's apparent policies toward Texas horrified Upshur, and he felt it necessary to seek Calhoun's opinion before he either acted "boldly" on his concerns or allowed them to subside. Upshur believed that Britain intended to bring about the abolition of slavery "throughout the American continent & islands" in order to destroy the competition with Britain's own colonies. He also believed that an independent Texas was too weak to stand on its own and would be forced to entrust its security to a greater power, either Britain or the United States. The South should "*demand*" the annexation of Texas, Upshur wrote, as "indispensable to their security." Otherwise Britain might bring abolition to Texas and threaten slavery along the southwestern frontier.[87]

Calhoun agreed entirely. In a reply marked "confidential," Calhoun wrote that he considered the danger from British abolitionism "great & menacing," a fact most recently confirmed by the second World Abolitionist Convention that had been held that year in London. He agreed that abolitionism simply masked Britain's commercial avarice and advised specific precautions. First, Calhoun suggested that Upshur publicly "demand" an explanation from Britain as to its intentions with Texas. Second, Upshur should send to France "an able minister, completely identified with the South," who could convince the French of the southern understanding of Britain's designs upon Texas. Finally, "the publick mind" in the United States had to be sensitized to the "danger" posed so that formal annexation could be agitated and ultimately accomplished. Calhoun believed that the arguments required to substantiate these charges could be based on public information, and he presumed that Upshur had access to more information

86. Duff Green to John Calhoun, August 2, 1843; Duff Green to Abel Upshur, August 3, 1843. Green's letter to Calhoun was enclosed in his letter to Upshur. The letter to Upshur is reprinted in Merk, *Slavery and Annexation*, 224–25; the letter to Calhoun is in *Calhoun Papers*, 17:329–32.

87. Abel Upshur to John Calhoun, August 14, 1843 in *Calhoun Papers*, 17:329–30, emphasis in the original. Upshur shared these opinions with William S. Murphy, the consul in Texas, and warned him to be aware of British intrigues. See Abel Upshur to William S. Murphy, August 8, 1843 in Manning, *Diplomatic Correspondence*, 11:44–49.

that shed even more light on British intentions.[88] Upshur already had such information from Harrison.

On September 28, 1843, Upshur sent two letters to Edward Everett (the brother of Alexander Everett), the U.S. minister to England. The first cited an exchange in Parliament between Aberdeen and the abolitionist M.P. Lord Brougham and instructed Everett to confront the British on their intentions toward Texas and American slavery. The second letter was marked "confidential" and attempted to convince Everett (a northerner) that abolitionism was merely a philanthropic mask worn by Britain to cloak a policy intended to "revive the industry of her East and West India colonies." Emancipation in the West Indies had failed, he explained, and Britain's pursuit of global abolition was a ploy to rob the slaveholding powers of the commercial advantage of the superior efficiency of slave labor. Furthermore, Upshur claimed that American concern with British intentions toward Texas should not be a sectional issue. He took it for granted that abolition in Texas would cause abolition in the South and offered Everett a worst-case scenario for the national ramifications of such an event. Employing now-classic proslavery logic, Upshur predicted that with emancipation the black population would be forced to move north, as "extermination" was inevitable if they attempted to remain in the South. What would happen, Upshur asked, if "*two and a half million*" blacks suddenly migrated to the North? Would white laborers agree to work alongside them? Surely Everett would agree that it was not American policy to "degrade" labor in this way, and so a foreign policy that secured Texas and thus the preservation of southern slavery was mandated. Upshur's argument to Everett was only one of many that would follow in the propaganda campaign to convince northerners of their interest in the annexation of Texas.[89]

Meanwhile, in Jamaica, Robert Harrison carried out Upshur's request for more information on Turnbull's intrigues against Cuba. General Marino was indeed in Jamaica and had resided on the island for some time. Moreover, American missionaries in the island had publicly stated that

88. John Calhoun to Abel Upshur, August 27, 1843, *Calhoun Papers*, 17:381–82.

89. Abel Upshur to Edward Everett, September 28, 1843 (two letters), Manning, *Diplomatic Correspondence*, 11:6–17. Upshur's argument was one variation of the "safety-valve thesis" that Frederick Merk has identified as central to the propaganda campaign to annex Texas. See Merk, "A Safety Valve Thesis and Texas Annexation," reprinted in Merk, *Fruits of Propaganda in the Tyler Administration* (Cambridge: Harvard University Press, 1971), 95–120.

American abolitionist societies would cooperate with Britain's plans. Harrison firmly believed that these "scoundrels" were fully capable of such a treasonous act. Upshur's blood must have boiled.[90]

The propaganda campaign to move American opinion toward accepting the need to annex Texas began in earnest in the fall of 1843. Upshur himself used the columns of the *Daily Madisonian* of Washington, D.C. One article described the "melancholy results" of emancipation in Jamaica and alleged that the British had created a "system of espionage" based in the islands that sought to divide the North from the South.[91] In October 1843 Upshur opened secret negotiations with Texas minister Isaac Van Zandt, and by January of the next year he was certain that a treaty with Texas could gain the necessary approval from two-thirds of the Senate.[92] Little did he know that he would not live to see the success of his efforts. On February 28, 1844, Upshur and a party of Washington elites spent the day on the Potomac on the battleship *Princeton*. The day's festivities included one too many demonstrations of the Peacemaker, a massive cast-iron cannon that fired 212-pound balls. Toward the end of an entertaining day of military spectacle, the cannon exploded, killing Upshur and several others on board.[93] After a short period of indecision, Tyler passed the quest for Texas to capable and informed hands—the next secretary of state was John Calhoun.

Progress toward annexation was well underway, and a treaty with Texas was signed on April 12. Calhoun's task was to secure its passage in the Senate. Upshur had believed this to be a sure thing, supposing that the propaganda campaign had diffused northern concerns that annexation was a purely southern measure, and Tyler had always talked of Texas annexation as a national, not a sectional, concern. One of the most effective and broadly disseminated arguments intended to allay northern anxiety had been put forth by Senator Robert Walker of Mississippi. Walker argued

90. R. M. Harrison to Abel Upshur, October 3, 1843, *Despatches from . . . Kingston, Jamaica*.

91. *Washington (DC) Daily Madisonian*, September 23, 1843. Claude Hall has argued that this article, as well as similar pieces in the *Madisonian*, were authored by Upshur, as the information conveyed could only have come from the State Department itself. See Hall, *Abel Upshur*, 256, n. 9 and 10. Other pieces in the *Madisonian* include: September 25, 27, 28, October 4, 19, 28, November 1, 7 1843.

92. Peterson, *The Presidencies*, 199; Merk, *Slavery and Annexation*, 36; Pletcher, *Diplomacy of Annexation*, 131.

93. Peterson, *The Presidencies*, 201–3.

that instead of expanding the domain of slavery, the annexation of Texas would actually reduce the extent of slavery. Walker pointed to the upper South states of Maryland and Virginia, both of which were selling slaves to the Southwest and thereby reducing their own slave populations. Soon, he argued, they would be free states. This was the continuation of the same process by which the North had been relieved of slavery, and Walker predicted that the annexation of Texas would enhance this process, as the cultivation of the virgin soils of Texas would continue to siphon off the excess slave population in the upper South so that even the Carolinas would soon be free states.[94]

Walker's portrayal of slavery as an institution that would gradually wither away could not have been an acceptable argument to Calhoun, who was slavery's most prominent apologist. He had long been concerned with Britain's abolitionist designs. Texas was Britain's next target, and Calhoun wanted to make it absolutely clear that it would be annexed as a matter of national security—not as part of some scheme to gradually remove slavery from the country. Calhoun's sudden rise to the State Department provided him with the ideal opportunity to place his proslavery mark upon national policy. The treaty with Texas was to be sent to the Senate with supporting documents, which Calhoun delayed in order to write his famous letter to Robert Pakenham and to stamp Texas annexation as a proslavery measure.[95]

When Calhoun combed through the files of the State Department, familiarizing himself with the official correspondence of his predecessor, he came upon a dispatch from Pakenham, which relayed a letter from Lord Aberdeen that set forth British policy toward Texas. Aberdeen denied the rumors of British "designs" on Texas, and in particular he wished to clarify Britain's position on slavery in Texas and the world. It was a matter of public record that Britain desired abolition throughout the globe, including in Texas, but it would only use "open and undisguised" means to accomplish this noble purpose.[96] Calhoun knew this assertion to be

94. *Letter of Mr. Walker of Mississippi, Relative to the Annexation of Texas.* Walker's letter is reprinted in Merk, *Fruits of Propaganda,* 221–52. For more on Walker's role in the annexation of Texas, see James P. Shenton, *Robert John Walker: A Politician from Jackson to Lincoln* (New York: Columbia University Press, 1961), 22–40.

95. For evidence that Calhoun delayed sending the treaty to the Senate, see John Tyler to Andrew Jackson, April 18, 1844 in Bassett., *Correspondence of Andrew Jackson,* 6:279.

96. Richard Pakenham to Abel Upshur, February 26, 1844, *Calhoun Papers,* 18:53–54.

false. He knew personally from his earlier correspondence with Alexander Everett that David Turnbull was responsible for the insurrections that had plagued Cuba over the past year, and Everett had written again with even more evidence of British activities there.[97] Robert Harrison's dispatches in the thick Jamaica file provided further evidence that Britain had designs upon the South, and Calhoun's response to Pakenham clearly expressed his distrust of Aberdeen's protestations. While it was perfectly acceptable for Britain to abolish slavery in its own possessions, Aberdeen's acknowledgement that Britain desired abolition in Texas was a serious matter. The United States could not allow such an outcome, for it would expose the "most vulnerable portion of our frontier" to British power—known to be used for abolitionist ends. Since Aberdeen had acknowledged the abolitionist dimension of British power, Calhoun felt it to be the "imperious duty" of the federal government to take measures that would permanently obstruct Britain's influence over Texas.

Perhaps, as his biographers have argued, Calhoun should have stopped there.[98] But he went on to lecture Pakenham on the humane superiority of southern slavery. The northern states had abandoned slavery, and the results had been horrendous. The census of 1840 had shown that one of every ninety-six black Americans in the North was either deaf, dumb, blind, insane, or an "idiot." In the South, however, the proportion of slaves so afflicted was only 1 in every 672, evidence that slavery achieved for the African race the highest "elevation in morals, intelligence, [and] civilization."[99] Calhoun's letter shattered all of the carefully wrought pretensions that annexation was not a sectional measure. He grounded U.S. policy toward Texas in the acerbic cadences of proslavery argument, and he was sure to let the Senate know that he had done so. The treaty and documents arrived in the Senate on April 22, and on the twenty-seventh the antislavery Democrat Benjamin Tappan leaked them to the *New York Evening Post*. That same day Martin Van Buren and Henry Clay, the presumed

97. Alexander Everett to John Calhoun, April 13, 1844, *Calhoun Papers*, 18:224–29. Everett also made these claims public in "The Texas Question," *United States Magazine, and Democratic Review* 15 (September 1844): 264–68; and "Present State of Cuba," *United States Magazine, and Democratic Review* 15 (November 1844): 475–83.

98. Wiltse, *John C. Calhoun*, 171; John Niven, *John C. Calhoun and the Price of Union* (Baton Rouge: Louisiana State University Press, 1988), 276–77.

99. John Calhoun to Richard Pakenham, April 18, 1844, *Calhoun Papers*, 19:273–78.

presidential candidates for the Democrats and the Whigs, respectively, published letters that renounced any intention to annex Texas. Calhoun could not have planned it better. Clay won the Whig nomination on an anti-annexation ticket; Van Buren lost the Democratic nomination because of his anti-annexation stance; and James Polk—Young Hickory from Tennessee—became the Democratic candidate on a pro-annexation ticket. The election of 1844 now turned on the question of Texas annexation, and, thanks to Calhoun, annexation was now a clear proslavery measure.[100]

In the midst of this partisan turmoil, the Senate debated the Texas treaty and rejected it decisively on June 8, 1844. At the same time developments in Europe provided Calhoun with the opportunity to advance his proslavery agenda at the international level. As the treaty failed in Washington, Lord Aberdeen made overtures to France to form a "Diplomatic Act" that would make Britain and France the guarantors of the Republic of Texas by coercing Mexico to acknowledge Texan independence. While historians have cast doubt upon the chances of the Diplomatic Act ever succeeding, Calhoun seized upon the information to communicate to the world the American position on the future of slavery.[101]

Early in August 1844, Calhoun received a dispatch from William King, a former senator from Alabama whom Calhoun had appointed minister to France. King Louis Phillippe desired that Texas remain independent for commercial considerations but assured the Alabamian that France would not contemplate any action the United States considered hostile. King was impressed with the French and considered their stance "essentially pacific and conservative," but Calhoun noticed the desire for an independent Texas and took the opportunity to write instructions to King that expanded upon the arguments he had made to Pakenham.[102]

Calhoun's audience was both domestic and international. To insure that all of Europe understood the American position, he included his letter to King in a series of instructions to the American ministers in the German States, Spain, Austria, Russia, Belgium, the Netherlands, and Brazil and

100. Fehrenbacher, *Slaveholding Republic*, 124–26; Merk, *Slavery and Annexation*, 68, 94–95; Pletcher, *Diplomacy of Annexation*, 139–45.

101. Pletcher, *Diplomacy of Annexation*, 156–62; Ephraim D. Adams, *British Interests and Activities in Texas, 1838–1846* (1910; reprint, Gloucester, MA: Peter Smith, 1968), 167–75.

102. William R. King to John Calhoun, July 13, 1844, *Calhoun Papers*, 19:334–38.

instructed each to defend the U.S. policy regarding Texas. The letter was also published as a pamphlet in South Carolina and was widely reprinted in newspapers on both sides of the Atlantic.[103]

Calhoun considered the division between the United States and Texas to be unnatural and believed that "destiny" would bring Texas into the American fold unless the European powers intervened. He acknowledged that the interests of France in Texas were purely commercial, but he warned that Great Britain joined commercial interests with a clear "political" agenda—abolitionism—which Calhoun believed would prove catastrophic to blacks and whites in Texas and in the United States. Only with black slavery, Calhoun argued, could the rich lands of Texas be cultivated to produce the wealth that all desired, and only white Americans with black slaves could do it.[104]

Calhoun's argument rested upon the proslavery interpretation of the failure of free labor to successfully replace slavery in the British West Indies and the belief that the British were not above violent means to spread abolition. As we have seen, Calhoun was convinced of this before he entered the State Department, and Harrison's dispatches would have further substantiated these views, providing direct evidence from the islands that emancipation had proved disastrous and British abolitionists were active in the West Indies.[105] By this time many British writers had also deemed emancipation a failure, and Calhoun had only to cite an article from *Blackwood's Magazine* of June 1844.[106] He noted that despite the enormity of British

103. Bruno Gujer, "Free Trade and Slavery: Calhoun's Defense of Southern Interests Against British Interference, 1811–1848," Ph.D. dissertation, University of Zurich, 1971, 181, n. 3. Calhoun's letter to King was reprinted as a pamphlet in South Carolina and in the following newspapers: *Washington (DC) Daily National Intelligencer,* December 9, 1844; *Washington (DC) Constitution,* December 11, 1844; *Washington (DC) Daily Madisonian,* December 11, 1844; *Baltimore Niles' Register,* December 21, 1844; *Columbus (GA) Times,* December 25, 1844, *New York National Anti-Slavery Standard,* January 2, 1845; it also appeared in the *London Times,* January 2, 1845. See *Calhoun Papers,* 19:578.

104. Calhoun to King, August 12, 1844, *Calhoun Papers,* 19:569–71.

105. In addition to the dispatches to Upshur that Calhoun would have read, Harrison wrote to Calhoun on several occasions before Calhoun penned his letter to King. On the failure of emancipation in Jamaica, see R. M. Harrison to John Calhoun, May 4, 1844, *Calhoun Papers,* 18:429–35; on British activity in the West Indies see R. M. Harrison to John Calhoun, June 5, 1844, *Despatches from . . . Kingston, Jamaica* (not included in the *Calhoun Papers*).

106. Calhoun cited James Macqueen, "Africa-Slave Trade-Tropical Colonies," *Blackwood's Edinburgh Magazine* 55 (June 1844): 731–48. Macqueen's article advocated estab-

possessions in the East and West Indian colonies, Britain was still being outproduced in sugar, coffee, and cotton by slaveholders in the Americas. This was a result of British abolition, which had left the island economies at the "brink of ruin" while stimulating the slave-based economies of Cuba, Brazil, and the United States, whose leaders had wisely disregarded the British example. Abolition had been so disastrous that some of Britain's West Indian colonies had even begun to import slave-grown sugar because it was cheaper than the local product grown by free labor. Britain's great experiment had proven itself a colossal failure, and anyone who could read a chart would see that slave labor was superior to free.[107]

The economic disaster in the West Indies explained Britain's desire to abolish slavery throughout the hemisphere. For Calhoun, it was "too late in the day" to accept claims that humanitarian sentiments motivated Britain's hope for abolition in the Americas. While he accepted that these admirable impulses may have been influential in 1808 when the slave trade was abolished, or even in 1833 when West Indian slavery was abolished, in 1844 he found the evidence overwhelming that greed and power now drove the British. Modern economic history had demonstrated that the wealth of the "civilized nations of the temperate zone" depended upon the exchange of manufactured goods for the natural products of the tropical regions. Nations acted in accord with their economic interests, and in 1833 the British had believed that free labor in the East and the West Indies would be more efficient than slave labor and thereby maintain Britain's commercial preeminence. "Experience" had now convinced them of the poverty of such logic, which led them to formulate a new plan to regain commercial dominion. Britain still wore the mask of philanthropy, but clear-eyed analysts like Calhoun could see that it simply sought to destroy its competition, which could only be done by abolishing black slavery in the Americas, beginning with Texas.[108]

There were some in Europe who did not share his view of the emancipation in the West Indies, and Calhoun moved on to dispel any notions

---

lishing British colonies in East Africa so Britain could regain dominance in the world market for tropical goods. Both Macqueen and Calhoun worked from the assumption that the trade in tropical products such as cotton and sugar were the key to wealth, but Calhoun implied that Macqueen's article revealed the master plan behind Britain's abolitionist activities in the Americas.

107. *Calhoun Papers*, 19:572–73.
108. Ibid., 571–72.

that Britain's experiment with abolition could provide a template for future emancipations.[109] Abolition in the British West Indies had occurred under the best possible circumstances, he wrote, which could never be replicated in another slave country. The most important factor in West Indian emancipation had been the military force that the British had been willing to exercise "to prevent or crush at once all insurrectionary movements on the part of the negroes." Furthermore, Britain's willingness to maintain white supremacy had been crucial in the maintenance of the social order that had characterized the West Indies over the past decade. It would not so happen in Cuba, Brazil, or the United States, especially if Britain were to succeed with its policy of exporting abolition. For Calhoun, a "correct conception" of the likely aftermath of emancipation could only be formed through the historical lens of Saint-Domingue, not Jamaica. The abolition of slavery would result in "unforgiving hate" between whites and blacks, resulting in a race war in which one or the other would be "subjugated, extirpated, or expelled" from the land. The result of course, would be Britain's rise to commercial dominance in the production of tropical staples—the fulfillment of her wicked design.[110]

The election of 1844 revealed the country fairly evenly split, but much of the antislavery vote in the North went to James Birney and the Liberty Party, giving Polk the election. Despite Polk's narrow victory, when Congress reconvened in December, Tyler made a final push for the joint resolution on the shallow ground that the election had "decisively manifested" the will of the people. Enough of Congress agreed, and by February 28, 1845, both houses passed Tyler's resolution. Texas became a state on May 5, 1845. Antislavery efforts had been silenced, and the "Texas junto" had won.[111]

Calhoun's urgent push to annex Texas was based on an interpretation of British abolitionism that synthesized a decade of southern commentary on Britain's act of emancipation in the West Indies. He had read the news reports on the failed economies of the West Indies, followed the in-

---

109. The French in fact, were considering abolishing slavery in the French West Indies and had evaluated the experiment in the British West Indies with the view to implementing a similar plan. See Lawrence C. Jennings, *French Reaction to British Slave Emancipation* (Baton Rouge: Louisiana State University Press, 1988).

110. *Calhoun Papers*, 19:574–75.

111. Fehrenbacher, *Slaveholding Republic*, 125–26; Merk, *Slavery and Annexation*, 121–66.

terference of British authorities in the coastal slave trade, and read the dispatches of Robert Monroe Harrison, all of which told him that emancipation had been a disaster that had left Britain economically disadvantaged. Calhoun was also aware of the growing abolitionist movement that saw this recent history from a very different perspective. For him, the most important fact about the United States was its status as a slaveholding nation faced with the mortal threat of abolitionism from within and without. The people needed to understand this, and Calhoun's letter to Pakenham, as well as his letter to King, should be seen in this light. In Calhoun's eyes, British interest in Texas could only be seen as a threat, and annexation became an imperative for the protection of American civilization as he saw it. In pursuit of this goal he formulated a policy toward annexation that he defended to the world and the nation as explicitly proslavery. America's face to the world was the face of a slaveholder, and not until the establishment of the Confederate States of America in 1861 would slavery be advocated at a higher level.

7

Rethinking Liberty

On August 1, 1849, African Americans in Columbus, Ohio, gathered to commemorate Britain's abolition of slavery in the West Indian colonies. The celebration had been planned months in advance, and while only the published toasts have survived (thanks to Frederick Douglass), accounts of celebrations in other communities suggest a program that would have been familiar to abolitionist communities throughout the country. The day often began with a procession through the major streets to a church or to a wooded grove on the outskirts of town. Here there would be a solemn reading of the British Parliament's Act of Abolition and, perhaps, the Declaration of Independence, and then there would be prayers, songs, a series of orations, and a picnic. Later in the evening organizers often held a private dinner, the occasion for toasts. By 1849 American abolitionists had been celebrating the First of August for eleven years, and Douglass's omission of such familiar details indicates his astute editorial selection of the most newsworthy information. The toasts were indeed remarkable.[1]

They began with "the 1st of August, the day we commemorate," an acknowledgment of the day in 1834 when Parliament's decree of abolition was enacted in the West Indies. This traditional first toast was a conscious echo of "the day we celebrate," the toast that had led white celebrations of the Fourth of July since at least the turn of the century. But there the resonance with the traditional American rite ended, for the toasts that followed trumpeted a radical abolitionism that cut to the hollow heart of white America's celebration of its love of freedom. "Slaveholding Christians" were damned as the "legitimate heirs and faithful commis-

1. *Rochester North Star,* June 29 and September 14, 1849.

saries of Satan." They condemned the war with Mexico as a "Slave-holding scheme," which had extended the "area of Despotism." They toasted Joshua Giddings and all others who "contend for the colored man's rights." But the most incredible toast was to "Nathaniel Turner, Cinque, and Madison Washington—They were great and mighty men; competent to lead the oppressed to Liberty: let us perpetuate their memory."[2]

It is hard to imagine a more radical toast in antebellum America. Most white Americans knew Nathaniel Turner by the more common—and diminutive—"Nat." They said he was the deranged lunatic whose hallucinations had inspired the bloody insurrection in Southampton, Virginia. When African Americans offered a formal toast in honor of Turner and replaced "Nat" with the proper "Nathaniel," they endowed Turner's leadership with a respectability generally reserved for George Washington or Lafayette. And to link Turner to the African Cinque and to Madison Washington, who had both led slave-ship rebellions off the U.S. coast within the past few years, was to commemorate the tradition of violent struggles for black freedom, an appropriate counterpoint to white America's celebration of its violent struggle for national freedom on the Fourth of July.

The toast to Joshua Giddings was equally significant. One of the most powerful Whigs in Ohio, Giddings represented the cutting edge of political abolitionism. In 1849 Giddings was in his sixth term as a representative of Ohio in the U.S. Congress and had gained national renown for his impassioned support for Madison Washington and the *Creole* rebels. But Giddings had also supported Zachary Taylor for the presidency in 1848. Taylor was a slaveholder from Louisiana and a hero of the Mexican War, but he was also a Whig. Giddings made deals with slaveholders so that he could maintain a position of power in the federal government and attack slavery on the national stage. Garrisonians disapproved of this cooperation with the devil, regardless of its end, but these black abolitionists in Columbus saw the value of political abolitionism, and they toasted Giddings and Nathaniel Turner in the same breath.[3]

These toasts in Cincinnati illuminate the sophisticated ideology in the late 1840s of black abolitionists who valued both violent rebellion and political compromise. They also reveal the importance of First of August celebrations in the intensifying exchange between radical abolitionism and

2. *Rochester North Star*, September 14, 1849.

3. James Brewer Stewart, *Joshua R. Giddings and the Tactics of Radical Politics* (Cleveland: Press of Case Western Reserve University, 1970).

party politics in the antebellum North. In the United States, First of August celebrations were created by the African American community.[4] While rooted in the festive traditions of the black community in the North, the celebrations also appropriated elements of the stylized rituals staged by white Americans every Fourth of July. In the antebellum decades, Whigs and Democrats celebrated the Fourth as the birthday of American freedom and styled themselves (in contrast to their opponents) as freedom's great protectors. Coming less than a month later, abolitionist celebrations of the First of August were a courageous response. African Americans and white abolitionists appropriated the forms of the Fourth of July—the banners, parades, orations, toasts, and community gatherings—and infused them with the subversive content of radical abolitionism. Thus, celebrations of West Indian emancipation were the civic rituals of American abolitionism. They were central to the core project of the movement—the molding of an antislavery constituency in the North. First of August celebrations, as well as the newspaper accounts that described them, fashioned an "imagined community" of abolitionism that sought a moral transformation of the United States. When Americans celebrated the First of August, they reminded their neighbors of the egregious hypocrisy of a thriving slavery in a nation that claimed freedom as its sustenance.[5]

THE FOURTH OF JULY

Fourth of July celebrations began during the Revolutionary War and by the time of British abolition were the dominant public celebrations in American life. The earliest ones arose from the desire among the rebellious colonists to forge the political unity necessary to win the war against Britain. David Waldstreicher has argued that these celebrations in the late 1770s laid the foundation for a national identity among the thirteen newly independent states. Drawing upon familiar British commemorations such as Guy Fawkes Day and Coronation Day, patriots invented commemo-

4. For a transnational analysis of these celebrations, which took place in the British West Indies, Canada, and Great Britain, in addition to the United States, see J. R. Kerr-Ritchie, *Rites of First of August: Emancipation Day in the Black Atlantic World* (Baton Rouge: Louisiana State University Press, 2007).

5. Benedict Anderson, *Imagined Communities: Reflections on the Origins and Spread of Nationalism* (London: Verso, 1983); Timothy P. McCarthy has also employed Anderson's work in "To Plead Our Own Cause": Black Print Culture and the Origins of American Abolitionism," in *Prophets of Protest: Reconsidering the History of American Abolitionism,* ed. McCarthy and John Stauffer (New York: New Press, 2007), 117.

rations of the movement for national independence. Each observance, as defined by the orations, the toasts, and the embroidered banners, contributed to the evolving definition of what it was to be an American. Newspaper accounts were particularly important, as readers throughout the rebellious colonies could relive the Fourth of July in Boston, Baltimore, or Charleston, and thereby get a sense of commonality with the far-flung populace of the emerging republic.[6]

The powerful fusion of celebration and print that emerged from the Revolution became the central praxis of early republican politics. As the suffrage began to expand in the 1790s and early 1800s, political power became linked to the amassing of votes and therefore influence over public opinion. Celebrations drew attention to candidates and garnered popularity, while newspaper editors built loyal constituencies of readers that worked to make the emerging parties national. Accounts of these celebrations were central to this process. While the Fourth of July remained the touchstone of political celebration, the fierce contests between Federalists and Democratic-Republicans spawned similar annual events that revealed the political flexibility of public celebrations. George Washington's birthday (February 22), for example, became an occasion for Federalists to strengthen the ties of party and disseminate their particular vision of the United States, past, present, and future. With the ascendancy of the Jeffersonian opposition in 1800, commemorations of Jefferson's inauguration (March 4) developed into a partisan event that sought not only to celebrate Jefferson's victory but also to define the Federalists as a misguided minority, beyond the limits of "true" Americanism. Celebration thus led to countercelebration as the two-party system began to structure the political calendar.[7]

6. David Waldstreicher, *In the Midst of Perpetual Fetes: The Making of American Nationalism, 1776–1820* (Chapel Hill: University of North Carolina Press, 1997), 32–35. More examples of accounts describing several celebrations in the antebellum period include: *Boston Advertiser,* July 6 and 7, 1840; *New York Times,* July 7, 1852, July 5, 1854, and July 7, 1855. The *New York Times* of July 7, 1855 described the Fourth of July celebration in thirty-five different communities. Other studies of the Fourth of July include Simon Newman, *Parades and the Politics of the Street: Festive Culture in the Early American Republic* (Philadelphia: University of Pennsylvania Press, 1997); Len Travers, *Celebrating the Fourth: Independence Day and the Rites of Nationalism in the Early Republic* (Amherst: University of Massachusetts Press, 1997).

7. Jeffrey L. Pasley, *"The Tyranny of Printers": Newspaper Politics in the Early American Republic* (Charlottesville: University of Virginia Press, 2001), 1–23; Newman, *Parades and the Politics of the Street,* 80–82; Waldstreicher, *In the Midst of Perpetual Fetes,* 214.

But public celebrations also served interests beyond the realm of partisan politics. Mary Ryan has shown that the traditional military parade arranged by regiment could be adapted to workingmen's organizations that lined up according to a set program. Through the act of marching, these organizations claimed their position in public life. In New York City, for example, artisans and workingmen participated in public occasions such as Evacuation Day (November 25). Proud of their work and eager to participate in national politics, artisans marched and toasted their crafts as essential to the success of the new republic. In the 1830s when tensions grew between masters and journeymen under the pressures of a growing capitalist economy, these celebrations became the locus for class expression, as masters emphasized individual responsibility while journeymen asserted the importance of their crafts and their role in the polity. Celebrations peopled the arena of politics and served as the auditorium for contested ideologies.[8]

By the 1830s, the big, city-sponsored Fourth of July celebrations were the most prominent on the summer calendar. These popular events mixed the raucous carousing of white workingmen with rhetoric about independence and a martial atmosphere that vividly recalled the battles of the Revolution. A ceremonial reading of the Declaration of Independence generally preceded orations about American freedom and the glories of national independence. Smaller, elite parties would also gather for private dinners that always featured a round of toasts. These were often printed in the newspapers, giving private gatherings a public dimension that voiced a strong political message, which Peter Thompson has described as a "verbal broadside." In the antebellum decades, "freedom" was a common theme for these toasts. In 1834, for example, Lafayette was toasted as the "friend of Washington—the Friend of Liberty." The celebrants at Tammany in 1854 toasted the "Freedom of Speech, of the Cross and of Religion." In 1855 President Franklin Pierce was toasted as the "instrument of freemen."[9]

8. Mary Ryan, *Civic Wars: Democracy and Public Life in the American City during the Nineteenth Century* (Berkeley and Los Angeles: University of California Press, 1997), 45–46, 64–65; Sean Wilentz, *Chants Democratic: New York City and the Rise of the American Working Class, 1788–1850* (New York: Oxford University Press, 1984), 87–97.

9. W. J. Rorabaugh, *The Alcoholic Republic: An American Tradition* (New York: Oxford University Press, 1979), 151–52; Peter Thompson, "The Friendly Glass": Drink and Gentility in Colonial Philadelphia," *Pennsylvania Magazine of History and Biography* 133 (October 1989): 560; *Boston Advertiser,* July 8, 1839 (Springfield, Mass.); *New York Times,* July 7, 1852 (Baltimore, MD); July 5, 1854 (Philadelphia and Utica, NY); July 5, 1855 (Tammany

According to a correspondent to the *Boston Daily Evening Transcript* in 1838, the celebration in New York had begun the night before with informal fireworks and drinking in the streets. Central Park saw the quick establishment of "temporary groggeries," simple booths that sold liquor by the dram. These were frequented by "the rowdies," and the evening air was filled with "the shouts of revelers and the firing of squibs, pistols," or anything else that could burn gunpowder. In the morning the tired and hungover were joined by fresher faces who came into the city on the "ferries, and the railroad" to observe the military parade and the evening fireworks. According to correspondents to the *New York Times,* the scene appeared to be similar in Philadelphia, Baltimore, and Washington in 1852. The Philadelphia correspondent observed "an incredible amount of gunpowder" wasted in the streets, along with a fine parade of the military and 150,000 people gathered on Broad Street to witness the evening fireworks display. In Baltimore there were "the usual quantity of fights, assaults, &c.," and fireworks in several parts of the city. In Washington, D.C., cannons were fired, and all of the city bells were rung at sunrise, noon, and sunset.[10]

The martial, alcoholic atmosphere at so many Fourth of July celebrations gave them a reputation that some citizens critiqued. In 1838, for example, the *Boston Daily Evening Transcript* juxtaposed an account of the celebration in Lowell, Massachusetts, with the above-mentioned description of the rowdy celebration in New York. Instead of gunshots and firecrackers, the predominant sounds were "church bells." The procession was of school children, not soldiers, and it was absent "the usual noisy accompaniment of martial music." The Lowell correspondent deemed this style of celebration "more patriotic" than any other. N. P. Rogers of Plymouth, Massachusetts, wrote to the (abolitionist) *Herald of Freedom* that the temperance and antislavery societies of Campton had replaced the "poor, old, rum-soaked, powder-smoked anniversary" with two celebrations— "Anti-drunkenness in the forenoon and anti-*slavery* in the afternoon." Only through celebrations like these could Americans become "a *sober* and a *free* people." One of William Lloyd Garrison's correspondents from Holliston, Massachusetts, wrote that the antislavery society there had celebrated the Fourth with a prayer meeting and an oration on immediate emancipation;

Hall in New York). Quotes are from *New York Times,* July 6, 1858; *Boston Daily Evening Transcript,* July 5, 1834; *New York Times,* July 5, 1854, and July 5, 1855.

10. *Boston Daily Evening Transcript,* July 6, 1838; *New York Times,* July 7, 1852.

it was far "more appropriate" than the usual Fourth, "profaned by drunkenness, revelry and hypocritical boasting."[11] As in the 1790s, reformers' embrace of the Fourth of July showed its political flexibility.

But when abolitionists embraced the Fourth, they sought to redefine its traditional meaning. Symbolically, the Fourth of July defined the United States as a freedom-loving nation despite the persistence of slavery and racism that denied freedom to African Americans. In 1831, Garrison reprinted an essay from the *Brooklyn Advertiser* that admonished white Americans for the "self gratulation" they practiced on the Fourth of July. It was a "delusion," the Brooklyn editor warned, that masked the enormous crime of slavery. The degradation of African Americans had also been quite tangibly manifested at some July Fourth celebrations. African Americans had been the victims of mob violence at Fourth of July celebrations in Philadelphia in 1805, New York in 1834, and Indianapolis in 1845, when white mobs attacked African Americans who had assembled in public spaces. Antipathy toward the Fourth of July, however, went beyond the fear of violence. African Americans and their white abolitionist allies rejected traditional Fourth of July rituals because they celebrated a nation that endorsed slavery and racism, a nation where black slavery was a prop for white men's freedom.[12]

THE FIRST OF AUGUST

In his seminal *Black Abolitionists,* the late Benjamin Quarles starkly noted that black Americans and white abolitionists "celebrated West Indian emancipation day because they did not have much to choose from." African Americans in the North did have a tradition of public celebration that stretched back to the eighteenth century, such as the Pinkster celebrations of New York and the Election Days of New England. But in the early nineteenth century, there were few landmarks of freedom for African Ameri-

11. *Boston Daily Evening Transcript,* July 6, 1838; *Concord (NH) Herald of Freedom,* undated, reprinted in *Boston Liberator,* July 14, 1837; *Boston Liberator,* July 14, 1837.

12. Gary Nash, *Forging Freedom: The Formation of Philadelphia's Black Community, 1720–1840* (Cambridge: Cambridge University Press, 1988), 177; *Boston Liberator,* July 23, 1831; Shane White, " 'It Was a Proud Day': African Americans, Festivals, and Parades in the North, 1741–1834," *Journal of American History* 81 (June 1994): 34; Leonard I. Sweet, "The Fourth of July and Black Americans in the Nineteenth Century: Northern Leadership Opinion within the Context of the Black Experience," *Journal of Negro History* 61 (1976): 260–63.

cans to commemorate. In 1808 black communities in New York and Philadelphia began to celebrate the abolition of the transatlantic slave trade on
January 1, an event that continued for several years; African Americans in
Boston celebrated the same occasion on July 14. Boston celebrations involved organized processions and banners and attracted the ire of whites
uncomfortable with such public displays of black pride. Broadsides showing gross caricatures of African Americans ridiculed the "Bobalition" proceedings, and angry white crowds began to harass the marchers until commemoration ceased in the late 1820s. In 1827 New York blacks began to
celebrate the end of slavery in their state, which had legislated gradual
abolition and fixed the Fourth of July as the day slaves born in 1799 became free. New York celebrations resembled those in Boston, but differences arose among black leaders concerning the appropriate relationship
between African Americans and the Fourth of July. Some believed that it
was appropriate to celebrate on the Fourth as a sign of respect to the legislature that had granted their freedom. Others, however, pointed to the
racist treatment meted out to blacks on the Fourth of July by intoxicated
whites. As a result, some black New Yorkers celebrated abolition on the
Fourth, but more chose to celebrate on the fifth.[13]

This tradition of freedom celebrations bears witness to the longstand-
ing efforts of free African Americans to politically engage with white
American society. As U.S. political culture matured, public celebrations
provided a clear means of advancing a political agenda such as abolitionism. In the 1830s, as black abolitionists convinced some antislavery whites
to abandon the American Colonization Society, a radical, interracial abolitionist movement emerged to challenge the white supremacist, proslavery
mainstream. When Great Britain abolished West Indian slavery on August 1, 1834, the fortuitous proximity of the Fourth of July and the First
of August (like the similar proximity of Washington's birthday and Jefferson's inauguration) allowed black and white abolitionists, often together,
to project their movement into the public square. The Fourth of July made

13. Benjamin Quarles, *Black Abolitionists* (New York: Oxford University Press, 1969),
118; Mitch Kachun, *Festivals of Freedom: Memory and Meaning in African American Emancipation Celebrations, 1808–1915* (Amherst: University of Massachusetts Press, 2003), 16–
53; Genevieve Fabre, "African American Commemorative Celebrations in the Nineteenth
Century" in *History and Memory in African American Culture,* ed. Genevieve Fabre and
Robert O'Meally (New York: Oxford University Press, 1994), 77–80; White, "It was a
Proud Day," 35–39; Waldstreicher, *In the Midst of Perpetual Fetes,* 328–44.

summer into the time of year when Americans affirmed their political identity. The First of August explicitly rejected the exclusive nationalism of the Fourth while the memory of that year's celebration was still quite fresh. Celebrations of the First of August made visible an interracial political collectivity of Americans who rejected the mainstream acceptance of slavery and racism publicly represented by celebrations of "American Freedom" on the Fourth of July.[14]

From the beginning, abolitionist leaders drew explicit links between the celebrations. The New York celebration in 1834, for example, began with an opening address by the black abolitionist David Ruggles, which was followed by solemn readings of the "DECLARATION OF INDEPENDENCE," the "Declaration of the National Anti-Slavery Convention," and the British Parliament's "Emancipation Act." The ceremonial recitation of the Declaration of Independence (and Garrison's capitalization in his newspaper account) followed the model of the Fourth of July, but the readings of key abolitionist texts challenged the definition of liberty as most white Americans understood it. After several orations, the assembly passed resolutions that continued the mirroring of the Fourth. The first resolution celebrated liberation, not of the United States from Britain's tyranny but of the enslaved of the West Indies from the tyranny of slavery. Where Fourth of July toasts and resolutions generally celebrated the United States, the New York meeting celebrated "generous-hearted Britain" and hoped that August 1, 1834, foreshadowed the day when "boasted 'free America'" would follow the British example. And just as accounts of Independence Day appeared in all the papers, black New Yorkers resolved that the proceedings of their meeting be "published in the newspapers," so all could read of the freedom they celebrated and the slavery they cursed. The resolutions projected a bold counterpoint to the patriotism of the Fourth of July and transposed the traditional opposition of Britain and the United States. Moreover, the celebrants' recitation of the Declaration of Independence signaled the embrace of the revolutionary moment that characterized political abolitionism. Just as partisan celebrations embraced nationalism while advancing a political agenda, abolitionist commemorations of the First of August

14. Paul Goodman, *Of One Blood: Abolitionism and the Origins of Racial Equality* (Berkeley and Los Angeles: University of California Press, 1998), 23–64; Richard S. Newman, *The Transformation of American Abolitionism: Fighting Slavery in the Early Republic* (Chapel Hill: University of North Carolina Press, 2002), 86–130.

celebrated the United States while demanding that the rhetoric of liberty be applied to African Americans. The Declaration of Independence may have stated that "all men are created equal," but only British abolition had begun to make it so, and only the abolition of slavery would make the United States live up to its pretensions.[15]

A celebration in Philadelphia in 1836 made the link with the Fourth of July even more explicit. In his introduction to the account, Garrison commented that black Philadelphians had carried on a "model" celebration that "might be imitated with advantage by the white celebrators of the anniversary of independence." Here the tables were turned. While the First of August celebration clearly followed the pattern of the Fourth of July, the rowdiness that had come to signify the Fourth led Garrison to suggest that the tone of the First of August should become a model for the Fourth of July. The celebration began with an address by the black abolitionist James Cornish followed by "appropriate public exercises" that included a procession through the city led by a banner made by the "Ladies of Philadelphia." Colorfully embroidered with gold-leaf lettering on a fine, white satin background framed with green tassels, the banner proclaimed "AUGUST FIRST, 1834. HAIL BIRTH DAY OF BRITISH EMANCIPATION" and called upon "our beloved country" to celebrate "the Lundys and Garrisons" of the United States who would "fan the like flame" in America until every slave was free.[16]

A dinner followed these events, which ended with a long series of "sentiments" proposed by more than a dozen participants and cheered by the audience with either "good, cool water" or "fine, pure lemonade." The Philadelphia "sentiments" played the same ideological role as toasts of wine or hard cider on the Fourth of July, while simultaneously offering a not-too-subtle critique of the drunkenness that often accompanied such occasions. Samuel C. Hutchins likened emancipation in the West Indies to a tree planted, which would grow until its branches "overshadowed the whole earth, and the fetters that now bind the sons and daughters of Africa be shaken off." Only then, Hutchins said, could "we universally celebrate the anniversary of Independence of these United States." Another, proposed by James M'Crummill, toasted the United States as "an unnatural

15. *Boston Liberator,* August 30, 1834. For more examples of African American commentary on the Fourth of July, see Kachun, *Festivals of Freedom,* 52–53, 86.

16. *Boston Liberator,* September 17, 1836.

mother to her natural children—still we love her." As in 1834, these black abolitionists recognized their American identity, but in the same breath they denounced their country's moral failures.[17]

WAITING FOR FULL FREEDOM

One toast at the Philadelphia celebration must have left its cheerers thinking. It was the first one—"The Day we celebrate"—and its call to honor all who advocated "universal and unconditional Emancipation to the enthralled of all nations."[18] As the audience knew very well, British abolition had been gradual, not immediate. West Indian slaveholders had been financially compensated—which implied that the government recognized the legitimacy of human property—and the former slaves of the West Indies still suffered the injustices of the apprenticeship system. Black Philadelphians did not celebrate the next First of August; in fact, of the six celebrations that took place in 1836, only two were repeated the next year. Emancipation was still compromised in the British West Indies, and American activists would wait for the abolition of the apprenticeship in 1838 to develop the First of August into the national celebration that it came to be.[19]

Full emancipation in 1838 inaugurated a significant geographic expansion of the celebration of the First of August in the northern and western United States. American abolitionists paid careful attention to their British counterparts' efforts to end the apprenticeship system, and in July 1838 the *Liberator* reported that Jamaica's House of Assembly had decided to forego enforcing the remaining years of apprenticeship.[20] Soon it was clear that the other colonies would follow Jamaica, and the abolition of the hated apprenticeship system was finally accomplished. Complete emancipation called for celebration, and in 1838 abolitionists staged events in thirty-six communities in New York, Massachusetts, Pennsylvania, Connecticut,

17. Ibid. Similar examples include *New York Colored American,* July 20 and August 17, 1839.

18. *Boston Liberator,* September 17, 1836.

19. William Green, *British Slave Emancipation: The Sugar Colonies and the Great Experiment, 1830–1865* (Oxford: Oxford University Press, 1976), 154–60; Kachun, *Festivals of Freedom,* 55.

20. *Boston Liberator,* July 6, 1838.

Ohio, New Hampshire, Rhode Island, and Vermont—precisely those regions of the North where political abolitionism would later emerge.[21]

Most of the towns that celebrated the First of August in 1838 for the first time were in rural areas of the North which had been settled by the descendents of New England emigrants and/or had significant African American communities. These towns were already connected to the centers of abolitionism through the network of newspapers and antislavery societies that had been growing since the early 1830s. The faint response to Britain's gradual abolition from 1834 to 1838 reveals abolitionist dedication to immediatism and the "unfree" character of the apprenticeship system, but we must also consider the hostile social climate that impinged on abolitionist activity during these years. As Mitch Kachun has observed, African Americans did not celebrate the Haitian Revolution for fear of violence, and according to Leonard Richards, antiabolitionist mobs began to appear in 1833, the very year of British abolition and the formation of the radical American Anti-Slavery Society. In 1835, proslavery mobs in the North and the South met the abolitionist mail campaign with organized violence. Gathering to the call to suppress "amalgamation," white mobs attacked abolitionist meetings in New York, Philadelphia, Boston, Utica, Cincinnati, and elsewhere throughout the North and West, making it particularly dangerous for African Americans or abolitionists to congregate publicly. While the frequency of mob activity decreased after 1835, the lingering threat likely dampened enthusiasm for public celebration.[22]

Perhaps the most elaborate celebration of 1838 took place in Cincinnati, Ohio. On the night of July 31, "a large and respectable assemblage" of

21. Based upon surveys of August through October in the *Boston Liberator* (1834–38), *New York Emancipator* (1836–38), *New York Colored American* (1837–38), and *Cincinnati Philanthropist* (1837–38); James Brewer Stewart, *Holy Warriors: The Abolitionists and American Slavery*, rev. ed. (New York: Hill and Wang, 1997), 78–79.

22. Mitch Kachun, "Antebellum African Americans, Public Commemorations, and the Haitian Revolution: A Problem of Historical Mythmaking," *Journal of the Early Republic* 26 (Summer 2006): 249–73; Leonard Richards, *"Gentlemen of Property and Standing": Anti-Abolition Mobs in Jacksonian America* (New York: Oxford University Press, 1970), 20–71. See also, James Brewer Stewart, "The Emergence of Racial Modernity and the Rise of the White North, 1790–1840," *Journal of the Early Republic* 18 (Summer 1998): 181–217; Stewart, " 'Modernizing 'Difference': The Political Meanings of Color in the Free States, 1776–1840," *Journal of the Early Republic* 19 (Winter 1999): 691–712.

Table 2. First of August Celebrations, 1834–1838

STATE	1834	1835	1836	1837	1838
New York	New York		Albany Catskill	New York (2)	Watertown Rochester Utica (2) Fort Ann Madison Byron Albany Germantown Skanteales Troy New York Mills Union Village New York (3)
Massachusetts	South Reading Amesbury & Salisbury	Boston	Fall River New Bedford & Fairhaven	Boston	Deerfield Wrentham Pawtucket Andover Chelsea Lynn Salem Fall River Boston (2)
Pennsylvania			Philadelphia (2)		Philadelphia Pittsburgh
Connecticut					Norwich
Ohio					Cincinnati Putnam
New Hampshire					Concord Dover
Rhode Island					Providence
Vermont					Brattleborough West Townshend

Source: Based upon surveys of August through October in the *Boston Liberator* (1834–38), *New York Emancipator* (1836–38), *New York Colored American* (1837–38), and *Cincinnati Philanthropist* (1837–38).

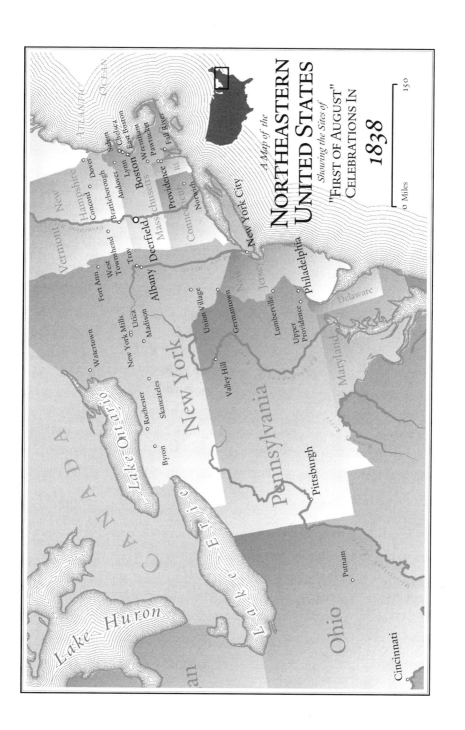

A Map of the

NORTHEASTERN UNITED STATES

Showing the Sites of
"FIRST OF AUGUST"
CELEBRATIONS IN
1838

0 Miles   150

the African American community gathered in the Bethel church. Fifteen minutes before midnight, the celebrant announced to the audience that "the joyful hour" of full emancipation was nigh. The congregation stood in "breathless silence" for the entire fifteen minutes, and when the midnight hour struck, all joined with the choir to sing the "jubilee hymn."

> Blow ye trumpet, blow!
> The gladly solemn sound.
> Let all the nations know,
> To earth's remotest bound
> The year of jubilee is come.

This first verse was followed by the chorus alone, "chanted vociferously."

> Watchman tell us of the night,
> What the signs of promise are.
> Travelers on yon mountain's height
> See that glory beaming star.

And then "the whole now shouted,"

> Praise ye the Lord, hallelujah!
> Praise ye the Lord, hallelujah!
> Praise ye the Lord, hallelujah!

It was a rousing opening. Solemn prayers followed, offered by the "elders of the various denominations," and then there were addresses by Mr. O. T. B. Nickens and Wallace Shelton. So the night went, with more singing, chanting, and praying until two o'clock in the morning.[23]

But the celebration had only begun. Perhaps sleepy, but clearly inspired, a "large number" gathered at ten the next morning and processed "through a portion of the city" to the Bethel church. Meanwhile, the Cincinnati Union Society met at the New Street Chapel, and, accompanied by a band of musicians, they too processed to the Bethel church to bring the entire community together. By eleven, the gathering had spilled into the street, and many likely found it difficult to hear the addresses of Mr. G. Q. Langston and Mr. Andrew J. Gordon, or the "declaration of sentiments" read by Nickens. Following these readings, a collection was taken to benefit the

23. *New York Colored American,* August 25, 1838.

New York Colored American, and some went home. But more than one hundred members of the Cincinnati Union Society continued the festivities at a "plain, economical, total abstinence dinner" at the residence of Mr. A. M. Sumner, where a series of "sentiments" were read and cheered with "great enthusiasm."[24]

As in Philadelphia in 1836, the first sentiment invoked "the event we celebrate this day," offered as the providential fulfillment of the scriptural injunction that "Ethiopia shall stretch forth her hand." All peoples of African descent would become "a people," united by their liberation from New World slavery. Full emancipation in the West Indies manifested "the budding" of this "glorious work." British abolitionism was cheered through sentiments admiring Britain's "philanthropists and statesmen" as well as the "Ladies of England." "The abolitionists of America" were cheered, as were John Quincy Adams and "the martyred Lovejoy" (the abolitionist editor of Alton, Illinois, who had been murdered while defending his press from a proslavery mob). Sentiments to groups within the community included: "the youth of our city of both sexes," as well as the Cincinnati Education Society and the Philomathean Institute. One sentiment celebrated the "Declaration of Independence" and the "Constitution of Ohio," which were both, the community agreed, "on the side of Liberty and Equality when not misinterpreted."[25] The dinner lasted well into the evening with more speeches and singing. Lewis B. Leach spoke on "civil and religious liberty," a Mr. Douse gave an address on "American slavery," there were performances by "several of the youth," and Sumner closed the day with some thoughts on the "Signs of the Times." A description of the day's proceedings was drawn up by George Cary, who sent them to be printed in the *Colored American,* along with a five dollar contribution to support the paper.[26]

The celebration ritually engaged three different audiences—white Cincinnati, the black community, and the transnational abolitionist movement. Within the broader public sphere of Cincinnati, the procession of African Americans through the streets from one church to another was a provocative spectacle for nonabolitionist citizens. Public processions were central to the Fourth of July, and many whites probably felt they were for

24. Ibid.
25. Ibid.
26. Ibid.

"whites only." As we have seen, Cincinnati's infamous "Black Laws" had attempted to limit the city's African American population, and violent white mobs had enforced these laws in 1829. Similar violence broke out in 1836 when James Birney established the *Philanthropist*, the first abolitionist newspaper to be published in the West. Well-heeled mobs destroyed the press and again attacked black neighborhoods.[27] So it took daring for black Cincinnatians to publicly celebrate the First of August in 1838. It was a bold political act that asserted their dedication to the abolition of American slavery, as well as their unflinching determination to remain in Cincinnati.

Within the community of celebrants, the Cincinnati celebration was designed to rejuvenate the community itself. Racist physical and verbal attacks had beaten down the strength of black Cincinnati, but full emancipation in the British West Indies in 1838 provided a source of hope. The focus on the empowering moment of West Indian emancipation was clearly evident in the midnight service, which recreated August 1, 1834 in Antigua. According to the famous description from James Thome and Horace Kimball's *Emancipation in the West Indies* (which had been reprinted by the *New York Colored American* in April), the freed people of Antigua had gathered in the mission chapel for a "watch-night" service to await the coming of freedom, and the hymn that opened the Cincinnati celebration was adapted from the "watch-night" hymn composed by Charles Wesley for celebrations of the New Year. In Antigua in 1834, as in Cincinnati in 1838, the congregations stood in silence during the moments before midnight, then broke into song when the bell struck, signifying the moment of emancipation in Antigua and the moment to celebrate emancipation in the United States. While such choreographed recreations of the moment of emancipation did not become a common practice, the celebration in Cincinnati poignantly illustrates the ritualized nature of commemorating West Indian Emancipation. The Cincinnati community's reenactment of this ritual reflected the linkages between black Christians in the United States and the West Indies, as well as the fusion of the religious and the political inherent in the First of August. While the ritual signified the end of slavery for black West Indians, it represented to black Americans the awesome reality that emancipation had been accomplished, and performing

27. Richards, *Gentlemen*, 34–35, 93–96.

the ritual in their own church fortified their belief that abolition could be accomplished in the United States as well.[28]

Finally, black Cincinnatians celebrated this act of Great Britain in unison with abolitionist communities throughout the Atlantic world, and when Cary penned his account of the celebration and sent it to the *Colored American*, he was communicating with the broader community of transatlantic abolitionism. Readers of the *Colored American* and those editors who might have reprinted Cary's account were thereby connected to the community in Cincinnati and enabled to partake in the celebration. Simultaneously, Cary's pen empowered the black community in Cincinnati to contribute to the articulation of American abolitionism. The "sentiments" offered to honored political leaders, institutions, and founding documents celebrated a complex set of allegiances that defined black Cincinnati's values and contributed to the national development of the meaning of the First of August. Black Cincinnatians celebrated the institutions of their community, the transatlantic link to Africa and the West Indies, and the complicated relationship with their nation and state. But most of the sentiments—seven of the twelve—were dedicated to the movement that stood against American slavery, the raison d'être of the First of August.

Cary's report also points to another parallel between the First of August and the Fourth of July as political rituals. While early American editors devoted attention to Fourth of July celebrations to cultivate patriotism and partisan identity, abolitionist editors described the multitude of First of August celebrations to describe for their readers the growing community of reform as it challenged the complacency of the white North. Abolitionist newspapers such as Garrison's *Liberator* in Boston, the *Colored American*, and Frederick Douglass's newspapers in Rochester reprinted detailed descriptions of the celebrations, with particular attention to geographic breadth. In 1838, for example, the *Liberator* cited or described ten different celebrations in Massachusetts, as well as celebrations in Providence, Rhode Island, West Townshend, Vermont, and Port au Prince, Haiti. In 1839, the *Colored American* printed descriptive accounts of celebrations in the city, as well as in Newark, New Jersey; Albany and Troy in upstate

28. James A. Thome and J. Horace Kimball, *Emancipation in the West Indies. A Six Months' Tour in Antigua, Barbadoes, and Jamaica, in the Year 1837* (New York, 1838), 36–37; *New York Colored American*, April 12, 1838.

New York; Detroit in the Michigan territory; and Wilmington, Delaware. In 1853, Douglass's description of the celebration in Rochester carefully noted that "Buffalo, Lockport, Leroy Bergen, and other towns" were also represented, and later issues described "two large picnics" in Cincinnati that included folks from as far away as Cleveland, as well as celebrations in Pittsburgh and Allegheny, Pennsylvania.[29]

In addition to emphasizing the growth of a constituency for reform, newspaper reports of First of August celebrations described the size and appearance of the crowds, especially with regard to race. Thus, the celebration in Newark in 1839 involved "thousands of persons, both white and colored." In 1848 Douglass estimated "some 1500 or 2000 persons" in attendance at the Rochester celebration, including "a great many colored people from the neighboring villages." In 1853, the *New York Tribune* noted about five hundred people—"an equal number of both sexes and colours"—at the celebration in Flushing on Long Island. Such clear evidence of editorial attention to the geography, size, sex, and racial composition of First of August celebrations reveals the deliberate efforts of abolitionist editors to educate their readers about the diversity and growth of the movement to abolish American slavery.[30]

THE FIRST OF AUGUST AND ABOLITIONIST IDENTITY

While abolitionist editors employed the First of August to cultivate the community of abolitionism, the celebrations themselves served an important psychological function for the individuals who participated, as well as a political role within a particular locale and ultimately at the national level. Celebrating the First of August enabled participants to reenact the moment of slavery's abolition in the West Indies, as we have seen in Cincinnati. Through this ritual of commemoration, dedicated abolitionists made the "imagined community" of transatlantic abolitionism part of a felt reality within individual abolitionists' hearts and within local abolitionist communities.[31] The personal journal of the white reformer Charles Spear

29. *Boston Liberator,* August 3, 10, 17, 24, and 31, September 14, 1838; *New York Colored American,* July 27, August 17, 24, September 28, 1839; *Rochester Frederick Douglass Paper,* August 5 and 26, 1853.

30. *New York Colored American,* August 24, 1839; *Rochester North Star,* August 11, 1848; *New York Tribune,* August 5, 1853.

31. John Stauffer's brilliant *The Black Hearts of Men: Radical Abolitionism and the Trans-*

and a reevaluation of the public career of Frederick Douglass illuminate this dual potency of First of August celebrations. Spear's private reflections reveal the profound individual experience of communal celebrations of the First of August, while Douglass's attention to First of August celebrations in upstate New York demonstrates their political function. While their roles in the movement were quite different, both men used the First of August to advance radical abolitionism and to question American identity.

Like most antebellum reformers, Spear's interests spanned a broad range of reforms including temperance, abolition, and banning capital punishment. Throughout his travels advancing career and cause, Spear attended celebrations of the Fourth of July and the First of August. The summer of 1843 found him traveling through northern New England selling his *Names and Titles of the Lord Jesus Christ* and speaking against capital punishment in churches that would allow him. On August 1 he was in Bangor, Maine, and as he entered the city he heard "a bell tolling" and inquired of a passerby the occasion. When he learned it was a celebration of West Indian Emancipation, his "soul was filled with joy." He "mingled with the crowd," and his "mind turned to America." Celebrating emancipation with the citizens of Bangor inspired in Spear a deep longing "for the hour to arrive when I should hear the notes of liberty sounding through our whole land." He had faith that "the hour will come" and thanked God that he had "embarked in the abolition cause."[32]

Spear's experiences in Bangor reveal the fusion of communal celebration and individual zeal embodied in First of August celebrations; they also show the conflicted feelings of national identity such occasions aroused. Reformers experienced great difficulties in antebellum America, and it is not hard to imagine the uncertainty Spear must have felt as he approached Bangor. The tolling bell could have been a wedding or a funeral, either of which might have inhibited Spear's ability to reach the town's inhabitants, or, it could have announced services at a church that rejected abolitionism. His response to hearing of the celebration of West Indian emancipation reveals the joy of finding acceptance, the pleasant discovery of

formation of Race (Cambridge: Harvard University Press, 2002) shows that the "heart" need not be a concept limited to love and romance.

32. Journal of Charles Spear, August 1, 1843, Boston Public Library, Boston, MA. For more on Spear, see Louis P. Masur, *Rites of Execution: Capital Punishment and the Transformation of American Culture, 1776–1865* (New York: Oxford University Press, 1989), 124–34.

a receptive audience for his message and a community to which he belonged. His mingling with the crowd manifested the community of reform, and like a journeying Christian attending services far from home, Spear found in Bangor's First of August celebration the opportunity to reaffirm his commitment to abolitionism within a community of believers. This joyful experience provoked Spear to reflect further upon the broader community of "America" itself. To celebrate emancipation in a nation that supported slavery provoked a longing for the moral perfection of his nation and steeled his commitment to the abolitionist cause.

The next summer Spear had the great "privilege" to be at home on the Fourth of July. He celebrated the day with his temperance society and listened to one Mr. Rontaul discuss "Intemperance [from] a political, moral and physical point of view." As Spear reflected in his diary, he was moved to write not on intemperance but on his disillusionment with the nation. Spear had once enjoyed the Fourth of July, but after his conversion to reform the celebration wore "a different aspect." He had once "thought our Revolution right," but he now believed "the whole affair ... a direct violation of Ch[ristianity]." While Spear was pleased that temperance had given a "new turn to the Celebrations" that allowed him to take part, even these had a military escort and he "would as soon have a corpse escort me."[33]

The contrast between Spear's reflections on the First of August and the Fourth of July illuminates the manner in which the First came to supercede the Fourth as a celebration of community for those Americans dedicated to the nation's moral reform. While Spear's experience in Bangor inspired joy, his Fourth of July at home evoked somber ruminations. As a stranger in Bangor he felt acceptance and rejuvenation. As a known member of the community in Boston, however, he felt alienated and despondent about the course of his nation. According to his diary, Spear attended only one more celebration of the Fourth of July—the next year at Dorchester Heights when he publicly denounced war. And in his journal at the end of that day, he wrote: "Goodbye to our national anniversary." The Fourth of July had come to represent the violence of war, and the persistence of slavery had revealed the corruption of America's much-vaunted "freedom." While Spear eventually focused upon the abolition of capital punishment as his central object of reform, he continued to travel and participate in First of August celebrations. Spear went to First of August celebrations in Waltham in 1845, in Worcester in 1846, in Canandaigua, New York, in 1847 (where

33. Journal of Charles Spear, July 4, 1844.

he noted the speech by Douglass), and in Lynn in 1848. Spear's dedication to celebrating West Indian emancipation reveals the potency of the First of August within the life to which he had been called. As he further dedicated his life to social reform, his very identity as an American became transformed. Spear abandoned the Fourth and embraced the First, the central ritual of the alternative political culture cultivated by American abolitionism.[34]

While Spear's diary reveals the personal meanings of the First of August, Douglass's embrace of First of August celebrations demonstrates their importance to the political agenda of American abolitionism. More than anyone, Douglass brought into the public arena the personal dedication to abolitionism cultivated on the First of August. Douglass's move to Rochester and his ideological break with Garrison were intimately linked to his conviction that abolitionists must engage the politics of the North. His change of heart can be traced through his increasing dedication to the First of August and, ultimately, the challenge it posed to the Fourth of July.

Douglass's first introduction to the First of August was probably in 1839 after he had escaped to the North. By 1842, he had already earned himself such a reputation as an orator that the *National Anti-Slavery Standard*, in its announcement of that year's celebration in Providence, Rhode Island, opined that it was worth a "walk of twenty miles" to hear Douglass speak. In New England in the early 1840s when Douglass began his abolitionist career, the celebrations in Providence, Boston, and New Bedford were organized by leaders of the black community and were based in the cities. The participants were mostly African American, but white abolitionists often attended as well. In 1842, however, the leadership of the American Antislavery Society resolved to stage picnics throughout the countryside as part of a campaign to broaden abolitionism through celebrations of the First of August. This effort gained immediate success. There were ten different celebrations in Massachusetts alone that year, and five thousand persons were reported to have attended the celebration in Lynn. Such growth in the movement would have important ramifications (which we investigate below), but for African Americans, it meant that many First of Augusts were no longer celebrations of the black community.[35]

34. Journal of Charles Spear, August 2, 1844, July 4, 1845, August 1, 1845, August 1, 1846, August 1, 1847, August 1, 1848. Spear's diary ends in April 1849.

35. *New York Anti-Slavery Standard*, July 28, 1842; *Boston Liberator*, June 24, July 29, August 5, 9, 12, September 9, 1842; Marian H. Studley, "An 'August First' in 1844," *New England Quarterly* 16 (December 1943): 567.

This did not mean that black celebrations of the First of August ended, but it did bring to the surface some of the racial tensions within the abolitionist movement. In 1844, for example, after describing the impressive procession of African American societies at the celebration in Boston, Garrison stated that the time had come for African Americans to "cease acting in an isolated and exclusive form." He argued that there had been a time when black celebrations had been necessary, but now that "prejudice has measurably abated . . . [it was] absurd and monstrous for persons of a certain complexion to swarm together" at distinct celebrations. A direct response to Garrison has not yet been uncovered, but the continuance of black celebrations was response enough. African Americans had no intention of simply folding their celebrations into the larger white picnics.[36]

This transformation of the celebrations in New England helps to explain Douglass's move to Rochester in the fall of 1847. He would have been uncomfortable with Garrison's statement in 1844, but he had larger problems at the time. In 1845 his former owner Hugh Auld learned of Douglass's whereabouts from the publication of his *Narrative*, so Douglass went abroad to escape possible recapture and to conduct a speaking tour that lasted until April 1847. He had tremendous success in Great Britain, where he was feted by leading abolitionists and cheered by approving white crowds, experiences impossible in the United States in the early 1840s. He raised enough money to pay off Auld and to finance the beginning of a newspaper of his own. When he returned to New England and discussed his plans with the AAS leaders, he was rebuffed. He moved to Rochester a few months later. There he would become a political abolitionist, and he would embrace the First of August with increasing enthusiasm for the rest of his abolitionist career.[37]

In December 1847 Douglass began publication of the *North Star*, and in the spring he alerted his readers to the first organizational meeting for that year's First of August. It was to be held on May 22 in the Zion's Church in Rochester, and his report described an "enthusiasm manifested" that foretold a celebration that "will exceed any of former years." In July, Douglass announced that "arrangements . . . on an extended scale"

36. *Boston Liberator*, August 9, 1844.

37. Stauffer, *The Black Hearts of Men*, 160; William S. McFeeley, *Frederick Douglass* (New York: Oxford University Press, 1991), 146–47; Waldo E. Martin, *The Mind of Frederick Douglass* (Chapel Hill: University of North Carolina Press, 1984), 56–58; Benjamin Quarles, *Frederick Douglass* (1948; reprint, New York: Oxford University Press, 1968), 57–59.

had been prepared for exercises in Washington Square, and he called upon "the friends of freedom" and "every colored man and woman within two hundred miles' distance of this city [to] see to it that at the appointed hour they are in Washington Square, Rochester." Douglass himself would speak. The next week he repeated his announcement, championing the organizing committee of "energetic business men" and calling on the entire abolitionist community to gather in Rochester to "devote one day to the honor of holy freedom" and advance "the cause of Emancipation in our own Land."[38]

A large attendance of "between two and three thousand persons . . . white and colored" rewarded his efforts, and descriptions of the days' events convey the enthusiasm that Douglass had hoped to elicit. All met at noon at the Ford Street Baptist Church to form a procession that marched through the city streets to Washington Square, which had been prepared with a speaker's platform and seats. "Adams' Brass Band" led the procession of carriages and marchers; the marshals wore ribbons, and the women wore their finest clothes. Banners included "Ethiopia stretches forth her hands to God"; "Knowledge is Power," carried by a group of African American schoolchildren; and "With this we overcome" painted above a representation of the Cross. As in Cincinnati, politics and religion were joined in the cause. The Washington Square proceedings began with readings of Britain's Act of Emancipation, as well as the decree of emancipation recently promulgated by the provisional government of revolutionary France, which had immediately abolished slavery in Martinique and Guadeloupe. These liberating documents set the tone for Douglass's speech.[39]

His opening lines mocked the empty rhetoric of the Fourth of July. The First of August was not the occasion for "partial patriotism," a day for the "the blood stained warrior," or a remembrance of the "obsolete antipathy" of 1776. It was "the Tenth Anniversary of West India Emancipation—a day, a deed, an event, all glorious in the annals of Philanthropy . . . as pure as the stars in heaven!" It was also 1848—"stirring times"—when recent events unveiled an America out of step with the progress of human liberty. Revolutions against monarchy had swept across Europe, and Douglass reminded his listeners that while they rejoiced "at the progress of freedom in France, Italy, [and] Germany . . . we are propagating slavery in . . . our

38. *Rochester North Star,* May 19 and 26, 1848, July 14 and 21, 1848.
39. *Rochester North Star,* August 4 and 11, 1848; Robin Blackburn, *The Overthrow of Colonial Slavery, 1776–1848* (London: Verso, 1988), 496.

blood-bought possessions" in Texas. "While our boast is loud and long of justice, freedom, and humanity," he cried, "the slavewhip rings to the mockery." Douglass's attention to world events shows how the celebration of the First of August enabled orators to harness American abolitionism to the transatlantic conversation on despotism and liberty.[40]

But Douglass had an even more radical message. Breaking ground for his brethren in Columbus, Ohio, Douglass spoke of Nathaniel Turner— "a man of noble courage"—who eighteen years before had invoked the name of "a God of justice" and led a rebellion against his oppressors. Douglass reminded his audience that Turner had been shot down "amid showers of American bullets" guided by a Constitution that guaranteed the slaveholder the powers of the federal government to suppress rebellion. Douglass charged his white listeners—"the voters of this city"—with the "awful responsibility of enslaving and imbruting my brothers and sisters in the Southern States." The Constitution provided the "bloody links in the chain of slavery," and northern whites' loyalty to its authority made them partners to its crime. Douglass's challenge to the white voters in his audience to recognize their culpability in American slavery revealed his own radicalization, as well as the political agenda he embraced. Slavery would not be abolished until a majority was willing to condemn it, and moving minds to abhor slavery and demand its abolition had become the fire that burned within him.[41]

Political developments in Washington pushed Douglass even further. The passage of the Fugitive Slave Act in 1850 would be the most radicalizing event for the black community during the antebellum decades. The law made the slave catcher's jurisdiction national and threatened the freedom of every African American in the North. In the summer of 1852, the Rochester Ladies Anti-Slavery Society invited Douglass to deliver their annual July oration. He politely declined to speak on the fourth but agreed to speak on the fifth in accordance with African American tradition in New York. Douglass's speech moved beyond the oblique allusions

40. *Rochester North Star*, August 4, 1848, reprinted in Philip S. Foner, ed., *Frederick Douglass: Selected Speeches and Writings* (Chicago: Lawrence Hill, 1999), 103–4. See also Mitch Kachun, " 'Our Platform Is as Broad as Humanity': Transatlantic Freedom Movements and the Idea of Progress in Nineteenth-Century African American Thought and Activism," *Slavery and Abolition* 24 (December 2003): 11–12.

41. Foner, *Frederick Douglass*, 109–10. It is interesting to note Douglass's portrayal of Turner's death as on the battlefield, rather than as the hanging that it was. This is emblematic of his radicalization during this period.

to the Fourth he had made in 1848 to a withering assault on the enslaving patriotism that pervaded the country every Fourth of July.

Douglass's July Fourth oration bridged the divide between the First and the Fourth, as the radicalism that had begun to emerge on the 1848 now sharpened his words on that fifth of July. Like countless orators before him, Douglass began in the noble cadences of commemoration. The founders were "wise men"; they were "brave men," who understood "the remedy for oppression." The patriots had been "harshly and unjustly treated"; Great Britain had been "unjust, unreasonable, and oppressive"; and the Revolution had been "simple, dignified, and sublime." The Declaration of Independence was the "ringbolt" that anchored the American "ship of state"; its "principles" would save the nation. But it was "your National Independence," Douglass told his white listeners. It was "your political freedom" celebrated on that day. His repeated use of the second person laid bare the "immeasurable distance" of race and slavery that barred him from his white listeners. "Why," he challenged them, "am I called upon to speak here today?" What had African Americans gained from national independence but "stripes and death?"[42]

The traditional opening was a classic rhetorical maneuver that set up the audience for Douglass's central theme: the relation of American slavery to the Fourth of July. To slaves it was a painful day. White Americans needed to listen, for above the "jubilee shouts" that sounded in every village droned the "mournful wail" of millions enslaved. Those discordant sounds were the paradox of the nation. "More than all the other days in the year," Douglass cried, the Fourth of July reminded America's slaves of "the gross injustice and cruelty" they suffered. The celebrations were a "sham." The liberty celebrated was the "unholy license" of slaveholders, those "shouts of liberty" were a "hollow mockery" of the Declaration's principles, and even those with "religious parade and solemnity" were "to *Him*, mere bombast, fraud, deception, impiety, and hypocrisy." God himself, Douglass argued, shared the views of the enslaved.[43]

Douglass portrayed America on its birthday with "scorching irony." He took his audience deep within the slave trade, orchestrated, as it was, by "well dressed" men of "captivating" manners. He forced his listeners to observe the auction, where the babe was sold from her young mother, where the men were "examined like horses," and the women were "brutally ex-

---

42. *Oration delivered in Corinthian Hall, Rochester, by Frederick Douglass, July 5, 1852* (Rochester, 1852) reprinted in Foner, *Frederick Douglass,* 188–90.

43. Ibid., 196–97. Emphasis in the original.

posed." He reminded them of the Fugitive Slave Act, by which "New York has become as Virginia" and the black person "a bird for the sportsmen's gun." And he condemned the churches as the "bulwark of American slavery" for protecting the slave system with biblical defenses and alleging the sanction of God. With his focus on the domestic slave trade, his attention to the national power of slavery, and his condemnation of the "whole slave system," Douglass unmasked individualist defenses of the "humane" master who claimed slaveholding was a Christian obligation. Such Christianity was "blasphemy," argued Douglass, and if Americans truly embraced the demands of their professed faith and principles, they would abolish slavery, the root of their corruption.[44]

Douglass's rhetorical finale embedded the crimes of American slavery in an international frame. Britain's churches, in contrast to America's, had not defended the slaveholder but had "bound up the wounds of the West Indian slave, and restored him his liberty." Americans, Douglass accused, boasted of their "love of liberty," condemning the "crowned headed tyrants of Russia and Austria," and yet they defended the "tyrants of Virginia and Carolina" with all the power of federal law. Americans were "all on fire" for the liberty of France or Ireland, but they were "cold as an iceberg" for the freedom of America's enslaved. This was dangerous hypocrisy, for the world had changed since the Revolution. "Oceans no longer divide, but link nations together," and the United States could not "shut itself up" from humanity's moral improvement. Douglass identified a transformation in world history whereby "long established customs of hurtful character" were increasingly subjected to the censure of the world. Only the founding principles of the Declaration, if embraced, could work along with the "obvious tendencies of the age" to erode the chains of America's slaves. Douglass brought the message of the First of August to his treatment of the Fourth of July. He embraced the moment of national independence not to celebrate American "freedom" but to redefine it.[45]

THE FIRST OF AUGUST AND THE ANTISLAVERY CONSTITUENCY

Douglass's embrace of the First of August and his critical engagement with white American nationalism reflected a significant development. Beginning in the early 1840s and throughout the antebellum period, First of

44. Ibid., 198–202.
45. Ibid., 202–5.

August celebrations were held in an increasing number of new communities throughout the North; they attracted ever larger audiences, including many whites; and they became engaged with party politics. First of August celebrations may have begun among the most radical wing of the abolitionist movement—black abolitionists and white Garrisonians—but beginning in 1842 these events began to attract a more politically diverse population. These celebrations provide a lens for historians to trace the emergence of an antislavery constituency in the North, and, more importantly, they played an important role in the creation of that constituency.

We have already seen the spread of the celebrations in New England beginning in 1842, their move to countryside, and the attendance of more whites. These trends continued until the eve of Civil War, not only in Massachusetts but also in New York, Ohio, Pennsylvania, and, to a lesser extent, in New Jersey, Connecticut, Maine, Michigan, and Wisconsin. Based upon a database of 274 descriptions of celebrations drawn from antislavery newspapers during the period 1834–60, the accompanying maps illustrate this geographic spread. This database does not include every celebration of the First of August, as many were not reported in the newspapers, but it is a large enough sample to illustrate the spread of the celebrations throughout the northern states. As noted above, the day began to be widely celebrated in 1838 with the abolition of the apprenticeship system in the British West Indies. Maps 3 and 4 show that celebrations continued to be embraced by new communities for the next twenty-one years. A community's adoption of the First of August does not necessarily signify the first manifestation of abolitionism in that community. It does, however, indicate a new level of dedication to the movement, as staging a celebration involved considerable time, effort, and resources on the part of local abolitionists. A new celebration of the First also signals a community decision to identify with transatlantic abolitionism. Celebrants saw their agitation against slavery in a world-historical frame.

The celebrations of the 1840s and 1850s were significantly larger, many with audiences in the thousands. The shift began in 1842 with the organizing efforts of the Massachusetts Antislavery Society. These were the first celebrations of the First of August that attracted significant numbers of citizens. Five hundred attended the celebration in Dedham, one thousand came to West Brookfield, twelve hundred gathered in Hubbardston, and estimates range from two to five thousand in Lynn. The Hingham, Massachusetts, event in 1844 drew between six and eight thousand people. In 1849, the celebration in Flushing, Ohio brought out between six hundred and a thousand people; only half were African American. Two thousand persons "of all shades" attended the celebration in Cass, Michigan, that same year. In 1853, the black abolitionist J. Mercer Langston reporting speaking before an audience of 2,500, most of them white, in Frankfort, Ohio, just south of Dayton. They listened to Langston for an hour and a half in the rain. In 1860 there were celebrations of five thousand people in Kennett, Pennsylvania, and in Hudson, New York. These First of Augusts brought together significant numbers of voters to celebrate abolitionism.[46]

As the celebrations grew, they drew from a wider hinterland with the cooperation of train and steamship companies. The Dedham celebration of 1843, which attracted between 1,500 and 2,000 persons, was attended by delegations from Boston, Salem, Lynn, Cambridge, Roxbury, Dorchester, Dedham, Milton, Walpole, Wrentham, and other places. So many people came that it was necessary to run extra cars on the Eastern and the Dedham Railroads. The New Bedford celebration of 1844 was organized with the help of the New Bedford and Providence Railroad Company, as well as the Nantucket Steamboat Company. Both companies reduced their rates for passengers going to the celebration, and they likely saw handsome profits, as the celebration attracted between 1,200 and 4,000 people. In 1851 the African American community of Long Island staged a picnic held between the "colored settlements" of Weeksville and Corsville. Organizers made preparations with the Long Island railroad for ten cars to carry people from Brooklyn, New York, Williamsburgh, and Flushing. In addition to these, several omnibuses were hired, and soon there were several thousand people assembled. The Cincinnati celebration in 1853 took place in Glendale, "about fifteen miles from Cincinnati, on the Hamilton and Dayton railway." Glendale's advantage as a central entrepôt was evident, as many from the Cincinnati region came to the celebration, with some from as far as Cleveland. In 1854 northern Ohio's celebration took place in Dayton, where "ten car loads" of people took the train up from Cincinnati, and more trekked in from Xenia, Hamilton, Troy, Piqua, and other towns. The seventeenth anniversary in 1857 in Poughkeepsie, New York, tapped an elaborate transportation network. In addition to the expected crowd that tramped in by foot or mule from the surrounding communi-

46. *Boston Liberator,* August 5 and 19, 1842, September 2, 1853; *New York Anti-Slavery Standard,* August 15, 1844, August 11, 1860; *Salem (OH) Anti-Slavery Bugle,* August 4, 1849; *Washington (DC) National Era,* September 13, 1849.

ties, people traveled on steamboats up the Hudson from Newburgh, Fishkill, and as far as Peekskill, while some took the same conveyance down the river from as far north as Coxsackie. Even more came in on the train from West Point and other towns. Such massive logistical operations reveal the place taken by the First of August on calendars throughout the country, as well as the involvement of a broadening segment of the population.[47]

As more and more people began to attend the celebrations, they moved out of the churches where they had originated and into wooded groves. Practically, most churches were small and antislavery sentiment had broadened, attracting sizable audiences. Groves enabled organizers to accommodate the larger crowds while maintaining the general pattern established in the 1830s. Groves were the sites for Evangelical revivals, an important source of abolitionism, and their physical beauty could be enhanced with decorations to transform these bucolic settings into sacred spaces. They were also reminiscent of the venues for the public lectures that became so popular in antebellum America.[48] With the exception of the celebration in Rochester (which took place in Washington Square in the center of town), all of the big regional celebrations mentioned above took place in groves on the towns' outskirts. In Massachusetts, for example, abolitionists in Springfield held a picnic in 1848 where five hundred sat for the dinner alone. The next year there was another picnic in Lynn, and again "a large audience was present." Abolitionists in Pittsburgh met in groves for the celebrations in 1849 and again in 1853.[49] Anna Studley recalled going to the Island Grove in Abington, Massachusetts, where "horses were tied to the hitching posts outside the grove as thick as they could stand."[50]

Organizers staged increasingly elaborate processions and ceremonies that maintained a public presence while avoiding urban centers. At the regional celebration at Hingham, Massachusetts, in 1844, participants came from various towns, and the procession was organized to meld each group

47. *New York Tribune*, August 7, 1843, August 5, 1857; *Boston Liberator*, August 9, 1844; *Rochester Frederick Douglass Paper*, September 4, 1851, August 26, 1853; *Washington (DC) National Era*, August 17, 1854. This development remains an unexplored element of the "transportation revolution."

48. Donald Scott, "The Popular Lecture and the Creation of a Public in Mid-Nineteenth Century America," *Journal of American History* 66 (March 1980): 793.

49. *Washington (DC) National Era*, August 19, 1847 (Springfield, MA); *Rochester North Star*, August 21, 1848 (Lynn, MA), August 31, 1849 (Pittsburgh, PA); *Rochester Frederick Douglass Paper*, August 26, 1853 (Pittsburgh, PA).

50. Studley, "An 'August First' in 1844," 570.

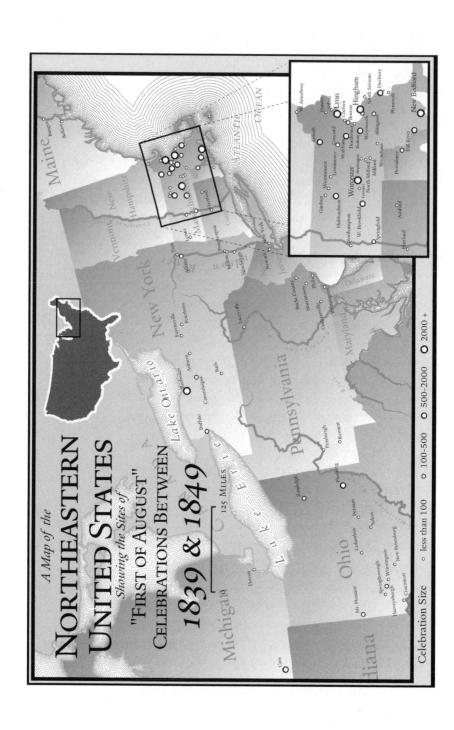

A Map of the
NORTHEASTERN
UNITED STATES
Showing the Sites of
"FIRST OF AUGUST"
CELEBRATIONS BETWEEN
1839 & 1849

125 MILES

Celebration Size   ∘ less than 100   ◦ 100-500   ○ 500-2000   ○ 2000 +

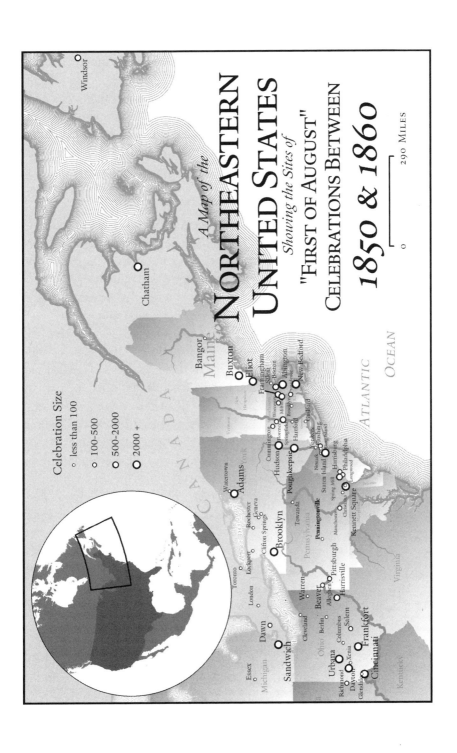

A Map of the

NORTHEASTERN UNITED STATES

Showing the Sites of

"FIRST OF AUGUST"
CELEBRATIONS BETWEEN

1850 & 1860

0   290 MILES

Celebration Size

○ less than 100

○ 100–500

○ 500–2000

○ 2000 +

OCEAN

ATLANTIC

CANADA

Windsor

Chatham

Bangor

Maine

Buxton

Eliot

Framingham

Salem

Boston

Abington

Worcester

New Bedford

Cummington

Hudson

Florence

Hartford

Watertown

Adams

Poughkeepsie

Newark

Flushing

Staten Island

Harrisburg

Philadelphia

Rochester

Geneva

Clifton Springs

Lockport

Brooklyn

Towanda

Penningtonville

Manchester

Kennett Square

Pennsylvania

Virginia

Warren

Pittsburgh

Beaver

Allegheny

Harrisville

Toronto

London

Cleveland

Berlin

Columbus

Xenia

Salem

Frankfort

Cincinnati

Ohio

Urbana

Richmond

Dayton

Glendale

Kentucky

Essex

Michigan

Sandwich

Dawn

Spring Mill

into a single abolitionist community. Part of the community arrived from Boston on the ferry, and as soon as they had assembled on shore, they "immediately formed a procession and marched, amidst the ringing of bells, to the centre of the village," where they met an equally numerous contingent who had come in from "the counties of Plymouth and Norfolk." In the center of town the groups combined and formed a "grand procession" under the direction of the chief marshal Jairus Lincoln, a lawyer from Hingham. According to the *Tribune*'s correspondent, the procession was "more than a mile in length" and led by "an escort" of thirty-six young women from Hingham, "dressed in white, bearing flowers, and tastefully decorated with wreathes of oak." There were numerous banners, "tasteful and quite imposing," which the writer did not describe but which probably represented the different societies participating in the day's festivities. The procession marched from the center of the town to "Tranquility Grove," a wide lawn "under the shadow of a forest of young oaks," which had been set up with a speaker's platform and seats for three thousand people.[51]

The regional celebration in Dayton in 1854 was equally impressive. The procession included the "United Colored Americans," the "Sons of Liberty," and several other African American organizations, all decked out in their "full regalia." Accompanied by "three bands of music," the participants marched through the "principal streets" of the city to a grove west of town where dinner and seating had been prepared for eleven hundred people. After the usual series of orations, the gathering repaired to City Hall, where a "grand ball" was held in the evening. The correspondent for the *Washington (D.C.) National Era* commented that the celebration displayed the intelligence and "general morality" of the free black population, evidence that gave "the lie ... to the slanders that have been propagated by the Southern press and politicians as to the social condition of the free colored population of the North."[52] Indeed, proslavery theorists consistently pointed to the "degraded" condition of free black people, in both the North and in the West Indies, which they styled as evidence that "proved" freedom to be the unnatural condition for peoples of African descent. First of August celebrations had become another means to undermine proslavery argument.

It is highly significant that the First of August celebrations in Hingham and in Dayton were covered, respectively, by the *New York Tribune* and the

51. *New York Tribune*, August 5, 1844.
52. *Washington (DC) National Era*, August 17, 1854.

National Era. The editors of both papers were devoted antislavery men, but in the 1840s neither was associated with the radical wing of abolitionism where the First of August had its roots. The *Tribune's* editor, Horace Greeley, was a Whig and later Republican who embraced abolitionism while maintaining his position as a major voice in party politics. *National Era* editor Gamaliel Bailey began his career as a nonvoting Garrisonian, but he became involved in party politics during the election of 1838 in Ohio and later helped found the Liberty Party. Like Douglass, political abolitionists such as Greeley and Bailey recognized that the national system of political parties would have to be engaged if slavery was to be abolished in the United States. Voters were important, and First of August celebrations attracted growing numbers to political antislavery.[53]

The earliest signs that the major parties were beginning to notice First of August celebrations appear in the abolitionist press. In the 1830s descriptions that appeared in the *Liberator* or the *Colored American* were written by attending abolitionists and forwarded to the editors for publication. Beginning in 1843, however, the first year after these celebrations had attracted audiences in the thousands, the political papers began to cover the First of August. In 1843, Garrison's source for the *Liberator's* coverage in Nantucket came from the *Nantucket Telegraph.* In 1847, the *Boston Atlas*, an organ of the Cotton Whigs, printed positive coverage of the African American celebration in the Boston. In 1848, Douglass noted coverage of the Rochester celebration in the *American*, the *Democrat*, and the *Advertiser* of that city. In 1854 First of Augusts were covered in the *Columbian* of Columbus, Ohio; the *Chronicle* of Warren, Ohio; and the *Portsmouth Messenger* in Maine. In 1859, First of Augusts were described in the *Cincinnati Commercial*, the *New York Evening Post*, the *Harrisburg Daily Telegraph*, the *Poughkeepsie Eagle* and the *Detroit Advertiser*. Coverage of the First of August indicates a political calculation on the part of mainstream editors. In previous years, the possibility of alienating antiabolitionist readers had inhibited the recognition of these celebrations. But as audiences on the First of August grew, editors for the political press recognized the expansion of antislavery sentiment and responded to their readers' interests.[54]

53. Sean Wilentz, *The Rise of American Democracy: Jefferson to Lincoln* (New York: W. W. Norton, 2005), 574, 678–79; Jonathan Earle, *Jacksonian Antislavery and the Politics of Free Soil, 1824–1854* (Chapel Hill: University of North Carolina Press, 2004), 147–51.

54. *Boston Liberator*, August 11, 1843, August 6, 1847, August 11, 1854, August 12 and 26, 1859; *Rochester North Star*, August 11, 1848; *Rochester Frederick Douglass' Paper*, August 25, 1854; *New York Evening Post*, August 4, 1860; *New York Anglo-African*, August 6, 1859.

In addition to newspaper editors, politicos involved with the mainstream parties, and especially activists in the Liberty Party and the Free Soil Party, also noticed First of August celebrations. In 1842, the *Liberator*'s account of the interracial celebration in Hubbardston, Massachusetts, a rural village in the northern part of the state, noted that "bystanders" had actually counted the audience at the celebration in order to know the "number of voters in H[ubbardston] belonging to 'the Abolition Party.'" Such an investigation into the audience at a First of August event could only be of interest to local chiefs from the mainstream parties concerned with the strength of antislavery sentiment in their district. In 1849, one O. Osborn wrote to the *National Era* in Washington of the "progress of the Free Soil movement" in his account of the First of August in Cass, Michigan. The free-soilers had "united with the Whigs" in the last election and, as a result, held the balance of power in the territory. The county judge, the sheriff of Cass, and their sole congressman were all dedicated to Free Soil, evidence that the "cause of Liberty" was gaining ground. Such political news was bolstered by the celebration of the First of August there, where "two thousand people of all *shades*" had attended. In 1852, Samuel Fleming, a Democratic candidate for the legislature, addressed a First of August celebration in Manchester, Pennsylvania (just north of York). In 1855 the Republican leaders Joshua Giddings and John Hale spoke at a First of August celebration in Buxton, Maine, which ended with "three cheers for the Republican Party!" We don't know how many attended the celebration, but we do know that a special train of ten cars was hired to bring people out from Portland.[55]

On August 1, 1859, the Democratic editor James Gordon Bennett attacked celebrations of the First of August in his influential *New York Herald.* Under the heading "Jubilees of the Abolitionists—What Has Emancipation Done for the West India Negroes," Bennett printed an editorial that ridiculed the celebrations as meaningless, called for their end, and claimed that it was "worse than idle twaddle to talk about the free negro working for wages." Bennett opined: "Surely the lesson taught us by the emancipation of the West India Negro should warn and dissuade all sensible men" from even considering the abolition of slavery in the United States. If Bennett read the *New York Times* the next day (and he probably

---

55. *Boston Liberator,* September 9, 1842, August 6, 1852, August 17, 1855; *Washington (DC) National Era,* September 13, 1849, emphasis in the original.

did), he would have discovered the pointed reply of the black abolitionist William Watkins of Rochester, who spoke at the First of August celebration in Poughkeepsie that year. Watkins read the *Herald* on the morning of his oration, and he responded directly to Bennett. After reciting the brilliant successes of the postemancipation West Indies, Watkins noted Bennett's attack and challenged him to a test of principles. Watkins sarcastically recommended that African Americans living in the city should apply to the *Herald* for employment to demonstrate their willingness to labor for wages. And if Bennett hired them, Watkins cried, he—a dedicated black abolitionist—would agree to give up celebrating the First of August. This exchange between Watkins and Bennett tells us that African American activists, through their invention of this hugely successful annual celebration, had insinuated themselves into the political discourse on slavery and abolition, despite the fact that most could not vote.[56]

On the eve of the most important election in U.S. history, First of August celebrations had become so large and widespread, such a fixture in the summer calendar, that even an established editor like James Gordon Bennett felt the need to lash out. Every summer thousands of Americans met in interracial assemblies to commemorate the abolition of slavery in the British West Indies and agitate for the destruction of slavery in the United States. Radical abolitionism and political antislavery had come together. The very existence of these celebrations clearly threatened a man like Bennett, because they represented everything he stood against as the editor of a major Democratic daily. Since 1854 the Democratic Party in the North had maintained its influence by race-baiting the "Black Republicans" and maintaining the alliance with the party's base in the South. The emergence of an antislavery constituency in the North represented a fatal threat, and every First of August that constituency took to the streets. In 1860 that constituency would vote, and the Black Republicans would win.

56. *New York Herald*, August 1, 1859; *New York Times*, August 2, 1859. See also *New York Anglo-African*, August 6, 1859, for a more lengthy response to Bennett.

8

British Abolition and the Coming of the Civil War

In October 1846 the opening article of the *United States Magazine and Democratic Review* was a message from President James Polk entitled "Slaves and Slavery." It had already been a remarkable year. That spring the United States had fought a war with Mexico, and in the summer David Wilmot, a Democratic congressman from Pennsylvania, attached a controversial amendment to the bill granting the president's request for a 2 million dollar appropriation to compensate Mexico for the vast southwestern region the administration sought to acquire. Wilmot's proviso required that "neither slavery nor involuntary servitude shall ever exist in any part" of the conquered territory—American slavery should not expand. Wilmot proposed his amendment late in the session, and it sent a clear signal that a significant minority of northern Democrats were not pleased with what had come to be known as the "Slave Power." The *Democratic Review* was the party's national organ, and Polk used its pages to make his case and to prepare the public mind for the midterm elections that fall.[1]

Polk's essay would later accompany a series of documents from American diplomats in Brazil and in Great Britain which he would submit to Congress, and the timing of its appearance in the *Democratic Review* speaks to the lasting potency of British abolition to shape the struggle over American slavery. Historians of the coming of the Civil War have seen 1846 as

---

1. [James Polk], "Slaves and Slavery," *United States Magazine and Democratic Review* 19 (October 1846): 243–54. Wilmot's proviso quoted in *Frederick J. Blue, No Taint of Compromise: Crusaders in Antislavery Politics* (Baton Rouge: Louisiana State University Press, 2005), 190.

a decisive year, as the war and Wilmot's proviso made the struggle over slavery a sectional issue within both parties which defined the political crises of the 1850s and lead to southern secession. Most historians of this era have neglected the international context; contemporaries such as Polk did not.[2] As slavery dominated U.S. politics in the 1850s, arguments about the recent history of emancipation in the British West Indies fueled both sides of the debate. Proslavery writers elaborated their interpretation of emancipation, analyzing every attempt of West Indian sugar planters to stay afloat. These writings helped to establish an impenetrable confidence in the permanence of American slavery, which grounded secessionist logic in the aftermath of Abraham Lincoln's election in 1860. Over the same ten years, new voices representing the emerging Republican Party seized upon the benefits of free labor. The journalists John Bigelow and William Sewell penned investigations of the postemancipation West Indies that drew attention to the emergence of an energetic free peasantry that validated the Republican slogan "free soil, free labor, and free men." These writings helped to broaden the antislavery constituency in the North already fostered by political abolitionism and the First of August.

Perhaps most importantly, the decades of political ferment in northern black communities led some to embrace physical responses to American slavery ranging from emigrating to rescuing recaptured fugitive slaves, to joining John Brown's band. British abolition created a geography of freedom in Canada, the British West Indies, and the British Isles that appealed to black Americans who were fed up with racism and decided to emigrate. The black communities that formed in these places became an international force against American slavery, and they facilitated the rescues of fugitive slaves by radicals willing to bear arms against slave catchers. Black radicalism, the proslavery belief in the permanence of American slavery, and the northern antislavery constituency collided in 1859 and 1860 with fatal consequences for the union and for American slavery. John

2. William Cooper, *The South and the Politics of Slavery, 1828–1856* (Baton Rouge: Louisiana State University Press, 1978), 269–374; Eric Foner, *Free Soil, Free Labor, Free Men: The Ideology of the Republican Party before the Civil War* (1970; reprint, New York: Oxford University Press, 1995), 1–102; Michael Holt, *The Political Crises of the 1850s* (New York: John Wiley, 1978), 3–4, 67–259. Thomas Bender has recently pointed out that in the immense historiography treating the Civil War, only five historians have ever placed it in a broader context. Bender himself neglects the role of Britain's abolition of slavery. See *A Nation Among Nations: America's Place in World History* (New York: Hill and Wang, 2006), 322, n. 13.

Brown's raid in the fall of 1859 can be seen as the ultimate manifestation of black radicalism. In the aftermath of Brown's trial and execution, leading northern intellectuals such as Ralph Waldo Emerson and Henry David Thoreau, both of whom had addressed First of August celebrations, celebrated Brown as a martyr for the abolitionist cause. During these same months the presidential canvass of 1860 began, and for the first time in the history of the United States, the winner of that election—Abraham Lincoln—held antislavery views. These were the events that led to the coming of civil war; all of them were shaped by British abolition.

AMERICAN SLAVERY AND THE POSTEMANCIPATION WEST INDIES

In his 1846 essay with which we began, President Polk began with a nod to antislavery sentiment, noting how "awful" it was that Africans had been transported by Great Britain to America to be slaves. His was a time-honored ploy to blame the British for slavery, but Polk also noted that it had existed "from the remotest of ages, and assumed different shapes under different circumstances in all countries." From this perspective, Polk argued, American slavery looked quite benign. At that very moment slavery existed not only in the United States but also in "Russia, Poland, Egypt, and British India." There were 21 million Russian slaves at the "absolute and uncontrolled disposal" of their noble masters. While the institution in Poland was milder, slaves there were still prohibited from ever leaving the lands of their lords. Egyptian slavery was far worse than in Poland, where 1.75 million men were the slaves of one man, Mohammed Ali, that "vigorous chief [who] has constituted himself the sole land-owner, manufacturer, and trader in his domains." And in British India, slavery was "more intense than any ever inflicted upon a people in any other country," demonstrating the hypocrisy of British abolitionism. This portrait of global misery stood in stark contrast to conditions in the American South, Polk claimed, where slaves were "the descendents of imported laborers, enjoying the same personal liberties as the free laborers in the British islands, and always receiving the full measure of their wants."[3]

The existence of slavery on a global scale, and the alleged exceptionalism of slavery in the United States, aimed to undermine arguments that slavery was somehow wrong. The reports from American diplomats, more-

3. [Polk], "Slaves and Slavery," 244–47.

over, indicated the failure of the abolitionist policies enacted by Great Britain. On the one hand, Britain's attempts to suppress the transatlantic slave trade to Cuba and Brazil had utterly failed, as planters in both regions continued to purchase slaves from transatlantic slavers. On the other hand, Britain's abolition had led to the near-collapse of the West Indian sugar industry, moving one member of Parliament to point out that planters "could not successfully cultivate their estates" without the immigration of foreign laborers. Polk showed that this labor shortage had led to a revival of the British slave trade, which authorities absurdly styled "voluntary emigration." British cruisers were seizing slave ships destined for the Americas and sending the Africans to the British West Indies as "free" laborers. According to Polk, "the whole operation to the poor black was only the difference of serving on an English plantation instead of Brazilian one."[4]

While contemporaries as well as modern historians have argued over the interpretation of British West Indian immigration policies as a renewed "slave trade," Polk accurately described British actions in the Atlantic world at this time. West Indian proposals to import laborers, based on the presumption that blacks would not work without the controls of slavery, had accompanied abolition in 1834. In the large colonies such as Jamaica, Trinidad, and Demerara, where sugar plantations had never monopolized all available land, ambitious former slaves had purchased land and declared their independence from the plantations as soon as they were able. Free black peasantries thus emerged which produced for subsistence and for local markets, and as former slaves embraced the freedom to work for themselves, many sugar planters could not find laborers to work for the wages planters wanted to pay. In 1841 British colonial authorities allowed for the importation of recaptured Africans from Sierra Leone. In 1843, the British foreign minister in Washington, D.C., Edward S. Fox, approached Secretary of State Abel Upshur with a proposal for an emigration agreement by which free African Americans could be encouraged to migrate to the British West Indies to work in the sugar plantations. Upshur was dumbfounded by such an open admission of the failure of emancipation, but by no means would he assent to such an agreement. Some West Indian planters finally got relief when immigration of indentured laborers from British India began in 1844. By 1850, more than 30,000 indentured Africans had arrived, and about 29,000 Indians had also been recruited for the

4. Ibid., 251–52.

harsh labor of the sugar plantation. Curiously, British abolitionists were just as outraged as Polk, albeit for different reasons. As one English correspondent wrote to William Lloyd Garrison, "beware of *Hill Coolies,* a new species of slavery."[5]

For abolitionists, the West Indian turn to indentured immigrant labor signaled the abandonment of the abolition principles of 1838, but to U.S. slaveholders and much of the white Atlantic the new policies revealed the failure of free black labor. The *National Intelligencer* (national organ of the Whigs) made this accusation in 1841, as did proslavery writers such as James Henry Hammond, whose 1844 letters to the venerable Thomas Clarkson heralded the failure of free labor and condemned immigration as a revival of the "AFRICAN SLAVE TRADE." The accusation contained a hint of truth. By the time Polk was writing in 1846, sugar production in the British West Indies had declined 35 percent from the average of the last decade of slavery. Immigration measures were justified with the same free labor ideology that had infused the abolition of slavery, but it was a clear acknowledgement that West Indian sugar was in decline.[6]

And it only got worse for West Indian planters. 1846 had been a year of western conquest in the United States, but in Great Britain it was the year of free trade. In June the corn laws that had long protected the agricultural interests of the British gentry were abolished, and in August Parliament approved the Sugar Duties Act, which legislated a gradual lowering of the import duties on foreign-grown sugars. The Sugar Duties Act opened the British market—and the West Indian sugar industry—to competition with the slave-grown sugars of Cuba and Brazil. The policy shift demon-

5. David Northrup, *Indentured Labor in the Age of Imperialism, 1831–1922* (Cambridge: Cambridge University Press, 1995), 24; Steven Heath Mitton, "The Free World Confronted: The Problem of Slavery and Progress in American Foreign Relations, 1833–1844" (Ph.D. diss., Louisiana State University, 2005), xii–xiii, 114–17; Anne Knight to William Lloyd Garrison, March 14, 1838, William Lloyd Garrison Papers, Boston Public Library, Boston, MA.

6. *National Intelligencer* quoted in "New Plan for Suppressing the Slave Trade and Obtaining Laborers for the British West India Colonies," *African Repository and Colonial Journal* 18 (May 15, 1841): 145–46; James Henry Hammond, "Letter to an English Abolitionist," in Drew Gilpin Faust, *The Ideology of Slavery: Proslavery Thought in the Antebellum South, 1830–1860* (Baton Rouge: Louisiana State University Press, 1981), 200; William Green, *British West Indian Slave Emancipation: The Sugar Colonies and the Great Experiment, 1830–1865* (Oxford: Oxford University Press, 1976), 246; Seymour Drescher, *The Mighty Experiment: Free Labor Versus Slavery in British Emancipation* (Oxford: Oxford University Press, 2002), 213–14.

strated the emergence of the free trade ideology that is still with us, but it also revealed the declining support in Britain for the "experiment" with free labor in the West Indian colonies. Eight years of full freedom made abolitionist predictions of the benefits of free labor look rather empty. The loss of protection exacerbated earlier trends in the West Indies, and worse, it coincided with economic depression in Europe. Slave-grown imports from Cuba and Brazil drove down the price of sugar on the British market, and consumers had less to spend. Both William Green and Seymour Drescher have characterized the remainder of the decade as years of "crisis" when profits tumbled, West Indian merchant houses collapsed, and entire estates went out of sugar production altogether. The postemancipation drift toward subsistence agriculture among the West Indian peasantries continued, and planter calls for the subsidized immigration of contract laborers became more strident. When the British Parliament called for a hearing of a select committee to assess the situation in 1849, Parliament was treated to a mass of evidence that described in excruciating detail the apparent failure of the "great experiment."[7]

Prominent British voices condemned the entire abolitionist project. The most callous of these was Thomas Carlyle, who applied his vaunted literary skills to popularizing the proslavery analysis of West Indian emancipation. Carlyle's *Occasional Discourse on the Nigger Question* placed the entire burden of the failed sugar industry upon a racialist caricature, "Quashee," the lazy freed black who refused to work. Carlyle described the luxuriance of the tropics and portrayed Quashee "up to the ears in pumpkins … grinders and incisor teeth ready for ever new work" while sugarcane rotted in the fields. Production had declined because blacks would not work unless forced to do so; it was congenital. Britain's experiment with freedom in the West Indies had shattered abolitionist theories by demonstrating that blacks did not respond to free labor incentives. Their physical needs were pumpkin and rum, and once those were obtained, they preferred idleness. Blacks had only one right, Carlyle argued, "the indisputable and perpetual right to be compelled" to labor.[8]

7. Green, *British Slave Emancipation,* 229–44; Drescher, *Mighty Experiment,* 176–78, and ch. 11.

8. Thomas Carlyle, *Occasional Discourse on the Nigger Question,* in Eugene R. August, ed., *Thomas Carlyle, The Nigger Question; John Stuart Mill, The Negro Question* (New York: Appleton Century Crofts, 1971), 4, 9. Carlyle's essay, "Occasional Discourse on the Negro Question," was first published anonymously in *Fraser's Magazine* 40 (December 1849):

White southerners had been saying this for years, and they controlled an economy that seemed to validate their ideas. The economy of the American South could not have been more different from the West Indies. While the West Indies were in crisis, the late 1840s saw the beginnings of an economic boom in the cotton South that would only end with the war. The power looms of Britain seemed insatiable, and with the exception of a short dip in 1848, the price of cotton on the British market was high enough to encourage planters to expand production. Slave prices rose, and the southern slave population became increasingly concentrated on large cotton plantations. Cotton exports continued to increase, and by 1860 the American South supplied 75 percent of the raw cotton on the British market. The cotton boom also provided the foundation for genuine economic development. The railroad and banking industries of the South Carolina upcountry and the black belt of Alabama saw tremendous growth during the 1850s, integrating previously isolated regions into the Atlantic economy.[9] In June 1850, New Orleans editor James De Bow gleefully reprinted Carlyle's essay, noting that the West Indian question had finally been put to the British people in its "true light." De Bow hoped that Carlyle's arguments would inspire "Northern fanaticism to pause and reflect." This was unlikely.[10]

THE ANTEBELLUM DEBATE ON BLACK EMANCIPATION

The economic divergence between the free labor West Indies and the slaveholding South was overwhelming by 1850, and pure economic logic would have guaranteed the perpetuation of slavery in the United States.

670–79, and later as a pamphlet with the racist title, *Occasional Discourse on the Nigger Question* (London, 1853). Carlyle's polemic received a stinging response from John Stuart Mill in "The Negro Question," *Fraser's Magazine* 41 (January 1850): 25–31. American readers had easy access to both essays through *Littell's Living Age,* a gleaning magazine published in Boston, which commented on the "grief" expected among Carlyle's admirers; Mill was not identified. See "Occasional Discourse on the Negro Question," *Littell's Living Age* 24 (February 9, 1850): 248–54 (quotation on p. 248); and "The Negro Question," *Littell's Living Age* 24 (March 9, 1850): 465–69. See also August's useful introduction in his edited volume, *Thomas Carlyle, The Nigger Question,* vii–xxxiii.

9. Lacy Ford, *Origins of Southern Radicalism: The South Carolina Upcountry, 1800–1860* (New York: Oxford University Press, 1988), 215–77; Robert Fogel, *Without Consent or Contract: The Rise and Fall of American Slavery* (New York: W. W. Norton, 1989, 70–71; David Eltis, *Economic Growth and the Ending of the Transatlantic Slave Trade* (New York: Oxford University Press, 1987), 39.

10. "Carlyle on West India Emancipation," *Commercial Review,* new ser. 2 (June 1850):

Nevertheless, the political fortunes of American slaveholders were far from certain. The election of 1848 brought Zachary Taylor to the White House, and while Taylor was a major slave owner himself, the Whig party he represented included radical abolitionists such as William Seward and Joshua Giddings. The thirty-first Congress of 1849–50 was riven by sectional conflict, and in the Deep South fire-eating secessionists organized the Southern Convention in Nashville in the fall of 1850 which almost precipitated sectional crisis. By the middle of the decade, the Republican Party had formed with the antislavery constituency of the North at its core, making the struggle over the future of slavery the central issue in U.S. political life. As white Americans debated the prospects of black emancipation, the recent history of the postemancipation West Indies held the most relevant lessons for contemplation.[11]

The South Carolinian planter and secessionist Edward Bryan, for example, argued that British abolition had provided a veritable scientific experiment that tested slave labor against free labor. Soil, climate, agricultural pursuits, and the "*race*" of the laborers had remained the same in the West Indies from 1830 until 1850, but with free labor, sugar cost the planter £20 per ton, while with slavery it had only cost £12. The transatlantic slave trade revealed the same truth. Although Britain had resorted to "ARMED PREVENTION" to end the transport of African slaves to Cuba and Brazil, the trade had "not even been diminished." Britain had actually increased the value of African slaves while at the same time impoverishing her own colonies. And now, Bryan noted, the British fanaticism for abolition had "wafted across the Atlantic" and settled in the North. Britain's experience proved abolitionism essentially irrational. South Carolina should secede now, Bryan argued, rather than wait for the rest of the South to recognize the gravity of the danger.[12]

Likewise, the Mobile jurist and Calhounite John Archibald Campbell penned a long article for the *Southern Quarterly Review* on the report of the Parliamentary Select Committee of 1849. Campbell quoted ex-

527–38 (quotations on pp. 534 and 529). Carlyle's essay was also reviewed in "British and American Slavery," *Southern Quarterly Review* 8 (October 1853), 369–411.

11. David M. Potter, *The Impending Crisis, 1848–1861* (New York: Harper and Row, 1976), 86–90; Sean Wilentz, *The Rise of American Democracy: Jefferson to Lincoln* (New York: W. W. Norton, 2005), 746; Manisha Sinha, *The Counter-Revolution of Slavery: Politics and Identity in Antebellum South Carolina* (Chapel Hill: University of North Carolina Press, 2000), chap. 4.

12. Edward B. Bryan, *The Rightful Remedy. Addressed to Slaveholders of the South* (Charleston, 1850): 59, 101, 109.

tensively from the committee's report, highlighting the struggles of West Indian planters to employ workers and their efforts to import laborers from Africa and India to make up for the inadequacies of free labor. He also stressed those arguments claiming a cultural reversion to barbarism. Campbell directly challenged abolitionist arguments that emancipation had brought the spread of education and Christian marriage. The missionary schools touted by abolitionist writers had been erected by British abolitionists for political—not moral—purposes, he claimed, and now that the experiment had clearly failed, the schools were "deserted" and West Indian blacks sank deeper into ignorance. And though Christian marriages had indeed increased, Campbell argued that this was only a factor of the blacks' fondness for public display. Legal marriages there may have been, but the "great dissoluteness in the morals of the females" and the "great ignorance" of marital duty on the part of the men rendered those marriages empty of moral integrity. West Indian emancipation had become a "frightful experiment" in economic and moral collapse. Nevertheless, Campbell warned, political abolitionism had advanced in the Atlantic world, ending slavery in the French, Danish, and Swedish West Indies and expanding in influence in the North. Could the South still afford union with the northern states when northerners were so blinded by abolitionism that they could not see the reality in the West Indies? Campbell did not think so and challenged his readers to ponder the South's future in the Union.[13]

While the arguments of Campbell and Bryan elaborated on earlier proslavery comparisons of the South and the free West Indies, the southern portrayal of Britain as an aggressive abolitionist power so important for the drive to annex Texas began to change. The collapse of the West Indies and the clear importance of American cotton to the British economy made southerners believe that instead of attempting to subvert the South through insurrection, Britain now depended upon the South for its cotton. This shift can be seen in *The Letters of Agricola*, written for the Greenville, S.C., *Southern Standard* by the Carolinian planter and Unionist William Elliot. Though he recited the old argument that Britain had abolished West Indian slavery to "stigmatize the institution" and "kindle a flame of fanatical discontent" that would divide the United States, Elliot argued that Britain was now more cautious, "restrained by the fear of injury to herself." Britain could no longer interfere with U.S. slavery because it could not "dispense

13. [John Archibald Campbell], "British West India Islands," *Southern Quarterly Review* 16 (January 1850): 342–77 (quotes on 349, 351, 358, 375).

with the cotton of the Southern States." That said, British abolitionism had already done its work, for in the North, Elliot warned, "the same spirit of fanaticism" had become a powerful force that could only be checked by the *"united action of the slaveholding States."*[14]

The ongoing relevance of Britain's "experiment" with free black labor made West Indian emancipation equally important among proslavery Democrats in the North and West. During the debates over Kansas-Nebraska, for example, James Shannon used the example of the post-emancipation West Indies in his 1855 address to the Proslavery Convention in Lexington, Missouri. Shannon's target was the "free soil fanaticism" that he believed would destroy the country if left unchecked. British abolition proved the folly of emancipation and even the respected *Blackwood's Magazine* of London had lamented the "two hundred millions sterling" lost by the British nation because of abolition. Financial ruin would hit the United States with even greater devastation, Shannon argued, as slaves represented a "vast amount of productive capital" that would vanish in an instant if the fanatics had their way. Who could consider such an act of economic suicide? Moreover, abolition would be the "greatest calamity" to America's slaves. "Look to St. Domingo and the British West Indies," Shannon implored. Both societies had lost the "guardianship of the white race" and "retrograded with rapid strides towards a savage, and even a brutal state" of civilization. Shannon believed it would be worse in the United States, as the white and black races were of equal populations and a race war would be the inevitable result of the imposition of "social and political equality." The abolition of American slavery could not be considered; the best evidence against it was the recent history of the British West Indies.[15]

British abolition played an equally important role in the arguments of Edmund Burke of New Hampshire, a Democrat faced with powerful Republican opposition in his home state. Democrats throughout the country tried to equate the Republicans with abolitionism, and Burke's *An Important Appeal to the People of the United States* warned of the dangers of disunion if abolitionism became ascendant. Burke proposed to his northern

14. [William Elliot], *The Letters of Agricola. Published in the Southern Standard, June 1851* (Greenville, SC, 1852).

15. [James Shannon], *An Address Delivered Before the Pro-Slavery Convention of the State of Missouri, Held in Lexington, July 13, 1855, on Domestic Slavery, as Examined in the Light of Scripture, of Natural Rights, of Civil Government, and the Constitutional Power of Congress* (St. Louis, 1855), i, 7–8.

audience the racial and geographic arguments already popular in the South. He argued that the "peculiar physical constitution" of black people allowed them to work in tropical regions such as the West Indies and the American South, regions where whites suffered harmful effects from physical labor. But blacks were congenitally "idle, dissolute, licentious, and filthy" and therefore required slavery and the "directing mind" of the white man to make use of their capacity to labor in the tropics. Burke argued that the economic demise of Haiti and the British West Indies (which he demonstrated with statistics) proved these fundamental truths of proslavery argument. Those who contemplated abolition ignored the "voice of history."[16]

But Burke's argument against the Republicans went beyond economics. An abolitionist-inspired disunion would invite war not only with the South but also with Great Britain. The British people might be abolitionists, but Britain was ruled by an "aristocracy," not the people, and the aristocrats sought the demise of the American republic and commercial dominion over the globe. As Calhoun had argued in 1844, Burke asserted that commercial supremacy was founded on the control of cotton and sugar, and in the case of civil war, Britain would support the South in exchange for a regular supply of cotton. Britain "depended" on Southern cotton, and war would firm up this supply while also providing the perfect opportunity to destroy "her manufacturing and commercial rivals in the free States of the North." An alliance with the South would also cause Britain to "reduce the black man in Jamaica" to slavery and restore the West Indian sugar industry. Britain could then regain dominance in the global sugar trade and, in league with the southern nation, would achieve the aristocrats' goals. Burke had simply reformulated for a northern audience the old proslavery assertion that Britain acted only for its own selfish interests. Republicanism, imperial paranoia, and the failure of West Indian emancipation intertwined in Burke's speech. The political moment may have been driven by immediate and local concerns, but Burke argued within the transatlantic debate.[17]

While the West Indian arguments of northern proslavery Democrats and Deep South secessionists asserted the permanence of American slav-

16. Edmund Burke, *An Important Appeal to the People of the United States. Slavery and Abolitionism. Union and Disunion* [1856], 2–3.

17. Burke, *An Important Appeal*, 12–13. For the real possibility that Britain would recognize the Southern Confederacy, see Richard Blackett, *Divided Hearts: Britain and the American Civil War* (Baton Rouge: Louisiana State University Press, 2001), 48–121.

ery, a growing cacophony of northern voices described an antislavery vision of the postemancipation West Indies which rejected that permanence. We have already seen the expansion of First of August celebrations, where the postemancipation West Indies were annually heralded as an unmitigated success. As abolitionist circles grew, the antislavery portrait of black emancipation in the British West Indies was further developed by professional journalists and disseminated in the political press. As fire-eaters considered secession in 1850, the antislavery Democrat John Bigelow wrote a series of essays on Jamaica for the *New York Evening Post,* and in 1859 and 1860—during that momentous presidential canvass—the Canadian journalist William Sewell wrote a similar series for the Republican *New York Times.* Both writers offered a nuanced portrait of the postemancipation West Indies which undermined proslavery argument and gave transatlantic validation to the free labor ideology embodied by the emerging Republican Party.

Bigelow toured Jamaica in the winter of 1850 to research some articles for William C. Bryant's *New York Evening Post* which later appeared as *Jamaica in 1850.* Bryant and Bigelow represented those northern Democrats who were increasingly unwilling to support the South on slavery, and Bigelow's articles on the West Indies showed the clear emergence of a new way for northerners to think about emancipation. Bigelow satisfied neither the abolitionists nor the proslavery writers. He acknowledged Jamaica's economic decline since the abolition of slavery but saw emancipation as only part of the problem. Moreover, he decried the long-term effects that slavery had had upon the culture of labor on the island. His was an argument for the superiority of free labor.[18]

As Eric Foner and others have recognized, promotion of the ideal of free labor enabled the emergent Republicans to attack slavery without embracing the abolitionism that was too intertwined with antiracism to be attractive to most white northerners.[19] Bigelow's work reinforced this complicated stance. His description of the island's three-tiered racial milieu would have surprised white readers unfamiliar with the West Indies. Bigelow reported that what racists called "amalgamation" was quite common among polite society in Jamaica. There were "colored" men in the legislature; they married white women; they worked as lawyers, editors,

---

18. John Bigelow, *Jamaica in 1850. Or, The Effects of Sixteen Years of Freedom on a Slave Colony* (1851; reprint, New York: Negro Universities Press, 1970).

19. Foner, *Free Soil,* ix–xxxix, 11–39.

and policemen; many were quite accomplished. But those who were accomplished were of lighter skin tone, and they disdained to mingle with those of darker complexion. Browns would not marry "a negro, or African" and considered it an "unpardonable insult" to be grouped among them. Bigelow sympathized. He noted that Jamaican blacks spoke a Creole "gibberish" that demonstrated their imbecility; it was speech heard only "from negroes and monkeys."[20] While shocking to modern ears, Bigelow's racist portrayal of Jamaican society was mild for his time and probably validated his authorial voice for white supremacist readers. Most white northerners rejected the racial egalitarianism of radical abolitionism, thus weakening the abolitionist assessment of black emancipation and enabling many Northern politicians to consistently side with the South on all things related to slavery. By distancing himself from unpopular racial views, Bigelow could widen the impact of his analysis of emancipation.

Bigelow argued that the collapse of the Jamaican sugar industry since emancipation stemmed from four principal causes: the degradation of agricultural labor resulting from slavery, the predominance of absentee ownership of sugar estates, the burden of debt carried by most planters since before emancipation, and the absence of a middle class. Each plank of Bigelow's argument drew attention away from the proslavery emphasis on emancipation's debilitating effect on the economy, while at the same time appealing to the Jacksonian ethos still central to northern Democrats. Because black slaves had been agricultural laborers, Jamaican whites would never match the energies of their white American counterparts, which Bigelow compared to the "degradation of free labor" in the South so evident to northern travelers. Because most estates were owned by absentee capitalists in Britain, white Jamaicans did not invest their "intellect" in their efficient operation, and black laborers had no intellect and the sugar estates struggled. And even if a conscientious white manager put forth his best efforts, there was no escape from the burden of debt to British bankers. Finally, as Jamaica was a society where the "moral influence of slavery" lived on, that class of "small proprietors so common throughout the northern part of the United States" had never developed. Thus, the bounty of the island could never be fully tapped. These conditions—not the end of slavery—explained Jamaica's economic prostration.[21]

Bigelow also sought to refute Carlyle, who had argued that though

20. Bigelow, *Jamaica in 1850*, 22–25, 128.
21. Ibid., 76–77.

wages were high, laborers would only work long enough to meet their basic needs. Bigelow described a very different situation. In his discussion of the absence of a middle class, Bigelow noted that so many market goods—grains, meats, cheese and butter, even lumber—were imported because no entrepreneurs had sought to fill these niches in the market. As a result, everyday goods in Jamaica were far more expensive than in U.S. markets. The wages in this economic milieu were barely sufficient for a worker to live. A day's labor for a grown man, for example, would not even buy a pound of ham. Women and boys were paid even less. The available wages, then, were hardly attractive to working people, especially when there were other options.[22]

And there were other options. The most compelling evidence Bigelow gathered to refute Carlyle lay in his account of the black-owned freehold properties in the countryside and the teeming Sunday markets they supplied. Bigelow estimated that throughout the island there were 100,000 of these freeholds. Ambitious laborers would work on the plantations during the harvest, save their earnings, and buy a piece of land that would supply their needs and even bring in some cash from the market. Bigelow described carefully tended farms with root crops, vegetables, and fruits of all descriptions. On market day he reported "an almost uninterrupted procession four or five miles in length" of independent proprietors bringing their surplus to the Kingston market. These men and women showed "neither anxiety, nor poverty, nor desire of gain" upon their faces. In comparison to plantation workers, independent freeholders enjoyed lives of "ease and independence," and it was hardly a surprise that so many laborers desired this approach to life rather than to work for wages. Blacks were not averse to work; they simply preferred to work for themselves.[23]

In the spring of 1859 and into the summer of 1860—the same months that saw the beginning of the presidential campaign—the *New York Times* published another series of essays on the postemancipation West Indies written by William Sewell. Sewell's work was later published as *The Ordeal of Free Labor* (1862,) and it remains a sophisticated analysis of the eman-

22. Ibid., 125.

23. Ibid., 116–17. In an extensive review of Bigelow's work, which opened the December number of the *Democratic Review*, an anonymous author agreed that the experience of Jamaica "afforded a valuable lesson to the United States," yet came to the opposite conclusions of Bigelow. The author instead endorsed Thomas Carlyle's interpretation. See "Jamaica," *United States Magazine and Democratic Review* 27 (December 1850), 481–96.

cipation process in the British West Indies. The *Times* had begun publication as a Whig paper in 1851 but had moved into the Republican camp by
1856 and represented conservative opinion within the Republican Party.
Like Bigelow, Sewell crafted his essays as letters from a traveler to appeal to nonabolitionist readers. Commenting on Sewell's series, the *Times*
noted the "great diversity of opinion" on the results of emancipation but
claimed that "the facts" had not yet been studied with sufficient precision.
Both the "advocates" and the "opponents of slavery" had simply projected
their own ideologies upon the history of emancipation in the West Indies.
The *Times* editors claimed that Sewell would be "eminently practical in
his observations and impartial in his reasoning," and while Sewell himself
did not comment in his letters on the debate over the future of American
slavery, accompanying editorials often did. This pairing of articles and editorials was innovative journalism that sought to validate the free labor,
antislavery positions of the Republican Party through an extended analysis
of the postemancipation West Indies. The series, as well as the responses to
it in the Democratic press, demonstrate that British abolition, on the cusp
of that pivotal election of 1860, continued to shape American public opinions on slavery and its abolition.[24]

Sewell's first dispatch from the West Indies focused almost entirely
on Barbados, one of the islands where the sugar industry had actually
prospered. The first scenes are from the "exhausted city" of Bridgetown,
the capital, where the old business center around the wharfs were mostly
vacant lots that had come to be known as the "burnt district." This de-
piction was Sewell's acknowledgement that the Barbadian economy had
suffered from emancipation, but his next subject was the energetic marketplace. It covered a full acre and was enclosed by a "neat row of butch-
er's stalls" that reminded him of New Orleans. The center was shaded by
"splendid evergreens," and "several scores of negro women" had gathered to
sell their crops of yams, sugarcane, sweet potatoes, oranges, and grapefruit.
The countryside, too, was thriving, and Sewell could not find "a single spot
which has not been cultivated even beyond what we should call perfec-

24. Sewell's series appeared in the *New York Times* from April 16, 1859, through July
21, 1860, and was later published as William Grant Sewell, *The Ordeal of Free Labor in the
British West Indies* (New York: Harper and Brothers, 1861). Harper and Brothers reprinted
Sewell's work in 1862 and 1863; it was also published in London. On the *Times* political af-
filiations, see Elmer Davis, *History of the New York Times, 1851–1921* (New York: New York
Times, 1921), 32–33.

tion." He combined his description of a boisterous local economy with racialist caricatures of black Barbadians. The "clatter of tongues" in the market was the "closest illustration of Sambo" Barbados had to offer. Likewise, when Sewell went for a cab to tour the countryside, he was besieged by a crowd of drivers and barely made his escape. Sewell found it "amusing to hear the successful driver denounce the "umperlite b'havor of dem niggers." Here was the same nod to white American racism that Bigelow had employed, and again it was linked to antislavery argument. For Republican antislavery to be successful, it needed the support of white racists. Sewell closed his letter by suggesting the argument that he would develop more fully over the next year. The results of emancipation had to be assessed island by island, and there were even differences from one plantation to the next on the same island. "Overcrowded Barbadoes" was very different from "sparsely settled" Trinidad.[25]

In July 1859, after several articles on the West Indies had appeared in the *Times*, James Gordon Bennett, the influential Democratic editor of the *New York Herald*, published a series of his own (albeit shorter) on the results of emancipation. Bennett's correspondent was in Jamaica, and unlike Sewell he focused entirely on that island. The *Herald's* letters described the series of riots that had recently taken place in Westmoreland parish. Historian Gad Heuman has argued that these riots were a prelude to the Morant Bay rebellion of 1865, as they illuminated the harsh economic injustices the free black peasantry of Jamaica still faced more than twenty years after emancipation.[26] But for the *Herald's* correspondent, the riots were evidence of the continuing disaster of emancipation. While justice had been done for some of the rioters, who now sat in prison, others—who had demolished the police station in Savanna-la-Mar and chased the judge from the courthouse—had not been tried because the jury called to sit at their trial had simply left town. Moreover, the *Falmouth Post*, a planter paper on the north coast, had received a letter under the pseudonym "Danton" (a reference to the French Revolutionist), which threatened that prosperity would not return until "the throats of the planters are cut and blood made to flow through the land." The letter had been traced to the leadership of the Ja-

25. *New York Times*, April 16, 1859.
26. The rioters targeted tollgates erected at the entrance of several market towns to collect a tax on peasant marketers. The colonial state in Jamaica, still controlled by the planters, had shifted the burden of taxation to the black peasantry. See Gad Heuman, *"The Killing Time": The Morant Bay Rebellion in Jamaica* (London: MacMillan, 1994), 41–42.

maican Reform Society, which was known to advocate for the abolition of slavery in the United States. The "notorious" Reverend Johnson, editor of the *Watchman*, an antislavery paper published by browns, had also been traveling the island "preaching sedition" and calling upon the laborers to abandon work and "demand for higher wages." The series closed this portrait of social chaos with an accounting of the collapse of Jamaica's sugar industry. When Bryan Edwards wrote his *History*, the correspondent reported, Jamaica exported more sugar and rum than the rest of the West Indies combined. Now Barbados and Demerara alone produced twice as much as Jamaica.[27]

Bennett followed his Jamaica letters with a threatening prediction that appeared just a week before the First of August: "Probable Re-enactment of the Slavery Laws in the Northern States." He claimed that the "black republican nigger-worshippers" were forced to confront this issue because of the improvidence and laziness of the black population in the North. Blacks in the North were losing out to white competitors and no longer held jobs as coachmen, barbers, and domestic servants. Bennett's explanation for this development rested on purely racist tenets that employed his recent coverage of the results of emancipation in the West Indies. Taking a page from Carlyle, Bennett argued that the African was genetically predisposed to live in a region of natural plenty, where work was unnecessary for life. In "Hayti and ... the West India islands," the climate of Africa was reproduced, and in those islands the blacks had "acquired the control of the social organization through the preponderance of numbers." At the same time, the island economies had collapsed because the former slaves had ceased to work and black society had relapsed into a "natural state of African barbarism." In the southern states, to the contrary, the persistence of slavery promised a hopeful future for blacks because of the "intimate association with the superior race." Slavery allowed blacks to learn from whites without competing with them, and the "logical deduction" for the northern states was to reimpose black slavery. Bennett repeated these charges in his attack on the First of August celebrations published the next week, and, as we've seen, the *Times* reprinted the pointed reply of William Watkins.[28]

On February 27, 1860, Abraham Lincoln delivered his famous address at the Cooper Union Institute in New York, in which he brilliantly laid out his antislavery views in conservative tones that appealed to a broad swath

27. *New York Herald*, July 10, 1859.
28. *New York Herald*, July 21, 1859, and see chap. 7, n. 57.

of white northerners.[29] Folks were deeply engaged with the jockeying of candidates for the upcoming election, and the *Times* had just returned to its series on the results of West Indian emancipation. Beginning in January 1860, Sewell devoted several articles to the history of emancipation in Jamaica, as that island remained the best evidence for proslavery writers like Bennett that black emancipation had failed. As he had done for Barbados, Sewell acknowledged the island's economic decline; indeed, he "knew of no country in the world where prosperity, wealth, and a commanding position have been so strangely subverted." Yet Sewell differed from the "partisans of Slavery" who attributed this sad decline to black emancipation. Sewell argued instead that Jamaica's decline had begun with the abolition of the slave trade in 1807 and the cause of decline was the poor management of the planters. They abused their slaves ruthlessly out of insatiable greed, and the laboring population was only maintained with imports from Africa, an annual supply of ten thousand. But even in the most prosperous period of Jamaica's history, the decade before 1807, Sewell found that more than 150 estates had gone bankrupt due to the improvidence of their owners. Sugar production began to decline when the flow of new slaves from Africa ended, and it had spiraled downward ever since.[30]

Like Bridgetown, Kingston was a city of "wreck and ruin." Its once beautiful churches were scarcely nicer than "the stables of some Fifth-avenue magnate," and it felt like a place "where money has been made, but can be made no more." But the countryside was starkly different. Sewell described the same hard-working peasantry he had seen in Barbados, and which Bigelow had observed in Jamaica ten years earlier. The fertile lands of the interior were "sparsely settled by small negro cultivators, who have been able to purchase their plots of land for £2 and £3 an acre." These black Jamaicans had saved their money, bought land, and could now earn "with a month's work on their own properties . . . as much as a year's labor on a sugar estate would yield them." Couldn't hard-working Americans appreciate the preference for independence rather than "labor for hire?" Emancipation had produced an independent peasantry that validated the superiority of free labor. Ironically, Sewell's recommendation for the island's

29. My reading of Lincoln has been influenced by James Oakes, *The Radical and the Republican: Frederick Douglass, Abraham Lincoln, and the Triumph of Antislavery Politics* (New York: W. W. Norton, 2007), 57–85.

30. *New York Times*, January 27, 1860. Other *Times* articles on Jamaica were printed on February 23, March 6, March 13, May 5, June 30, July 20, July 21, 1860.

sugar industry was precisely the same as the planters he ridiculed. Jamaican planters wanted Parliament to extend them loans to facilitate the immigration of East Indian laborers, a strategy that planters in Trinidad and Demerara had used with some success but that abolitionists and southern slaveholders attacked as slavery under another name. Sewell pointed out that there were eleven acres for each person in Jamaica, in comparison to one and a half persons per acre in Barbados. If Jamaica were as populated as Barbados, there would be 5 million people on the island, rather than 378,000. Immigration would help to alleviate this difference. The Jamaican economy might be in decline, but emancipation was not at fault.[31]

ANTEBELLUM BLACK RADICALISM

The debate among whites about the results of emancipation in the British West Indies seemed irrelevant to most black Americans, who became increasingly focused upon acting directly to end slavery. Antebellum black thinkers developed the transnational frame of resistance laid down in the 1820s, and the organic connections between the black communities of the United States and the British West Indies (particularly with Jamaica) continued to develop. The importance of British abolition to American black radicalism extended far beyond a day of celebration, or even the fact of progress in the international movement to abolish chattel slavery; it changed the tangible reality of being black in the Atlantic world. Slavery was now illegal according to the laws of a powerful empire, yet in the United States slaveholders were a powerful group who skillfully maneuvered their nation's democratic system to protect their right to own and exploit black slaves. Moreover, as Martin Delany would point out in 1854, Great Britain was "decidedly a commercial and money-making nation" that privileged economic relations rather than any set of values.[32] Great Britain might enforce its laws within its empire, but it would not use its power to liberate all black people from slavery. As David Walker had proclaimed a quarter-century before, "the colored citizens of the world" had to free themselves.

The transnational quality of antebellum black radicalism drew its most powerful strain from the history and impact of British abolition and was

31. *New York Times*, January 27, 1860.
32. Martin R. Delany, *The Political Destiny of the Colored Race* [1854], in Sterling Stuckey, *The Ideological Origins of Black Nationalism* (Boston: Beacon Press, 1972), 232.

most clearly articulated within the political discourse that modern scholars have associated with the origins of Black Nationalism. In the winter of 1841, for example, a series of essays appeared under the pseudonym "Sidney" in the *Colored American*, probably written by Henry Highland Garnet.[33] Like other black nationalist writing of this era, the central thrust of Sidney's essays was the mode of fighting slavery and racist society, and significantly, he found inspiration in the experience of "our brethren in the British West Indies." He pointed to the enfranchisement of the free coloreds in the 1820s and to the abolition of slavery, arguing that both liberations were accomplished "chiefly through the influence of colored men—the oppressed." Sidney called particular attention to Jamaica, where the slaves had become "insurgent runaways," an allusion to the Baptist war, and where the editor Edward Jordan (whom Sidney named) had performed some of the "most daring and heroic acts in the annals of the race." Sidney acknowledged that both liberations had been enacted legislatively, but lawmakers had been "compelled, forced to it, by the combined exertions of the oppressed." Black Jamaicans had charted a course of active pursuit of their rights, and they had won their liberation. Sidney called upon his readership to heed the West Indian example, to agitate and "force" American legislators to acknowledge African American rights.[34]

Mob violence in Philadelphia on the First of August 1842 demonstrated that African Americans faced significantly greater obstacles than had their brethren in the West Indies. As they had since 1838, black Philadelphians planned a celebration, which began with a procession through the city to the banks of the Schuylkill River. As the procession approached the city market, it was attacked by a group of white men and boys, who hurled "offal" at the marchers. The parade quickly dispersed, but a mob of "several thousand" pursued the fleeing paraders into the black neighborhood of Moyamensing. Some tried to defend their homes from the mob, but this resistance fed the violence, and a "melee" ensued that ended only with the arrival of the police. The police did little. They arrested one "deaf and dumb colored man" and several of the white ringleaders, but these men were forcibly released by the mob and violence continued unabated. Black

33. Sterling Stuckey, Introduction to *Ideological Origins*, 16. Stuckey writes that "Sidney" could be either Garnet or Alexander Crummel, but definitive evidence has not emerged to indicate either.

34. "Four Letters by Sidney," from *New York Colored American*, February 20, 1841, in Stuckey, *Ideological Origins*, 154.

Philadelphians had little choice but to flee. Most left without belongings, some without shirts or shoes, and they hid as refugees in the "woods and swamps" of New Jersey.[35] Others were less fortunate. Charles Black, an old man who had not participated in the procession, was sitting in his home when some from the mob burst inside, dragged him into the street, and beat him senseless with clubs and stones. Isaac Reed, sixty-five, had been sawing wood when a group of rioters came upon him and beat him nearly to death with the wood that he had been working on. Bitsey Lewis, an "old colored woman," was found knocked out on the street, her head cut and her jaw broken.[36]

Violence continued into the night. Around nine o'clock, as crowds still filled the streets, arsonists set fire to a large unfinished building known as Smith's Hall, which had been built to replace Pennsylvania Hall, destroyed in similar violence in 1838.[37] Soon after firemen arrived at the scene, the African American Presbyterian Church, only a few blocks away, also started to burn. According to a *New York Tribune* correspondent, the firemen thoroughly doused all the buildings that surrounded the hall and the church, not allowing a "particle of water" to cool the fires that burned these edifices of the black community. The correspondent described the fireman's actions as a "concession to the fierce revenge of the mob" intended to "soothe" the crowd's anger, but the church and the meeting hall were havens to the fight against slavery and racism, and their firing and subsequent neglect show the resolve of one sector of Philadelphia's white population to destroy these sites of black activism.

According to press reports, the alleged catalyst of the initial attack involved a banner created by the Young Men's Vigilant Society which offended white observers. The banner portrayed an emancipated slave pointing with one hand to the word "Liberty" in embroidered gold letters above his head, and with the other to broken manacles that lay beside his feet. In the background was a rising sun and a sinking ship, which the *Philadelphia Public Ledger* (Democrat) took as a representation of the "dawn of liberty and the wreck of tyranny" and the *New York Tribune* described as a "burning slave ship." News of the mutiny on the *Creole* was still fresh and may have inspired the image. The rioters claimed that the banner presented the

35. *Philadelphia Public Ledger*, August 5, 1842.

36. Ibid., August 2 and 3, 1842.

37. Gary Nash, *Forging Freedom: The Formation of Philadelphia's Black Community, 1720–1840* (Cambridge: Harvard University Press, 1988), 277–78.

slogan "Liberty or Death" over the visage of a black man, with "the conflagration of a town in St. Domingo" painted into the background, commemorating the "massacre of the whites by their slaves."[38] Perhaps it did. Either way, the maritime setting of the banner and the occasion of the First of August suggest a Caribbean motif, an artistic expression of the transnational black imagination invoked by Sidney the previous year.

The next August, at the annual convention of African American leaders in Buffalo, Henry Highland Garnet's *Address to the Slaves* transformed the vision of the Young Men's Vigilant Society into some of the boldest oratory black Americans had ever heard. Garnet's clear endorsement of slave violence was rejected by a slim majority of the convention. His speech would not be published for another five years, and his most thorough biographer has puzzled at Garnet's stance, noting his rejection of violence early in 1842.[39] But if we consider the Emancipation Day violence in Philadelphia (especially the burning of the Presbyterian Church and Garnet's position as a Presbyterian minister), the likelihood that Garnet was "Sidney," and Garnet's own references to the British West Indies, then his radical position makes sense, inspired as it was by the transnational black imagination and the painful reality of African American oppression.

Garnet called upon the slaves to "appeal" to their masters' "sense of justice, and tell them that they have no more right to oppress you, than you have to enslave them." Tell your masters to "remunerate you for your labor," Garnet said, and "promise them renewed diligence" in your work if they agree. "Point them to the increase of happiness and prosperity in the British West Indies since the Act of Emancipation," he suggested, and tell them in clear language that slavery is a moral abomination, that "all you desire is FREEDOM, and that nothing else will suffice." Then, Garnet advised, refuse to work for them unless they accept your demands, and "if they then commence the work of death, they, and not you will be responsible for the consequences." It was better to "*die immediately*—than live slaves, and entail your wretchedness upon your posterity." Garnet had no illusions about the "sense of justice" among slaveholders. His strategy called for a strike action that, when rejected, would place the onus of responsibility for the bloodletting that would follow on the oppressor, not the oppressed. Garnet cited the precedents of Toussaint L'Ouverture, "Denmark Veazie,"

38. *Philadelphia Public Ledger,* August 4, 1842; *New York Tribune,* August 6, 1842.

39. Joel Schor, *Henry Highland Garnet: A Voice of Black Radicalism in the Nineteenth Century* (Westport, CT: Greenwood, 1977), 53.

"Nathaniel Turner," Cinque,, and Madison Washington, but his strategy was nothing like the plans of these rebels.[40] Instead, Garnet's approach to rebellion echoed the initial tactics of Samuel Sharpe in the Baptist War of 1831. Sharpe had also planned for a strike action with a promise to return to work in exchange for wages and the abolition of slavery. But he had never established enough discipline among his followers to carry out this strategy; rebellion had been the consequence. Yet that rebellion had led to emancipation and the "happiness and prosperity" of the British West Indies. We cannot be sure that Garnet was directly inspired by Sharpe, but the similarity in their approaches to resistance is striking.[41]

Another transnational strain of black radicalism argued that African Americans had no future in the United States. Racism was too deeply rooted; blacks should emigrate to a friendlier political climate in order to achieve emancipation. The most prominent spokesman of this position—Martin Delany—made the clearest statement of emigrationist sentiment in his *Political Destiny of the Colored Race,* written in 1854. Whereas Walker and Garnet emphasized the oppression of African Americans and the coordinated resistance necessary to overcome it, Delany accepted the permanence of racism in white American culture and looked outward for a permanent solution to black empowerment.[42]

Delany set his agenda for African Americans within a global history of human societies, which taught him that the "great principle of political economy [was] that no people can be free who themselves do not constitute an essential part of the *ruling element* of the country in which they live." Political power was essential, and for Delany the ability to exercise political power derived from the history of races and demographic balance. "For more than two thousand years," he argued, "the determined aim of the whites has been to crush the colored races wherever found." Whites had conquered an enormous amount of terrain, and the most aggressive had been the "Anglo American." Like Walker, Delany acknowledged the "existence of great and good" white people who genuinely sought the well-being of humanity, regardless of race. Nevertheless, it was not "the moralist, Christian, [or] philanthropist" who determined national destinies but

40. Henry Highland Garnet, *An Address to the Slaves of the United States of America* [1848], in Stuckey, *Ideological Origins,* 170–72.

41. See chap. 4. For contemporary evidence that Sharpe's plan was widely known, see *Kingston (JA) Watchman, and Jamaica Free Press,* January 4, 1832.

42. Delany, *Political Destiny,* 195–236.

"the politician, the civil engineer, [and] the skilful economist." These were the professions with the power to "direct and control the machinery" that moved great nations forward, and these were the professions that African Americans needed to engage. Emigration then, was a strategy not to evade the battle foreseen by Walker and Garnet but to take the struggle to a transnational level, whereby African Americans could obtain "adequate means for the conflict." Black Americans were barred from positions of power in the United States; they were not of the "ruling element." Emigration would allow blacks to become a part of the ruling element elsewhere.[43]

Delany looked south to the West Indies and to Central and South America. He gathered pages of demographic statistics on these societies, indicating (he thought) that people of color formed the "ruling element" in all of these places. Delany argued that whites were only "one-seventh" of the population in this vast region, creating a geography of freedom where black Americans might find opportunity. Moreover, the populations of the southern Americas were "a noble race of people, generous, sociable, and tractable" who desired "all the improvements of North America," suggesting that African American immigrants in these societies would likely take positions of leadership.[44] Delany's prospectus thus carried an assumption of superiority that was not unlike that of many white Americans toward Latin America and the Caribbean, and his understanding of these societies was at best ill informed. Whites (or at least those who saw themselves as white) held the preponderance of political power throughout this vast region, despite being demographic minorities among the far larger mestizo and Indian populations. But Delany's broader argument shows that African Americans not only looked outward for inspiration in their struggle but also considered acting beyond the boundaries of the United States to elevate their war against slavery to a transnational level.

There is considerable evidence that African Americans acted on these ideas, particularly with respect to Jamaica; moreover, black Jamaicans were more than willing to cooperate. As we have seen, organic connections between the black communities of the northern United States and the British West Indies had formed by the late 1820s, if not earlier. As emigrationist ideas gained more credence, small numbers of African Americans sought refuge in the West Indies in the years after British abolition, a trend

43. Ibid., 197, 204.
44. Ibid., 206–9, 210, 222.

that expanded in the 1840s and 1850s. Black abolitionist James Pennington, for example, sought refuge in Jamaica in 1846 after his presence in the
North as a fugitive slave became known to his former master. Pennington
remained in Jamaica for the next two years, touring the various missionary
stations and giving public lectures. He also worked at building connections
between Jamaicans and African Americans, efforts that bore fruit with the
formation of the "Jamaica Hamic Association," which Pennington represented at the African American convention in Troy, New York, in 1847.
A group of Jamaican merchants, the Hamic Association sought to create business connections between the black communities of Jamaica and
the United States that would not only create wealth but also work against
American slavery. If black merchants could prosper in the West Indian
trade, the white Americans who now dominated that trade would have to
"transact business" with people of color and thereby develop "a more humane and rational" view of black people that would counteract American
racism. "The reaction upon North American slavery would be irresistibly
great," their spokesman believed. While the healing powers of commerce
were perhaps overstated, the emergence of such an association speaks to a
growing transnationalism in both communities.[45]

While the Jamaica Hamic Association does not seem to have flourished, efforts to build links between the United States and Jamaica continued. With the passage of the Fugitive Slave Law in 1850, thousands of
African Americans fled for British Canada, fearful of federally empowered
slave catchers. Garnet, however, traveled to safer ground in Great Britain
and after a speaking tour sought appointment as a missionary to Jamaica
under the auspices of the Scottish Presbyterian Church. Garnet arrived in
Kingston in December 1852 and on the seventeenth of that month lectured to a "large audience" on the effect of the Fugitive Slave Law on African American life. The *Kingston Dispatch* admired Garnet's "vividness of
description," and from the advocate of rebellion (Garnet published his *Address to the Slaves* in 1848) we can presume some fiery oratory. Garnet's
principal duties were to serve as pastor to the Sterling Presbyterian Church

45. Richard J. Blackett, *Beating Against the Barriers: The Lives of Six Nineteenth Century
Afro-Americans* (Ithaca: Cornell University Press, 1986), 32–35; *Proceedings of the National
Convention of Colored People . . . held in Troy, N.Y., 1847*, in Howard Holman Bell, ed., *Minutes of the Proceedings of the National Negro Conventions, 1830–1864* (New York: Arno, 1969),
23. A small group of blacks from Baltimore also settled in Trinidad and British Guiana during this same period.

in Grange Hill in Westmoreland parish, which had been the epicenter of the Baptist War of 1831. Garnet took his duties quite seriously. In addition to preaching in Grange Hill, he also served a more isolated congregation in the country and began a Sunday school that had more than 150 pupils by the end of his first year.[46]

Garnet also became involved in coordinating African American emigration to Jamaica. In June 1853 he wrote an open letter to African Americans on behalf of the planters George Porteus and Benjamin Vickers, which was published in the *New York Tribune*, the *Frederick Douglass Paper* in Rochester, and perhaps others. Porteus was an elder in Garnet's congregation; Vickers owned a plantation adjoining Garnet's residence. Both planters hoped to recruit farm laborers for "cleaning canes," who would be paid $2.50 per acre. Garnet claimed that "an active man or woman" could clear half an acre a day, and he advertised the proximity of Methodist and Baptist congregations, as well as his own church. Garnet wanted persons of "good moral and religious character" only, and he seemed to believe that native Jamaicans could benefit from the positive example of the American worker. Jamaicans were "naturally indolent," he claimed, and an American worker "would do four times the amount" of work that Jamaicans did in a day. Such a comparison echoed that of sixteenth-century Spanish colonists who argued that an African slave could perform four times as much labor as Native Americans; it also communicated the same assumption of American superiority expressed by Martin Delany. Douglass condemned Garnet's "Jamaica schemes," and his most recent biographer has argued that Garnet's pandering indicates he had a financial incentive.[47] Whatever Garnet's motive, his missionary work and his efforts to promote emigration reveal a black consciousness that transcended national boundaries. The common goal remained to challenge American slavery, through abolitionist agitation, racial uplift, and the successful example of postemancipation Jamaica.

Two rescues—one of a free Jamaican in Pittsburgh and one of a Baltimore slave in Kingston—demonstrate the coordination of these black communities in the fight against American slavery. Their dedication to radical abolitionism transcended cultural difference. In May 1853, the members of the Pittsburgh Vigilance Committee, which included Delany,

46. *Frederick Douglass Paper*, January 21, 1853.

47. *Frederick Douglass Paper*, September 2, 1853; Martin B. Pasternak, *Rise Now and Fly to Arms: The Life of Henry Highland Garnet* (New York: Garland, 1995), 75.

wrote an open letter of warning to the editors of the *Kingston Morning Journal,* Edward Jordan and Richard Osborne. They told of their rescue of Alexander Hendrickure, a Jamaican youth of only fourteen who had been kidnapped in Kingston by an American slave trader, Thomas Adams. Adams had been in California, and he was en route back to the East Coast on the steamer *Uncle Sam,* which stopped in Jamaica. He seduced the young man with new clothes and a promise to take him home to Nashville, where Hendrickure could earn money on Adams's cattle farm to pay his passage to California, where he would get rich. The Pittsburgh abolitionists had been alerted by their counterparts in Philadelphia, where Adams and Hendrickure had landed, and they were waiting for the slave trader and his prey when the pair arrived on the evening train. The abolitionists were also fortunate to have the cooperation of the city authorities, particularly Judge Thomas Williams, a prominent Whig and later a radical Republican congressman. When the abolitionists confronted Adams and had Hendrickure arrested for his own safety, the slave trader fled and was not seen again. For Hendrickure, it had been a very close call.[48]

Safe but startled to learn of the danger he had faced, Hendrickure shared his story with the abolitionists, who discovered "a new and alarming species of the slave trade" that sold free Jamaicans into American slavery. Hendrickure had been fooled once before in the winter of 1851, when an American had made similar promises and brought him to Norfolk, Virginia. Hendrickure had stayed on ship when the man went ashore to do some business (presumably to sell the boy), and, fortunately for Hendrickure, the ship left for New York before the man returned. On his arrival in New York, Hendrickure was handed over to the British authorities and sent back to Jamaica. Hendrickure also testified that on his recent trip three other young men had accompanied him and Adams on the *Uncle Sam,* but the others had disembarked in New York, and the abolitionists presumed that they were now enslaved. The Pittsburgh merchant Samuel Cuthbert had witnessed a similar tragedy when returning from California on the *Illinois,* which had also stopped in Jamaica. Two American women were traveling from Jamaica to New York with at least two Jamaican girls (perhaps three). Like Adams, the American women claimed that after a

48. "Martin R. Delay, John C. Peck, William Webb, and Thomas Burrows to Editor, Kingston *Morning Journal*" [*Pittsburgh Saturday Visiter,* May 31, 1853] in C. Peter Ripley et al., eds., *The Black Abolitionist Papers,* 5 vols. (Chapel Hill: University of North Carolina Press, 1991), 4:157–60.

sojourn on the East Coast the girls would also head for California. The abolitionists presumed this too was a fabrication and feared the girls were already enslaved. Obviously, there existed "a regular system of *decoying, kidnapping, and selling into hopeless bondage, in the United States, the free subjects of Great Britain.*" The abolitionists called upon the editors to publicize this information and to be cautious of American steamers to their islands, for what had happened in Jamaica probably occurred elsewhere in the West Indies. "No colored person in the United States is really free," they warned, and it would be better to struggle with poverty in the West Indies than to be a slave in the United States.[49]

Two years later a group of Jamaicans in Savanna-la-Mar, a small port in Westmoreland, returned the favor to the Pittsburgh abolitionists. The *Young America,* a brig out of Baltimore, had arrived under the command of one Captain Rodgers. The ship's cook was a slave named James Anderson, who was owned by a Mr. Robinson of Baltimore. Wary that the slave in his charge might be freed if he landed, Captain Rodgers "took great pains" to keep him on board for the duration of their stay. Local abolitionists, however, heard of Anderson's presence—no doubt from a free black seaman—and "took the matter into their own hands." Five "stalwart Negroes" took canoes, made their way to the brig and "boarded her by main force, and seizing the slave, bore him off in triumph." The activists also had the cooperation of a local magistrate, Justice R. F. Thomas, who greeted Anderson when he came ashore, asking him "Are you a free man or a slave?" When Anderson replied that he was a slave, the judge told him, "Then in the name of her Majesty the Queen, I now declare that you are free and at liberty, having landed on British soil." Robert Monroe Harrison, now eighty-five, demanded redress from the governor, but Judge Thomas's decision was confirmed the next day and presumably Anderson went free.[50]

The rescues of Hendrickure and Anderson shed light on the abolitionist radicalization that had been shaping these black communities since the 1820s. African American spokesmen had framed the struggle against slavery in transnational terms for this entire period, and in this final antebellum decade, wherever black activists formed a critical mass, they acted against American slavery. Radical abolitionists in Pittsburgh and Savanna-

49. Ibid.

50. *Washington (DC) National Era,* July 5, 1855; *Rochester Frederick Douglass Paper,* July 27, 1855.

la-Mar were connected by their dedication to the fight against American slavery which threatened black people everywhere, not only in the United States. American slavery was racial slavery and because of the shared history that linked the peoples of the United States and the British Empire, no person of African descent was safe until it was abolished. While Alexander Hendrickure was illegally kidnapped and therefore protected by law, black activists in the United States who seized recaptured slaves violated federal law. In the British West Indies, however, those who made the same daring rescues were supported by Great Britain's abolition of chattel slavery in 1833. The struggle against slavery linked these societies across the Atlantic, and as long as the power of the U.S. government defended slaveholders, it would collide with international abolitionism.

THE COMING OF CIVIL WAR

On January 1, 1860, David Christy sat down to write the introduction to the election year reprinting of his best-selling *Cotton is King*, which now appeared as the lead title in a compendium of proslavery literature edited by E. N. Elliot. In the months preceding, John Brown and a small company of black abolitionists had attacked the federal arsenal at Harper's Ferry, Virginia, sending panic throughout southern communities and moving prominent northerners such as Thoreau and Emerson to proclaim Brown a martyr for the abolitionist cause. Christy wrote that a few weeks earlier he had acquired a copy of the Chatham (Canada West) *Weekly Pilot*, an African American newspaper, which had in October reported on a community meeting about emigration which had been addressed by an agent from Jamaica. Christy probably liked the idea of black emigration, but he was alarmed by the printed resolutions the meeting had produced, one of which alluded to "the crisis [that] will soon occur in the United States" and hailed the "enslaved bondmen upon their deliverance." Christy saw a connection between the resolution and John Brown's attack, which, he believed, was "known to the leaders of the meeting . . . [who] desired to co-operate in the movement." The meeting in Chatham had been held on October 3; Brown had attacked less than two weeks later. Brown did have extensive contacts among radical black abolitionists, and he had presented his plan to revolutionize the South at a meeting in Chatham in the spring of 1858. Christy rightly perceived the radicalization of a black community that transcended national boundaries. Now they had tried to instigate a slave rebellion, and white northerners had cooperated. It was time for southern slaveholders to calculate the value of maintaining the Union.[51]

In 1860 the United States faced an election that turned on the question of slavery, for, as Christy put it, "the negro is to American politics what cotton is to European manufactures and commerce—the controlling element." Historians have long recognized the election of Abraham Lincoln in 1860 as the decisive event that led to southern secession and the American Civil War. Slavery had emerged as the central and most divisive subject in the nation's political discourse, and Lincoln's Republican Party included many who had considered themselves abolitionists for quite some time. While most historians of this era have neglected the international context, contemporaries such as David Christy did not. Christy sought to awaken the public mind to the permanence of American slavery and "to convince the abolitionists of the utter failure of their plans." He noted that British and American abolitionists had "destroyed tropical cultivation" in the West Indies and that by rejecting colonization, abolitionists had missed the opportunity to promote tropical cultivation in Africa as a challenge to the South, which had "given to slavery in the United States its prosperity and power." Slavery was governed by "the laws of Political Economy," and as white southerners had been saying for years, the tropical cultivation of the world's most valuable commodities—sugar and cotton—was the core of the world economy, and it could only flourish with white masters and black slaves.[52]

Christy offered a history of the early republic ensconced in the Atlantic world of commerce yet infused with the futile spirit of abolitionism. He moved back and forth between the emancipations in the northern states and the progress of cotton, noting, for example, that the formation of the New York Abolition Society took place during the same year that James Watt had applied the steam engine to the spinning of cotton. When New Hampshire abolished slavery, the first shipments of cotton were exported,

51. David Christy, "Preface to the Third Edition," in E. N. Elliot, ed., *Cotton is King, and Pro-Slavery Arguments* (1860; reprint, New York: Negro Universities Press, 1969), 23. Christy's work was first published in 1855 in Cincinnati by Moore, Wilstach, Keys & Co. A second, expanded edition was published the next year in New York by Derby & Jackson, and again in Cincinnati by H.W. Derby & Co. The third edition was published in Augusta, Georgia, by Pritchard, Abbot & Loomis, in 1860; Stephen B. Oates, *To Purge This Land with Blood: A Biography of John Brown* (Amherst: University of Massachusetts Press, 1970), 243–44.

52. Christy, *Cotton is King*, in Elliot, *Cotton is King*, 22, 24.

and when Vermont abolished slavery, the cotton gin was invented. During these years of northern emancipation, whites in the North discovered to their horror the problems posed by the "degraded character of the colored population" when not enslaved. The number of black convicts soared, burdening the northern states, and the benevolent efforts of northern philanthropists failed to raise them to civility. Southern whites, however, understood the "negro character" and learned from the mistakes of their northern neighbors. They began to prohibit emancipations and formed the American Colonization Society "as the only means for accomplishing anything" for the betterment of African peoples. But this noble effort was hindered by British abolition, which "gave a great impulse to the abolition cause in the United States"; inspired the abolitionist attack on the ACS; and deceived the North, where "everywhere resounded with the cry of 'Immediate Abolition.'" Christy's reading of American history saw two inexorable forces—the progress of slave-grown cotton and the deceptions of abolitionism—which brought that dangerous moment of the election of 1860.[53]

To the glory of cotton and the deceptions of abolitionism, Christy and his fellow authors dedicated their entire tome; both threads of proslavery argument led to Great Britain. On the one hand, cotton had become so central to British commerce that the *Economist* of London had warned that any "convulsion" in the American economy would send shock waves through the United Kingdom, as "the lives of nearly two millions of our countrymen are dependent upon the cotton crops of America." Christy provided numbers, endless quotations, and seventeen pages of tables to demonstrate the tremendous value of slave-grown cotton to the global economy.[54]

On the other hand, Britain's experiment with free labor in the British West Indies offered the "conclusive arguments" against the deceptions of the abolitionists, tangible proof that emancipation had not only failed to uplift the former slaves but had also devastated the fortunes of the planters. The *American Missionary* reported that the spread of missions had done nothing to improve the morals of the people. A man would be welcomed in chapel, for example, even if he were "a drunkard, a liar, a Sabbath-breaker, a profane man, [or] a fornicator." The *London Times* had observed that

53. Ibid., 35–36, 50–52.
54. Ibid., 62, 250–67.

"the negro has not acquired, with his freedom, any habits of industry or morality." And John Bigelow, who in 1850 had expressed such admiration for the effects of sixteen years of freedom in Jamaica, had noted in 1853 the "alarming" decline of the island's economy wreaking "distress and misery" on thousands of people." Christy provided tables from *Blackwood's Magazine* that showed the decline in sugar production in Jamaica and another table that illuminated the "free labor deficit" based on the production of sugar, coffee, and cotton in the British West Indies and Haiti. These were "facts," Christy argued, that American slaveholders had "closely watched." The moral degradation of freed people of color, in the North and in the West Indies, demonstrated the impossibility of emancipation without colonization, and "with the example of West India emancipation before them . . . it cannot be expected that Southern statesmen will ever risk the liberation of their slaves."[55]

The election of 1860 brought to the White House a man who believed in free labor and the long-standing axiom that slavery would someday wither and die. Abraham Lincoln was hardly an abolitionist. In his famous debates with Stephen Douglas, Lincoln had suggested the plausibility of "systems of gradual emancipation" but had also stated that he could not "judge" the South for failing to adopt one. Yet in the political context of 1860, Lincoln was antislavery enough for the radical abolitionist Wendell Phillips to declare that "for the first time in our history, the *slave* has chosen a President for the United States." There were "cheers" from the packed crowd in the Tremont Temple in Boston, and leading southerners, steeped in the rhetoric of King Cotton and wary of the West Indian example, moved to strike for independence.[56]

As the Confederacy formed, secessionist commissioner Stephen Hale of Alabama invoked the "horrors of a San Domingo servile insurrection" as well as the "scenes of West Indian emancipation, with its attendant horrors and crimes (that monument of British fanaticism and folly" when he urged Governor Beriah Magoffin of Kentucky to join with the seceding states. On August 1, 1861, during the first summer of war and with no hint of a Union policy of emancipation, Wendell Phillips addressed the annual celebration in Framingham, Massachusetts. His words filled the entire front page of Horace Greeley's *Tribune*. The West Indies, Phillips cried, had not

55. Ibid., 137–39, 142, 149.

56. Harold Holzer, ed., *The Lincoln-Douglas Debates* (New York: Harper Collins, 1993), 61; *New York Anti-Slavery Standard*, November 17, 1860.

seen a day of violence after their emancipation; it offered the example of a "peaceful, moral emancipation by ordinary force of law" which America had witnessed and "dashed aside." Emancipation could now be had only through "the mouth of a cannon." America's "lesson to-day is ... St. Domingo," and as the French had paid for emancipation with the "blood of seventy thousand," so too would the United States. Phillips believed in the "personal courage" of the southern states, and like Poland, Hungary, and Italy, they would fight for independence.[57]

Phillips argued for a war of emancipation. Only a war for emancipation could bring volunteers to the Union army, stave off international intervention, and endow the Union cause with justice worthy of abolitionist support. In addition to the efforts of abolitionists like Phillips, Republican activists such as Franklin Sanborn, Richard Hinton, and William Sewell, and abolitionists like Lewis Tappan and Lydia Maria Child cooperated in a massive public relations campaign that again pushed the example of the West Indies before the northern mind. There were few new arguments, but in pamphlet after pamphlet the northern public was presented with the successful experiment in the free West Indies as evidence of the safety and good policy of emancipation.[58] Likewise, in 1862 the Democratic editor John Van Evrie reprinted his *Free Negroism; Or, Results of Emancipation*, which echoed the arguments of *Cotton is King*, warning of the social, economic, and political disasters history taught would accompany emancipation. For Americans at war, the history of the modern world showed two paths to emancipation—the peaceful route of the British West Indies and the violent struggle of Haiti—both so close to American shores. For twenty-seven years American abolitionists had advocated the peaceful path, but the rest of the country had not listened, and now the war had come.[59]

57. Stephen F. Hale to Governor Beriah Magoffin, December 27, 1860, quoted in Charles B. Dew, *Apostles of Disunion: Southern Secession Commissioners and the Causes of the Civil War* (Charlottesville: University of Virginia Press, 2001), 98–99; *New York Tribune*, August 5, 1861.

58. James M. McPherson, "Was West Indian Emancipation a Success? The Abolitionist Argument During the American Civil War," *Caribbean Studies* 4 (1964): 28–34.

59. [John Van Evrie], *Free Negroism: Or, Results of Emancipation in the North and West India Islands, with Statistics of the Decay of Commerce, Idleness of the Negro, His Return to Savageism, and the Effect of Emancipation upon the Farming, Mechanical, and Laboring Classes* (New York: Van Evrie, Horton & Co., 1862). This work was originally written in the 1850s, and in addition to the 1862 printing, reappeared in 1863 and 1866; see Forest Wood, *Black Scare: The Racist Response to Emancipation and Reconstruction* (Berkeley and Los Angeles: University of California Press, 1968), 36.

The Morant Bay Rebellion and Radical Reconstruction

On October 7, 1865, an altercation at the courthouse in Morant Bay led to a widespread rebellion that violently illuminated the gross inequities of free Jamaica. The violence stemmed from two cases, connected only by the deep resentment they inspired among the black community. Free of slavery for almost thirty years now, black Jamaicans were poor, disenfranchised, and angry. While many embodied John Bigelow's portrait of a hard-working black peasantry with their own freeholds, the legal security of those freeholds was uncertain, and many still depended upon the low and irregular wages of the plantations. Moreover, political power remained in the hands of the planter elite. There were no racial barriers to prevent the former slaves from voting, but property qualifications were so high that only a miniscule percentage of the population had the vote. The planters used their power to shift the burden of governance to the working poor. A farmer's cart, for example, was taxed at eighteen shillings per year; the same cart used on a plantation was not taxed. Lately, times had been even harder. There had been drought followed by floods, destroying crops, and the Union blockade of Confederate ports had cut off much of the American trade, increasing the prices of necessary imports. The price of sugar in Britain had also fallen, putting downward pressure on already low wages for sugar workers.[1]

Peasant groups requested that lands be made available to them, Baptist missionaries publicized their plight in Great Britain, and in the As-

---

1. The narrative in the following paragraphs draws from Thomas Holt, *The Problem of Freedom: Race, Labor, and Politics in Jamaica and Britain, 1832–1938* (Baltimore: Johns Hopkins University Press, 1992), 263–309, and Gad Heuman, *"The Killing Time": The Morant Bay Rebellion in Jamaica* (London: MacMillan, 1994).

sembly in Kingston the colored planter George William Gordon champi-
oned black rights. But the official response echoed the theories of Thomas
Carlyle. In a memorandum penned by the colonial secretary Henry Taylor,
which came to be known as "the Queen's Advice," those who were suffering were told that their "prosperity" depended upon "working for Wages,
not uncertainly, or capriciously, but steadily and continuously, at the times
when their labor is wanted, and for so long as it is wanted." The recently
appointed Governor Eyre agreed. He had fifty thousand copies printed
and posted throughout the island and comforted himself that he had dealt
with the problem of those lazy blacks.[2]

The signal case at Morant Bay was an accusation of trespass against
Lewis Miller, a peasant farmer whose claim to his freehold was contested
by Wellwood Maxwell Anderson, colored assemblyman, agent-general of
immigration, and the proprietor of Middleton Pen. Anderson claimed that
Miller was a squatter on his land. Land disputes between Anderson and
the black community had been frequent since the late 1850s—indeed, land
disputes were frequent throughout the island—and a large crowd had assembled to observe the case. The presiding magistrates were both proprietors, and when they decided in favor of Anderson and slapped Miller with
a heavy fine, the crowd was outraged. They called on Lewis to appeal; he
did so, and his bond was posted by Paul Bogle, the black Baptist preacher
in Miller's community of Stony Gut, a village in the hills.

But the case that started the melee involved the petty assault of one
black boy against another, resulting in a fine of twelve shillings—five weeks
pay for a grown man. A black spectator, James Geoghegen, urged the boy
not to pay, and when the magistrate ordered Geoghegen arrested for dis-
rupting the court, several of the crowd intervened, escorted Geoghegen
outside, and beat the policemen on the courthouse steps. The next day a
contingent of black policemen were sent up to Stony Gut to arrest the men
involved in the fisticuffs and Bogle, whom the authorities assumed had
been behind the whole confrontation. When the police arrived in Bogle's
yard and attempted to arrest him, hundreds of Bogle's supporters turned
out, armed with cutlasses, clubs, and pikes. They quickly overpowered the
police, beat them, and forced them to take an oath that they would "join
their colour" and "cleave to the black." They sent the policemen back down
to town with the message that Bogle would come down the next day. Baron

2. Quoted in Holt, *Problem of Freedom*, 277–78.

von Ketelhodt, a planter and *custos* of the parish, called out the militia and sent for troops from Kingston, a day's journey to the west. The call of shells blowing could already be heard in the hills above Morant Bay.

Bogle's supporters came in force the following morning. Several hundred men and women, marching in two long columns and armed as they had been the day before, came down from the hills blowing shells and beating drums. Their numbers grew as they approached Morant Bay, and upon arrival they attacked the police station, emptying its arsenal. The parish vestry was meeting in the courthouse, and a small company of militia was gathered in the schoolhouse. As the rebels approached the courthouse, the militia filed out. Von Ketelhodt came out on the courthouse steps and attempted to read the Riot Act, but he was answered with a volley of curses and stones. The militia opened fire, killing several rebels, but before they could reload, the rebels charged and unleashed their fury. The militia retreated back into the courthouse and began to fire on the crowd. The rebels set fire to the courthouse and the surrounding structures, and when these fell the terrified militia and vestrymen were lost to the crowd. Some ran and escaped; others were beaten to death; von Ketelhodt's body was found mutilated.

The rebellion spread throughout the eastern half of the island and lasted several days. Governor Eyre declared martial law and sent troops and militia throughout the region to quell the violence. The suppression was brutal. All told, the rebels had killed twenty-two and wounded thirty-four; they burnt down five buildings in Morant Bay and plundered twenty plantations in the surrounding region. British soldiers and militiamen killed 354 people; some were shot and others hung at impromptu court-martials. They flogged more than six hundred and burned a thousand freehold properties. Paul Bogle was captured and hung, and in an extraordinary abuse, George William Gordon was accused of instigating the revolt, arrested, and transported to Morant Bay where he could be tried under martial law. He was hung on October 23, 1865.

The first reports of "negro insurrection" appeared in American newspapers over the next few days. By November 3 Paul Bogle had been identified and a reward offered for his arrest, and the next day's papers reported that the insurgents were "besieging Kingston." The Spanish authorities in Cuba had become so concerned with the contagion of rebellion that they had sent warships to aid in the suppression. Another early report in the *Lynchburg Daily Virginian* described a "band of negroes, numbering 800 men, thoroughly organized . . . sweeping everything before them." The rebellion was growing: "troops are wanted. There is no time to be lost." A widely reprinted letter from William A. Isles (who worked for a brokerage firm that traded in the island) placed the revolt in a broader perspective and was highly sympathetic to the planters. Ever since emancipation, Isles wrote, "the authorities have experienced considerable opposition in attempting to collect the taxes from the negroes." Black Jamaicans were "mostly squatters" who, as Carlyle had suggested, were incapable of the "ordinary industry" that would have made the lands they used productive. They were therefore unable to pay, due to their own laziness. Isles situated the initial riot at the courthouse around a contest over tax collection and described the killing of Baron von Ketelhodt, not sparing gruesome details of "thumbs" sliced off and bowels "ripped open." The rebellion "was still in progress" when he wrote (the letter was dated October 23), and the white population feared for their lives.[3]

Some of the first connections made between the rebellion in Jamaica and the postwar United States appeared in the *New York World* (the major Democratic daily later bought by Joseph Pulitzer), and the *Lynchburg Daily Virginian*, which reprinted the *World*'s analysis and suggested some lessons for the defeated South. According to the *World*, the precise "cause" for the rebellion was unclear, but the political complexion of the island would make any white man shudder. The Jamaican Assembly was "virtually and to all purposes a negro assembly, as not more than one-fifth of the members belong to the despised white race." The black population of the island outnumbered the whites "twenty to one." The mayor of Kingston was a "colored man . . . more than three-fourths of the magistrates and officers of the Colonial Government are colored men, and several of the best educated and most prominent journalists of the island are also colored men. The police . . . belong to the same race." Moreover, the political dominance of the black population in Jamaica was compounded by "an infernal feeling of hatred displayed toward the white minority, on the part of the negroes." Incredibly, the *World* attributed the "principal cause" of this racial enmity to the agitation of "emissaries from the Northern United States, who go about among the half-educated and debased blacks, instilling false and

3. *New York Times,* October 25, November 3, 4, 1865; *Lynchburg Daily Virginian,* November 1, 8, 1865. William A. Isles's letter appeared first in the *Boston Traveller* and was reprinted in the *New York Times,* November 12, 1865, and the *Lynchburg Daily Virginian,* November 16, 1865.

pernicious ideas into the craniums of their too-willing hearers." American abolitionists (or perhaps "black" Republicans) were espousing the idea of a "free and independent negro republic," and they would invite "the brutal Souloque" (the recently overthrown tyrant of Haiti) to take power and "follow in the footsteps of the inhuman butchers of 1793." Here was yet another formulation of the Edwards thesis, after more than sixty years, and now combined with the specter of black political power which white supremacists North and South had long feared. The *World* ended its account ominously, predicting "an indiscriminate massacre of white women and children" if the rebellion was not crushed soon.[4]

The *Daily Virginian* reprinted this account in full, adding that "later reports" described "terrible massacres of the whites." And if the *World's* account was true, the *Virginian* opined, and northern abolitionists had been behind these developments, "it is but one more melancholy proof of the baleful influence of that mischievous set of disorganizers." These dangerous men had started the terrible war that destroyed slavery, and now they "would transfer the scenes of Jamaica and San Domingo to the Southern States of this Union." The rebellion in Jamaica revealed to white southerners that the "spirit of old John Brown still lives though 'his body is a mouldering.'" The *Virginian* "shudder[ed] to think of what would be the effect of these incendiary teachings in the lately populous slave regions of the South." The lessons of emancipation in the British West Indies were even more potent after the war than they had been when the white South still had slavery to defend. The focus on the political power held by Jamaican blacks foreshadowed white southern fears of a Reconstruction controlled by the "black" Republicans in Congress and at home, and the frenzied perception of "terrible massacres" looked backward to the fear of slave rebellions and forward to the paramilitary violence of the Ku Klux Klan. Northern Democratic organs like the *World* stirred up these fears with misleading portrayals of the origins of the revolt. Defeated and powerless, the news from Jamaica exacerbated white southern paranoia.[5]

News from Jamaica also shaped the Republican shift toward Radical Reconstruction, which developed over precisely the same period of time. As we have seen, the *New York Times* paid careful attention to the rebel-

4. *Lynchburg Daily Virginian,* November 11, 1865. For more examples of the New York Democratic coverage, see Forest Wood, *Black Scare: The Racist Response to Emancipation and Reconstruction* (Berkeley and Los Angeles: University of California Press, 1968), 121.

5. Ibid.

lion in Jamaica, and the first detailed account, drawn from the "Kingston papers" and published November 17, was highly sympathetic to Jamaica's white population, with no expression of outrage at the brutality of the suppression. The rebels were "deluded wretches" who carried out their depredations in a drunken "madness [that] overcame every feeling of humanity and prudence." The rebellion had begun with a "furious attack" of a force of five hundred men led by Paul Bogle, followed by days of "plunder and murder" until a "perfect reign of terror prevailed everywhere." The rebels' war cry was "death to the white man," and only the "summary measures" of the military had slowed their rage. While Bogle was named as the military leader, the "master spirit of the revolt was a white man, GEORGE GORDON, who for sake of revenging a private wrong, had for months been fomenting a spirit of discontent among the peasants." The *Times* opined that "had there been no such tampering with their loyalty, the black population of the island would probably have remained contented and quiet."[6]

The misrepresentation of Gordon was corrected on November 30, when he was described as "a black man of mark—a Baptist preacher," but sympathy for the threatened whites continued. Foreshadowing the stance of conservative Republicans who would retreat from radical reconstruction over the next decade, the *Times* stated: "The life of the white man is not safe, without an active police and a strong military force—an energetic and despotic government. Either that must be organized for all the British West Indies, or the whites must abandon their possessions and give them up to the great barbaric negro empire, that may be destined to spread over those Central American regions." While the paper's reports do not reveal it, it seems likely that editors at the *Times* had caught wind of Governor Eyre's proposal, delivered to the Jamaica Assembly on November 7, that the assembly give up its legislative powers and transform Jamaica into a Crown colony directly under the authority of the Colonial Office in London. As William Green has shown, even those assemblymen who had been sympathetic to the plight of Jamaica's impoverished black population were terrified by the revolt, and the establishment of a "despotic government" to protect the planter class became a plausible solution. If we consider these attitudes of Jamaican legislators in light of the Republican abandonment of Radical Reconstruction in 1877, we can see clear parallels in the postemancipation histories of these very different slave societies. The *Times* as-

6. *New York Times*, November 17, 1865.

sessment of the threats that faced Jamaica reveal the same fear of black power and the same white supremacist identification with the white South that would reunite the United States over the final decades of the nineteenth century.[7]

But it was still 1865. The Radical Republicans were ascendant in Washington, and in early December reports began to arrive of the tremendous public outcry in Great Britain over the brutal suppression authorized by Governor Eyre. In the first December number of *Littell's Living Age*, the New York magazine that had covered the debate over West Indian emancipation between Thomas Carlyle and John Stuart Mill, reports reprinted from the *London Spectator* showed that many Britons doubted the legitimacy of fears of island-wide rebellion and were disgusted with the "bloody suppression" that may have taken, they believed, more than 400 lives. The reports from the *Spectator* explored the socioeconomic background of the revolts; they castigated the assembly with its "slaveholding morality," its slender democratic legitimacy, and its blunt use of government power to oppress the peasantry with taxes, laws, and the denial of justice in the courts.[8]

The *Spectator* came to the same conclusion as Governor Eyre, although from a completely different perspective. The rebellion and its brutal suppression revealed that "the planting class is alike by hereditary feeling and by circumstance disqualified for the possession of absolute power." The "mulattoes" were not capable of governance, the blacks were too ignorant to be "trusted with the franchise," and there was "no iron necessity, as in the Southern States of America" to entrust the blacks with power "in order that they not be trampled on" by the dominant white population. It had therefore become the "duty" of the Crown to assert its authority and demand the dissolution of the assembly, so that a society founded on British justice could be formed. The defeated Confederacy, now in the midst of its own ordeal of emancipation, had become the comparative point in the *Spectator*'s exploration of Jamaican governance. A strong and centralized

7. *New York Times*, November 30, 1865; William Green, *British Slave Emancipation: The Sugar Colonies and the Great Experiment, 1830–1865* (Oxford: Oxford University Press, 1976), 396; David W. Blight, *Race and Reunion: The Civil War in American Memory* (Cambridge: Harvard University Press, 2001).

8. *Littell's Living Age* 31 (December 9, 1865): 506–14 (quotes on 507, 509); later reports from *Littell's* appeared in the next two issues: December 23, 1865, 572–74, and December 30, 1865, 622–29.

authority was required, but its purpose would be to raise up the ignorant black population to that undetermined moment of capable self-governance. Radical Republicans would embrace a similar endeavor, and, as Demetrius Eudell has shown, they thought about it in the same paternalistic way.[9]

Curiously, the coverage of the *New York Times* changed its tone. The report of December 13 referred to the "so-called Jamaica insurrection," and rather than emphasizing the alleged demagoguery of Gordon, the *Times* now explored the oppressions suffered by the black peasantry at the hands of the "old slaveowners." Now echoing the *Spectator* rather than the Jamaican planter press, the *Times* report explored the severity of emancipation—the abusive "apprenticeship," the planters' unwillingness to pay "fair wages," the bias of the courts, the oppressive taxes and laws, and the denial of suffrage. The results of this emancipation, controlled as it was by former slaveholders, had "rendered [the black population] permanently suspicious of . . . the employers of the island." Black Jamaicans were in a state of "profound ignorance" that freedom had not removed, and as they had "no part or lot in the government, they attribute all their disasters and misfortunes to their old masters, so that their discontent and anger have been smoldering for many years." It was this state of injustice that had led to the rebellion, and the proposed transfer of authority to London would be, according to the *Times*, "a vast improvement" that would "insure the Negroes a nearer approach to justice than they can ever hope for from the present governing classes." Similar arguments would be used in Congress justifying the direct authority of the federal government over the southern states.[10]

The *Times* also discovered its outrage at the depredations of the British military in suppressing the revolt. The "measures" that had once been presented as wise and necessary were now "not at all creditable to the humanity" of British soldiers. A later report described London headlines that read "TWO THOUSAND NEGROES KILLED—EIGHT MILES OF DEAD BODIES!" and described British soldiers making "a regular sport" out of their orders to quell the rebellion. In fact, the *Times* now used that weighty phrase "reign of terror" to describe the official repression, "quite equal to the worst excesses of despotism of the first French Revolution." The news was dividing British society, and the *Times* quoted the opinions of a broad spectrum

9. *Littell's Living Age* 31 (December 9, 1865): 508; Demetrius Eudell, *The Political Languages of Emancipation in the British Caribbean and the U.S. South* (Chapel Hill: University of North Carolina Press, 2002).

10. *New York Times*, December 13, 1865.

of British newspapers, observing that "the men and the journals that took the part of the North in the late war now take the part of the negroes in Jamaica, while those who sympathized with the South defend Gov. Eyre and the civil and military authorities." The *Times* editors must have felt rather uncomfortable with their earlier coverage, sympathizing as they had with the supporters of the Confederacy. Their next report quoted from a letter from a merchant in Kingston, who could "quite understand the feeling in America among the pro-slavery men, who are only too glad of affairs here, to use as a handle against liberating [the blacks]; but I expect that when the facts connected with the affairs here have seen the light of day ... people will arrive at a different conclusion." As we have seen, those facts had come to light, and powerful members of Congress had come to a different conclusion that had already been suggested by the *Spectator*.[11]

On February 6, 1866, the *Times* devoted ample space to the latest developments in the Senate debates on the policy of Reconstruction then being hammered out between the conservative and radical wings of the Republican Party. Congress had already refused the admittance of the southern members elected under Andrew Johnson's generous guidelines for ex-Confederates, and on January 5, 1866, Senator Lyman Trumbull of Illinois introduced the Civil Rights Bill, intended to extend the rights of citizenship, as well as the suffrage, to the former slaves of the South. Early in February the conservative senator William Fessenden of Maine introduced an amendment that would penalize states that denied the suffrage "on account of race or color" by excluding "all persons therein of such race or color ... from the basis of representation." The amendment created a loophole, of course, for northern states that had disfranchised blacks, as well as for southern states that did not wish to empower former slaves with the vote, and would have accepted the penalty of lessened representation to accomplish this aim. On February 4, Charles Sumner, the most radical of Republicans, launched a three-day oration entitled "The Equal Rights of All" which blasted the amendment and laid out the principles of Radical Reconstruction. The rebellion in Jamaica bolstered his case.[12]

For three generations now, Americans had framed the abolition of slavery with the Haitian revolution, and "only recently," Sumner reminded his audience, "we have listened to a similar tragedy from Jamaica, thus

11. *New York Times,* December 15, 26, 1865.

12. *New York Times,* February 6, 1866; David Donald, *Charles Sumner and the Rights of Man* (New York: Knopf, 1970), 245–47.

swelling the terrible testimony" of justice denied to former slaves. Drawing from the abolitionist arguments of Thomas Clarkson, William Jay, and Lydia Maria Child, Sumner argued that the rebellions in Haiti and Jamaica stemmed from "the denial of rights to colored people," first by Napoleon and more recently by the planters of Jamaica. Imagine the unfolding of a similar history in the American South, "the unhappy freedman blasted by the ban of exclusion." If the former slave, and not the "Rebel master," were to suffer the change of slavery into freedom, "he must be discontented, restless, anxious, and smarting with . . . consciousness of rights denied." The freedmen of the South were "not unlike the freedmen of San Domingo or Jamaica," Sumner argued, "they have the same . . . sense of wrong, and the same revenge." He predicted the "terrible war of races foreseen by Jefferson" if the freedmen of the South were not "enfranchised" with the full rights of American citizens. As the debate moved on, the Republican Congress came to agree with Sumner, and with Radical Reconstruction black southerners were empowered with those rights, averting the rebellions of the West Indies and establishing the only interracial democracy of the nineteenth century, tragically short-lived.[13]

The end of American slavery extended a process of "creative destruction" that remade the nineteenth-century Atlantic world. The Haitian Revolution had opened the sugar markets for planters of the Caribbean, Brazil, and Louisiana, fortifying slavery's economic base and allowing it to expand. But the Haitian Revolution had also strengthened the hands of slaves and abolitionists with the example of slavery overthrown—abolitionists agitated, the slaves rebelled, and slavery in the British West Indies was also destroyed. American slaveholders were in tune with this world, deeply aware of the political weaknesses of their West Indian counterparts. Southern slaveholders learned from British abolition; they focused on building their political strength and constructed an ideology that saw a modernized slavery that would last for hundreds of years. But British abolition had also inspired American abolitionists—black and white—and after twenty-seven years of organization and agitation they moved the northern mind against slavery. The two-party compromises that sustained slavery collapsed, and war ensued, destroying slavery in the American South.

13. New York Times, February 6, 1866; [Charles Sumner], Charles Sumner, His Complete Works, 20 vols. (Boston: Lee and Shepard, 1874), 131–33.

The abolition of slavery was a transatlantic process that was never the work of the markets alone. Slaves and abolitionists, planters and politicians were dynamic participants in this transformation of global significance. But as Sumner and the rebels at Morant Bay understood, the destruction of slavery led to new forms of exploitation that impoverished the freedom of emancipation. As the exploitation of Atlantic slaves expanded after Haitians rebelled, and Great Britain abolished, so the end of American slavery propelled new forms of exploitation for the "free" laborers in the cotton fields of Egypt, India, and equatorial Africa. Moreover, the poverty of Haitian peasants after slavery led to decades of tyranny, military occupation, and a lasting desperation that still plagues that island. And while perhaps not as desperate, the postslavery histories of the African peoples of the Anglo-Atlantic have been struggles against poverty, racism, and legalized oppression which have continued to mock those cherished values that "all men are created equal . . . endowed by their creator with certain unalienable rights." Only the legacy of abolitionism—that lasting movement for the extension of human rights—offers hope from this history.

Bibliography

PRIMARY SOURCES

Manuscript Collections

Dall, Caroline H. Papers. Massachusetts Historical Society, Boston.
Channing, William Ellery. Papers. Massachusetts Historical Society, Boston.
Garrison, William Lloyd. Papers. Antislavery Manuscripts. Boston Public Library.
Hammond, James Henry. Papers. Library of Congress, Washington, DC.
Sedgewick, Charles. Family Papers. Massachusetts Historical Society, Boston.
Spear, Charles. Journal. Boston Public Library
Smith, William. Papers. Perkins Library, Duke University, Durham, NC.
Wright, Elizur. Papers. Library of Congress, Washington, DC.

Government Publications

Annals of the Congress of the United States, 1789–1824. 42 vols. Washington, DC, 1834–56.
Congressional Globe. 46 vols. Washington, DC, 1834–73.
Despatches from U.S. Consuls in Kingston, Jamaica, 1796–1906. Record Group 59, T 31. National Archives, College Park, MD.
Diplomatic Instructions of the Department of State, Great Britain, 1801–1906. Record Group 59, M77. National Archives, College Park, MD.
Executive Documents. 27th Cong., 2nd sess., 1841–1842, no. 215 (ser. 404).
Irish University Press Series of British Parliamentary Papers. Slave Trade. 95 vols. Shannon: Irish University Press, 1969.
Senate Documents. 27th Cong., 2nd sess., 1841–1842, no. 51 (ser. 396).
Senate Documents. 34th Cong., 1st sess., 1855–1856, no. 102 (ser. 824).

Newspapers

Annapolis Maryland Gazette, 1832
Baltimore American & Commercial Advertiser, 1823
Baltimore Freeman's Banner, 1832
Baltimore Niles' Register, 1816–35
Baltimore Patriot and Mercantile Advertiser, 1832–35
Bennington Vermont Gazette, 1832
Boston Advertiser, 1839–40
Boston Christian Watchman, 1831–32
Boston Courier, 1833–35
Boston Daily Advertiser, 1841
Boston Daily Evening Transcript, 1834–38
Boston Liberator, 1831–60
Boston Recorder, 1829–38
Boston Statesman, 1832
Bermuda Gazette, 1823
Charleston City Gazette and Commercial Advertiser, 1816
Charleston Mercury, 1823–35
Chatham (Canada West) Provincial Freeman, 1854–57
Cincinnati Philanthropist, 1837–40
Concord (NH) Herald of Freedom, 1837
Hartford Christian Secretary, 1823–24
Hartford Connecticut Courant, 1832
Kingston Watchman and Jamaica Free Press, 1832
Lenox Massachusetts Eagle, 1834–35
Lynchburg Virginian, 1834–65
New Orleans Bee, 1833–35
New York Albion, 1823–32
New York Antislavery Standard, 1840–60
New York Christian Advocate and Journal and Zion's Herald, 1831–32
New York Christian Index, 1830–32
New York Colored American, 1837–41
New York Commercial Advertiser, 1816
New York Emancipator, 1834–39
New York Evening Post, 1816–23
New York Freedom's Journal, 1827–29
New York Herald, 1859–60
New York Morning Courier and Enquirer, 1834–35
New York Times, 1852–66
New York Tribune, 1842–53
New York Weekly Anglo-African, 1859

Newport Mercury, 1831–35
Philadelphia Pennsylvanian, 1834–35
Philadelphia Public Ledger, 1842
Providence Daily Journal, 1838
Raleigh North Carolina Standard, 1838
Raleigh Star and North Carolina Gazette, 1838
Richmond Constitutional Whig, 1831–35
Richmond Enquirer, 1816–35
Rochester Frederick Douglass Paper, 1853–55
Rochester North Star, 1848–49
Salem (OH) Anti-Slavery Bugle, 1849–50
Sandwich (Canada West) Voice of the Fugitive, 1851–52
Warren (RI) Northern Star and Constitutionalist, 1834–35
Washington (DC) Daily Madisonian, 1843
Washington (DC) Daily National Intelligencer, 1816–34
Washington (DC) National Era, 1849–57
Washington (DC) United States Telegraph, 1833–34
Wilmington (NC) Peoples' Press and Wilmington Advocate, 1835

Books and Articles

Abdy, Edward S. *Journal of a Residence in the United States of North America, from April, 1833 to October, 1834.* 3 vols. 1835. Reprint, New York: Negro Universities Press, 1969.

Address to the People of Beaufort and Colleton Districts, upon the Subject of Abolition, by Robert Barnwell Rhett, January 15, 1838. N.p, 1838.

Alexander, J. E. *Transatlantic Sketches, Comprising Visits to the Most Interesting Scenes in North and South America, and the West Indies. With Notes on Negro Slavery and Canadian Emigration.* London, 1833.

An Appeal to the Good Sense of a Great People. Charleston, 1835.

August, Eugene R., ed. *Thomas Carlyle, The Nigger Question; John Stuart Mill, The Negro Question.* New York: Appleton Century Crofts, 1971.

[Austin, James Trecothick]. *Remarks on Dr. Channing's Slavery, by a citizen of Massachusetts.* Boston, 1835.

[Barskett, James]. *History of the Island of St. Domingo, from its First Discovery by Columbus to the Present Period.* London, 1818.

Bassett, John Spencer, ed. *Correspondence of Andrew Jackson.* 6 vols. Washington, DC: Carnegie Institution, 1926–33.

Bell, Howard Holman, ed. *Minutes of the Proceedings of the National Negro Conventions, 1830–1864.* New York: Arno, 1969.

Bellinger, Edmund Jr. *A Speech on the Subject of Slavery; delivered 7th Sept'r, 1835. At* a Public Meeting of the Citizens of Barnwell District, South Carolina. Charleston, 1835.

Bigelow, John. 1851. Jamaica in 1850. Or, The Effects of Sixteen Years of Freedom on a Slave Colony. Reprint, New York: Negro Universities Press, 1970.

Birney, James. Letter on Colonization, addressed to the Rev. Thornton J. Mills, Corresponding Secretary of the Kentucky Colonization Society. New York, 1834.

Blassingame, John W., ed. Frederick Douglass Papers. Ser. 1. 3 vols. New Haven: Yale University Press, 1979–).

Bleby, Henry. Death Struggles of Slavery. London, 1853.

"British and American Slavery." Southern Quarterly Review 8 (October 1853): 369–41.

Bryan, Edward B. The Rightful Remedy. Addressed to Slaveholders of the South. Charleston, 1850.

Burke, Edmund. An Important Appeal to the People of the United States. Slavery and Abolitionism. Union and Disunion. N.p., [1856].

[Campbell, John Archibald]. "British West India Islands." Southern Quarterly Review 16 (January 1850): 342–77.

"Carlyle on West India Emancipation." Commercial Review, new series, 2 (June 1850): 527–38.

[Carlyle, Thomas]. "Occasional Discourse on the Negro Question." Fraser's Magazine 40 (December 1849): 670–79. Reprinted in Littell's Living Age 24 (February 9, 1850): 248–54.

"Case of the late Rev. John Smith, Missionary at Demerara." Religious Monitor and Evangelical Repository 1 (September 1824): 197–98.

A Catalogue of The Books Belonging to the Charleston Library Society, January, 1811. Charleston, 1811.

Celebration of West Indian Emancipation, by the Hingham and Weymouth Anti Slavery Societies. In Hingham, August 1, 1842. N.p, 1842.

Channing, William E. Slavery. Boston, 1835.

———. The Works of William Ellery Channing, D.D. Boston: American Unitarian Association, 1878.

Channing, William Henry, ed. Memoir of William Ellery Channing, with Extracts from his Correspondence and Manuscripts. 2 vols. Boston, 1848.

Child, David. Oration in Honor of Universal Emancipation in the British Empire, Delivered at South Reading, August First, 1834. Boston, 1834.

Child, Lydia Maria. 1833. An Appeal in Favor of that Class of Americans Called Africans. Facsimile of 1st ed., with introduction by Carolyn L. Karcher. Amherst: University of Massachusetts Press, 1996.

Clarkson, Thomas. Thoughts on the Necessity of Improving the Condition of the Slaves in the British Colonies, with a view to their Ultimate Emancipation; and on the Practicality, the Safety, and the Advantages of the Later Measure. London, 1823.

———. *The True State of the Case, Respecting the Insurrection at St. Domingo.* Ipswich [U.K.], 1792

Columbian. *A Series of Numbers Addressed to the Public, on the Subject of the Slaves and Free People of Color: First Published in the South Carolina State Gazette, in the Months of September and October, 1822.* Columbia, 1822.

Correspondence between the Hon. F. H. Elmore, One of the South Carolina Delegation in Congress and James G. Birney, One of the Secretaries of the American Anti-Slavery Society. New York, 1838.

Cropper, James. *Letters to the Liverpool Society for Promoting the Abolition of Slavery, on the injurious effects of high prices of produce, and the beneficial prospects of low prices on the condition of Slaves.* London, 1823.

De Lacroix, Pamphile. *Mémoir pour servir á l'histoire de la Révolucion de Saint-Domingue.* 1819. Reprint, Paris, 1995.

"Demerara." *Christian Advocate* 2 (May 1824): 237–38.

"Demerara." *Religious Intelligencer . . . Containing the Principal Transactions of the Various Bible and Missionary Societies, with Particular Accounts of Revivals of Religion* 8 (April 1824): 730.

Dew, Thomas R. 1832. "Abolition of Negro Slavery." Reprinted in Drew Gilpin Faust, ed., *The Ideology of Slavery: Proslavery Thought in the Antebellum South, 1830–1860.* Baton Rouge: Louisiana State University Press, 1981.

Drescher, Seymour, ed. and trans. *Tocqueville and Beamont on Social Reform.* New York: Harper and Row, 1968.

Dumond, Dwight L., ed. *Letters of James Gillespie Birney, 1835–1857.* 2 vols. New York: D. Appleton-Century Co., 1938.

East and West India Sugar. London, 1823.

"East India Cotton." *Southern Quarterly Review* 1 (1842): 446–93.

Edwards, Bryan. *Thoughts on the Late Proceedings of the Government respecting the Trade of the West India Islands and the United States of North America.* London, 1784.

———. *The History, Civil and Commercial, of the British Colonies in the West Indies.* 4 vols. Philadelphia, 1805.

Elliot, E. N., ed., *Cotton is King, and Pro-Slavery Arguments.* 1860. Reprint, New York: Negro Universities Press, 1969.

[Elliot, William]. *The Letters of Agricola. Published in the Southern Standard, June 1851.* Greenville, SC, 1852.

"Emancipation in the West Indies." *Quarterly Christian Spectator* 10 (August, 1838): 440–67.

"The Episcopal Plan of Christian Instruction for the Slaves in the West Indies." *Gospel Messenger and Southern Episcopal Register* 11 (June 1834): 175–81.

Everett, Alexander. "Present State of Cuba." *United States Magazine, and Democratic Review* 15 (November 1844): 475–83.

———. "The Texas Question." *United States Magazine, and Democratic Review* 15 (September 1844): 264–68.

Foner, Philip S., ed. *Frederick Douglass: Selected Speeches and Writings*. Chicago: Lawrence Hill Books, 1999.

Franklin, Benjamin. 1868. *The Autobiography of Benjamin Franklin*. Reprint, Mineola, NY: Dover, 1996.

Franklin, James. *The Present State of Hayti*. London, 1828.

"From the West Indies." *United Brethren's Missionary Intelligencer and Religious Miscellany* 4 (1832): 357–71.

Greenberg, Kenneth S., ed. *The Confessions of Nat Turner and Related Documents*. Boston: Bedford Books of St. Martin's Press, 1996.

Grimke, A[ngelina]. "Letter to Christian Women of the South." *Anti-Slavery Examiner* 1 (September 1836): 1–36.

Gurney, Joseph John. *Familiar Letters to Henry Clay of Kentucky, Describing a Winter in the West Indies*. New York, 1840.

[Hammond, James Henry]. *Remarks of Mr. Hammond of South Carolina on the Question of Receiving Petitions for the Abolition of Slavery in the District of Columbia*. Washington [DC], 1836.

Harvey, W. W. *Sketches of Hayti: From the Expulsion of the French to the Death of Christophe*. London: L. B. Seeley and Son, 1827.

Heyrick, Elizabeth. *Immediate, not Gradual Abolition; or, An Inquiry into the Shortest and Most Effective Means of Getting Rid of West Indian Slavery*. London, 1824.

Hicks, Granville. "Dr. Channing and the Creole Case." *American Historical Review* 37 (April 1932): 516–25.

Hinks, Peter P., ed., *David Walker's Appeal to the Coloured Citizens of the World*. University Park: Pennsylvania State University Press, 2000.

Hinton, John Howard. *Memoir of William Knibb, Missionary in Jamaica*. London, 1847.

Holzer, Harold, ed. *The Lincoln-Douglas Debates*. New York: Harper Collins, 1993.

Hopkins, James F., and Mary W. M. Hargreaves, eds. *The Papers of Henry Clay*. 11 vols. Lexington: University of Kentucky Press, 1959–92.

"Jamaica." *United States Magazine and Democratic Review* 27 (December 1850): 481–96.

Jay, William. 1853. *Miscellaneous Writings on Slavery*. Reprint, New York: Negro Universities Press, 1968.

Julian, George. *Political Recollections, 1840 to 1872*. 1884. Reprint, New York: Negro Universities Press, 1970.

Killens, John Oliver, ed. *The Trial Record of Denmark Vesey*. Boston: Beacon Press, 1970.

The Late Insurrection in Demerara, and Riot in Barbadoes. N.p., 1824.

Le Breton, Anna Letitia., ed. *Correspondence of William Ellery Channing, D.D. and Lucy Aikin, from 1826 to 1842.* Boston, 1874.

Letters to Wilberforce, recommending the Encouragement of the Cultivation of Sugar in our Dominions in the East Indies, as the natural and certain means of effecting the general and total abolition of the Slave Trade. London, 1822.

Lewis, Mathew Gregory. 1834. *Journal of a West Indian Proprietor, Kept during a Residence in the Island of Jamaica.* Facsimile of 1st edition, with an introduction by Judith Terry. New York: Oxford University Press, 1999.

Liele, George, et al. "Letters Showing the Rise and Progress of the Early Negro Churches of Georgia and the West Indies." *Journal of Negro History* 1 (January 1916): 69–92.

Llaverias y Martinez, Joaquin, ed., *Centon Epistolario de Domingo Del Monte.* 7 vols. Havana: Academia de la Historia Cuba, 1923–57.

Macqueen, James. "Africa-Slave Trade-Tropical Colonies." *Blackwood's Edinburgh Magazine* 55 (June 1844): 731–48.

Malenfant, [Colonel]. *Des Colonies, Particuliérement de celle de Saint-Domingue; Mémoire Historique et Politique.* Paris, 1814.

Malloy, Daniel, ed. *The Life and Speeches of Henry Clay.* 2 vols. New York: Robert P. Bixby and Co., 1843.

Manning, William R., ed. *Diplomatic Correspondence of the United States: Inter-American Affairs, 1831–1860.* 12 vols. Washington, DC: Carnegie Endowment for International Peace, 1936–39.

May, Samuel J. *Emancipation in the British W. Indies, August 1, 1834. An Address, delivered in the First Presbyterian Church in Syracuse on the First of August, 1845.* Syracuse, 1845.

———. *Recollections of the Antislavery Conflict.* Boston: Fields, Osgood and Co., 1869.

Memminger, C. G. *Lecture delivered before the Young Men's Library Association, of Augusta, April 10th, 1851. Showing African Slavery to be Consistent with the Moral and Physical Progress of a Nation.* Augusta, GA, 1851.

Meriwether, Robert L., W. Edwin Hemphill, and Clyde N. Wilson, eds. *The Papers of John C. Calhoun.* 20 vols. Columbia: University of South Carolina Press, 1959–2001.

Merrill, Walter M., ed. *The Letters of William Lloyd Garrison, 1822–1835.* 6 vols. Cambridge, MA: Harvard University Press, 1971.

Mill, John Stuart. "The Negro Question." *Fraser's Magazine* 41 (January 1850): 25–31. Reprinted in *Littell's Living Age* 24 (March 9, 1850): 465–69.

Murat, Achille. *The United States of North America.* London, 1833.

Nevins, Allan, and Milton Halsey Thomas, eds. *The Diary of George Templeton Strong: Young Man in New York, 1835–1875.* 4 vols. 1952. Reprint, New York: Octagon Books, 1974.

"New Plan for Suppressing the Slave Trade and Obtaining Laborers for the British West India Colonies." *African Repository and Colonial Journal* 18 (May 15, 1841): 145–50.

A Particular Account of the Commencement and Progress of the Insurrection of the Negroes in St. Domingo, which began in August, 1791: Being a Translation of the Speech made to the National Assembly, the 3d of November, 1791 by the Deputies from the General Assembly of the French Part of St. Domingo. 2d ed. London, 1792.

Phillippo, James M. *Jamaica: Its Past and Present State.* London, 1843.

Phipps, John. *Treatise on the principal Products of Bengal,–Indigo, Sugar, Cotton, Hemp, Silk and Opium.* Calcutta, 1832.

Pickens, Francis. *Speech of Mr. Pickens, of South Carolina, in the House of Representatives, January 21, 1836, on the Abolition Question.* Washington [DC], 1836.

[Pinckney, Thomas]. *Reflections, Occasioned by the late Disturbances in Charleston. By Achates.* Charleston, 1822.

Pitkin, Timothy. *A Statistical View of the Commerce of the United States of America.* New Haven, 1835.

[Polk, James]. "Slaves and Slavery." *United States Magazine and Democratic Review* 19 (October 1846): 243–54.

Pratt, Minot. *A Friend of the South in Answer to Remarks on Dr. Channing's Slavery.* Boston, 1836.

Proceedings of the Citizens of Charleston on the Incendiary Machinations, Now in Progress Against the Peace and Welfare of the Southern States. Charleston, 1835.

Rainsford, Marcus. *An Historical Account of the Black Empire of Hayti: Comprehending a View of the Principal Transactions in the Revolution in Saint Domingo with its Antient and Modern State.* London, 1805.

"Religious Instruction of Slaves in Jamaica." *Gospel Messenger and Southern Episcopal Register* 10 (June 1833): 188. *Reply to the Reviewer of the Remarks on Dr. Channing's Slavery.* Boston, 1836.

"Rev. John Smith—Missionary to Demerara." *Religious Intelligencer* 8 (May 1824): 775–77.

Riot in Barbadoes, and Destruction of the Wesleyan Chapel and Mission House. N.p., [1823].

Ripley, C. Peter, ed. *The Black Abolitionist Papers.* 5 vols. Chapel Hill: University of North Carolina Press, 1985–92.

Rutland, Robert A., et al., eds. *The Papers of James Madison.* 17 vols. Chicago: University of Chicago Press; Charlottesville: University Press of Virginia, 1962–91.

Schade, Louis. *A Book for the "Impending Crisis!"... "Helperism" Annihilated! The "Irrepressible Conflict" and its Consequences!* Washington [DC], 1860.

Sewell, William Grant. *The Ordeal of Free Labor in the British West Indies.* New York: Harper and Brothers, 1861.

[Shannon, James]. *An Address Delivered Before the Pro-Slavery Convention of the State of Missouri, Held in Lexington, July 13, 1855, on Domestic Slavery, as Examined in the Light of Scripture, of Natural Rights, of Civil Government, and the Constitutional Power of Congress.* St. Louis, 1855.

Simmons, George Frederick. *Review of the Remarks on Dr. Channing's Slavery, by a Citizen of Massachusetts.* Boston, 1836.

A Slaveholder [pseud.]. *Remarks upon Slavery and the Slave-Trade, Addressed to the Hon. Henry Clay.* N.p., 1839.

"South America.—Demerara." *Christian Herald and Seaman's Magazine* 11 (February 1824): 113–16.

"Speculations Upon the Consequences of a War with Great Britain." *Southern Literary Messenger* 8 (July 1842): 444–47.

Speech of Thomas Marshall (of Fauquier) in the House of Delegates of Virginia, on the Policy of the State in Relation to Her Coloured Population. Richmond, 1832.

State Papers on Nullification. Boston, 1834.

Stuckey, Sterling, ed. *The Ideological Origins of Black Nationalism.* Boston: Beacon Press, 1972.

Sullivan, T[homas] R. *Letters against the Immediate Abolition of Slavery; Addressed to the Free Blacks of the Non-Slaveholding States. Comprising a Legal Opinion on the power of legislatures in Non-Slaveholding States to prevent measures tending to immediate and general emancipation.* Boston, 1835.

Sumner, Charles. *Charles Sumner, His Complete Works.* 20 vols. Boston: Lee and Shepard, 1874.

Thomas, Isaiah. *The History of Printing in America, with a Biography of Printers, and an Account of Newspapers.* 2 vols. 1810. Reprint, Albany, 1874.

Thome, James A., and J. Horace Kimball. *Emancipation in the West Indies. A Six Months' Tour in Antigua, Barbadoes, and Jamaica, in the Year 1837.* New York, 1838.

de Toqueville, Alexander. *Democracy in America.* 2 vols. 1840. Reprint, New York, 1990.

Turnbull, David. *Travels in the West: Cuba with Notices of Porto Rico and the Slave Trade.* London, 1841.

[Turnbull, Robert J.]. *The Crisis: Or, Essays on the Usurpations of the Federal Government. By Brutus.* Charleston: A. E. Miller, 1827.

[Turnbull, Robert J., and Isaac Edward Holmes]. *Caroliniensis.* Charleston, [1824].

[Evrie, John Van]. *Free Negroism: Or, Results of Emancipation in the North and West India Islands, with Statistics of the Decay of Commerce, Idleness of the Negro, His Return to Savageism, and the Effect of Emancipation upon the Farming, Mechanical, and Laboring Classes.* New York: Van Evrie, Horton and Co., 1862.

Wallbridge, Edwin Angel. *The Demerara Martyr: Memoirs of the Reverend John Smith, Missionary to Demerara.* London, 1848.

Wheaton, Henry. "Our Relations with England." *Southern Literary Messenger* 8 (June 1842): 390–96.

SECONDARY SOURCES

Books

Anderson, Benedict. *Imagined Communities: Reflections on the Origins and Spread of Nationalism.* London: Verso, 1983.

Armitage, David, and Michael J. Braddick, eds. *The British Atlantic World, 1500–1800.* Hampshire, UK: Palgrave Macmillan, 2002.

Ayers, Edward L. *What Caused the Civil War? Reflections on the South and Southern History.* New York: W. W. Norton, 2005.

Bailyn, Bernard. *The New England Merchants in the Seventeenth Century.* Cambridge, MA: Harvard University Press, 1955.

Barnes, Gilbert Hobbs. *The Anti-Slavery Impulse, 1830–1844.* 1933. Reprint, New York: Harcourt, Brace and World, 1964.

Beckles, Hilary M. *Natural Rebels: A Social History of Enslaved Black Women in Barbados.* New Brunswick, NJ: Rutgers University Press, 1989.

Bemis, Samuel Flagg. *John Quincy Adams and the Foundations of American Foreign Policy.* New York: Alfred A. Knopf, 1949.

——. *John Quincy Adams and the Union.* New York: Alfred A. Knopf, 1956.

Bender, Thomas. *A Nation Among Nations: America's Place in World History.* New York: Hill and Wang, 2006.

Benns, F. Lee. *The American Struggle for the British West India Carrying Trade, 1815–1830.* 1923. Reprint, Clifton, NJ: Augustus M. Kelley Publishers, 1972.

Blackburn, Robin. *The Overthrow of Colonial Slavery.* London: Verso, 1988.

Blackett, Richard. *Beating Against the Barriers: The Lives of Six Nineteenth Century Afro-Americans.* Ithaca: Cornell University Press, 1986.

——. *Building an Antislavery Wall: Black Americans in the Atlantic Abolitionist Movement, 1830–1860.* Ithaca: Cornell University Press, 1983.

——. *Divided Hearts: Britain and the American Civil War.* Baton Rouge: Louisiana State University Press, 2001.

Blue, Frederick J. *No Taint of Compromise: Crusaders in Antislavery Politics.* Baton Rouge: Louisiana State University Press, 2005.

Bolster, Jeffrey. *Black Jacks: African American Seamen in the Age of Sail.* Cambridge, MA: Harvard University Press, 1997.

Brathwaite, Edward K. *The Development of Creole Society in Jamaica, 1770–1820.* Oxford: Clarendon, 1971.

Breen, T. H. *The Marketplace of Revolution: How Consumer Politics Shaped American Independence.* New York: Oxford University Press, 2004.

Brown, Arthur W. *Always Young for Liberty: A Biography of William Ellery Channing.* Syracuse: Syracuse University Press, 1956.

Brown, Christopher L. *Moral Capital: Foundations of British Abolitionism.* Chapel Hill: University of North Carolina, 2006.

Brown, Richard D. *Knowledge is Power: The Diffusion of Information in Early America, 1700–1865.* New York: Oxford University Press, 1989.

———. *The Strength of a People: The Idea of an Informed Citizenry in America, 1650–1870.* Chapel Hill: University of North Carolina Press, 1996.

Burrows, Edwin G., and Mike Wallace. *Gotham: A History of New York City to 1898.* New York: Oxford University Press, 1999.

Butler, Kathleen Mary. *The Economics of Emancipation: Jamaica and Barbados, 1823–1843.* Chapel Hill: University of North Carolina Press, 1995.

Carey, James W. *Communication as Culture: Essays in Media and Society.* New York: Routledge, 1992.

Clarke, Erskine. *Dwelling Place: A Plantation Epic.* New Haven: Yale University Press, 2005.

Colley, Linda. *Britons: Forging the Nation, 1707–1837.* New Haven: Yale University Press, 1992.

Cooper, William J. Jr. *The South and the Politics of Slavery, 1828–1856.* Baton Rouge: Louisiana State University Press, 1978.

da Costa, Emilia Viotti. *Crowns of Glory, Tears of Blood: The Demerara Slave Rebellion of 1823.* New York: Oxford University Press, 1994.

Craton, Michael. *Testing the Chains: Resistance to Slavery in the British West Indies.* Ithaca: Cornell University Press, 1982.

Davis, David Brion. *Challenging the Boundaries of Slavery.* Cambridge, MA: Harvard University Press, 2002.

———. *From Homicide to Slavery.* New York: Oxford University Press, 1986.

———. *Inhuman Bondage: The Rise and Fall of Slavery in the New World.* New York: Oxford University Press, 2006.

———. *Slavery and Human Progress.* New York: Oxford University Press, 1984.

———. *The Problem of Slavery in the Age of Revolution, 1770–1823.* Ithaca: Cornell University Press, 1975. Reprint, New York: Oxford University Press, 1999.

———. *The Problem of Slavery in Western Culture.* Ithaca: Cornell University Press, 1966. Reprint, New York: Oxford University Press, 1988.

Davis, Elmer. *History of the New York Times, 1851–1921.* New York: New York Times, 1921.

Delbanco, Andrew. *William Ellery Channing: An Essay on the Liberal Spirit in America.* Cambridge, MA: Harvard University Press, 1981.

Dew, Charles B. *Apostles of Disunion: Southern Secession Commissioners and the Causes of the Civil War.* Charlottesville: University of Virginia Press, 2001.

Donald, David Herbert. *Charles Sumner and the Coming of the Civil War.* Chicago: University of Chicago Press, 1960.

———. *Charles Sumner and the Rights of Man.* New York: Alfred A. Knopf, 1970.

Dorchester, Daniel. *Christianity in the United States from the First Settlement down to the Present Time.* New York: Hunt and Eaton, 1890.

Drescher, Seymour. *Capitalism and Antislavery: British Mobilization in Comparative Perspective.* New York: Oxford University Press, 1987.

———. *Econocide: British Slavery in the Era of Abolition.* Pittsburgh: University of Pittsburgh Press, 1977.

———. *The Mighty Experiment: Free Labor Versus Slavery in British Emancipation.* Oxford: Oxford University Press, 2002.

———. *From Slavery to Freedom: Comparative Studies in the Rise and Fall of Atlantic Slavery.* New York: New York University Press, 1990.

Dubois, Laurent. *Avengers of the New World: The Story of the Haitian Revolution.* Cambridge: Harvard University Press, 2004.

———. *A Colony of Citizens: Revolution and Slave Emancipation in the French Caribbean, 1787–1804.* Chapel Hill: University of North Carolina Press, 2004.

Duckett, Alvin Laroy. *John Forsyth: Political Tactician.* Athens: University of Georgia Press, 1962.

Dunn, Richard S. *Sugar and Slaves: The Rise of the Planter Class in the English West Indies, 1624–1713.* Chapel Hill: University of North Carolina Press, 1972.

Earle, Jonathan. *Jacksonian Antislavery and the Politics of Free Soil, 1824–1854.* Chapel Hill: University of North Carolina Press, 2004.

Eaton, Clement. *The Freedom of Thought Struggle in the Old South.* Revised. 1940. Reprint, New York: Harper Torchbooks, 1964.

Egerton, Douglas R. *He Shall Go Out Free: The Lives of Denmark Vesey.* Madison: Madison House, 1999.

Elkins, Stanley, and Eric McKitrick. *The Age of Federalism.* New York: Oxford University Press, 1993.

Eltis, David. *Economic Growth and the Ending of the Transatlantic Slave Trade.* New York: Oxford University Press, 1987.

———. *The Rise of African Slavery in the Americas.* Cambridge: Cambridge University Press, 2000.

Eudell, Demetrius. *The Political Languages of Emancipation in the British Caribbean and the U.S. South.* Chapel Hill: University of North Carolina Press, 2002.

Fehrenbacher, Don E. *The Slaveholding Republic: An Account of the United States Government's Relations to Slavery.* New York: Oxford University Press, 2001.

Filler, Louis. *Crusade Against Slavery: Friends, Foes, and Reforms, 1820–1860.* Algonac, MI: Reference Publications, 1986.

Finkleman, Paul. *Slavery and the Founders: Race and Liberty in the Age of Jefferson.* Armonk, NY: M. E. Sharpe, 1996

Fladeland, Betty. *Men and Brothers: Anglo-American Antislavery Cooperation.* Urbana: University of Illinois Press, 1972.

Fogel, Robert. *Without Consent or Contract: The Rise and Fall of American Slavery.* New York: W. W. Norton, 1989.

Foner, Eric. *Free Soil, Free Labor, Free Men: The Ideology of the Republican Party Before the Civil War.* 1970. Reprint, New York: Oxford University Press, 1995.

———. *Nothing But Freedom.* Baton Rouge: Louisiana State University Press, 1983.

Ford, Lacy. *Origins of Southern Radicalism: The South Carolina Upcountry, 1800–1860.* New York: Oxford University Press, 1988.

Fredrickson, George M. *The Black Image in the White Mind: The Debate on Afro-American Character and Destiny, 1817–1914.* Hanover, NH: Wesleyan University Press, 1971.

Freehling, Alison. *Drift Toward Dissolution: The Virginia Slavery Debate of 1831–1832.* Baton Rouge: Louisiana State University Press, 1982.

Freehling, William F. *Prelude to Civil War: The Nullification Controversy in South Carolina, 1816–1836.* New York: Harper and Row, 1965.

———. *The Reintegration of American History: Slavery and the Civil War.* New York: Oxford University Press, 1994.

———. *The Road to Disunion.* Vol. 1, *Secessionists at Bay, 1776–1854.* New York: Oxford University Press, 1990.

———. *The Road to Disunion.* Vol. 2, *Secessionists Triumphant, 1854–1861.* New York: Oxford University Press, 2007.

Frey, Sylvia R., and Betty Wood. *Come Shouting to Zion: African American Protestantism in the American South and the British Caribbean to 1830.* Chapel Hill: University of North Carolina Press, 1998.

Geggus, David. *Slavery, War, and Revolution: The British Occupation of Saint Domingue, 1793–1798.* New York: Oxford University Press, 1982.

Genovese, Eugene. *From Rebellion to Revolution: Afro-American Slave Revolts in the Making of the Modern World.* Baton Rouge: Louisiana State University Press, 1979.

———. *Roll Jordan Roll: The World the Slaves Made.* New York: Vintage, 1976.

Goodman, Paul. *Of One Blood: Abolitionism and the Origins of Racial Equality.* Berkeley and Los Angeles: University of California Press, 1998.

Goudie, Sean X. *Creole America: The West Indies and the Formation of Literature and Culture in the New Republic.* Philadelphia: University of Pennsylvania Press, 2006.

Goveia, Elsa. *Slave Society in the British Leeward Islands at the End of the Eighteenth Century.* New Haven: Yale University Press, 1965.

Gray, Lewis Cecil. *History of Agriculture in the Southern United States to 1860.* 2 vols. 1932. Reprint, Gloucester, MA: Peter Smith, 1958.

Green, William. *British West Indian Slave Emancipation: The Sugar Colonies and the Great Experiment, 1830–1865.* Oxford: Oxford University Press, 1976.

Greenberg, Kenneth S. *Masters and Statesmen: The Political Culture of American Slavery.* Baltimore: Johns Hopkins University Press, 1985.

Greene, Jack. *Pursuits of Happiness: The Social Development of Early Modern British Colonies and the Formation of American Culture.* Chapel Hill: University of North Carolina Press, 1988.

Hall, Claude H. *Abel Upshur: Conservative Virginian, 1790–1844.* Madison: State Historical Society of Wisconsin, 1964.

Hall, Neville A. T. *Slave Society in the Danish West Indies, St. Thomas, St. John, and St. Croix.* Baltimore: Johns Hopkins University Press, 1992.

Heuman, Gad. *Between Black and White: Race, Politics, and the Free Coloreds in Jamaica, 1792–1865.* Westport, CT: Greenwood, 1981.

———. *"The Killing Time": The Morant Bay Rebellion in Jamaica.* London: Macmillan, 1994.

Hietala, Thomas. *Manifest Design: Anxious Aggrandizement in Late Jacksonian America.* Ithaca: Cornell University Press, 1985.

Hinks, Peter P. *To Awaken My Afflicted Brethren: David Walker and the Problem of Antebellum Slave Resistance.* University Park: Pennsylvania State University Press, 1997.

Hofstadter, Richard. *The Paranoid Style in American Politics and Other Essays.* New York: Alfred A. Knopf, 1965.

Holt, Michael. *The Political Crises of the 1850s.* New York: John Wiley and Sons, 1978.

Holt, Thomas C. *The Problem of Freedom: Race, Labor, and Politics in Jamaica and Britain, 1832–1938.* Baltimore: Johns Hopkins University Press, 1992.

Hornsby, Stephen J. *British Atlantic, American Frontier: Spaces of Power in Early Modern British America.* Hanover: University Press of New England, 2005.

Horton, James Oliver, and Lois E. Horton. *In Hope of Liberty: Culture, Community and Protest Among Northern Free Blacks, 1700–1860.* New York: Oxford University Press, 1997.

Hunt, Alfred. *Haiti's Influence on Antebellum America: Slumbering Volcano in the Caribbean.* Baton Rouge: Louisiana State University Press, 1988.

Isaac, Rhys. *The Transformation of Virginia, 1740–1790.* Chapel Hill: University of North Carolina Press, 1982.

James, C. L. R. *The Black Jacobins: Touissaint L'Ouverture and the San Domingo Revolution.* 1938. Reprint, New York: Vintage, 1989.

Jennings, Lawrence C. *French Reaction to British Slave Emancipation.* Baton Rouge: Louisiana State University Press, 1988.

John, Richard. *Spreading the News: The American Postal System from Franklin to Morse.* Cambridge, MA: Harvard University Press, 1995.

Jones, Howard. *To the Webster-Ashburton Treaty: A Study in Anglo-American Relations, 1783–1843.* Chapel Hill: University of North Carolina Press, 1977.

Jones, Howard, and Donald A. Rakestraw. *Prologue to Manifest Destiny: Anglo-American Relations in the 1840s.* Wilmington, DE: Scholarly Resources, Inc, 1997.

Jordan, Winthrop. *Tumult and Silence at Second Creek: An Inquiry into a Civil War Slave Conspiracy.* Baton Rouge: Louisiana State University Press, 1993.

Kachun, Mitch. *Festivals of Freedom: Memory and Meaning in African American Emancipation Celebrations, 1808–1915.* Amherst: University of Massachusetts Press, 2003.

Karcher, Carolyn L. *The First Woman in the Republic: A Cultural Biography of Lydia Maria Child.* Durham: Duke University Press, 1994.

Kerr-Ritchie, J. R. *Rites of First of August: Emancipation Day in the Black Atlantic World.* Baton Rouge: Louisiana State University Press, 2007.

Lemire, Beverly. *Fashion's Favorite: The Cotton Trade and the Consumer in Britain, 1660–1800.* Oxford: Oxford University Press, 1991.

Littlefield, Daniel C. *Rice and Slaves: Ethnicity and the Slave Trade in Colonial South Carolina.* Baton Rouge: Louisiana State University Press, 1981.

Litwack, Leon. *North of Slavery: The Negro in the Free States, 1790–1860.* Chicago: University of Chicago Press, 1961.

Logan, Rayford W. *The Diplomatic Relations of the United States with Haiti, 1776–1891.* Chapel Hill: University of North Carolina Press, 1941.

Luxon, Noval N. *Niles' Weekly Register: News Magazine of the Nineteenth Century.* Baton Rouge: Louisiana State University Press, 1947.

Lyerly, Cynthia Lynn. *Methodism and the Southern Mind, 1770–1810.* Oxford: Oxford University Press, 1998.

Martin, Waldo E. *The Mind of Frederick Douglass.* Chapel Hill: University of North Carolina Press, 1984.

Masur, Louis P. *Rites of Execution: Capital Punishment and the Transformation of American Culture, 1776–1865.* New York: Oxford University Press, 1989.

Mayer, Henry. *All on Fire: William Lloyd Garrison and the Abolition of Slavery.* New York: St. Martin's Griffin, 1998.

McColley, Robert. *Slavery and Jeffersonian Virginia.* 2d ed. Chicago: University of Illinois Press, 1973.

McFeeley, William. *Frederick Douglass.* New York: W. W. Norton, 1991.

Mendolsohn, Jack. *Channing: The Reluctant Radical.* Westport, CT: Greenwood, 1971.

Merk, Frederick. *Fruits of Propaganda in the Tyler Administration.* Cambridge, MA: Harvard University Press, 1971.

———. *Slavery and the Annexation of Texas.* New York: Alfred A. Knopf, 1972.

Maier, Pauline. *American Scripture: Making the Declaration of Independence.* New York: Alfred A. Knopf, 1997.

Mathieson, William Law. *British Slavery and Its Abolition, 1823–1838.* London: Longmans, Green and Co., 1926.

Matthews, Gelien. *Caribbean Slave Revolts and the British Abolitionist Movement.* Baton Rouge: Louisiana State University Press, 2006.

Matthewson, Tim. *A Proslavery Foreign Policy: Haitian American Relations During the Early Republic.* Westport, CT: Praeger, 2003.

McCusker, John J., and Russell R. Menard. *The Economy of British America, 1607–1789.* Chapel Hill: University of North Carolina Press, 1985.

McKivigan, John. *The War Against Proslavery Religion: Abolitionism and the Northern Churches, 1830–1865.* Ithaca: Cornell University Press, 1984.

McPherson, James. *Battle Cry of Freedom: The Civil War Era.* New York: Oxford University Press, 1988.

Meinig, D. W. *Atlantic America, 1492–1800.* New Haven: Yale University Press, 1986.

Miller, William Lee. *Arguing About Slavery: The Great Battle in the United States Congress.* New York: Alfred A. Knopf, 1996.

Morgan, Donald G. *Justice William Johnson the First Dissenter: The Career and Constitutional Philosophy of a Jeffersonian Judge.* Columbia: University of South Carolina Press, 1954.

Murry, David R. *Odious Commerce: Britain, Spain and the Abolition of the Cuban Slave Trade.* Cambridge: Cambridge University Press, 1980.

Nash, Gary B. *Forging Freedom: The Formation of Philadelphia's Black Community, 1720–1840.* Cambridge, MA: Harvard University Press, 1988.

Newman, Richard S. *The Transformation of American Abolitionism: Fighting Slavery in the Early Republic.* Chapel Hill: University of North Carolina Press, 2002.

Niven, John. *John C. Calhoun and the Price of Union.* Baton Rouge: Louisiana State University Press, 1988.

North, Simon Dexter. *History and Present Condition of the Newspaper and Periodical Press of the United States.* Washington: Government Printing Office, 1884.

Northrup, David. *Indentured Labor in the Age of Imperialism, 1834–1922.* Cambridge: Cambridge University Press, 1995.

Oakes, James. *The Radical and the Republican: Frederick Douglass, Abraham Lincoln, and the Triumph of Antislavery Politics.* New York: W. W. Norton, 2007.

Oates, Stephen B. *To Purge This Land With Blood: A Biography of John Brown.* Amherst: University of Massachusetts Press, 1970.

O'Brien, Michael. *Conjectures of Order: Intellectual Life and the American South, 1810–1860.* 2 vols. Chapel Hill: Univ. of North Carolina Press, 2004.

O'Shaughnessy, Andrew Jackson. *An Empire Divided: The American Revolution and the British Caribbean.* Philadelphia: University of Pennsylvania Press, 2000.

Palmer, R. R. *The Age of Democratic Revolution.* 2 vols. Princeton: Princeton University Press, 1959–64.

Pares, Richard. *Yankees and Creoles: The Trade Between North America and the West Indies before the American Revolution.* Cambridge: Harvard University Press, 1956.

Pasley, Jeffrey L. *"The Tyranny of Printers": Newspaper Politics in the Early Republic.* Charlottesville: University Press of Virginia, 2001.

Pasternak, Martin B. *Rise Now and Fly to Arms: The Life of Henry Highland Garnet.* New York: Garland, 1995.

Peterson, Merrill D. *The Great Triumvirate: Webster, Clay, and Calhoun.* New York: Oxford University Press, 1987.

Peterson, Norma Lois. *The Presidencies of William Henry Harrison and John Tyler.* Lawrence: University Press of Kansas, 1989.

Phillips, Derrick. *"Past Historic, Graphic Present and Future Present," or, "All Roads Lead to Bombay"—The Story of My Ancestors, Family, Relatives and Descendants, and My In-Laws.* Unpublished manuscript.

Pletcher, David. *The Diplomacy of Annexation: Texas, Oregon, and the Mexican War.* Columbia: University of Missouri Press, 1973.

Potter, David. *The Impending Crisis, 1848–1861.* New York: Harper and Row, 1976.

Quarles, Benjamin. *Black Abolitionists.* Oxford: Oxford University Press, 1969.

———. *Frederick Douglass.* 1948. Reprint, New York: Athenaeum, 1968.

———. *The Negro in the American Revolution.* 1961. Reprint, New York: W. W. Norton, 1973.

Raboteau, Albert J. *Slave Religion: The "Invisible Institution" in the American South.* New York: Oxford University Press, 1978.

Rael, Patrick. *Black Identity and Black Protest in the Antebellum North.* Chapel Hill: University of North Carolina Press, 2002.

Ragatz, Lowell B. *The Fall of the Planter Class in the British Caribbean, 1763–1833: A Study in Social and Economic History.* 1928. Reprint, New York: Octagon, 1971.

Remini, Robert V. *The Election of Andrew Jackson.* Westport, CT: Greenwood, 1963.

Richards, Leonard L. *"Gentlemen of Property and Standing": Anti-Abolition Mobs in Jacksonian America.* New York: Oxford University Press, 1970.

———. *The Slave Power: The Free North and Southern Domination, 1780–1860.* Baton Rouge: Louisiana State University Press, 2000.

Rodgers, Daniel T. *Atlantic Crossings: Social Politics in a Progressive Age.* Cambridge, MA: Harvard University Press, 1998.

Rorabaugh, W. J. *The Alcoholic Republic: An American Tradition.* New York: Oxford University Press, 1979.

Ryan, Mary. *Civic Wars: Democracy and Public Life in the American City during the Nineteenth Century.* Berkeley and Los Angeles: University of California Press, 1997.

Schlesinger, Arthur M. *Prelude to Independence: The Newspaper War on Britain, 1764–1776.* New York: Alfred A. Knopf, 1958.

Schor, Joel. *Henry Highland Garnet: A Voice of Black Radicalism in the Nineteenth Century.* Westport, CT: Greenwood, 1977.

Schudson, Michael. *Discovering the News: A Social History of American Newspapers.* New York: Basic Books, 1978.

Sellers, Charles. *The Market Revolution: Jacksonian America, 1815–1846.* New York: Oxford University Press, 1991.

Sensbach, Jon J. *A Separate Canaan: The Making of an Afro-Moravian World in North Carolina, 1763–1840.* Chapel Hill: University of North Carolina Press, 1998.

Shenton, James P. *Robert John Walker: A Politician from Jackson to Lincoln.* New York: Columbia University Press, 1961.

Sidbury, James. *Ploughshares into Swords: Race, Rebellion, and Identity in Gabriel's Virginia.* Cambridge: Cambridge University Press, 1997.

Sinha, Manisha. *The Counterrevolution of Slavery: Politics and Ideology in Antebellum South Carolina.* Chapel Hill: University of North Carolina Press, 2000.

Siskind, Janet. *Rum and Axes: The Rise of a Connecticut Merchant Family, 1795–1850.* Ithaca: Cornell University Press, 2002.

Snay, Mitchell. *Gospel of Disunion: Religion and Separatism in the Antebellum South.* Chapel Hill: University of North Carolina Press, 1997.

Staudenraus, P. J. *The African Colonization Movement, 1816–1865.* New York: Columbia University Press, 1961.

Stauffer, John. *The Black Hearts of Men: Radical Abolitionism and the Transformation of Race.* Cambridge: Harvard University Press, 2002.

Stewart, James Brewer. *Joshua R. Giddings and the Tactics of Radical Politics.* Cleveland: Press of Case Western Reserve University, 1970.

———. *Holy Warriors: The Abolitionists and American Slavery.* Rev. ed. New York: Hill and Wang, 1996.

———. *Wendell Phillips: Liberty's Hero.* Baton Rouge: Louisiana State University Press, 1986.

———. *William Lloyd Garrison and the Challenge of Emancipation.* Arlington Heights, IL: Harland Davidson, 1992.

Stout, Harry S. *The Divine Dramatist: George Whitefield and the Rise of Modern Evangelicalism.* Grand Rapids, MI: William B. Eerdmans, 1991.

Tadman, Michael. *Speculators and Slaves: Masters, Traders, and Slaves in the Old South.* Madison: University of Wisconsin Press, 1989.

Tannenbaum, Frank. *Slave and Citizen: The Negro in the Americas.* New York: Vintage, 1946.

Taylor, Frank. *To Hell with Paradise: A History of the Jamaican Tourist Industry.* Pittsburgh: University of Pittsburgh Press, 1993.

Temperley, Howard. *British Antislavery, 1833–1870.* London: Longman, 1972.

Thistlethwaite, Frank. *The Anglo-American Connection in the Early Nineteenth Century.* Philadelphia: University of Pennsylvania Press, 1959.

Thomas, John L. *The Liberator: William Lloyd Garrison: A Biography.* Boston: Little, Brown and Co., 1963.

Thornton, John. *Africa and Africans in the Making of the Atlantic World.* 2d ed. Cambridge: Cambridge University Press, 1998.

Travers, Len. *Celebrating the Fourth: Independence Day and the Rites of Nationalism in the Early Republic.* Amherst: University of Massachusetts Press, 1997.

Trouillot, Michel-Rolph. *Silencing the Past: Power and Production of History.* Boston: Beacon Press, 1995.

Turner, Mary. *Slaves and Missionaries: The Disintegration of Jamaican Slave Society, 1787–1834.* Urbana: University of Illinois Press, 1982.

Von Frank, Albert J. *The Trials of Anthony Burns: Freedom and Slavery in Emerson's Boston.* Cambridge: Harvard University Press, 1998.

Waldstreicher, David. *In the Midst of Perpetual Fetes: The Making of American Nationalism, 1776–1820.* Chapel Hill: University of North Carolina Press, 1997.

Walvin, James. *England, Slaves and Freedom, 1776–1838.* Jackson: University Press of Mississippi, 1986.

Ward, J. R. *British West Indian Slavery: The Process of Amelioration, 1750–1834.* Oxford: Clarendon Press, 1988.

Watts, David. *The West Indies: Patterns of Development, Culture and Environmental Change since 1492.* Cambridge: Cambridge University Press, 1987.

Wigger, John H. *Taking Heaven by Storm: Methodism and the Rise of Popular Christianity in America.* New York: Oxford University Press, 1998.

Wilentz, Sean. *Chants Democratic: New York City and the Rise of the American Working Class, 1788–1850.* New York: Oxford University Press, 1984.

———. *The Rise of American Democracy: Jefferson to Lincoln.* New York: W. W. Norton, 2005.

Williams, Eric. *Capitalism and Slavery.* 1944. Reprint, Chapel Hill: University of North Carolina Press, 1994.

Wiltse, Charles M. *John C. Calhoun: Sectionalist, 1840–1850.* New York: Bobbs-Merrill Co., Inc., 1951.

Winks, Robin. *The Blacks in Canada: A History.* Montreal: McGill-Queens University Press, 1971.

Wood, Forrest G. *The Racist Response to Emancipation and Reconstruction.* Berkeley and Los Angeles: University of California Press, 1968.

Wood, Peter. *Black Majority: Negroes in Colonial South Carolina from 1670 through the Stono Rebellion*. New York: Alfred A. Knopf, 1974.

Wright, Philip. *Knibb "the Notorious": Slaves' Missionary 1803–1845*. London: Sidgwick and Jackson, 1973.

Wyatt-Brown, Bertram. *Lewis Tappan and the Evangelical War Against Slavery*. New York: Athenaeum, 1971.

Young, Jeffrey Robert. *Domesticating Slavery: The Master Class in Georgia and South Carolina, 1670–1837*. Chapel Hill: University of North Carolina Press, 1999.

Articles

Abzug, Robert H. "The Influence of Garrisonian Abolitionists' Fear of Slave Violence on the Antislavery Argument, 1829–1840." *Journal of Negro History* 55 (January 1970): 15–26.

Adams, Randolph G. "Abel Parker Upshur." In *American Secretaries of State and Their Diplomacy*, 20 vols., ed. Samuel Flag Bemis et. al., 5, 67–124. New York: Alfred A. Knopf, 1928–.

Blackett, Richard. "The Hamic Connection: African Americans and the Caribbean, 1820–1865." In *Before and After 1865: Education, Politics, and Regionalism in the Caribbean, in Honour of Sir Roy Augier*, ed. Roy Augier, Brian L. Moore, Swithin R. Wilmot, 317–29. Kingston, Jamaica: Ian Randle, 1998.

Blouet, Olwyn M. "Bryan Edwards and the Haitian Revolution." In *The Impact of the Haitian Revolution in the Atlantic World*, ed. David Geggus, 44–57. Columbia: University of South Carolina Press, 2001.

Botein, Stephen. "Printers and the American Revolution." In *The Press and the American Revolution*, ed. Bernard Bailyn and John B. Hench, 11–57. Worcester: American Antiquarian Society, 1980.

Brown, Richard. "The Missouri Crisis, Slavery, and the Politics of Jacksonianism." *South Atlantic Quarterly* 65 (Winter 1966): 55–72.

Carrington, Selwyn. "The American Revolution and the British West Indies Economy." *Journal of Interdisciplinary History* 17 (Spring 1987): 823–50.

Cassell, Frank A. "Slaves of the Chesapeake Bay Area and the War of 1812." *Journal of Negro History* 57 (April 1972): 144–55.

Clark, Charles E. "Early American Journalism: News and Opinion in the Popular Press." In *The Colonial Book in the Atlantic World*, ed. Hugh Amory and David D. Hall, 347–65. Cambridge: Cambridge University Press, 2000.

Coatsworth, John H. "American Trade with European Colonies in the Caribbean and South America, 1790–1812." *William and Mary Quarterly*, 3d ser., 24 (April 1967): 243–66.

Coclanis, Peter A. "Distant Thunder: The Creation of a World Market in Rice and the Transformations It Wrought." *American Historical Review* 98 (October 1993): 1050–78.

Davis, David Brion. "The Emergence of Immediatism in British and American Antislavery Thought." *Mississippi Valley Historical Review* 49 (September 1962): 209–30

———. Introduction to *The Fear of Conspiracy: Images of Un-American Subversion from the Revolution to the Present*, ed. David Brion Davis, xiii–xxiv. Ithaca: Cornell University Press, 1971.

Drescher, Seymour. "The Limits of Example." In *The Impact of the Haitian Revolution in the Atlantic World*, ed. David Geggus. 10–14. Columbia: University of South Carolina Press, 2001.

———. "Whose Abolition? Popular Pressure and the Ending of the British Slave Trade." *Past and Present* 143 (May 1994): 136–66.

Egerton, Douglas R. "It's Origin Is Not A Little Curious": A New Look at the American Colonization Society." *Journal of the Early Republic* 5 (Winter 1985): 463–80.

Engerman, Stanley. "Economic Adjustments to Emancipation in the United States and British West Indies." *Journal of Interdisciplinary History* 13 (Autumn 1982): 191–220.

Fabre, Genevieve. "African American Commemorative Celebrations in the Nineteenth Century." In *History and Memory in African American Culture*, ed. Genevieve Fabre and Robert O'Meally, 72–91. New York: Oxford University Press, 1994.

Farris, Sara Guertler. "Wilmington's Maritime Commerce: 1775–1807." *Delaware History* 14 (1970): 22–51.

Friedman, Lawrence J. "Purifying the White Man's Country: The American Colonization Society Reconsidered, 1816–1840." *Societas* 6 (Winter 1976): 1–24.

Geggus, David. "British Opinion and the Emergence of Haiti, 1791–1805." In *Slavery and British Society, 1776–1846*, ed. James Walvin, 123–49. Baton Rouge: Louisiana State University Press, 1982.

Gellman, David. "Pirates, Sugar, Debtors, and Slaves: Political Economy and the Case for Gradual Abolition in New York." *Slavery and Abolition* 22 (August 2001): 51–68.

Goveia, Elsa. "The West Indian Slave Laws of the Eighteenth Century." In *Caribbean Slave Society and Economy: A Student Reader*, ed. Hilary Beckles and Verene Shepherd, 346–62. New York: New Press, 1991.

Green, Fletcher M. "Duff Green, Militant Journalist." *American Historical Review* 52 (January 1947): 247–64.

Greene, Jack P. "Colonial South Carolina and the Caribbean Connection." *South Carolina Historical Magazine* 88 (1987): 192–210.

Hamer, Philip M. "Great Britain, the United States, and the Negro Seaman Acts, 1822–1848." *Journal of Southern History* 1 (February 1935): 3–28.

Harding, Vincent. "Symptoms of Liberty and Blackhead Signposts, David Walker and Nat Turner." In *Nat Turner: A Slave Rebellion in History and Memory*, ed. Kenneth S. Greenberg, 79–102. Oxford: Oxford University Press, 2003.

Haynes, Sam W. "Anglophobia and the Annexation of Texas: The Quest for National Security." In *Manifest Destiny and Empire: American Antebellum Expansion*, ed. Sam W. Haynes and Christopher Morris, 115–45. College Station: Texas A&M University Press, 1997.

Hickey, Donald. "America's Response to the Slave Revolt in Haiti, 1791–1806." *Journal of the Early Republic* 2 (Winter 1982): 361–79.

Higman, B. W. "Jamaican Port Towns in the Early Nineteenth Century." In *Atlantic Port Cities: Economy, Culture, and Society in the Atlantic World, 1650–1850*, ed. Franklin W. Knight and Peggy K. Liss, 117–37. Knoxville: University of Tennessee Press, 1991.

Jackson, Harvey H. "Hugh Bryan and the Evangelical Movement in Colonial South Carolina." *William and Mary Quarterly* 43 (October 1986): 594–614.

January, Alan F. "The South Carolina Association: An Agency for Race Control in Antebellum Charleston." *South Carolina Historical Magazine* 78 (July 1977): 191–201.

Jervey, Edward D., and C. Harold Huber. "The Creole Affair." *Journal of Negro History* 65 (Summer 1980): 196–211.

Johnson, Michael P. "Denmark Vesey and His Co-conspirators." *William and Mary Quarterly*, 3rd ser., 58 (October 2002): 933–71.

Johnson, Walter. "The Pedestal and the Veil: Rethinking the Capitalism/Slavery Question." *Journal of the Early Republic* 24 (Summer 2004): 299–308.

Kachun, Mitch. "Antebellum African Americans, Public Commemorations, and the Haitian Revolution: A Problem of Historical Mythmaking." *Journal of the Early Republic* 26 (Summer 2006): 249–73.

———. " 'Our Platform Is as Broad as Humanity': Transatlantic Freedom Movements and the Idea of Progress in Nineteenth-Century African American Thought and Activism." *Slavery and Abolition* 24 (December 2003): 1–23.

Kornblith, Gary. "Rethinking the Coming of the Civil War: A Counterfactual Exercise." *Journal of American History* 90 (June 2003): 76–105.

Lachance, Paul. "Repercussions of the Haitian Revolution in Louisiana." In *The Impact of the Haitian Revolution in the Atlantic World*, ed. David Geggus, 209–30. Columbia: University of South Carolina Press, 2001.

Lewis, Andrew. " 'An Incendiary Press': British West Indian Newspapers During the Struggle for Abolition." *Slavery and Abolition* 16 (December 1995): 346–61.

Little, Thomas J. "George Liele and the Rise of Independent Black Baptist Churches in the Lower South and Jamaica." *Slavery and Abolition* 16 (August 1995): 188–204.

Mathews, Donald G. "The Methodist Mission to the Slaves, 1829–1844." *Journal of American History* 51 (March 1965): 615–31.

———. "The Second Great Awakening as an Organizing Process, 1780–1830." *American Quarterly* 21 (Spring 1969): 23–43.

McCarthy, Timothy P. " 'To Plead Our Own Cause': Black Print Culture and the Origins of American Abolitionism." In *Prophets of Protest: Reconsidering the History of American Abolitionism,* ed. Timothy P. McCarthy and John Stauffer, 114–44. New York: New Press, 2007.

McCormac, Eugene I. "John Forsyth." In *American Secretaries of State and Their Diplomacy,* 20 vols., ed. Samuel Flag Bemis et al., 4, 301–43. New York: Alfred A. Knopf, 1928–.

McCusker, John J., and Russel R. Menard. "The Sugar Industry in the Seventeenth Century: A New Perspective on the Barbadian "Sugar Revolution." In *Tropical Babylons: Sugar and the Making of the Atlantic World, 1450–1680,* ed. Stuart B. Schwartz, 289–330. Chapel Hill: University of North Carolina Press, 2004.

McPherson, James M. "Was West Indian Emancipation a Success? The Abolitionist Argument During the American Civil War." *Caribbean Studies* 4 (1964): 28–34.

Merk, Frederick. "A Safety Valve Thesis and Texas Annexation." *Mississippi Valley-Historical Review* 49 (December 1962): 413–36.

Mitton, Steven Heath. "The Upshur Inquiry: Lost Lessons of the Great Experiment." *Slavery and Abolition* 27 (April 2006): 89-124.

Paley, Ruth. "After Somerset: Mansfield, Slavery, and the Law in England, 1772–1830." In *Law, Crime and English Society, 1660–1830,* ed. Norma Landau, 165–84. Cambridge: Oxford University Press, 2002.

Paquette, Robert L. "The Everett-Del Monte Connection: A Study in the International Politics of Slavery." *Diplomatic History* 11 (Winter 1987): 1–21.

———. "From Rebellion to Revisionism: The Continuing Debate about the Denmark Vesey Affair." *Journal of the Historical Society* 4 (Fall 2004): 291–334.

Paquette, Robert L., and Douglas R. Egerton. "Of Facts and Fables: New Light on the Denmark Vesey Affair." *South Carolina Historical Magazine* 105 (January 2004): 8–48.

Quarles, Benjamin. "Antebellum Free Blacks and the "Spirit of '76." *Journal of Negro History* 61 (July 1976): 229–42.

Roberts, William. "The Losses of a Loyalist Merchant During the Revolution," *Georgia Historical Quarterly* 52 (1968): 270–76.

Rugemer, Edward B. "Robert Monroe Harrison, British Abolition, Southern Anglophobia, and the Annexation of Texas," *Slavery and Abolition* 28 (Aug. 2007): 169-91.

———. "The Southern Response to British Abolitionism: The Maturation of Pro-slavery Apologetics." *Journal of Southern History* 70 (May 2004): 221–48.

Schudson, Michael. "Preparing the Minds of the People: Three Hundred Years of the American Newspaper." In *Three Hundred Years of the American Newspaper*, ed. John B. Hench, 421–43. Worcester: American Antiquarian Society, 1991.

Scott, Donald. "The Popular Lecture and the Creation of a Public in Mid-Nineteenth Century America." *Journal of American History* 66 (March 1980): 791–809.

———. "Print and the Public Lecture System, 1840–1860." In *Printing and Society in Early America,* ed. William L. Joyce et al., 278–99. Worcester: American Antiquarian Society, 1983.

Sharrer, G. Terry. "Flour Milling in Baltimore: 1750–1830." *Maryland Historical Magazine* 71 (Fall 1976): 322–23.

Sheehan, Colleen. "Madison and the French Enlightenment: The Authority of Public Opinion." *William and Mary Quarterly,* 3d ser., 59 (October 2002): 925–56.

Sheridan, Richard B. "The Crisis of Slave Subsistence in the British West Indies During and After the American Revolution." *William and Mary Quarterly,* 3d ser., 33 (October 1976): 615–41.

Sioussat, St. George L. "Duff Green's 'England and the United States': With an Introductory Study of American Opposition to the Quintuple Treaty of 1841." *Proceedings of the American Antiquarian Society* 40 (1930): 175–276.

Stewart, James Brewer. "Abolitionists, Insurgents, and Third Parties: Sectionalism and Partisan Politics in Northern Whiggery, 1836–1844." In *Crusaders and Compromisers: Essays on the Relationship of the Antislavery Struggle to the Antebellum Party System,* ed. Alan M. Kraut, 25–43. Westport: Greenwood, 1983.

———. "The Emergence of Racial Modernity and the Rise of the White North, 1790–1840." *Journal of the Early Republic* 18 (Summer 1998): 181–217.

———. "Modernizing "Difference": The Political Meanings of Color in the Free States, 1776–1840." *Journal of the Early Republic* 19 (Winter 1999): 691–712;

———. "Peaceful Hopes and Violent Experiences: The Evolution of Reforming and Radical Abolitionism, 1831–1837." *Civil War History* 17 (December 1971): 293–309.

Studley, Marian H. "An 'August First' in 1844." *New England Quarterly* 16 (December 1943): 567–77.

Sweet, Leonard I. "The Fourth of July and Black Americans in the Nineteenth Century: Northern Leadership Opinion within the Context of the Black Experience." *Journal of Negro History* 61 (1976): 256–75.

Thompson, Peter. " 'The Friendly Glass': Drink and Gentility in Colonial Philadelphia." *Pennsylvania Magazine of History and Biography* 133 (Oct. 1989): 549–574.

Thornton, John. "African Dimensions of the Stono Rebellion." *American Historical Review* 96 (October 1991): 1101–13.

Troutman, Phillip. "Grapevine in the Slave Market: African American Geopolitical Literacy and the 1841 Creole Revolt." In *The Chattel Principle: Internal Slave Trades in the Americas,* ed. Walter Johnson, 203–33. New Haven: Yale University Press, 2004.

Waldstreicher, David. "Rites of Rebellion, Rites of Assent: Celebrations, Print Culture, and the Origins of American Nationalism." *Journal of American History* 82 (June 1995): 37–61.

White, Shane. 'It was a Proud Day': African Americans, Festivals, and Parades in the North, 1741–1834." *Journal of American History* 81 (June 1994): 13–50.

Wyly-Jones, Susan. "The 1835 Anti-Abolition Meetings in the South: A New Look at the Controversy over the Abolition Postal Campaign." *Civil War History* 47 (2001): 289–309.

Young, Sandra Sandiford. "John Brown Russwurm's Dilemma: Citizenship or Emigration." In *Prophets of Protest: Reconsidering the History of American Abolitionism,* ed. Timothy Patrick McCarthy and John Stauffer, 90–113. New York: The New Press, 2006.

Dissertations

Dellamura, Fred A. "The Harrison Report and its Role in the British American Controversy over the West India Carrying Trade, 1827–1828." M.A. thesis, University of Kentucky, 1972.

Forbes, Robert. "Slavery and the Meaning of America, 1819–1837." Ph.D. diss., Yale University, 1994.

Gujer, Bruno. "Free Trade and Slavery: Calhoun's Defense of Southern Interests Against British Interference, 1811–1848." Ph.D. diss., University of Zurich, 1971.

McDaniel, William Caleb. "Our Country is the World: Radical American Abolitionists Abroad." Ph.D. diss., Johns Hopkins University, 2006.

Mitton, Steven Heath. "The Free World Confronted: The Problem of Slavery and Progress in American Foreign Relations, 1833–1844." Ph.D. diss., Louisiana State University, 2005.

Scott, Julius S. "The Common Wind: Currents of Afro-American Communication in the Era of the Haitian Revolution." Ph.D. diss., Duke University, 1986.

Wilkins, Joe Bassette Jr. "Window on Freedom: The South's Response to the Emancipation of the Slaves in the British West Indies, 1833–1861." Ph.D. diss., University of South Carolina, 1977.

Reference Works

Appleton's Cyclopedia of American Biography. New York, 1888.

The Biographical Dictionary of America. Boston: American Biographical Society, 1906.

Yrigoyen, Charles Jr., and Susan E. Warrick, eds. *Historical Dictionary of Methodism.* Lanham, MD: Scarecrow Press, 1996.

Index

Note: page numbers in *italics* refer to tables or illustrations; those followed by "n" indicate footnotes.